MOLINE

MYSPACE
DARK HORSE
PRESENTS

5

FRIENDSHIP

FEATURING THE

5

MYSPACE
DARK HORSE
PRESENTS
WORK OF

Scott Allie, Sergio Aragonés, John Arcudi, Aaron Conley, M. S. Corley,
Guy Davis, Felicia Day, Todd Demong, Ben Dewey, Jane Espenson,
Mark Evanier, Adam Gallardo, Rick Geary, Damon Gentry, Cody Goodfellow,
Matt Kindt, David Malki!, Brian Maruca, Kevin McGovern, Karl Moline,
Dean Motter, Roman Muradov, Yuko Ota, Ananth Panagariya, Jeff Parker,
Jesse Reklaw, Darick Robertson, Jim Rugg, Matt Sundstrom,
Jill Thompson, and Jeff Wamester

Dark Horse Books®

President and Publisher
Mike Richardson

Editors
Scott Allie
Sierra Hahn

Assistant Editors
Freddye Lins
Brendan Wright

Collection Designer
Scott Cook

Cover Art
Guy Davis
with Dave Stewart

NEIL HANKERSON executive vice president TOM WEDDLE chief financial officer RANDY STRADLEY vice president of publishing MICHAEL MARTENS vice president of business development ANITA NELSON vice president of marketing, sales, and licensing DAVID SCROGGY vice president of product development DALE LAFOUNTAIN vice president of information technology DARLENE VOGEL director of purchasing KEN LIZZI general counsel DAVEY ESTRADA editorial director SCOTT ALLIE senior managing editor CHRIS WARNER senior books editor DIANA SCHUTZ executive editor CARY GRAZZINI director of design and production LIA RIBACCHI art director CARA NIECE director of scheduling

"Dalton: Promise Kept"; "The Gax of Life: A Wondermark Tale"; and "Exurbia: No Return" edited by Dave Land.

"Our Boarding House" edited by Dave Land with Patrick Thorpe.

"The Secret Files of the Giant Man in Egypt" edited by Diana Schutz with Brendan Wright.

"Mister X: The Vanishing Breed" edited by Dave Marshall with Brendan Wright.

"Solomon Kane: All the Damned Souls at Sea" and "Conan and the Mad King of Gaul" edited by Philip R. Simon with Patrick Thorpe.

"Groo: The Hogs of Horder" edited by Katie Moody.

"The Horror Robber" edited by Brendan Wright.

"Callie Eats Feathers" edited by Samantha Robertson.

MYSPACE DARK HORSE PRESENTS™ VOLUME FIVE

This volume reprints the online comic-book anthology *MySpace Dark Horse Presents* #25–#30, as well as "Callie Eats Feathers" from issue #31.

Published by Dark Horse Books
A division of Dark Horse Comics, Inc.
10956 SE Main Street
Milwaukie, OR 97222

darkhorse.com

To find a comics shop in your area, call the Comic Shop Locator Service toll-free at (888) 266-4226.

First edition: August 2010
ISBN 978-1-59582-570-4

10 9 8 7 6 5 4 3 2 1
Printed at Midas Printing International, Ltd., Huizhou, China

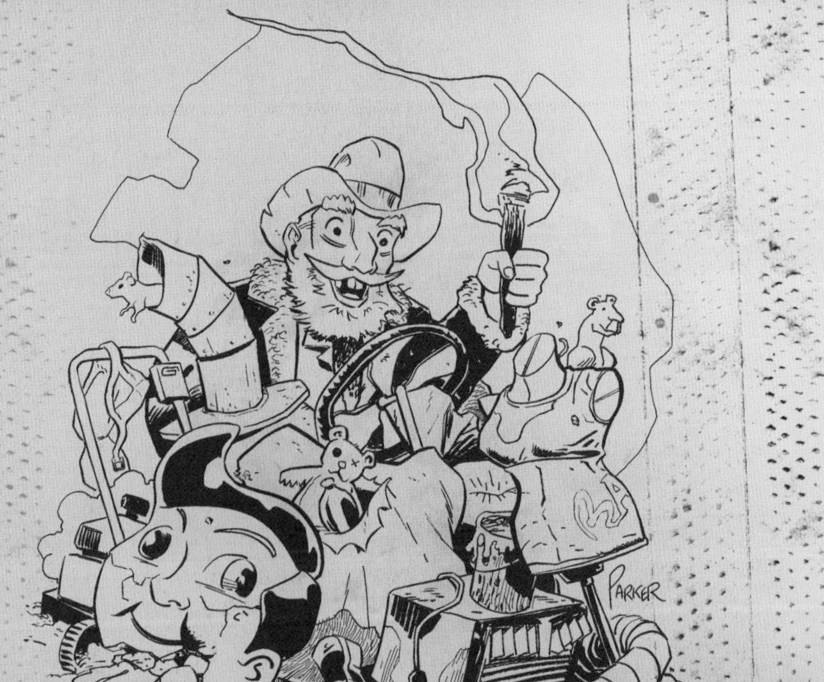
PARKER

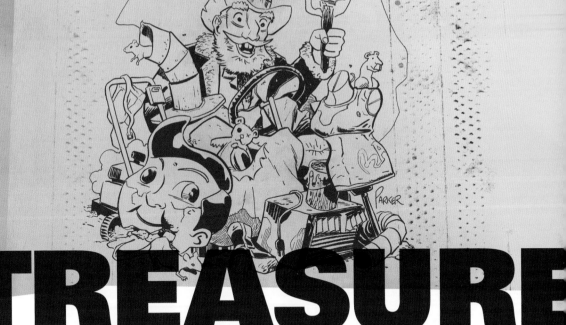

TREASURE

THE CONTENTS OF MDHP VOLUME 5

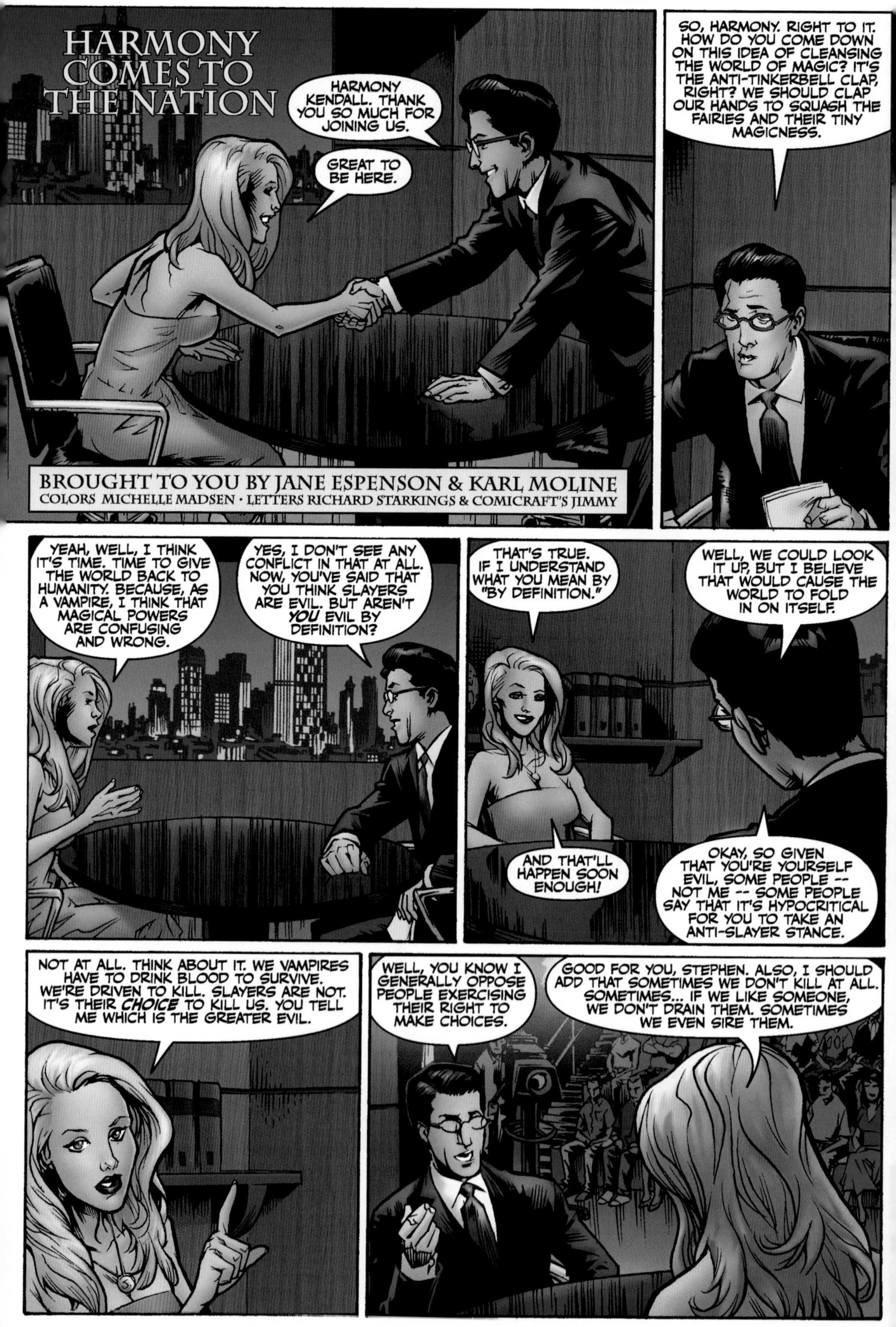
HARMONY COMES TO THE NATION
HARMONY KENDALL. THANK YOU SO MUCH FOR JOINING US.
GREAT TO BE HERE.
BROUGHT TO YOU BY JANE ESPENSON & KARL MOLINE
COLORS MICHELLE MADSEN · LETTERS RICHARD STARKINGS & COMICRAFT'S JIMMY
SO, HARMONY. RIGHT TO IT. HOW DO YOU COME DOWN ON THIS IDEA OF CLEANSING THE WORLD OF MAGIC? IT'S THE ANTI-TINKERBELL CLAP, RIGHT? WE SHOULD CLAP OUR HANDS TO SQUASH THE FAIRIES AND THEIR TINY MAGICNESS.
YEAH, WELL, I THINK IT'S TIME. TIME TO GIVE THE WORLD BACK TO HUMANITY. BECAUSE, AS A VAMPIRE, I THINK THAT MAGICAL POWERS ARE CONFUSING AND WRONG.
YES, I DON'T SEE ANY CONFLICT IN THAT AT ALL. NOW, YOU'VE SAID THAT YOU THINK SLAYERS ARE EVIL. BUT AREN'T *YOU* EVIL BY DEFINITION?
THAT'S TRUE. IF I UNDERSTAND WHAT YOU MEAN BY "BY DEFINITION."
WELL, WE COULD LOOK IT UP, BUT I BELIEVE THAT WOULD CAUSE THE WORLD TO FOLD IN ON ITSELF.
AND THAT'LL HAPPEN SOON ENOUGH!
OKAY, SO GIVEN THAT YOU'RE YOURSELF EVIL, SOME PEOPLE -- NOT ME -- SOME PEOPLE SAY THAT IT'S HYPOCRITICAL FOR YOU TO TAKE AN ANTI-SLAYER STANCE.
NOT AT ALL. THINK ABOUT IT. WE VAMPIRES HAVE TO DRINK BLOOD TO SURVIVE. WE'RE DRIVEN TO KILL. SLAYERS ARE NOT. IT'S THEIR *CHOICE* TO KILL US. YOU TELL ME WHICH IS THE GREATER EVIL.
WELL, YOU KNOW I GENERALLY OPPOSE PEOPLE EXERCISING THEIR RIGHT TO MAKE CHOICES.
GOOD FOR YOU, STEPHEN. ALSO, I SHOULD ADD THAT SOMETIMES WE DON'T KILL AT ALL. SOMETIMES... IF WE LIKE SOMEONE, WE DON'T DRAIN THEM. SOMETIMES WE EVEN SIRE THEM.

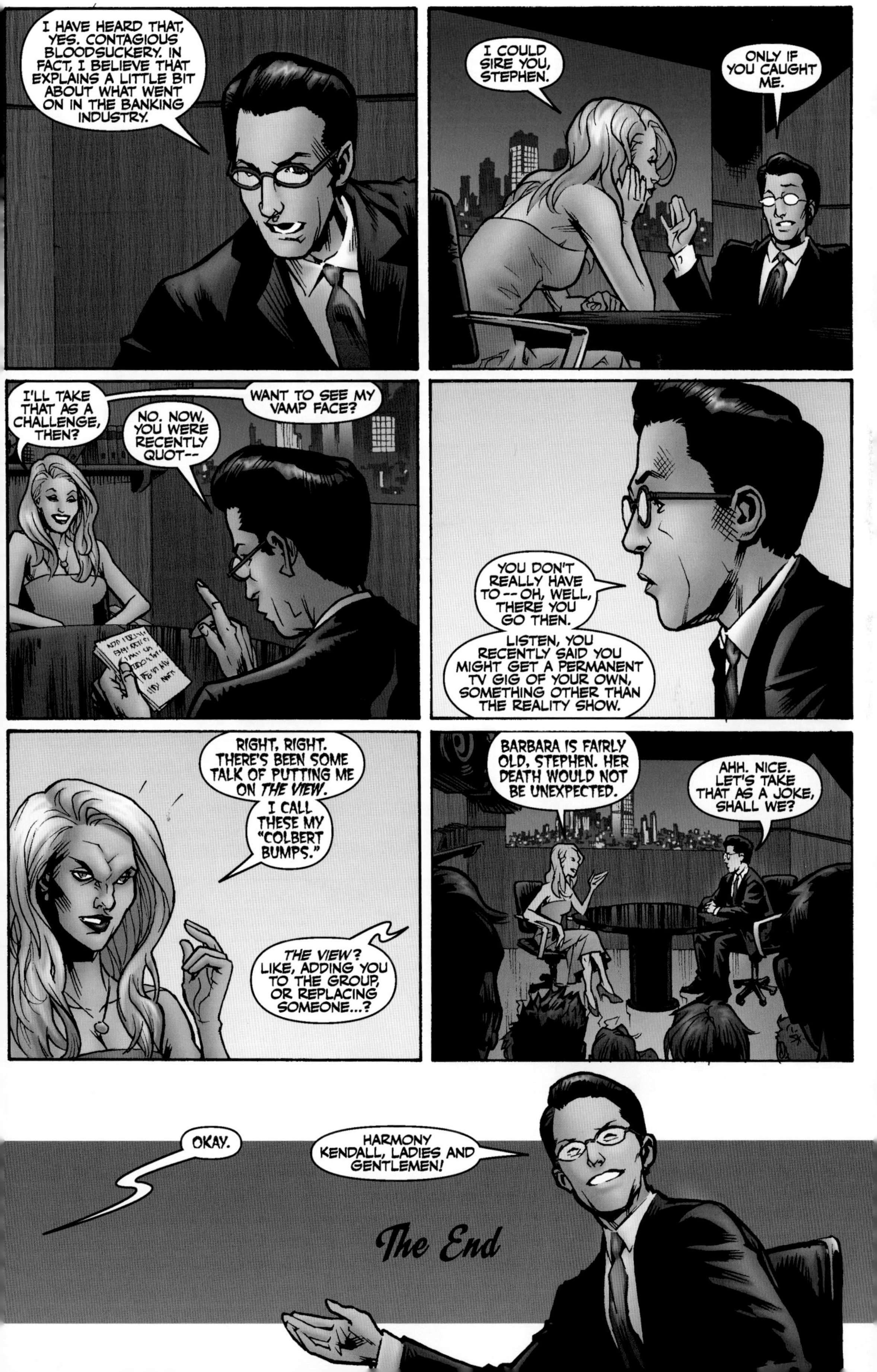
I HAVE HEARD THAT, YES. CONTAGIOUS BLOODSUCKERY. IN FACT, I BELIEVE THAT EXPLAINS A LITTLE BIT ABOUT WHAT WENT ON IN THE BANKING INDUSTRY.
I COULD SIRE YOU, STEPHEN.
ONLY IF YOU CAUGHT ME.
I'LL TAKE THAT AS A CHALLENGE, THEN?
NO. NOW, YOU WERE RECENTLY QUOT--
WANT TO SEE MY VAMP FACE?
YOU DON'T REALLY HAVE TO--OH, WELL, THERE YOU GO THEN.
LISTEN, YOU RECENTLY SAID YOU MIGHT GET A PERMANENT TV GIG OF YOUR OWN, SOMETHING OTHER THAN THE REALITY SHOW.
RIGHT, RIGHT. THERE'S BEEN SOME TALK OF PUTTING ME ON *THE VIEW*.
I CALL THESE MY "COLBERT BUMPS."
THE VIEW? LIKE, ADDING YOU TO THE GROUP, OR REPLACING SOMEONE...?
BARBARA IS FAIRLY OLD, STEPHEN. HER DEATH WOULD NOT BE UNEXPECTED.
AHH. NICE. LET'S TAKE THAT AS A JOKE, SHALL WE?
OKAY.
HARMONY KENDALL, LADIES AND GENTLEMEN!
The End

The GUILD BY FELICIA DAY & JIM RUGG with JUAN FERREYRA, DAN JACKSON, and BLAMBOT'S NATE PIEKOS

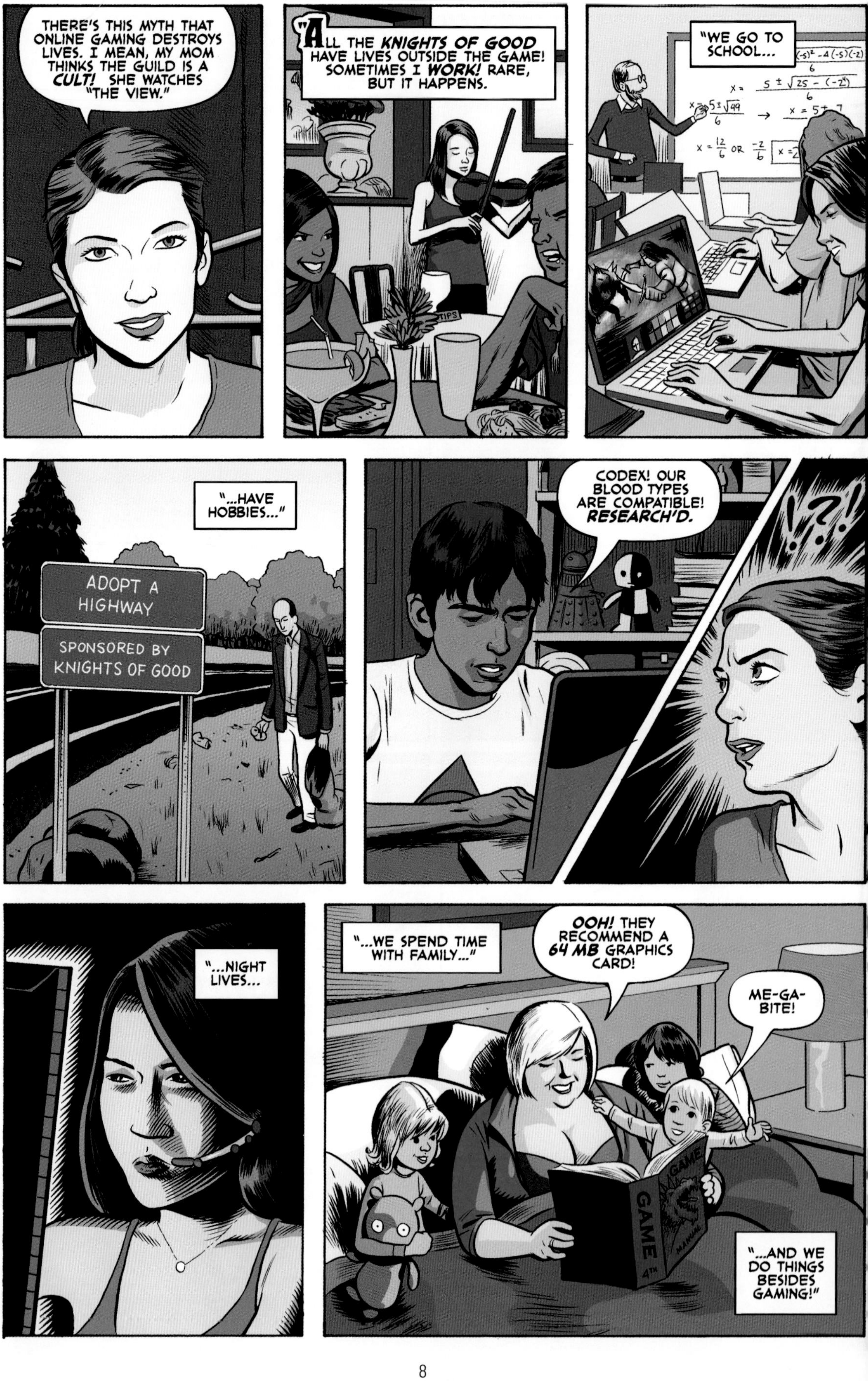

THERE'S THIS MYTH THAT ONLINE GAMING DESTROYS LIVES. I MEAN, MY MOM THINKS THE GUILD IS A CULT! SHE WATCHES "THE VIEW."
"ALL THE KNIGHTS OF GOOD HAVE LIVES OUTSIDE THE GAME! SOMETIMES I WORK! RARE, BUT IT HAPPENS.
TIPS
"WE GO TO SCHOOL...
"...HAVE HOBBIES..."
ADOPT A HIGHWAY
SPONSORED BY KNIGHTS OF GOOD
CODEX! OUR BLOOD TYPES ARE COMPATIBLE! RESEARCH'D.
!?!
"...NIGHT LIVES...
"...WE SPEND TIME WITH FAMILY..."
OOH! THEY RECOMMEND A 64 MB GRAPHICS CARD!
ME-GA-BITE!
GAME
GAME 4TH MANUAL
"...AND WE DO THINGS BESIDES GAMING!"

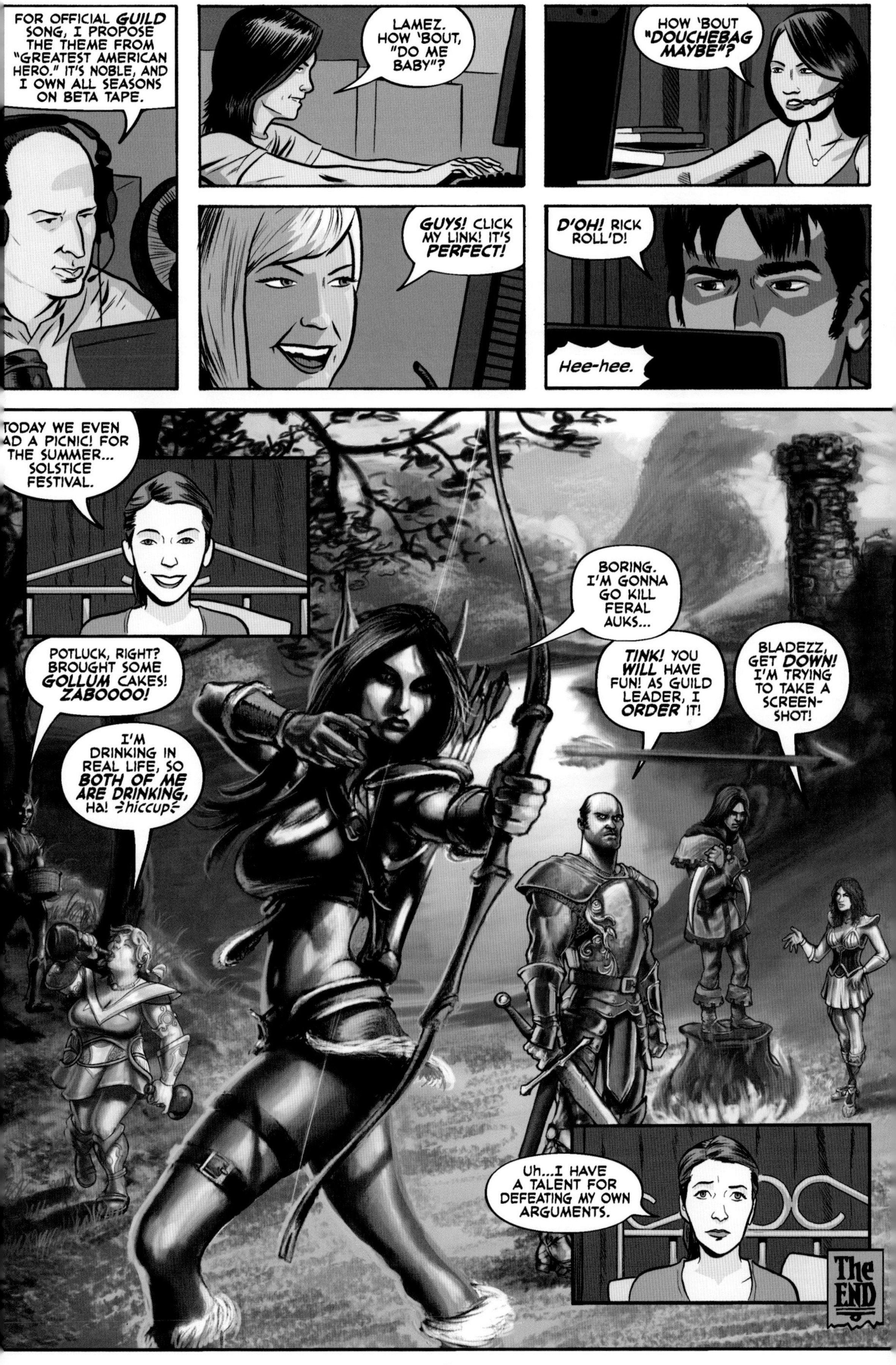

FOR OFFICIAL GUILD SONG, I PROPOSE THE THEME FROM "GREATEST AMERICAN HERO." IT'S NOBLE, AND I OWN ALL SEASONS ON BETA TAPE.
LAMEZ. HOW 'BOUT, "DO ME BABY"?
HOW 'BOUT "DOUCHEBAG MAYBE"?
GUYS! CLICK MY LINK! IT'S PERFECT!
D'OH! RICK ROLL'D!
Hee-hee.
TODAY WE EVEN AD A PICNIC! FOR THE SUMMER... SOLSTICE FESTIVAL.
BORING. I'M GONNA GO KILL FERAL AUKS...
POTLUCK, RIGHT? BROUGHT SOME GOLLUM CAKES! ZABOOOO!
TINK! YOU WILL HAVE FUN! AS GUILD LEADER, I ORDER IT!
BLADEZZ, GET DOWN! I'M TRYING TO TAKE A SCREEN-SHOT!
I'M DRINKING IN REAL LIFE, SO BOTH OF ME ARE DRINKING, Ha! hiccup
Uh...I HAVE A TALENT FOR DEFEATING MY OWN ARGUMENTS.
The END

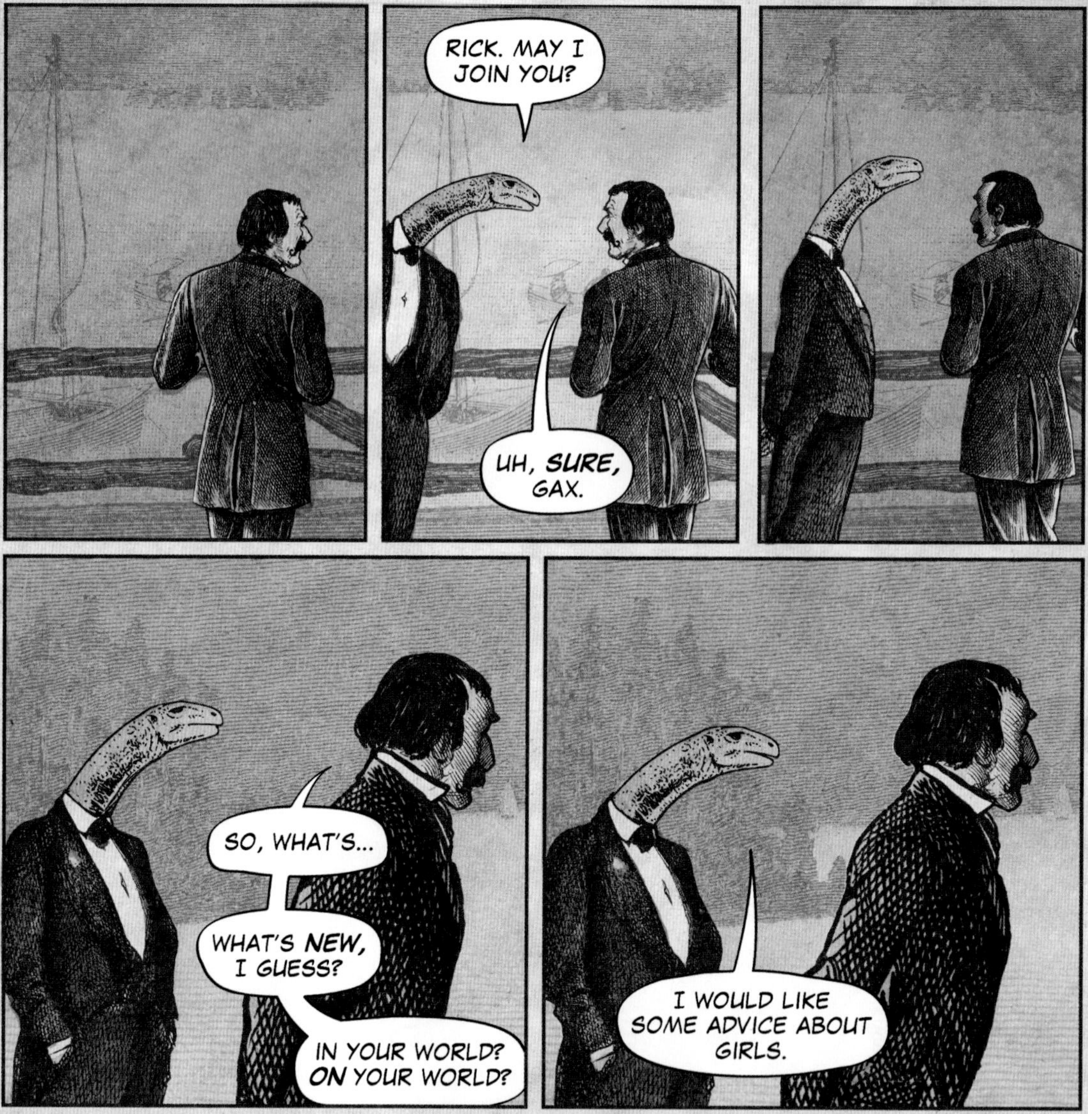
RICK. MAY I JOIN YOU?
UH, SURE, GAX.
SO, WHAT'S...
WHAT'S NEW, I GUESS?
IN YOUR WORLD? ON YOUR WORLD?
I WOULD LIKE SOME ADVICE ABOUT GIRLS.

"The Gax of Life"

A WONDERMARK TALE BY *David Malki !* COLOR BY *Marcus Thiele*

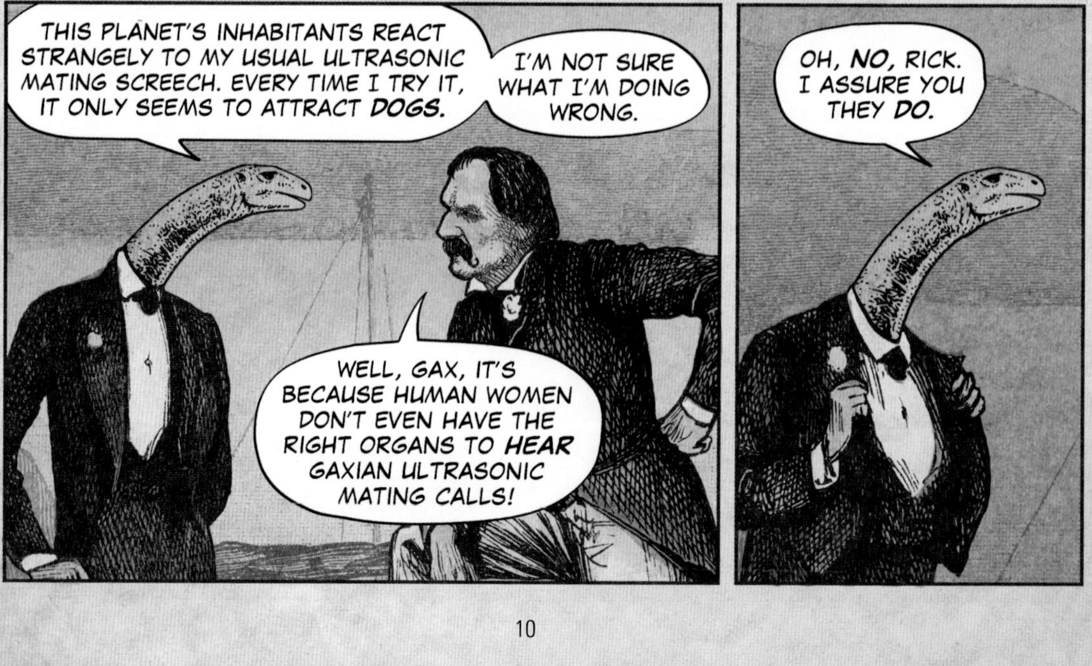
THIS PLANET'S INHABITANTS REACT STRANGELY TO MY USUAL ULTRASONIC MATING SCREECH. EVERY TIME I TRY IT, IT ONLY SEEMS TO ATTRACT DOGS.
I'M NOT SURE WHAT I'M DOING WRONG.
WELL, GAX, IT'S BECAUSE HUMAN WOMEN DON'T EVEN HAVE THE RIGHT ORGANS TO HEAR GAXIAN ULTRASONIC MATING CALLS!
OH, NO, RICK. I ASSURE YOU THEY DO.

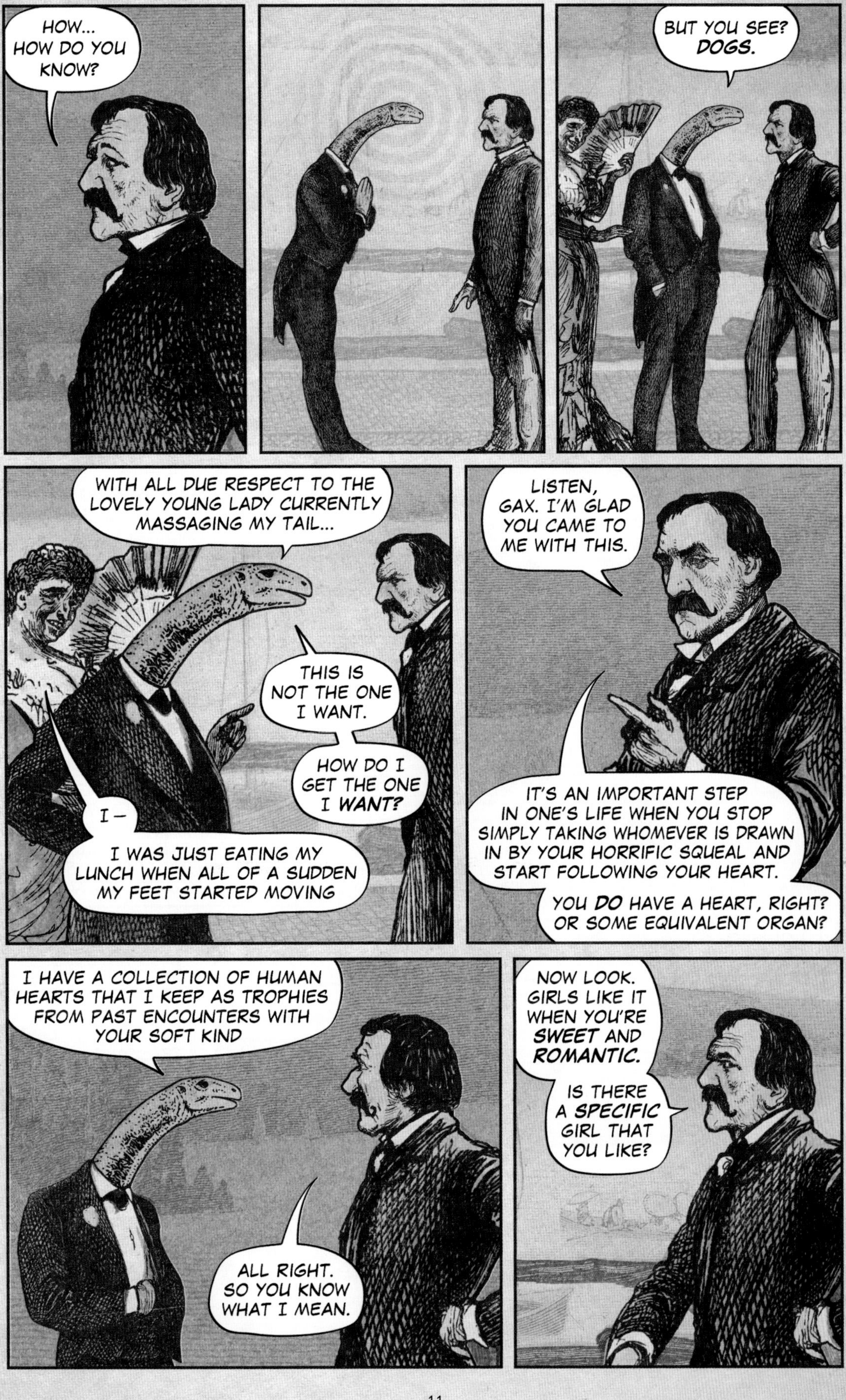
HOW... HOW DO YOU KNOW?
BUT YOU SEE? DOGS.
WITH ALL DUE RESPECT TO THE LOVELY YOUNG LADY CURRENTLY MASSAGING MY TAIL...
THIS IS NOT THE ONE I WANT.
HOW DO I GET THE ONE I WANT?
I —
I WAS JUST EATING MY LUNCH WHEN ALL OF A SUDDEN MY FEET STARTED MOVING
LISTEN, GAX. I'M GLAD YOU CAME TO ME WITH THIS.
IT'S AN IMPORTANT STEP IN ONE'S LIFE WHEN YOU STOP SIMPLY TAKING WHOMEVER IS DRAWN IN BY YOUR HORRIFIC SQUEAL AND START FOLLOWING YOUR HEART.
YOU DO HAVE A HEART, RIGHT? OR SOME EQUIVALENT ORGAN?
I HAVE A COLLECTION OF HUMAN HEARTS THAT I KEEP AS TROPHIES FROM PAST ENCOUNTERS WITH YOUR SOFT KIND
ALL RIGHT. SO YOU KNOW WHAT I MEAN.
NOW LOOK. GIRLS LIKE IT WHEN YOU'RE SWEET AND ROMANTIC.
IS THERE A SPECIFIC GIRL THAT YOU LIKE?

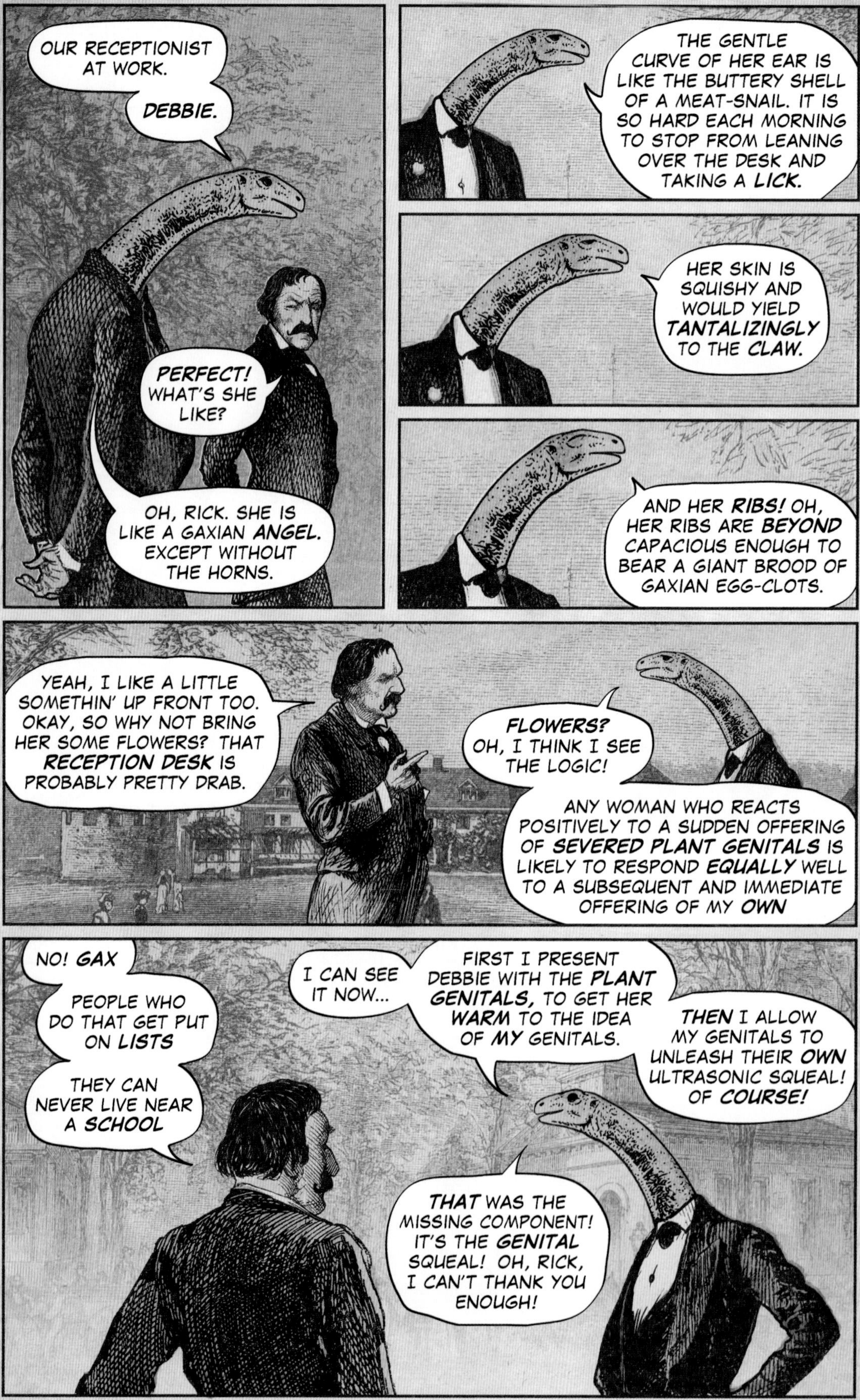
OUR RECEPTIONIST AT WORK.
DEBBIE.
PERFECT! WHAT'S SHE LIKE?
OH, RICK. SHE IS LIKE A GAXIAN ANGEL. EXCEPT WITHOUT THE HORNS.
THE GENTLE CURVE OF HER EAR IS LIKE THE BUTTERY SHELL OF A MEAT-SNAIL. IT IS SO HARD EACH MORNING TO STOP FROM LEANING OVER THE DESK AND TAKING A LICK.
HER SKIN IS SQUISHY AND WOULD YIELD TANTALIZINGLY TO THE CLAW.
AND HER RIBS! OH, HER RIBS ARE BEYOND CAPACIOUS ENOUGH TO BEAR A GIANT BROOD OF GAXIAN EGG-CLOTS.
YEAH, I LIKE A LITTLE SOMETHIN' UP FRONT TOO. OKAY, SO WHY NOT BRING HER SOME FLOWERS? THAT RECEPTION DESK IS PROBABLY PRETTY DRAB.
FLOWERS? OH, I THINK I SEE THE LOGIC!
ANY WOMAN WHO REACTS POSITIVELY TO A SUDDEN OFFERING OF SEVERED PLANT GENITALS IS LIKELY TO RESPOND EQUALLY WELL TO A SUBSEQUENT AND IMMEDIATE OFFERING OF MY OWN
NO! GAX
PEOPLE WHO DO THAT GET PUT ON LISTS
THEY CAN NEVER LIVE NEAR A SCHOOL
I CAN SEE IT NOW...
FIRST I PRESENT DEBBIE WITH THE PLANT GENITALS, TO GET HER WARM TO THE IDEA OF MY GENITALS.
THEN I ALLOW MY GENITALS TO UNLEASH THEIR OWN ULTRASONIC SQUEAL! OF COURSE!
THAT WAS THE MISSING COMPONENT! IT'S THE GENITAL SQUEAL! OH, RICK, I CAN'T THANK YOU ENOUGH!

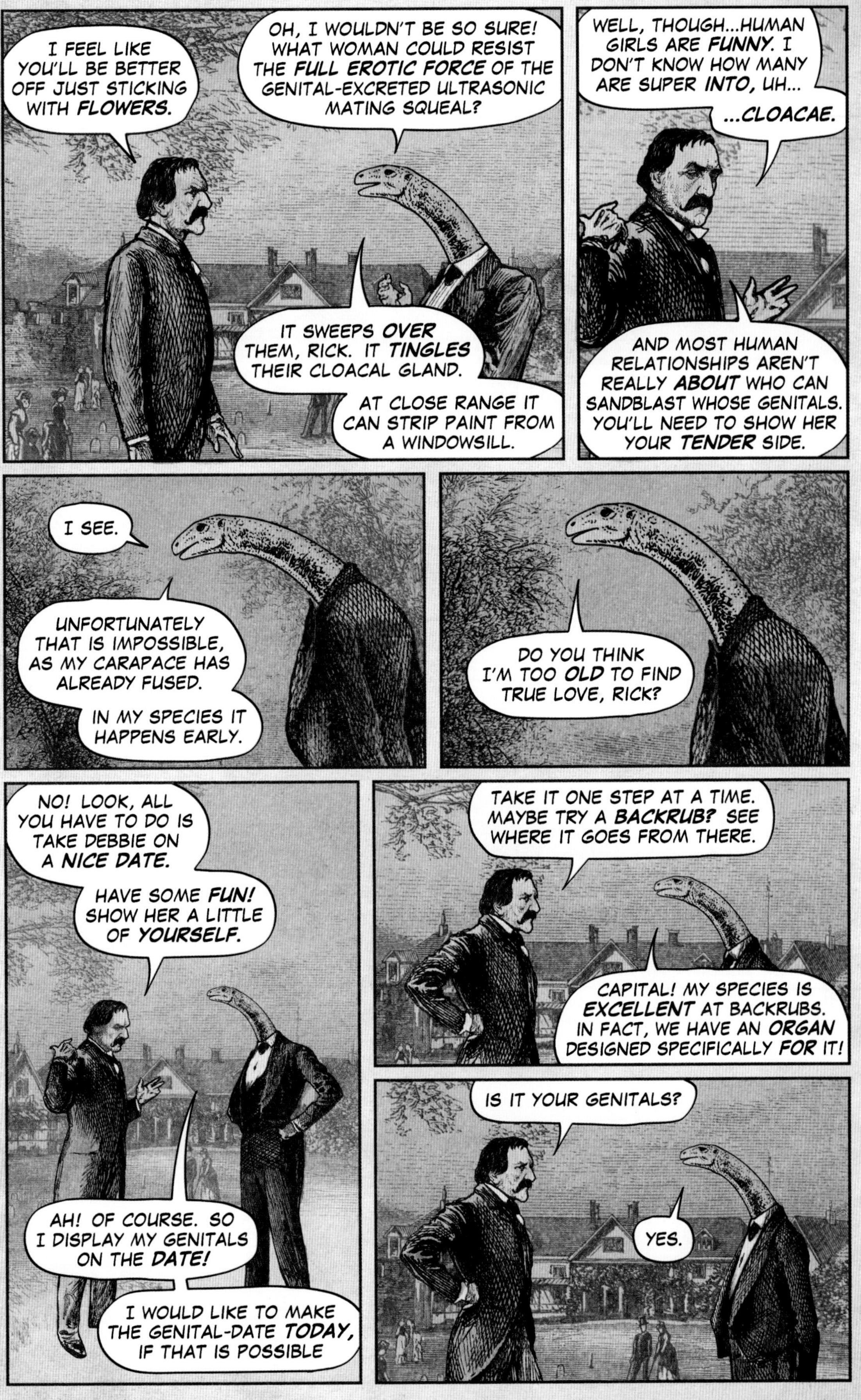

I FEEL LIKE YOU'LL BE BETTER OFF JUST STICKING WITH FLOWERS.
OH, I WOULDN'T BE SO SURE! WHAT WOMAN COULD RESIST THE FULL EROTIC FORCE OF THE GENITAL-EXCRETED ULTRASONIC MATING SQUEAL?
IT SWEEPS OVER THEM, RICK. IT TINGLES THEIR CLOACAL GLAND.
AT CLOSE RANGE IT CAN STRIP PAINT FROM A WINDOWSILL.
WELL, THOUGH...HUMAN GIRLS ARE FUNNY. I DON'T KNOW HOW MANY ARE SUPER INTO, UH...
...CLOACAE.
AND MOST HUMAN RELATIONSHIPS AREN'T REALLY ABOUT WHO CAN SANDBLAST WHOSE GENITALS. YOU'LL NEED TO SHOW HER YOUR TENDER SIDE.
I SEE.
UNFORTUNATELY THAT IS IMPOSSIBLE, AS MY CARAPACE HAS ALREADY FUSED.
IN MY SPECIES IT HAPPENS EARLY.
DO YOU THINK I'M TOO OLD TO FIND TRUE LOVE, RICK?
NO! LOOK, ALL YOU HAVE TO DO IS TAKE DEBBIE ON A NICE DATE.
HAVE SOME FUN! SHOW HER A LITTLE OF YOURSELF.
AH! OF COURSE. SO I DISPLAY MY GENITALS ON THE DATE!
I WOULD LIKE TO MAKE THE GENITAL-DATE TODAY, IF THAT IS POSSIBLE
TAKE IT ONE STEP AT A TIME. MAYBE TRY A BACKRUB? SEE WHERE IT GOES FROM THERE.
CAPITAL! MY SPECIES IS EXCELLENT AT BACKRUBS. IN FACT, WE HAVE AN ORGAN DESIGNED SPECIFICALLY FOR IT!
IS IT YOUR GENITALS?
YES.

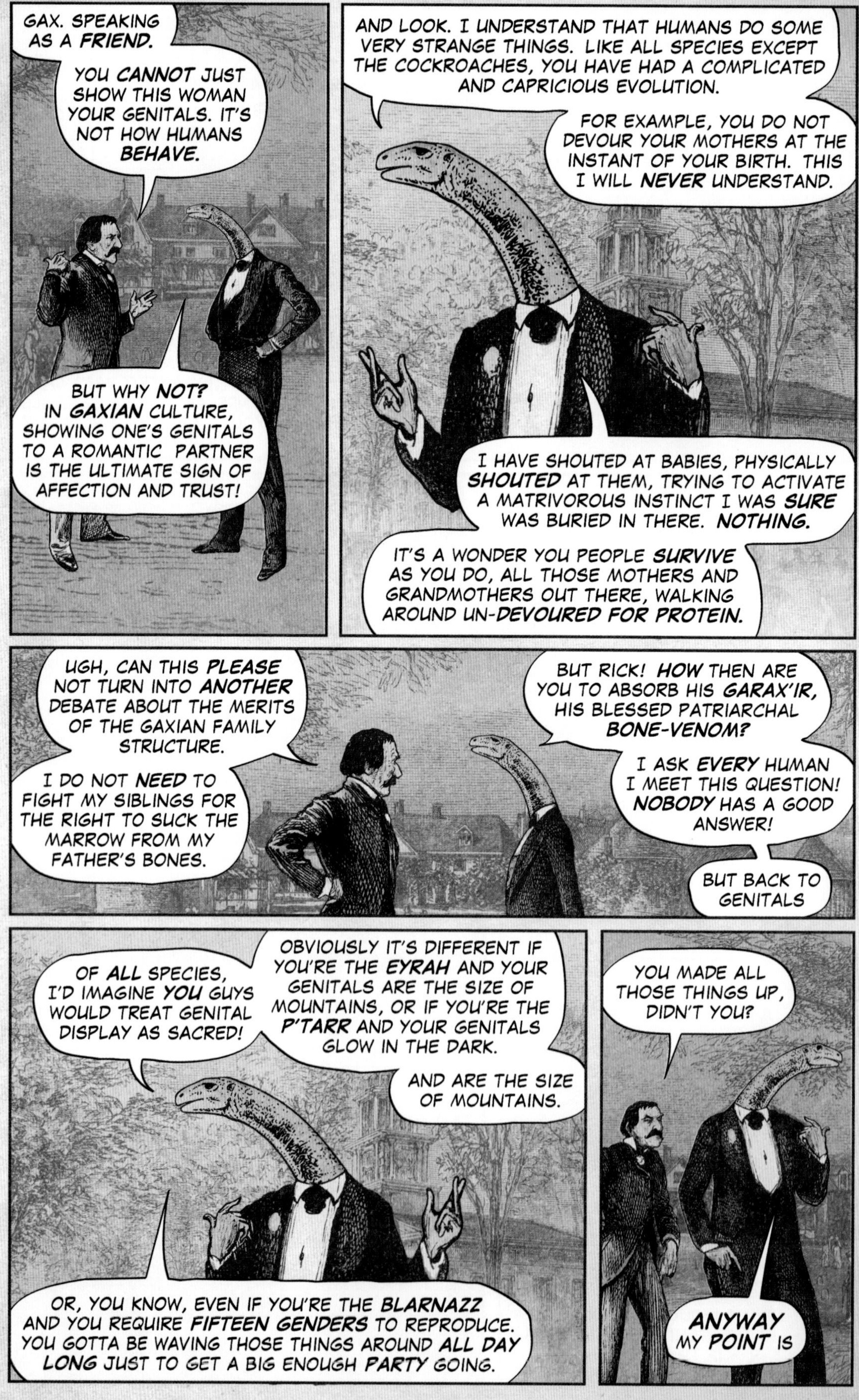
GAX. SPEAKING AS A FRIEND.
YOU CANNOT JUST SHOW THIS WOMAN YOUR GENITALS. IT'S NOT HOW HUMANS BEHAVE.
BUT WHY NOT? IN GAXIAN CULTURE, SHOWING ONE'S GENITALS TO A ROMANTIC PARTNER IS THE ULTIMATE SIGN OF AFFECTION AND TRUST!
AND LOOK. I UNDERSTAND THAT HUMANS DO SOME VERY STRANGE THINGS. LIKE ALL SPECIES EXCEPT THE COCKROACHES, YOU HAVE HAD A COMPLICATED AND CAPRICIOUS EVOLUTION.
FOR EXAMPLE, YOU DO NOT DEVOUR YOUR MOTHERS AT THE INSTANT OF YOUR BIRTH. THIS I WILL NEVER UNDERSTAND.
I HAVE SHOUTED AT BABIES, PHYSICALLY SHOUTED AT THEM, TRYING TO ACTIVATE A MATRIVOROUS INSTINCT I WAS SURE WAS BURIED IN THERE. NOTHING.
IT'S A WONDER YOU PEOPLE SURVIVE AS YOU DO, ALL THOSE MOTHERS AND GRANDMOTHERS OUT THERE, WALKING AROUND UN-DEVOURED FOR PROTEIN.
UGH, CAN THIS PLEASE NOT TURN INTO ANOTHER DEBATE ABOUT THE MERITS OF THE GAXIAN FAMILY STRUCTURE.
I DO NOT NEED TO FIGHT MY SIBLINGS FOR THE RIGHT TO SUCK THE MARROW FROM MY FATHER'S BONES.
BUT RICK! HOW THEN ARE YOU TO ABSORB HIS GARAX'IR, HIS BLESSED PATRIARCHAL BONE-VENOM?
I ASK EVERY HUMAN I MEET THIS QUESTION! NOBODY HAS A GOOD ANSWER!
BUT BACK TO GENITALS
OF ALL SPECIES, I'D IMAGINE YOU GUYS WOULD TREAT GENITAL DISPLAY AS SACRED!
OBVIOUSLY IT'S DIFFERENT IF YOU'RE THE EYRAH AND YOUR GENITALS ARE THE SIZE OF MOUNTAINS, OR IF YOU'RE THE P'TARR AND YOUR GENITALS GLOW IN THE DARK.
AND ARE THE SIZE OF MOUNTAINS.
OR, YOU KNOW, EVEN IF YOU'RE THE BLARNAZZ AND YOU REQUIRE FIFTEEN GENDERS TO REPRODUCE. YOU GOTTA BE WAVING THOSE THINGS AROUND ALL DAY LONG JUST TO GET A BIG ENOUGH PARTY GOING.
YOU MADE ALL THOSE THINGS UP, DIDN'T YOU?
ANYWAY MY POINT IS

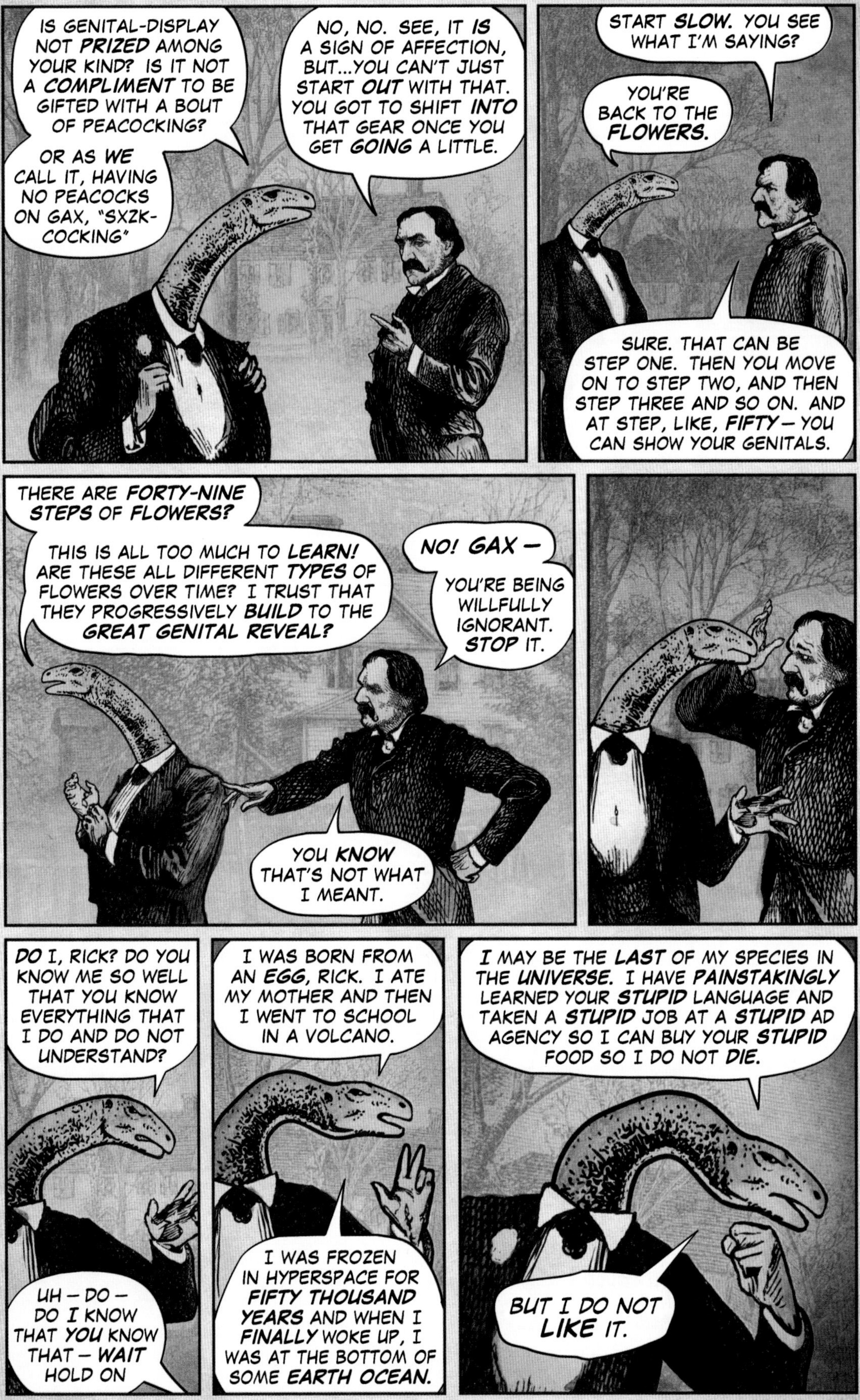
IS GENITAL-DISPLAY NOT PRIZED AMONG YOUR KIND? IS IT NOT A COMPLIMENT TO BE GIFTED WITH A BOUT OF PEACOCKING?
OR AS WE CALL IT, HAVING NO PEACOCKS ON GAX, "SXZK-COCKING"
NO, NO. SEE, IT IS A SIGN OF AFFECTION, BUT...YOU CAN'T JUST START OUT WITH THAT. YOU GOT TO SHIFT INTO THAT GEAR ONCE YOU GET GOING A LITTLE.
START SLOW. YOU SEE WHAT I'M SAYING?
YOU'RE BACK TO THE FLOWERS.
SURE. THAT CAN BE STEP ONE. THEN YOU MOVE ON TO STEP TWO, AND THEN STEP THREE AND SO ON. AND AT STEP, LIKE, FIFTY— YOU CAN SHOW YOUR GENITALS.
THERE ARE FORTY-NINE STEPS OF FLOWERS?
THIS IS ALL TOO MUCH TO LEARN! ARE THESE ALL DIFFERENT TYPES OF FLOWERS OVER TIME? I TRUST THAT THEY PROGRESSIVELY BUILD TO THE GREAT GENITAL REVEAL?
YOU KNOW THAT'S NOT WHAT I MEANT.
NO! GAX —
YOU'RE BEING WILLFULLY IGNORANT. STOP IT.
DO I, RICK? DO YOU KNOW ME SO WELL THAT YOU KNOW EVERYTHING THAT I DO AND DO NOT UNDERSTAND?
UH — DO — DO I KNOW THAT YOU KNOW THAT — WAIT HOLD ON
I WAS BORN FROM AN EGG, RICK. I ATE MY MOTHER AND THEN I WENT TO SCHOOL IN A VOLCANO.
I WAS FROZEN IN HYPERSPACE FOR FIFTY THOUSAND YEARS AND WHEN I FINALLY WOKE UP, I WAS AT THE BOTTOM OF SOME EARTH OCEAN.
I MAY BE THE LAST OF MY SPECIES IN THE UNIVERSE. I HAVE PAINSTAKINGLY LEARNED YOUR STUPID LANGUAGE AND TAKEN A STUPID JOB AT A STUPID AD AGENCY SO I CAN BUY YOUR STUPID FOOD SO I DO NOT DIE.
BUT I DO NOT LIKE IT.

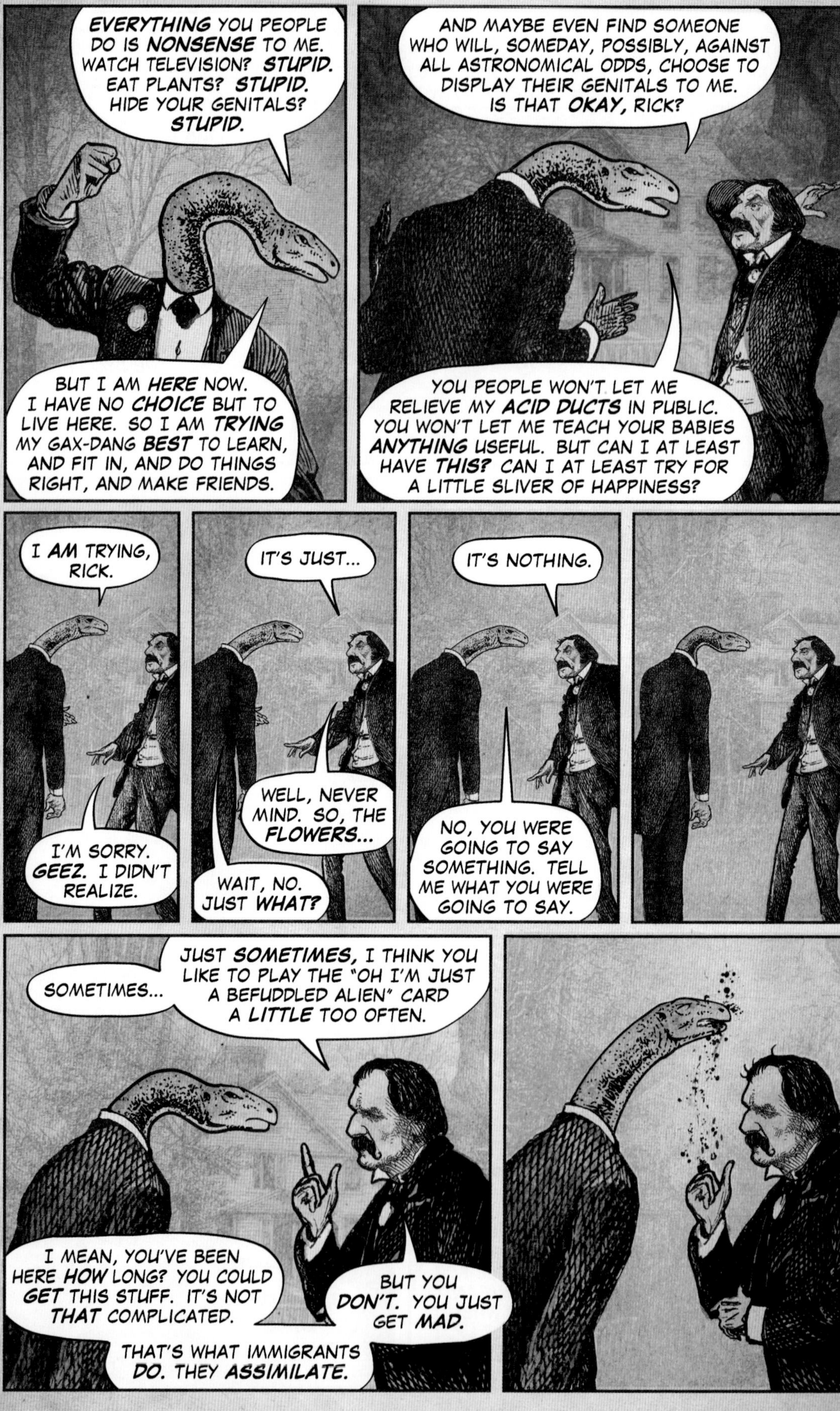
EVERYTHING YOU PEOPLE DO IS NONSENSE TO ME. WATCH TELEVISION? STUPID. EAT PLANTS? STUPID. HIDE YOUR GENITALS? STUPID.
BUT I AM HERE NOW. I HAVE NO CHOICE BUT TO LIVE HERE. SO I AM TRYING MY GAX-DANG BEST TO LEARN, AND FIT IN, AND DO THINGS RIGHT, AND MAKE FRIENDS.
AND MAYBE EVEN FIND SOMEONE WHO WILL, SOMEDAY, POSSIBLY, AGAINST ALL ASTRONOMICAL ODDS, CHOOSE TO DISPLAY THEIR GENITALS TO ME. IS THAT OKAY, RICK?
YOU PEOPLE WON'T LET ME RELIEVE MY ACID DUCTS IN PUBLIC. YOU WON'T LET ME TEACH YOUR BABIES ANYTHING USEFUL. BUT CAN I AT LEAST HAVE THIS? CAN I AT LEAST TRY FOR A LITTLE SLIVER OF HAPPINESS?
I AM TRYING, RICK.
I'M SORRY. GEEZ. I DIDN'T REALIZE.
IT'S JUST...
WELL, NEVER MIND. SO, THE FLOWERS...
WAIT, NO. JUST WHAT?
IT'S NOTHING.
NO, YOU WERE GOING TO SAY SOMETHING. TELL ME WHAT YOU WERE GOING TO SAY.
SOMETIMES...
JUST SOMETIMES, I THINK YOU LIKE TO PLAY THE "OH I'M JUST A BEFUDDLED ALIEN" CARD A LITTLE TOO OFTEN.
I MEAN, YOU'VE BEEN HERE HOW LONG? YOU COULD GET THIS STUFF. IT'S NOT THAT COMPLICATED.
THAT'S WHAT IMMIGRANTS DO. THEY ASSIMILATE.
BUT YOU DON'T. YOU JUST GET MAD.

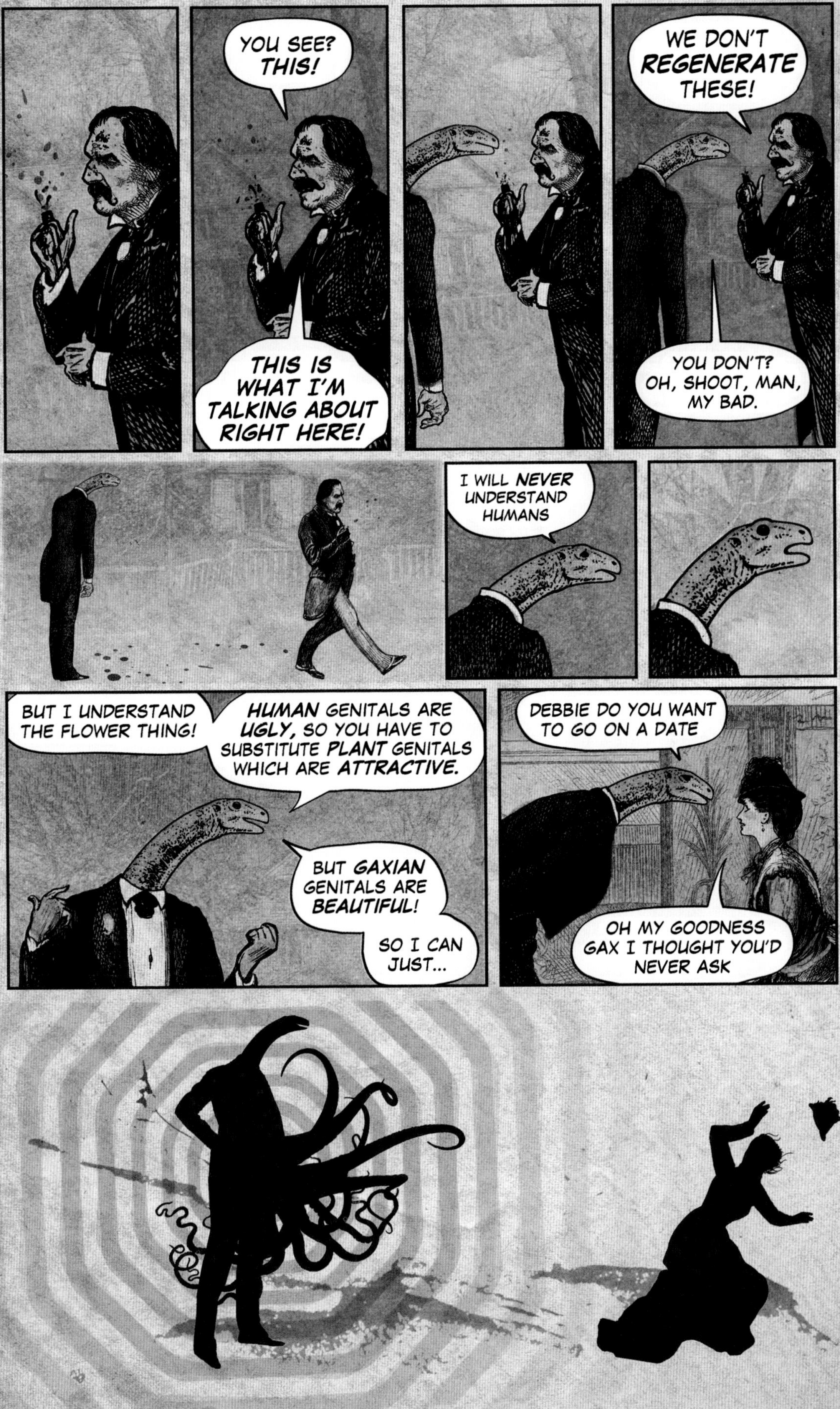

YOU SEE? THIS!
THIS IS WHAT I'M TALKING ABOUT RIGHT HERE!
WE DON'T REGENERATE THESE!
YOU DON'T? OH, SHOOT, MAN, MY BAD.
I WILL NEVER UNDERSTAND HUMANS
BUT I UNDERSTAND THE FLOWER THING!
HUMAN GENITALS ARE UGLY, SO YOU HAVE TO SUBSTITUTE PLANT GENITALS WHICH ARE ATTRACTIVE.
BUT GAXIAN GENITALS ARE BEAUTIFUL!
SO I CAN JUST...
DEBBIE DO YOU WANT TO GO ON A DATE
OH MY GOODNESS GAX I THOUGHT YOU'D NEVER ASK

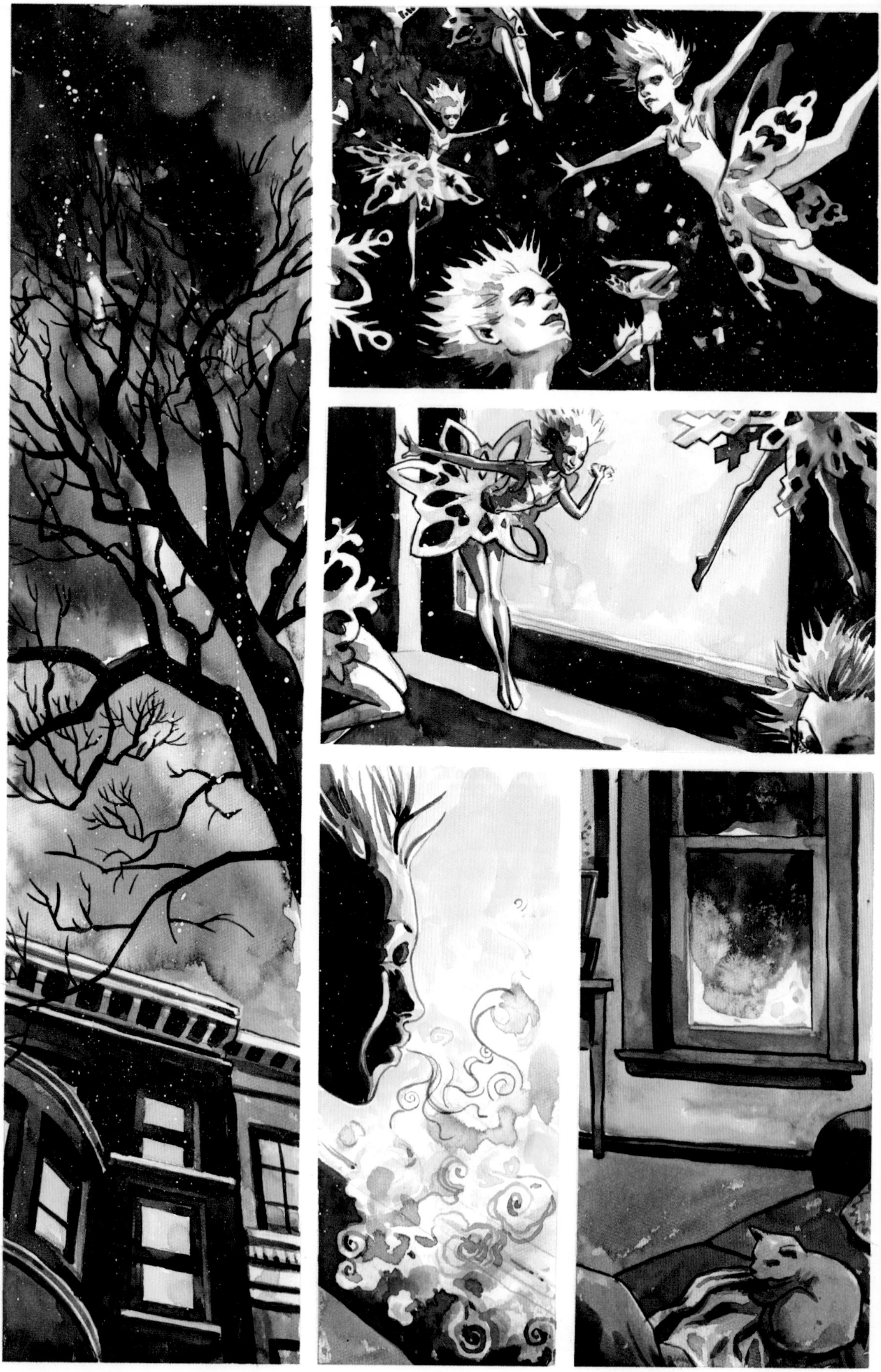

"Here comes suzy snowflake" -by JILL THOMPSON

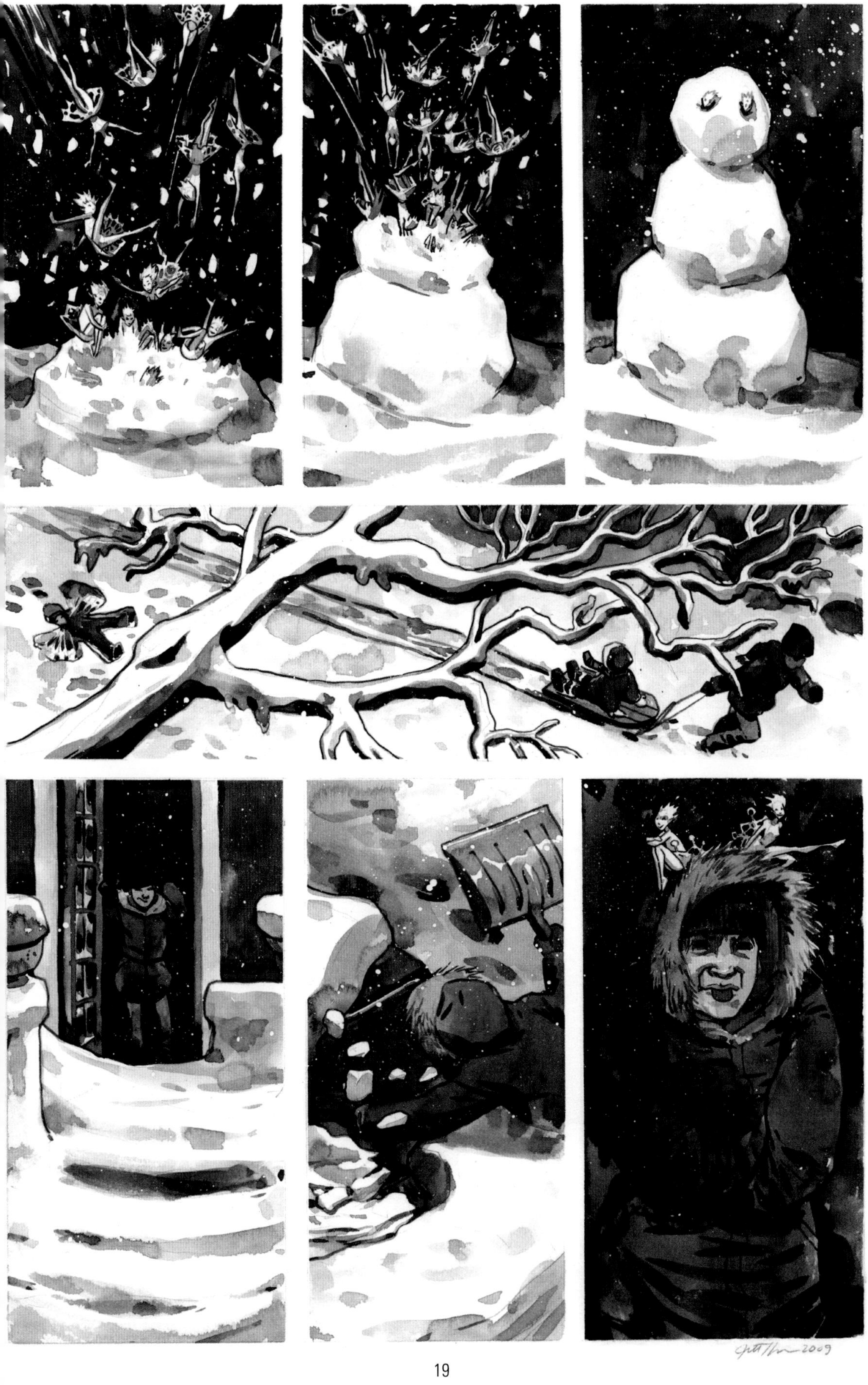

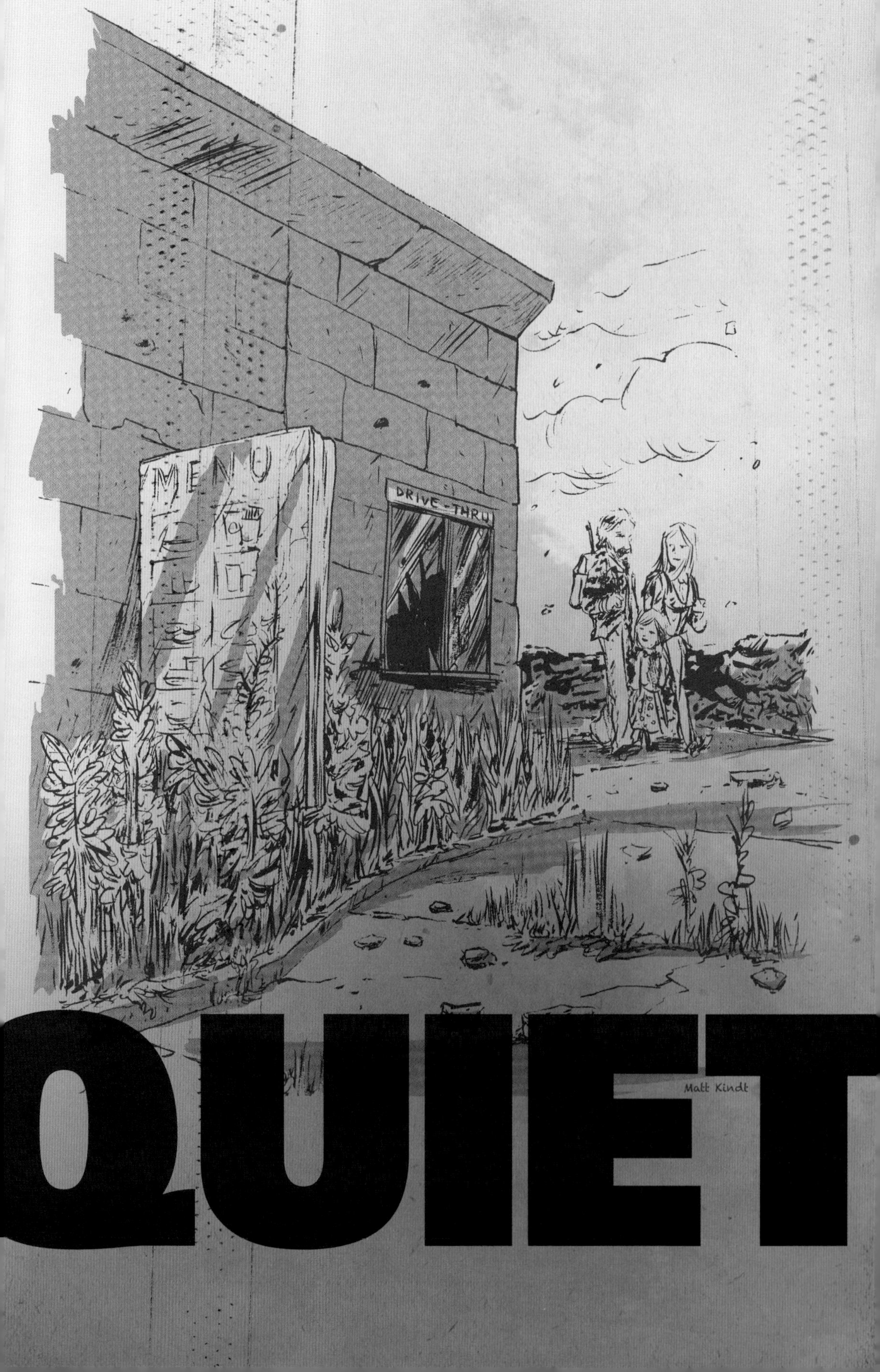
MENU
DRIVE-THRU

QUIET

Matt Kindt

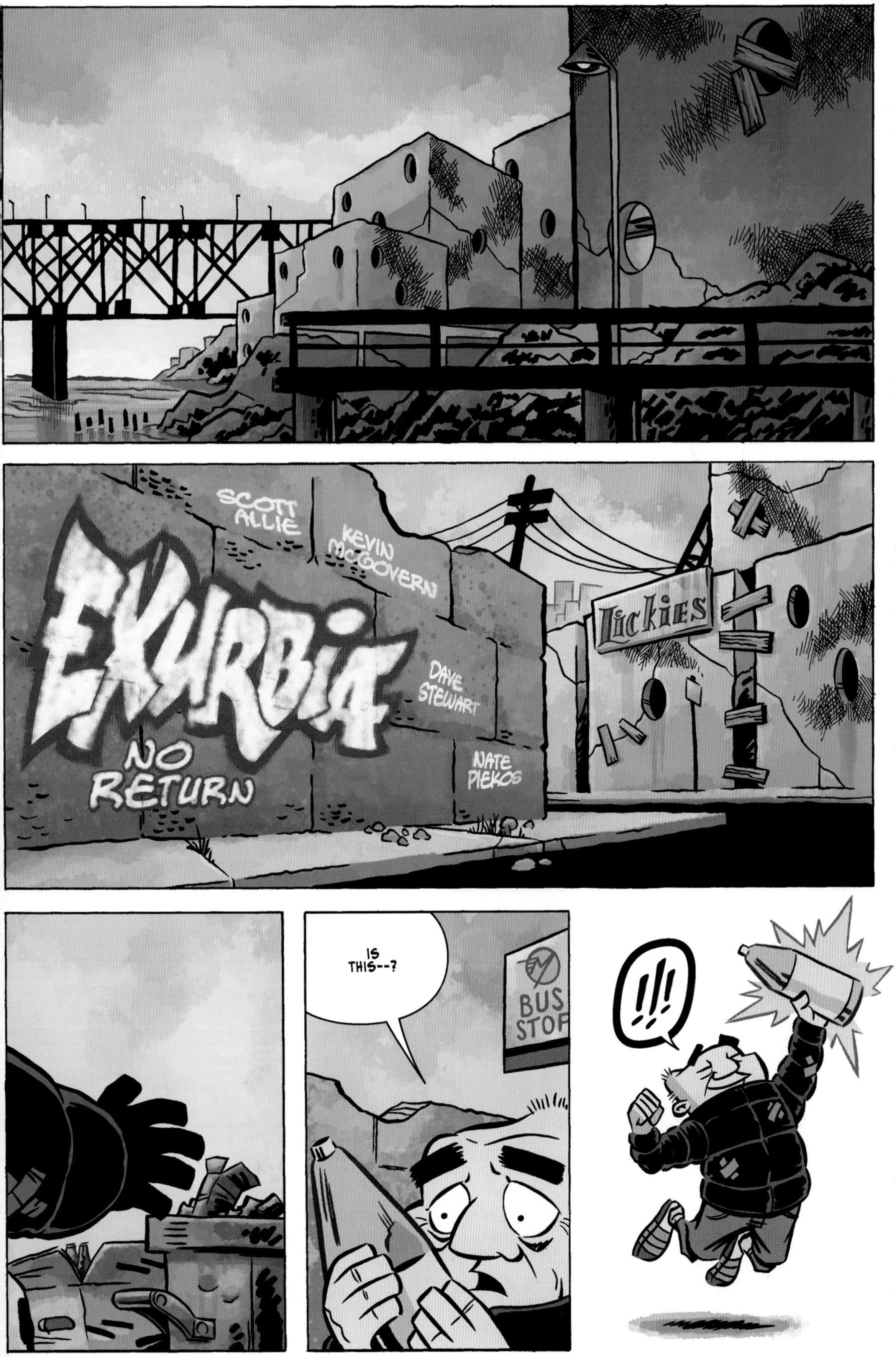
EXURBIA
NO RETURN
SCOTT ALLIE
KEVIN McGOVERN
DAVE STEWART
NATE PIEKOS
LICKIES
IS THIS--?
BUS STOP
!!!

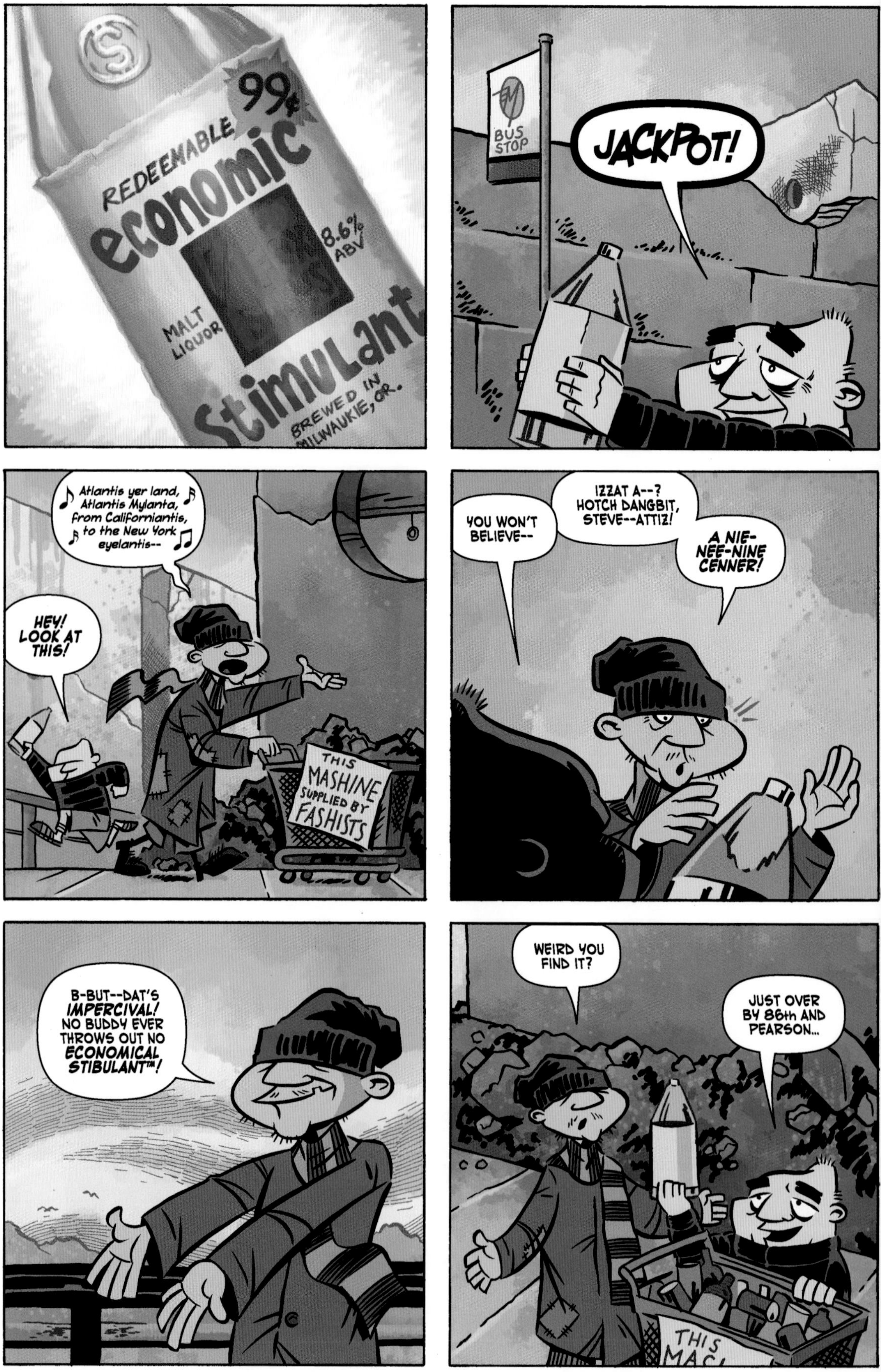
99¢
REDEEMABLE
economic
8.6% ABV
MALT LIQUOR
stimuLant
BREWED IN MILWAUKIE, OR.
BUS STOP
JACKPOT!
Atlantis yer land, Atlantis Mylanta, from Californiantis, to the New York eyelantis--
HEY! LOOK AT THIS!
THIS MASHINE SUPPLIED BY FASHISTS
YOU WON'T BELIEVE--
IZZAT A--? HOTCH DANGBIT, STEVE--ATTIZ!
A NIE-NEE-NINE CENNER!
B-BUT--DAT'S IMPERCIVAL! NO BUDDY EVER THROWS OUT NO ECONOMICAL STIBULANT™!
WEIRD YOU FIND IT?
JUST OVER BY 86th AND PEARSON...

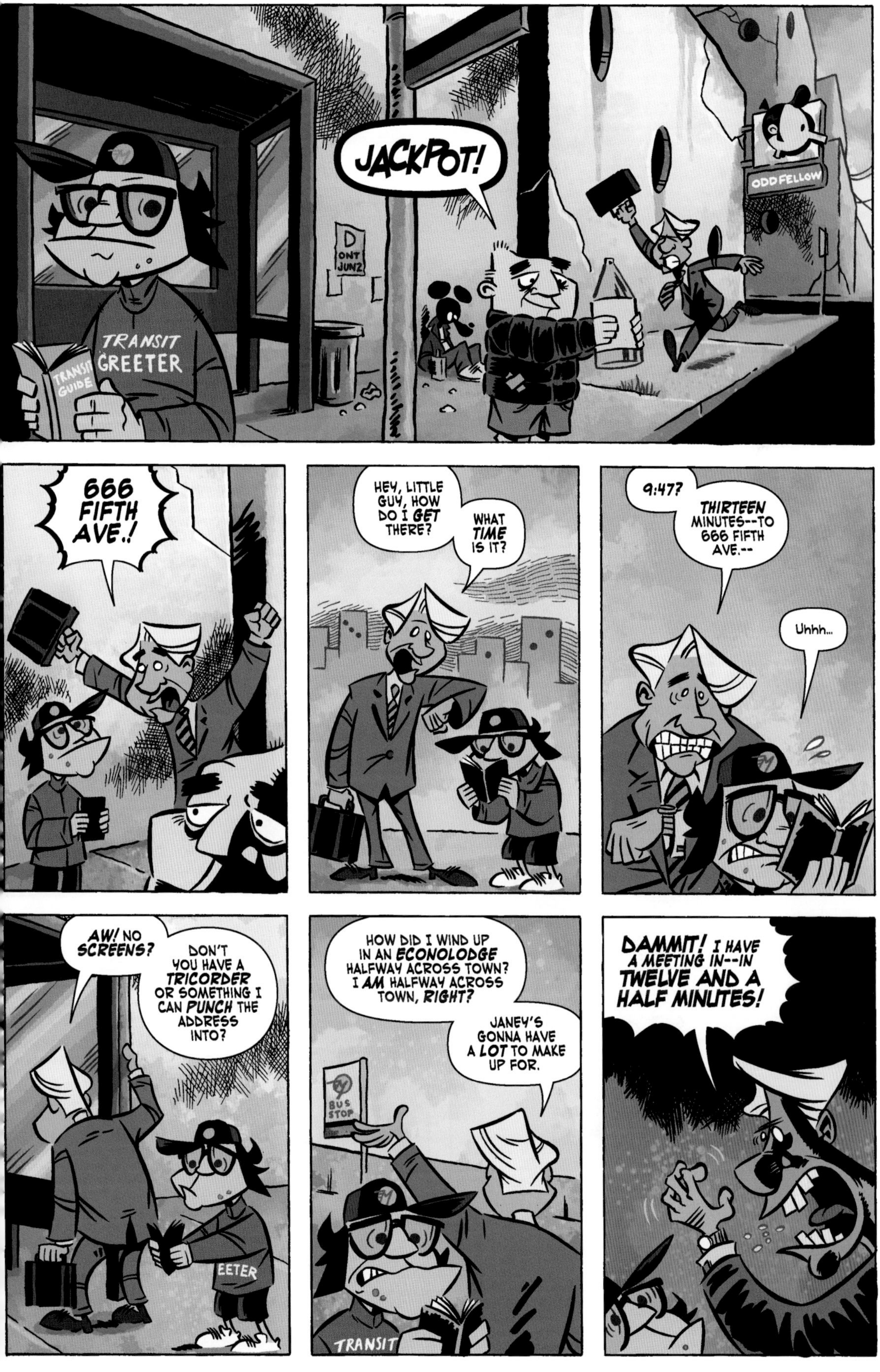

TRANSIT GREETER
TRANSIT GUIDE
JACKPOT!
D ONT JUNZ
ODD FELLOW
666 FIFTH AVE.!
HEY, LITTLE GUY, HOW DO I GET THERE?
WHAT TIME IS IT?
9:47?
THIRTEEN MINUTES--TO 666 FIFTH AVE.--
Uhhh...
AW! NO SCREENS?
DON'T YOU HAVE A TRICORDER OR SOMETHING I CAN PUNCH THE ADDRESS INTO?
EETER
HOW DID I WIND UP IN AN ECONOLODGE HALFWAY ACROSS TOWN? I AM HALFWAY ACROSS TOWN, RIGHT?
JANEY'S GONNA HAVE A LOT TO MAKE UP FOR.
BUS STOP
TRANSIT
DAMMIT! I HAVE A MEETING IN--IN TWELVE AND A HALF MINUTES!

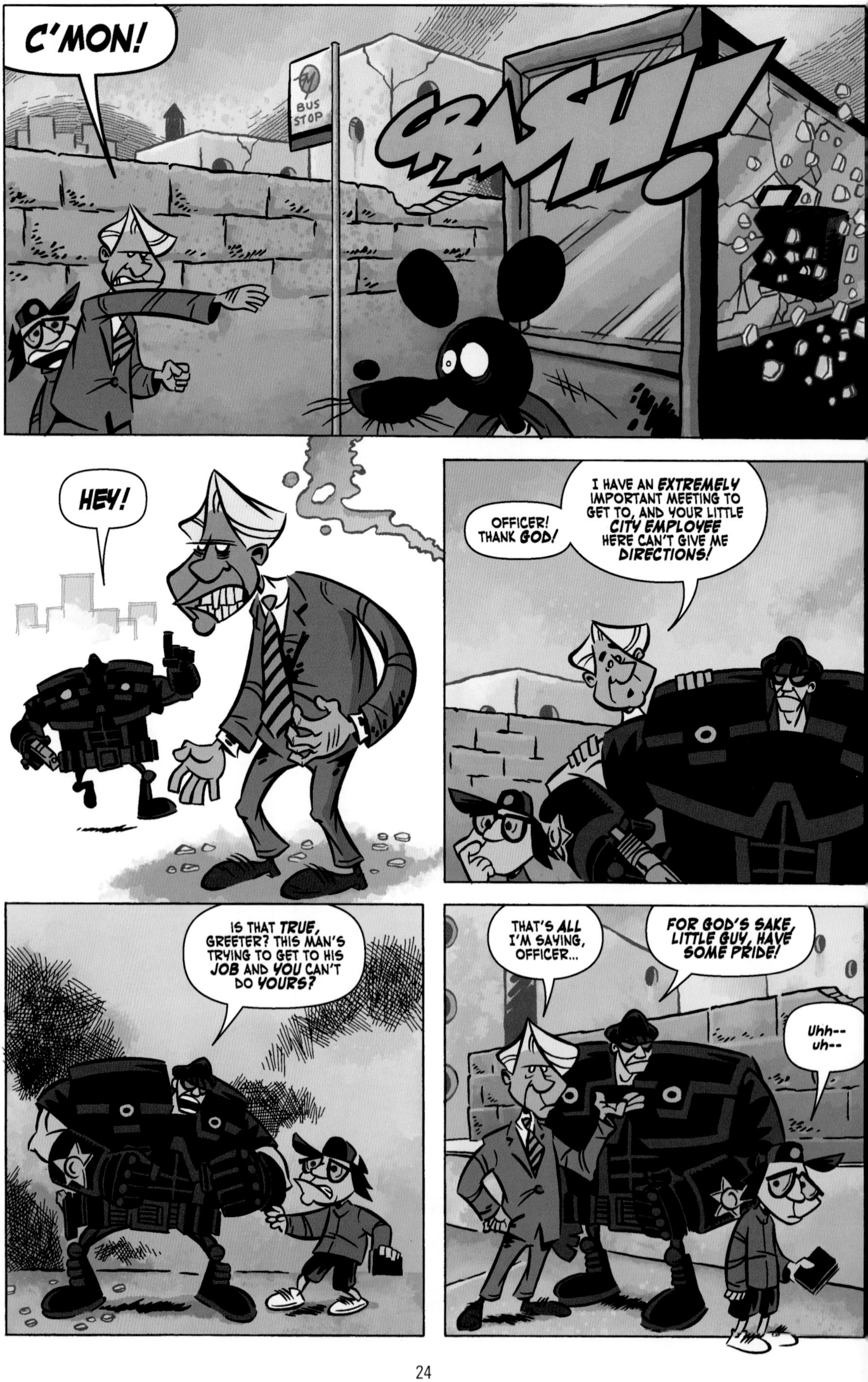
C'MON!
BUS STOP
CRASH!
HEY!
OFFICER! THANK GOD!
I HAVE AN EXTREMELY IMPORTANT MEETING TO GET TO, AND YOUR LITTLE CITY EMPLOYEE HERE CAN'T GIVE ME DIRECTIONS!
IS THAT TRUE, GREETER? THIS MAN'S TRYING TO GET TO HIS JOB AND YOU CAN'T DO YOURS?
THAT'S ALL I'M SAYING, OFFICER...
FOR GOD'S SAKE, LITTLE GUY, HAVE SOME PRIDE!
Uhh-- uh--

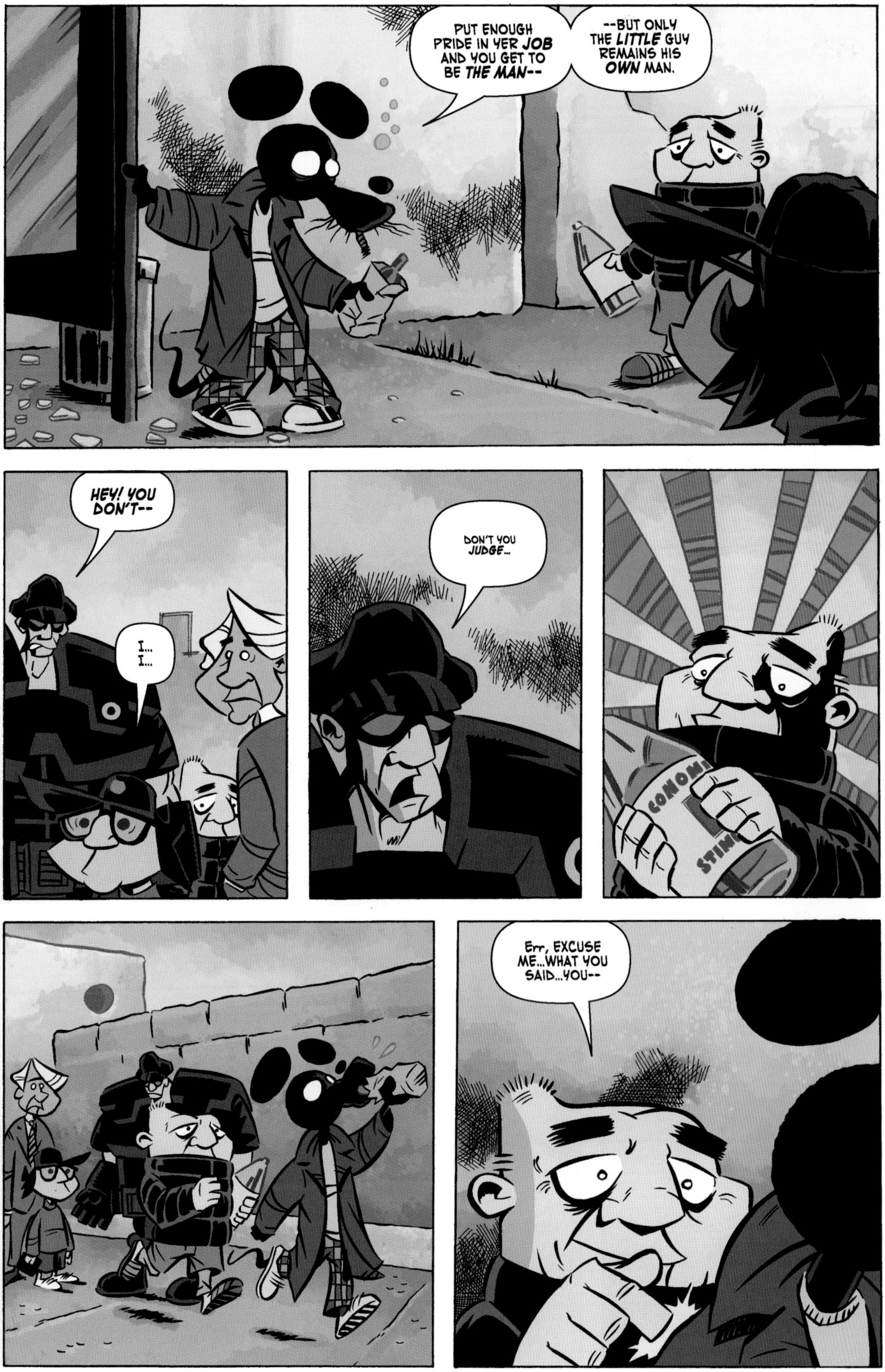
PUT ENOUGH PRIDE IN YER JOB AND YOU GET TO BE THE MAN--
--BUT ONLY THE LITTLE GUY REMAINS HIS OWN MAN.
HEY! YOU DON'T--
I... I...
DON'T YOU JUDGE...
Err, EXCUSE ME...WHAT YOU SAID...YOU--

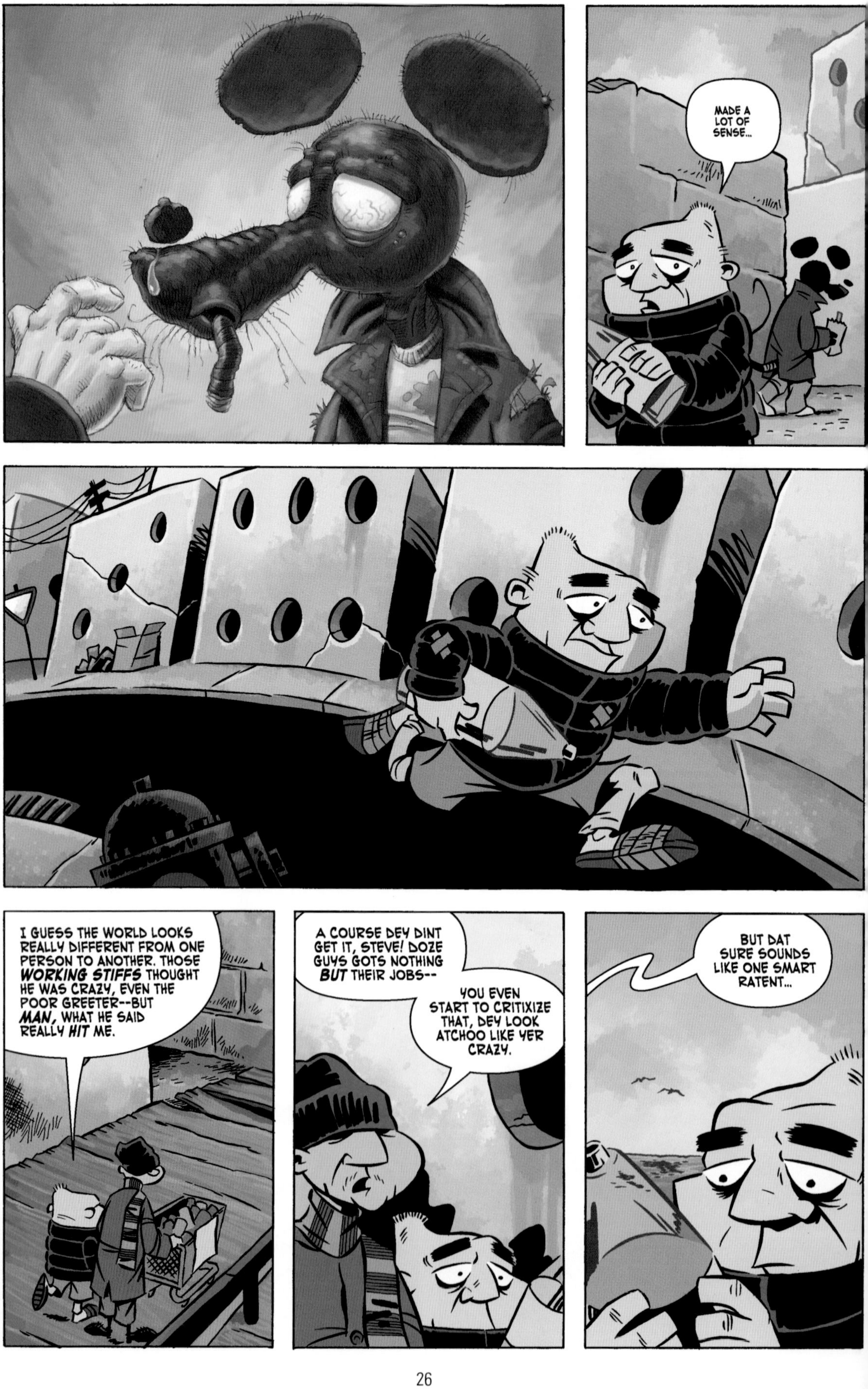
MADE A LOT OF SENSE...
I GUESS THE WORLD LOOKS REALLY DIFFERENT FROM ONE PERSON TO ANOTHER. THOSE WORKING STIFFS THOUGHT HE WAS CRAZY, EVEN THE POOR GREETER--BUT MAN, WHAT HE SAID REALLY HIT ME.
A COURSE DEY DINT GET IT, STEVE! DOZE GUYS GOTS NOTHING BUT THEIR JOBS--
YOU EVEN START TO CRITIXIZE THAT, DEY LOOK ATCHOO LIKE YER CRAZY.
BUT DAT SURE SOUNDS LIKE ONE SMART RATENT...

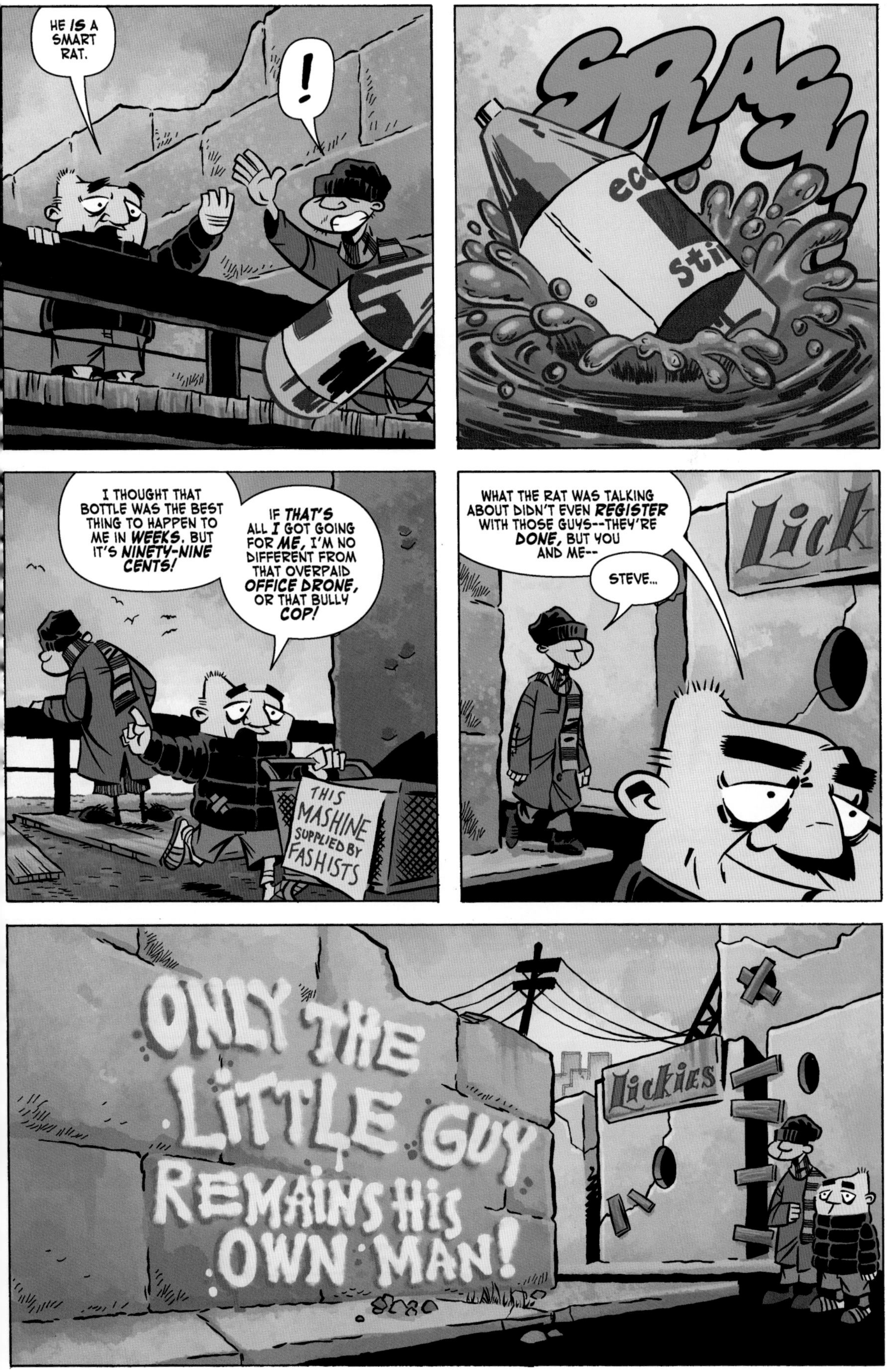
HE IS A SMART RAT.
!
SRASH
eco
Sti
I THOUGHT THAT BOTTLE WAS THE BEST THING TO HAPPEN TO ME IN WEEKS. BUT IT'S NINETY-NINE CENTS!
IF THAT'S ALL I GOT GOING FOR ME, I'M NO DIFFERENT FROM THAT OVERPAID OFFICE DRONE, OR THAT BULLY COP!
THIS MASHINE SUPPLIED BY FASHISTS
WHAT THE RAT WAS TALKING ABOUT DIDN'T EVEN REGISTER WITH THOSE GUYS--THEY'RE DONE, BUT YOU AND ME--
STEVE...
Lick
ONLY THE LITTLE GUY REMAINS HIS OWN MAN!
Lickies

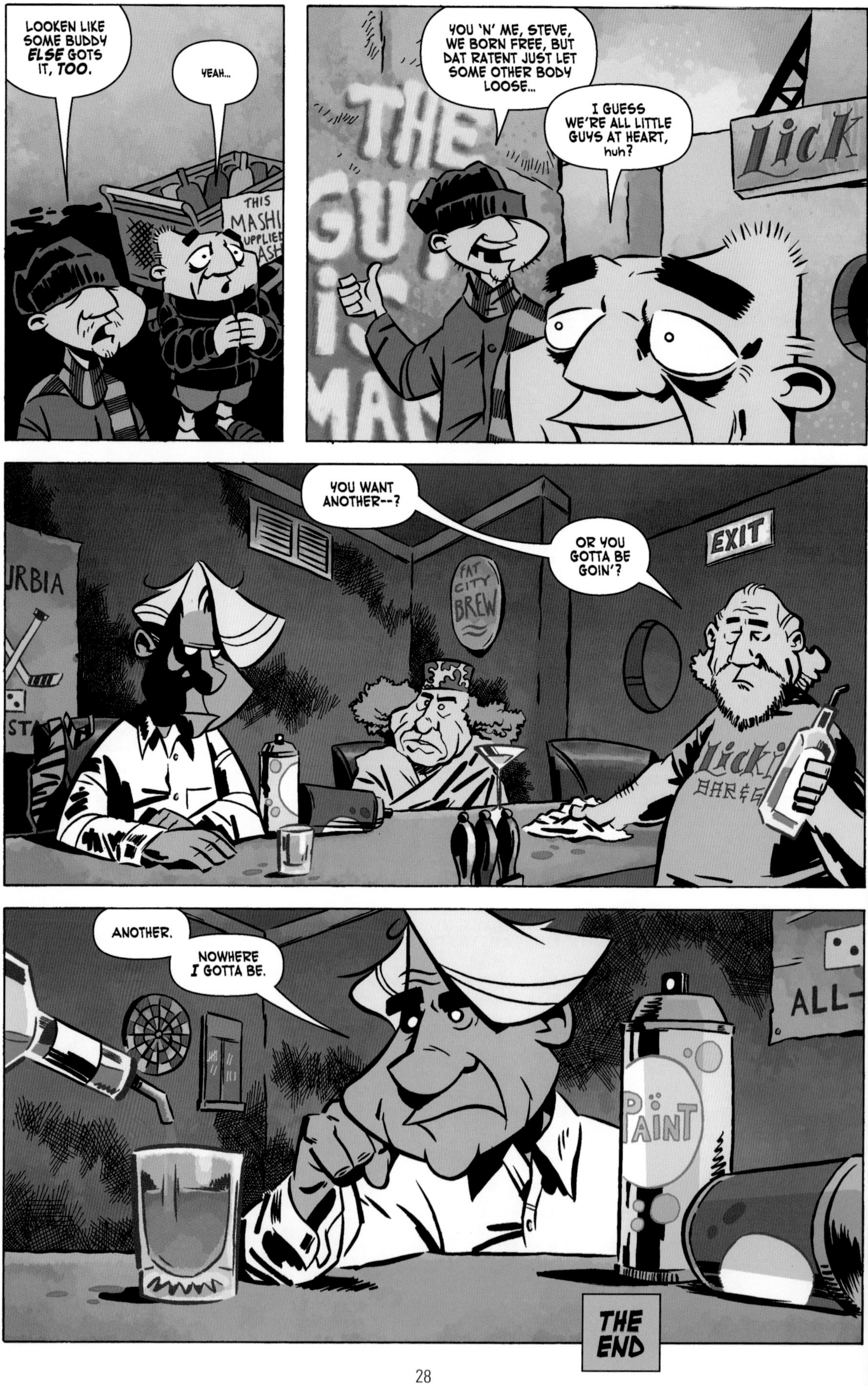
LOOKEN LIKE SOME BUDDY *ELSE* GOTS IT, *TOO*.
YEAH...
THIS
YOU 'N' ME, STEVE, WE BORN FREE, BUT DAT RATENT JUST LET SOME OTHER BODY LOOSE...
I GUESS WE'RE ALL LITTLE GUYS AT HEART, huh?
Lick
YOU WANT ANOTHER--?
OR YOU GOTTA BE GOIN'?
EXIT
FAT CITY BREW
URBIA
ANOTHER.
NOWHERE *I* GOTTA BE.
ALL-
PAINT
THE END

BASED ON THE TRUE CRIMES OF A "VULTURE CAPITALIST"

"GOING TO WORK"

JESSE REKLAW

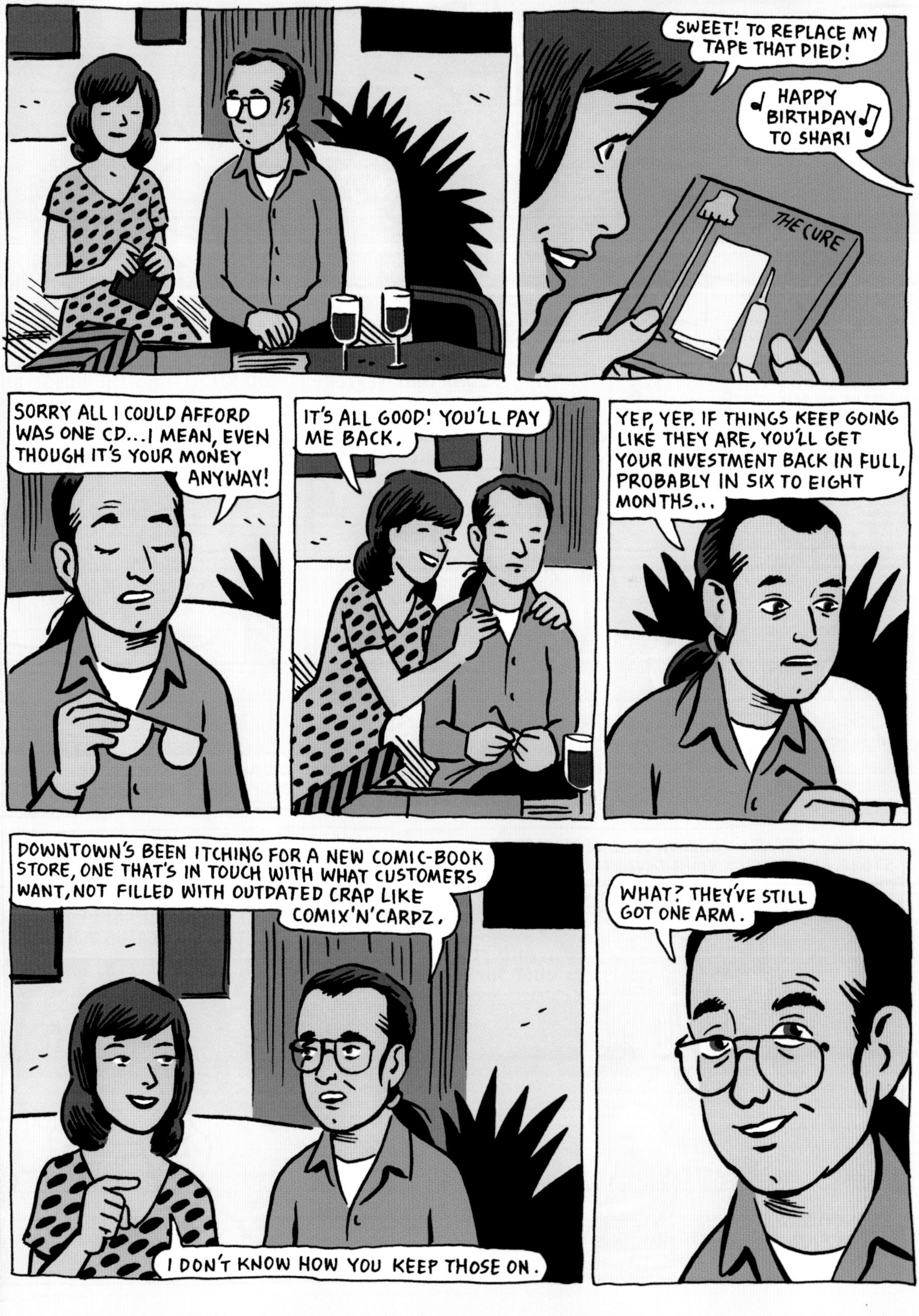

SWEET! TO REPLACE MY TAPE THAT DIED!
HAPPY BIRTHDAY TO SHARI
THE CURE
SORRY ALL I COULD AFFORD WAS ONE CD...I MEAN, EVEN THOUGH IT'S YOUR MONEY ANYWAY!
IT'S ALL GOOD! YOU'LL PAY ME BACK.
YEP, YEP. IF THINGS KEEP GOING LIKE THEY ARE, YOU'LL GET YOUR INVESTMENT BACK IN FULL, PROBABLY IN SIX TO EIGHT MONTHS...
DOWNTOWN'S BEEN ITCHING FOR A NEW COMIC-BOOK STORE, ONE THAT'S IN TOUCH WITH WHAT CUSTOMERS WANT, NOT FILLED WITH OUTDATED CRAP LIKE COMIX'N'CARDZ.
I DON'T KNOW HOW YOU KEEP THOSE ON.
WHAT? THEY'VE STILL GOT ONE ARM.

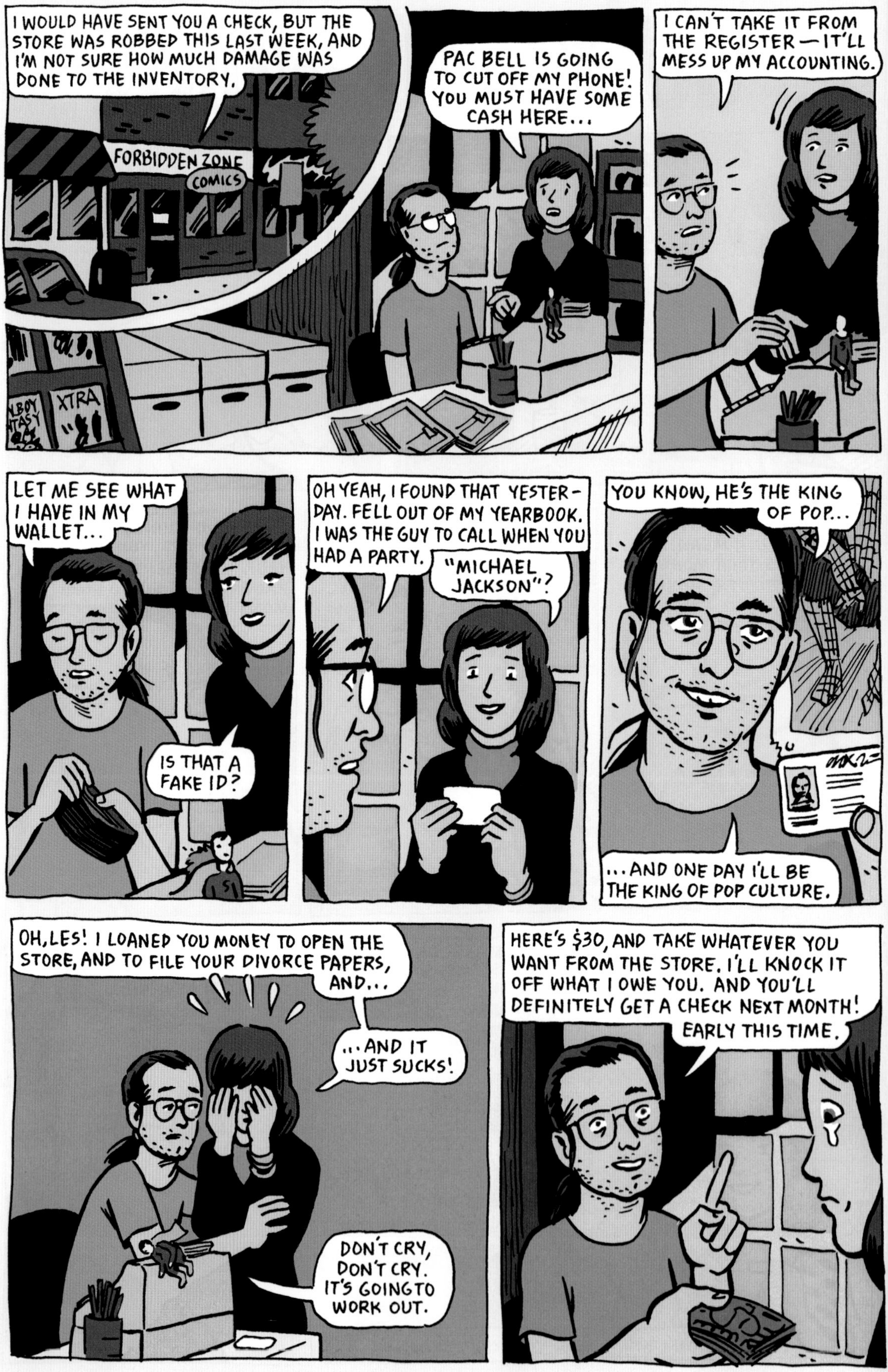
I WOULD HAVE SENT YOU A CHECK, BUT THE STORE WAS ROBBED THIS LAST WEEK, AND I'M NOT SURE HOW MUCH DAMAGE WAS DONE TO THE INVENTORY.
FORBIDDEN ZONE
COMICS
PAC BELL IS GOING TO CUT OFF MY PHONE! YOU MUST HAVE SOME CASH HERE...
I CAN'T TAKE IT FROM THE REGISTER—IT'LL MESS UP MY ACCOUNTING.
LET ME SEE WHAT I HAVE IN MY WALLET...
IS THAT A FAKE ID?
OH YEAH, I FOUND THAT YESTERDAY. FELL OUT OF MY YEARBOOK. I WAS THE GUY TO CALL WHEN YOU HAD A PARTY.
"MICHAEL JACKSON"?
YOU KNOW, HE'S THE KING OF POP...
...AND ONE DAY I'LL BE THE KING OF POP CULTURE.
OH, LES! I LOANED YOU MONEY TO OPEN THE STORE, AND TO FILE YOUR DIVORCE PAPERS, AND...
...AND IT JUST SUCKS!
DON'T CRY, DON'T CRY. IT'S GOING TO WORK OUT.
HERE'S $30, AND TAKE WHATEVER YOU WANT FROM THE STORE. I'LL KNOCK IT OFF WHAT I OWE YOU. AND YOU'LL DEFINITELY GET A CHECK NEXT MONTH!
EARLY THIS TIME.

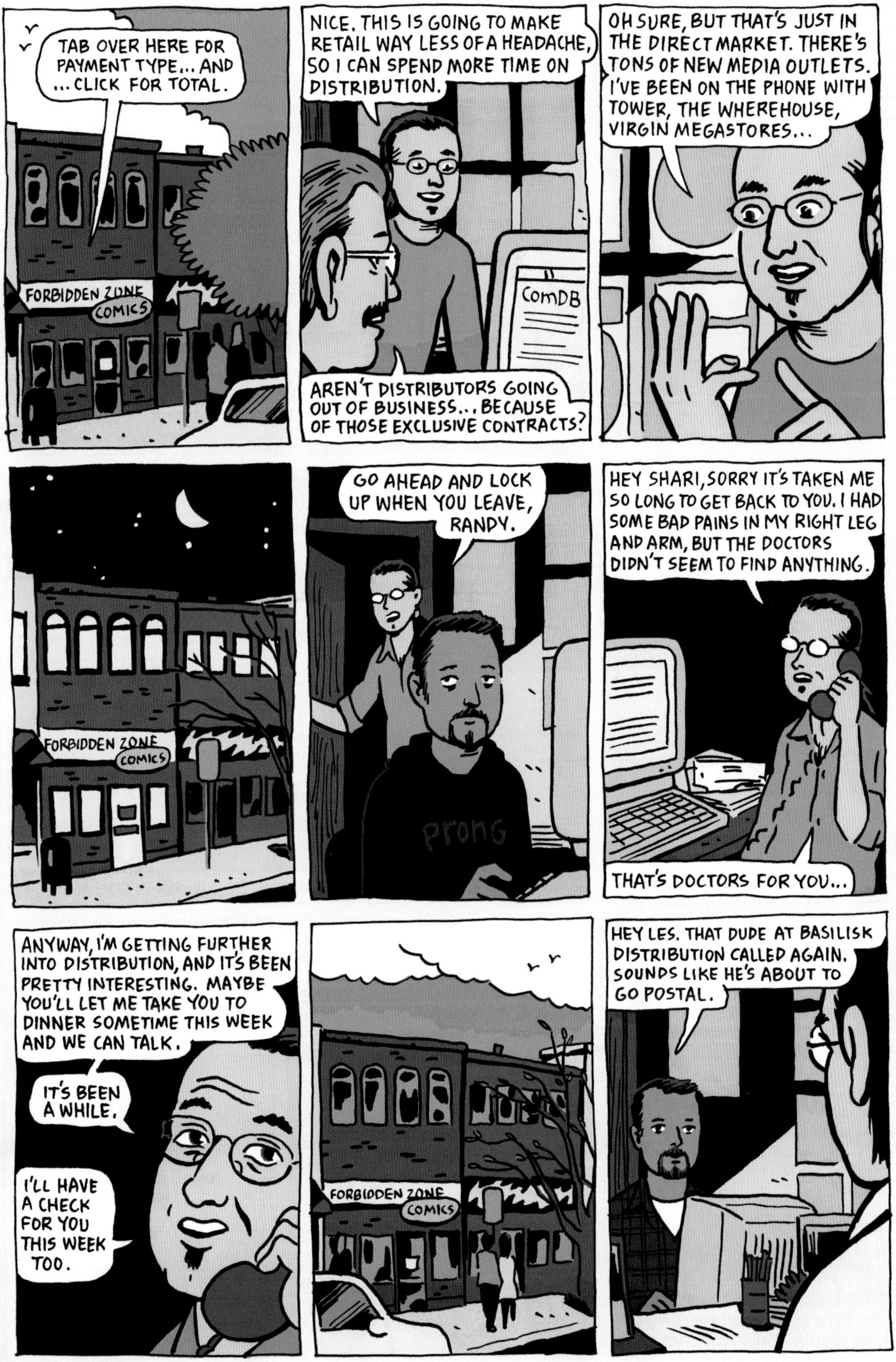
TAB OVER HERE FOR PAYMENT TYPE... AND ...CLICK FOR TOTAL.
FORBIDDEN ZONE COMICS
NICE. THIS IS GOING TO MAKE RETAIL WAY LESS OF A HEADACHE, SO I CAN SPEND MORE TIME ON DISTRIBUTION.
ComDB
AREN'T DISTRIBUTORS GOING OUT OF BUSINESS... BECAUSE OF THOSE EXCLUSIVE CONTRACTS?
OH SURE, BUT THAT'S JUST IN THE DIRECT MARKET. THERE'S TONS OF NEW MEDIA OUTLETS. I'VE BEEN ON THE PHONE WITH TOWER, THE WHEREHOUSE, VIRGIN MEGASTORES...
FORBIDDEN ZONE COMICS
GO AHEAD AND LOCK UP WHEN YOU LEAVE, RANDY.
Prong
HEY SHARI, SORRY IT'S TAKEN ME SO LONG TO GET BACK TO YOU. I HAD SOME BAD PAINS IN MY RIGHT LEG AND ARM, BUT THE DOCTORS DIDN'T SEEM TO FIND ANYTHING.
THAT'S DOCTORS FOR YOU...
ANYWAY, I'M GETTING FURTHER INTO DISTRIBUTION, AND IT'S BEEN PRETTY INTERESTING. MAYBE YOU'LL LET ME TAKE YOU TO DINNER SOMETIME THIS WEEK AND WE CAN TALK.
IT'S BEEN A WHILE.
I'LL HAVE A CHECK FOR YOU THIS WEEK TOO.
FORBIDDEN ZONE COMICS
HEY LES. THAT DUDE AT BASILISK DISTRIBUTION CALLED AGAIN. SOUNDS LIKE HE'S ABOUT TO GO POSTAL.

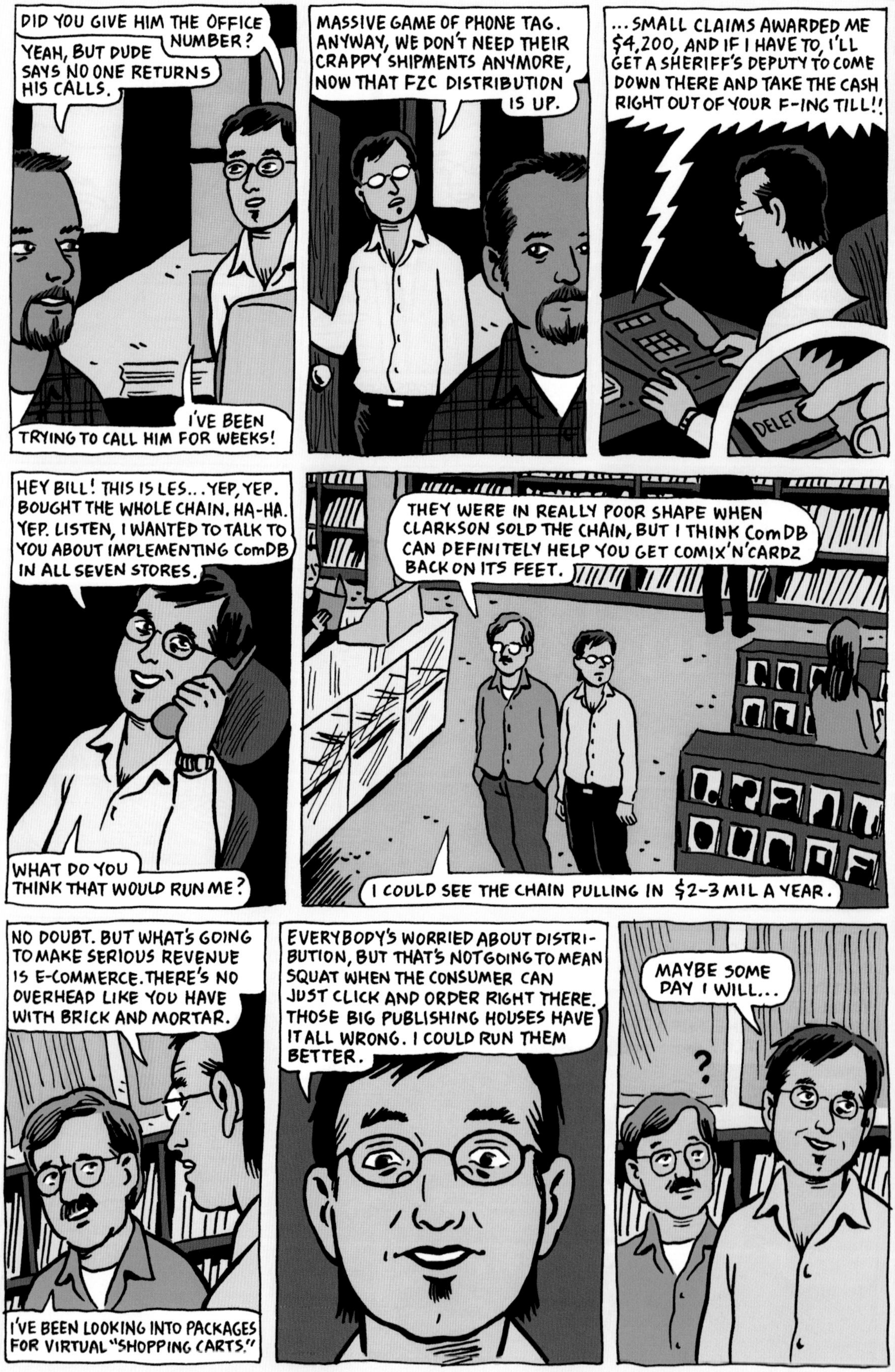
DID YOU GIVE HIM THE OFFICE NUMBER?
YEAH, BUT DUDE SAYS NO ONE RETURNS HIS CALLS.
I'VE BEEN TRYING TO CALL HIM FOR WEEKS!
MASSIVE GAME OF PHONE TAG. ANYWAY, WE DON'T NEED THEIR CRAPPY SHIPMENTS ANYMORE, NOW THAT FZC DISTRIBUTION IS UP.
...SMALL CLAIMS AWARDED ME $4,200, AND IF I HAVE TO, I'LL GET A SHERIFF'S DEPUTY TO COME DOWN THERE AND TAKE THE CASH RIGHT OUT OF YOUR F-ING TILL!!
DELET
HEY BILL! THIS IS LES... YEP, YEP. BOUGHT THE WHOLE CHAIN. HA-HA. YEP. LISTEN, I WANTED TO TALK TO YOU ABOUT IMPLEMENTING ComDB IN ALL SEVEN STORES.
WHAT DO YOU THINK THAT WOULD RUN ME?
THEY WERE IN REALLY POOR SHAPE WHEN CLARKSON SOLD THE CHAIN, BUT I THINK ComDB CAN DEFINITELY HELP YOU GET COMIX'N'CARDZ BACK ON ITS FEET.
I COULD SEE THE CHAIN PULLING IN $2-3 MIL A YEAR.
NO DOUBT. BUT WHAT'S GOING TO MAKE SERIOUS REVENUE IS E-COMMERCE. THERE'S NO OVERHEAD LIKE YOU HAVE WITH BRICK AND MORTAR.
I'VE BEEN LOOKING INTO PACKAGES FOR VIRTUAL "SHOPPING CARTS."
EVERYBODY'S WORRIED ABOUT DISTRIBUTION, BUT THAT'S NOT GOING TO MEAN SQUAT WHEN THE CONSUMER CAN JUST CLICK AND ORDER RIGHT THERE. THOSE BIG PUBLISHING HOUSES HAVE IT ALL WRONG. I COULD RUN THEM BETTER.
MAYBE SOME DAY I WILL...
?

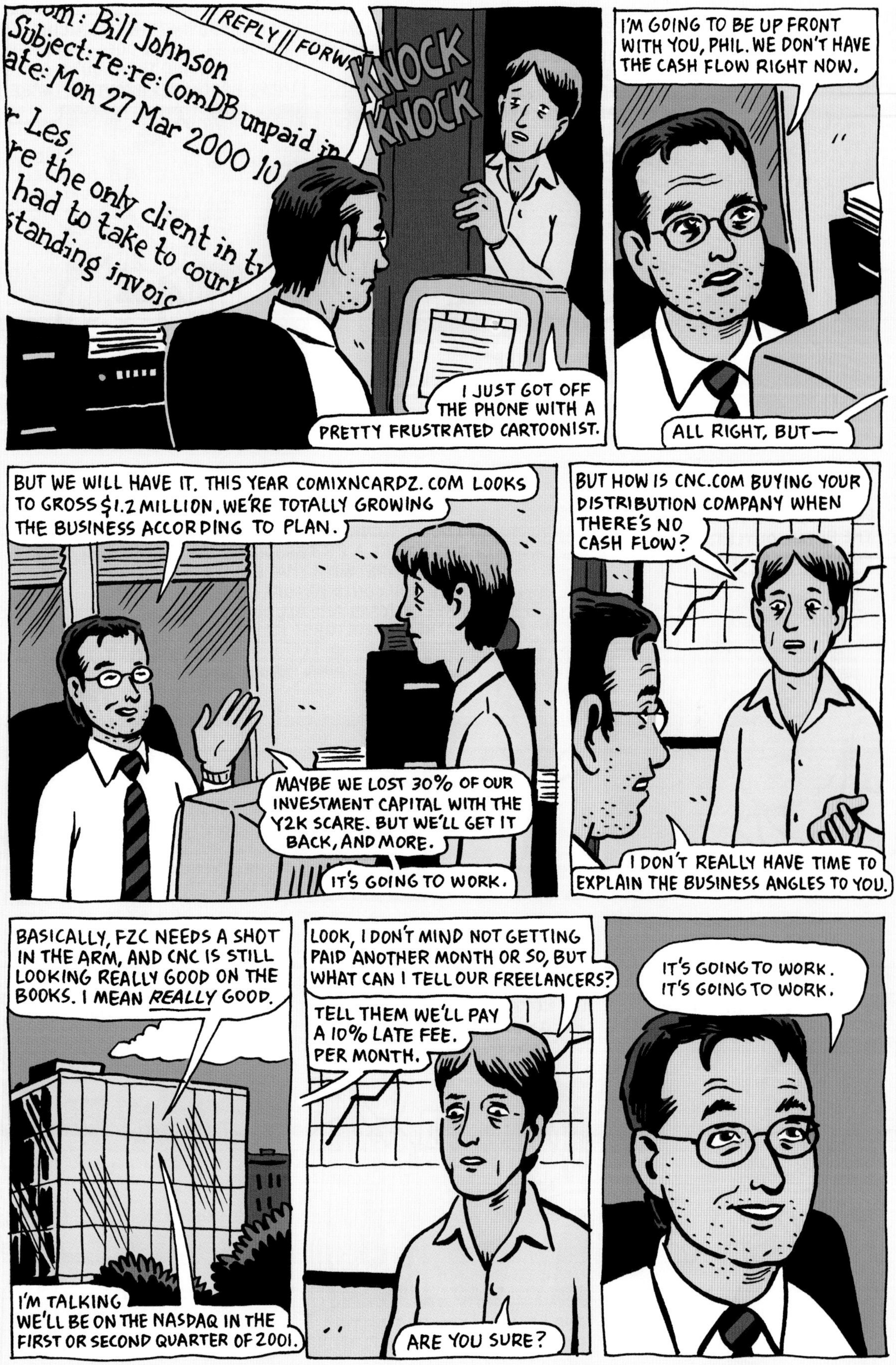

om: Bill Johnson
Subject: re: re: ComDB unpaid in
ate: Mon 27 Mar 2000 10
r Les,
re the only client in t
had to take to court
standing invoic
REPLY
FORW
KNOCK KNOCK
I JUST GOT OFF THE PHONE WITH A PRETTY FRUSTRATED CARTOONIST.
I'M GOING TO BE UP FRONT WITH YOU, PHIL. WE DON'T HAVE THE CASH FLOW RIGHT NOW.
ALL RIGHT, BUT—
BUT WE WILL HAVE IT. THIS YEAR COMIXNCARDZ.COM LOOKS TO GROSS $1.2 MILLION. WE'RE TOTALLY GROWING THE BUSINESS ACCORDING TO PLAN.
MAYBE WE LOST 30% OF OUR INVESTMENT CAPITAL WITH THE Y2K SCARE. BUT WE'LL GET IT BACK, AND MORE.
IT'S GOING TO WORK.
BUT HOW IS CNC.COM BUYING YOUR DISTRIBUTION COMPANY WHEN THERE'S NO CASH FLOW?
I DON'T REALLY HAVE TIME TO EXPLAIN THE BUSINESS ANGLES TO YOU.
BASICALLY, FZC NEEDS A SHOT IN THE ARM, AND CNC IS STILL LOOKING REALLY GOOD ON THE BOOKS. I MEAN REALLY GOOD.
I'M TALKING WE'LL BE ON THE NASDAQ IN THE FIRST OR SECOND QUARTER OF 2001.
LOOK, I DON'T MIND NOT GETTING PAID ANOTHER MONTH OR SO, BUT WHAT CAN I TELL OUR FREELANCERS?
TELL THEM WE'LL PAY A 10% LATE FEE. PER MONTH.
ARE YOU SURE?
IT'S GOING TO WORK. IT'S GOING TO WORK.

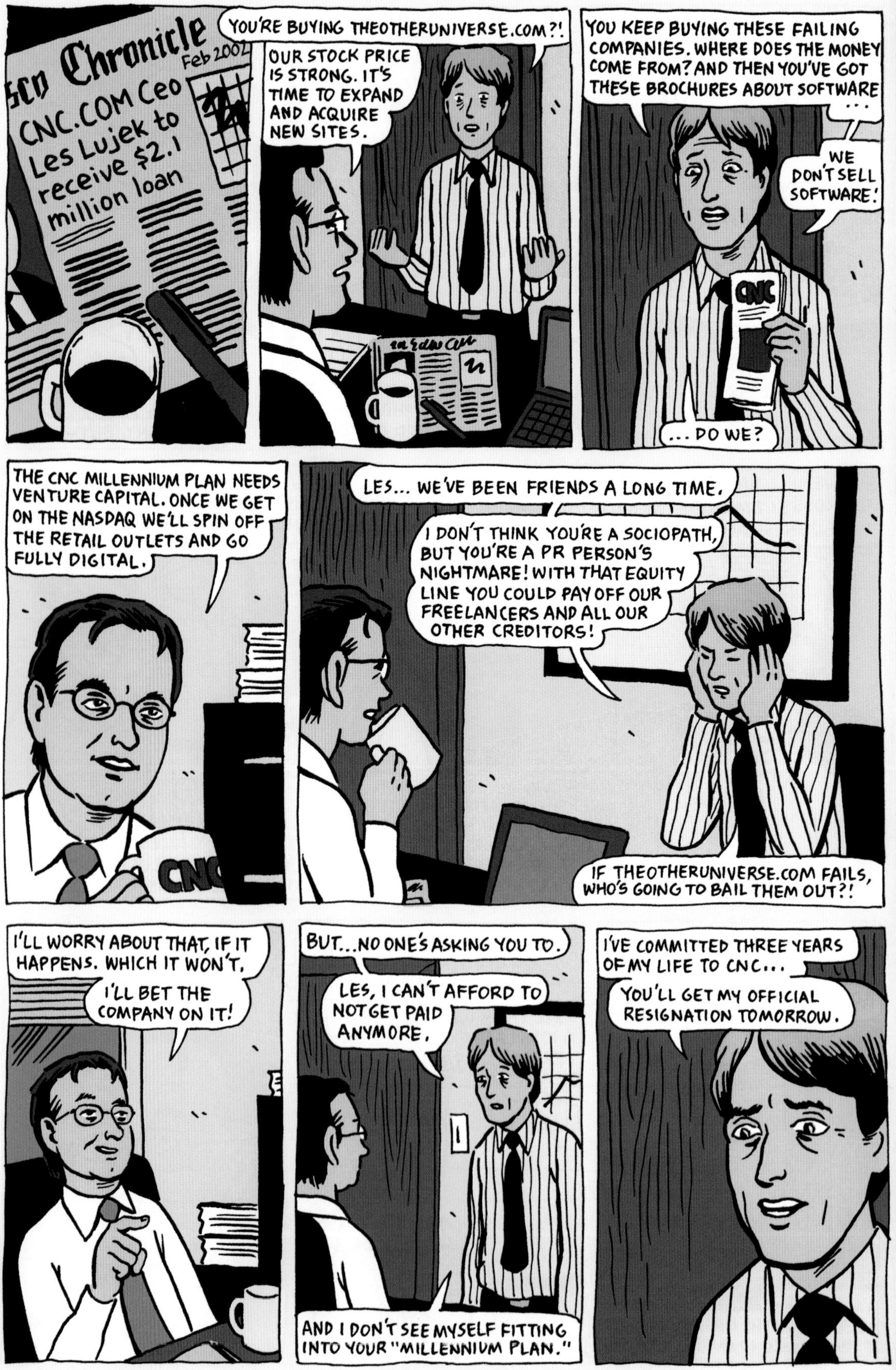

Chronicle
Feb 2002
CNC.COM Ceo Les Lujek to receive $2.1 million loan
YOU'RE BUYING THEOTHERUNIVERSE.COM?!
OUR STOCK PRICE IS STRONG. IT'S TIME TO EXPAND AND ACQUIRE NEW SITES.
YOU KEEP BUYING THESE FAILING COMPANIES. WHERE DOES THE MONEY COME FROM? AND THEN YOU'VE GOT THESE BROCHURES ABOUT SOFTWARE...
WE DON'T SELL SOFTWARE!
CNC
... DO WE?
THE CNC MILLENNIUM PLAN NEEDS VENTURE CAPITAL. ONCE WE GET ON THE NASDAQ WE'LL SPIN OFF THE RETAIL OUTLETS AND GO FULLY DIGITAL.
CNC
LES... WE'VE BEEN FRIENDS A LONG TIME.
I DON'T THINK YOU'RE A SOCIOPATH, BUT YOU'RE A PR PERSON'S NIGHTMARE! WITH THAT EQUITY LINE YOU COULD PAY OFF OUR FREELANCERS AND ALL OUR OTHER CREDITORS!
IF THEOTHERUNIVERSE.COM FAILS, WHO'S GOING TO BAIL THEM OUT?!
I'LL WORRY ABOUT THAT, IF IT HAPPENS. WHICH IT WON'T.
I'LL BET THE COMPANY ON IT!
BUT...NO ONE'S ASKING YOU TO.
LES, I CAN'T AFFORD TO NOT GET PAID ANYMORE.
AND I DON'T SEE MYSELF FITTING INTO YOUR "MILLENNIUM PLAN."
I'VE COMMITTED THREE YEARS OF MY LIFE TO CNC...
YOU'LL GET MY OFFICIAL RESIGNATION TOMORROW.

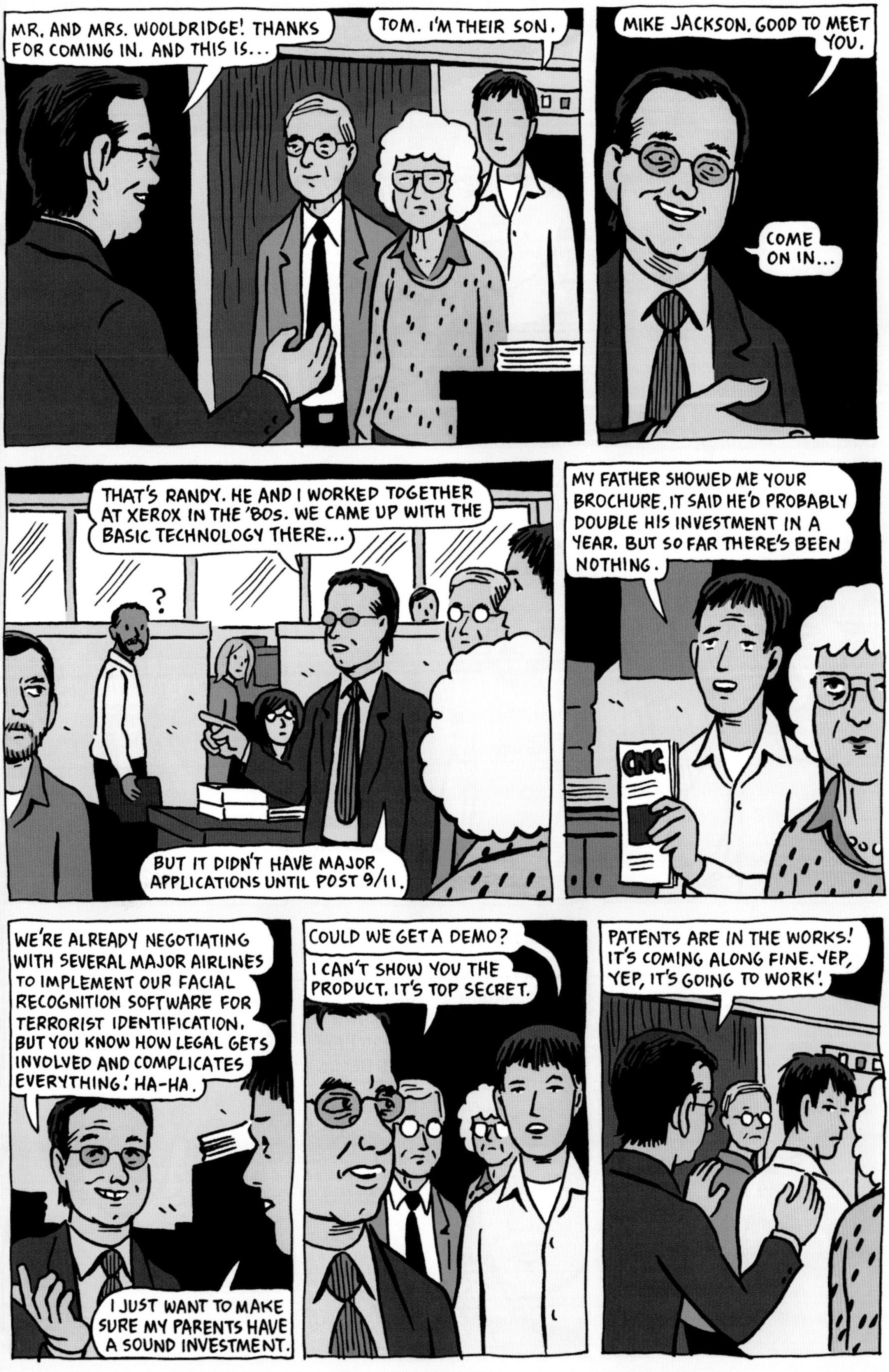
MR. AND MRS. WOOLDRIDGE! THANKS FOR COMING IN. AND THIS IS...
TOM. I'M THEIR SON.
MIKE JACKSON. GOOD TO MEET YOU.
COME ON IN...
THAT'S RANDY. HE AND I WORKED TOGETHER AT XEROX IN THE '80S. WE CAME UP WITH THE BASIC TECHNOLOGY THERE...
?
BUT IT DIDN'T HAVE MAJOR APPLICATIONS UNTIL POST 9/11.
MY FATHER SHOWED ME YOUR BROCHURE. IT SAID HE'D PROBABLY DOUBLE HIS INVESTMENT IN A YEAR. BUT SO FAR THERE'S BEEN NOTHING.
CNC
WE'RE ALREADY NEGOTIATING WITH SEVERAL MAJOR AIRLINES TO IMPLEMENT OUR FACIAL RECOGNITION SOFTWARE FOR TERRORIST IDENTIFICATION. BUT YOU KNOW HOW LEGAL GETS INVOLVED AND COMPLICATES EVERYTHING! HA-HA.
I JUST WANT TO MAKE SURE MY PARENTS HAVE A SOUND INVESTMENT.
COULD WE GET A DEMO?
I CAN'T SHOW YOU THE PRODUCT. IT'S TOP SECRET.
PATENTS ARE IN THE WORKS! IT'S COMING ALONG FINE. YEP, YEP, IT'S GOING TO WORK!

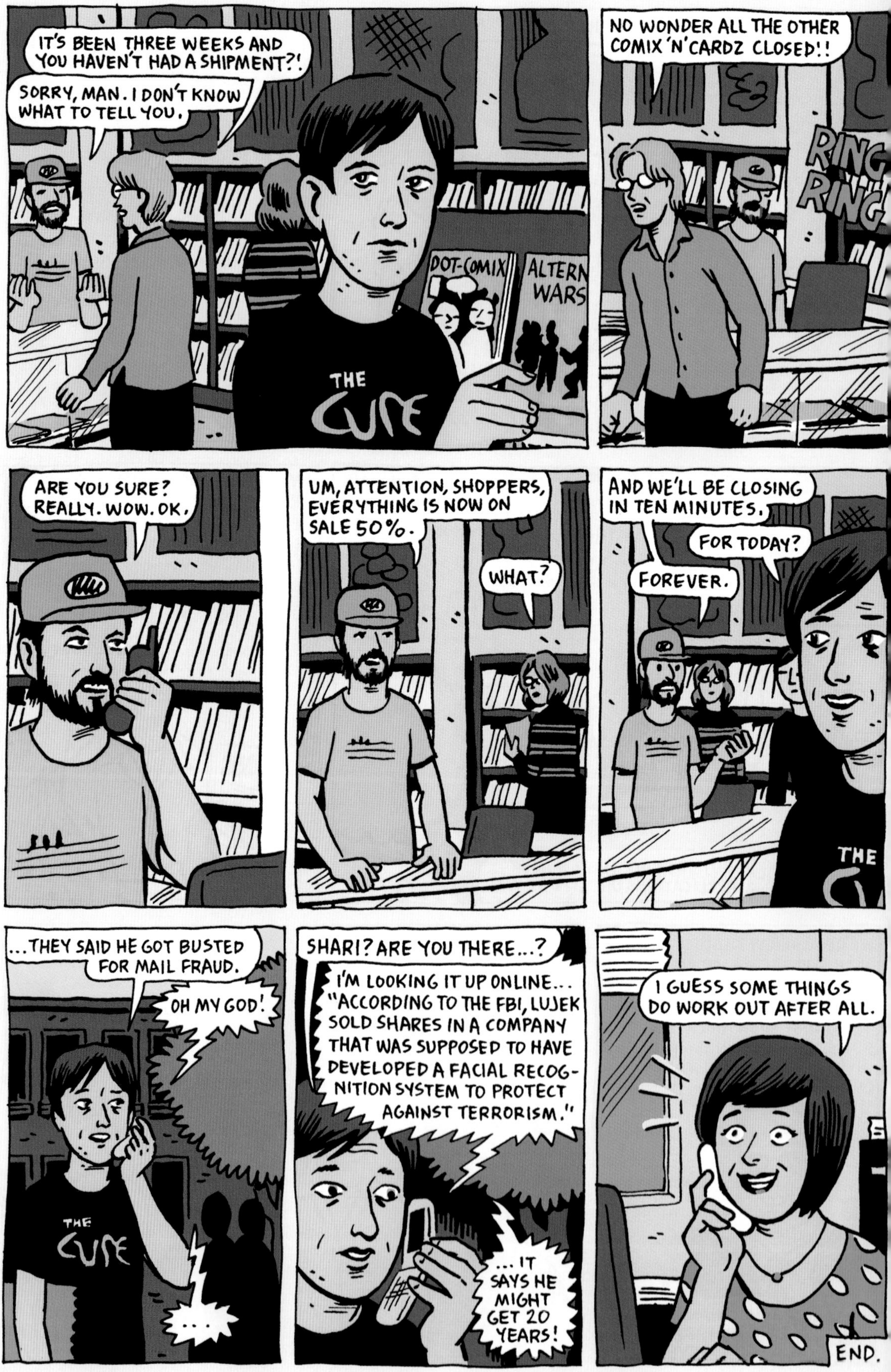
IT'S BEEN THREE WEEKS AND YOU HAVEN'T HAD A SHIPMENT?!
SORRY, MAN. I DON'T KNOW WHAT TO TELL YOU.
DOT-COMIX
ALTERN WARS
THE CURE
NO WONDER ALL THE OTHER COMIX 'N' CARDZ CLOSED!!
RING RING
ARE YOU SURE? REALLY. WOW. OK.
UM, ATTENTION, SHOPPERS, EVERYTHING IS NOW ON SALE 50%.
WHAT?
AND WE'LL BE CLOSING IN TEN MINUTES.
FOR TODAY?
FOREVER.
THE
...THEY SAID HE GOT BUSTED FOR MAIL FRAUD.
OH MY GOD!
THE CURE
...
SHARI? ARE YOU THERE...?
I'M LOOKING IT UP ONLINE... "ACCORDING TO THE FBI, LUJEK SOLD SHARES IN A COMPANY THAT WAS SUPPOSED TO HAVE DEVELOPED A FACIAL RECOGNITION SYSTEM TO PROTECT AGAINST TERRORISM."
...IT SAYS HE MIGHT GET 20 YEARS!
I GUESS SOME THINGS DO WORK OUT AFTER ALL.
END.

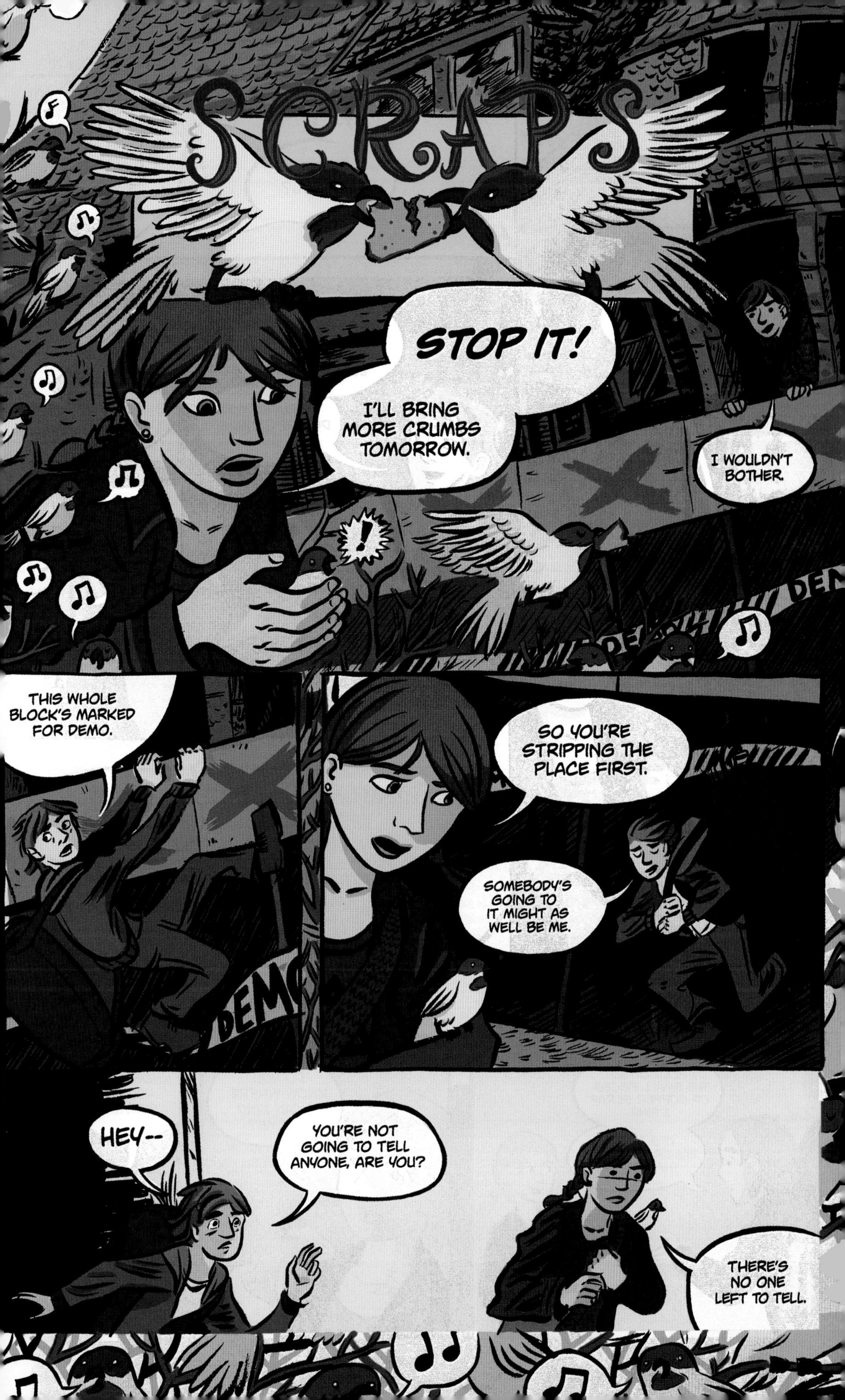
SCRAPS
STOP IT!
I'LL BRING MORE CRUMBS TOMORROW.
I WOULDN'T BOTHER.
!
THIS WHOLE BLOCK'S MARKED FOR DEMO.
SO YOU'RE STRIPPING THE PLACE FIRST.
SOMEBODY'S GOING TO IT MIGHT AS WELL BE ME.
HEY--
YOU'RE NOT GOING TO TELL ANYONE, ARE YOU?
THERE'S NO ONE LEFT TO TELL.

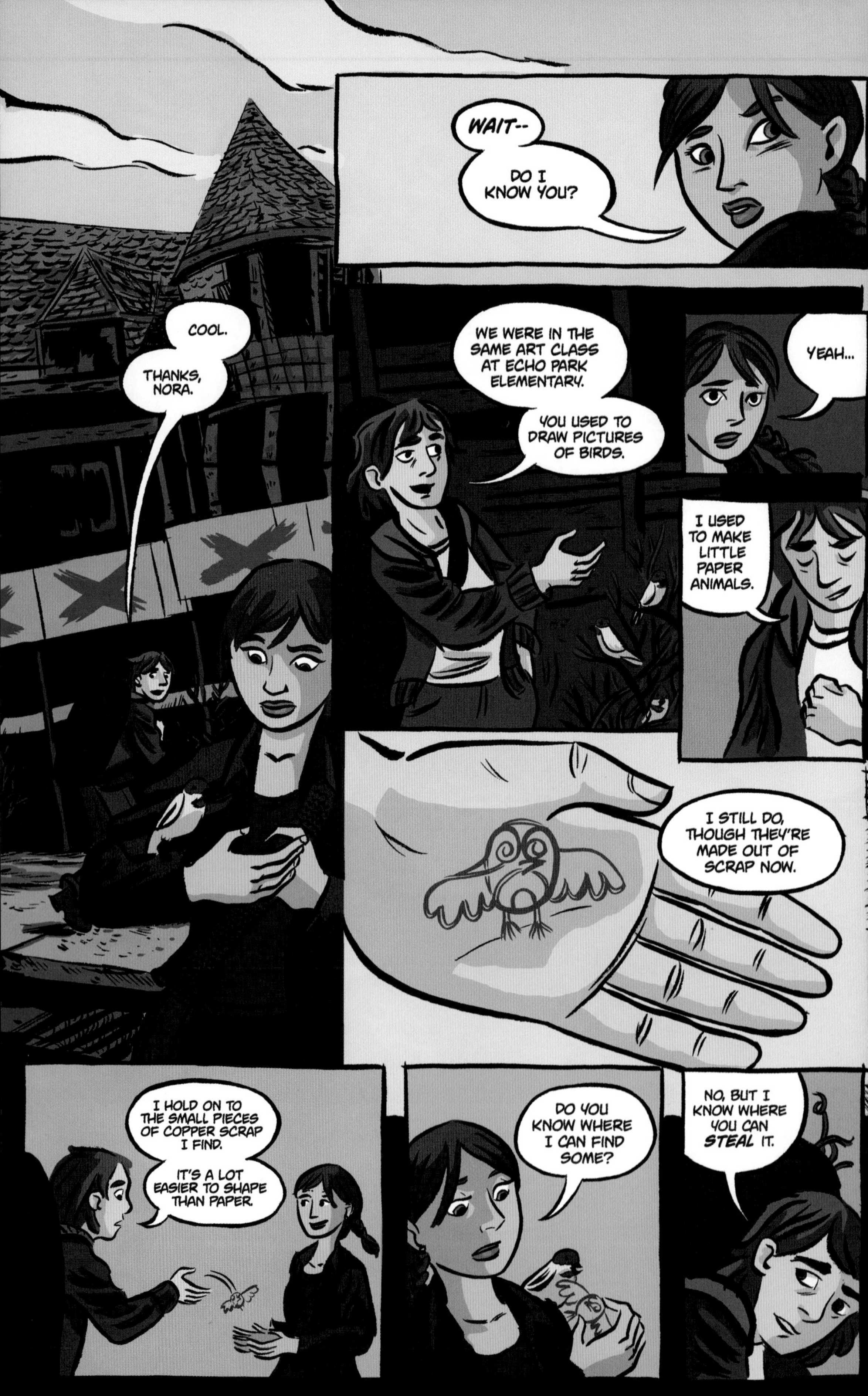
WAIT--
DO I KNOW YOU?
COOL.
THANKS, NORA.
WE WERE IN THE SAME ART CLASS AT ECHO PARK ELEMENTARY.
YOU USED TO DRAW PICTURES OF BIRDS.
YEAH...
I USED TO MAKE LITTLE PAPER ANIMALS.
I STILL DO, THOUGH THEY'RE MADE OUT OF SCRAP NOW.
I HOLD ON TO THE SMALL PIECES OF COPPER SCRAP I FIND.
IT'S A LOT EASIER TO SHAPE THAN PAPER.
DO YOU KNOW WHERE I CAN FIND SOME?
NO, BUT I KNOW WHERE YOU CAN *STEAL* IT.

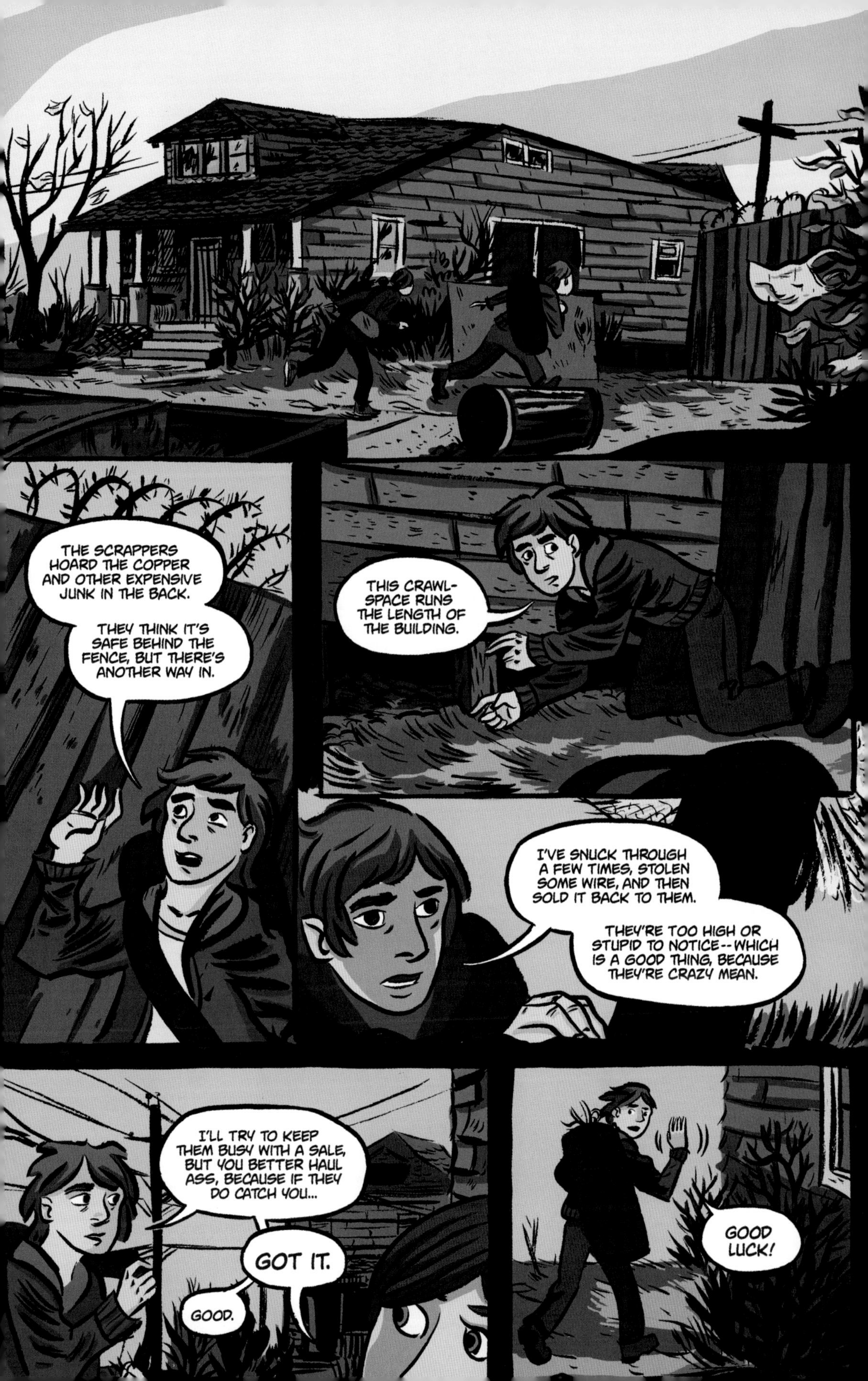
THE SCRAPPERS HOARD THE COPPER AND OTHER EXPENSIVE JUNK IN THE BACK.
THEY THINK IT'S SAFE BEHIND THE FENCE, BUT THERE'S ANOTHER WAY IN.
THIS CRAWL-SPACE RUNS THE LENGTH OF THE BUILDING.
I'VE SNUCK THROUGH A FEW TIMES, STOLEN SOME WIRE, AND THEN SOLD IT BACK TO THEM.
THEY'RE TOO HIGH OR STUPID TO NOTICE--WHICH IS A GOOD THING, BECAUSE THEY'RE CRAZY MEAN.
I'LL TRY TO KEEP THEM BUSY WITH A SALE, BUT YOU BETTER HAUL ASS, BECAUSE IF THEY DO CATCH YOU...
GOT IT.
GOOD.
GOOD LUCK!

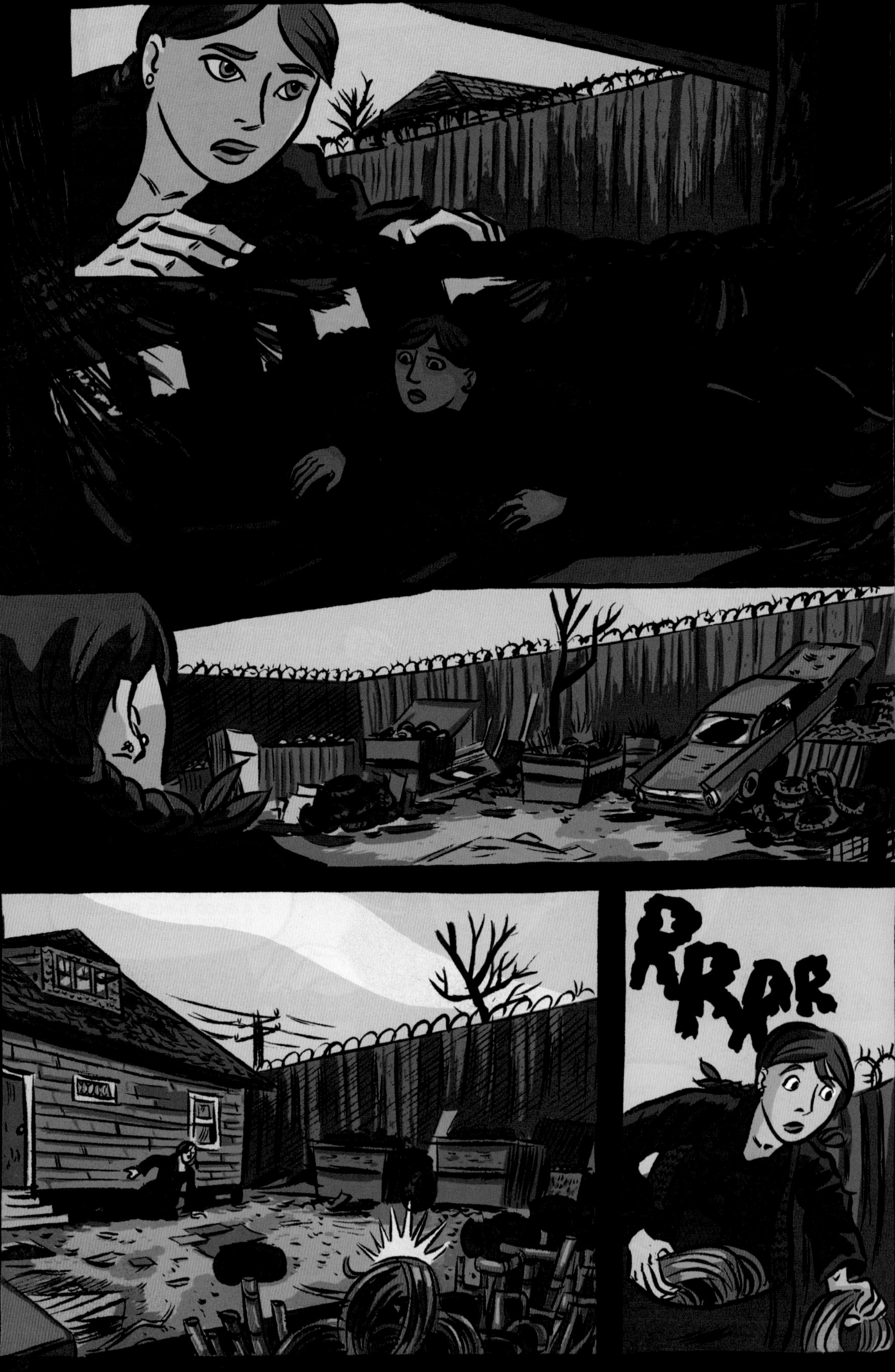
RRAR

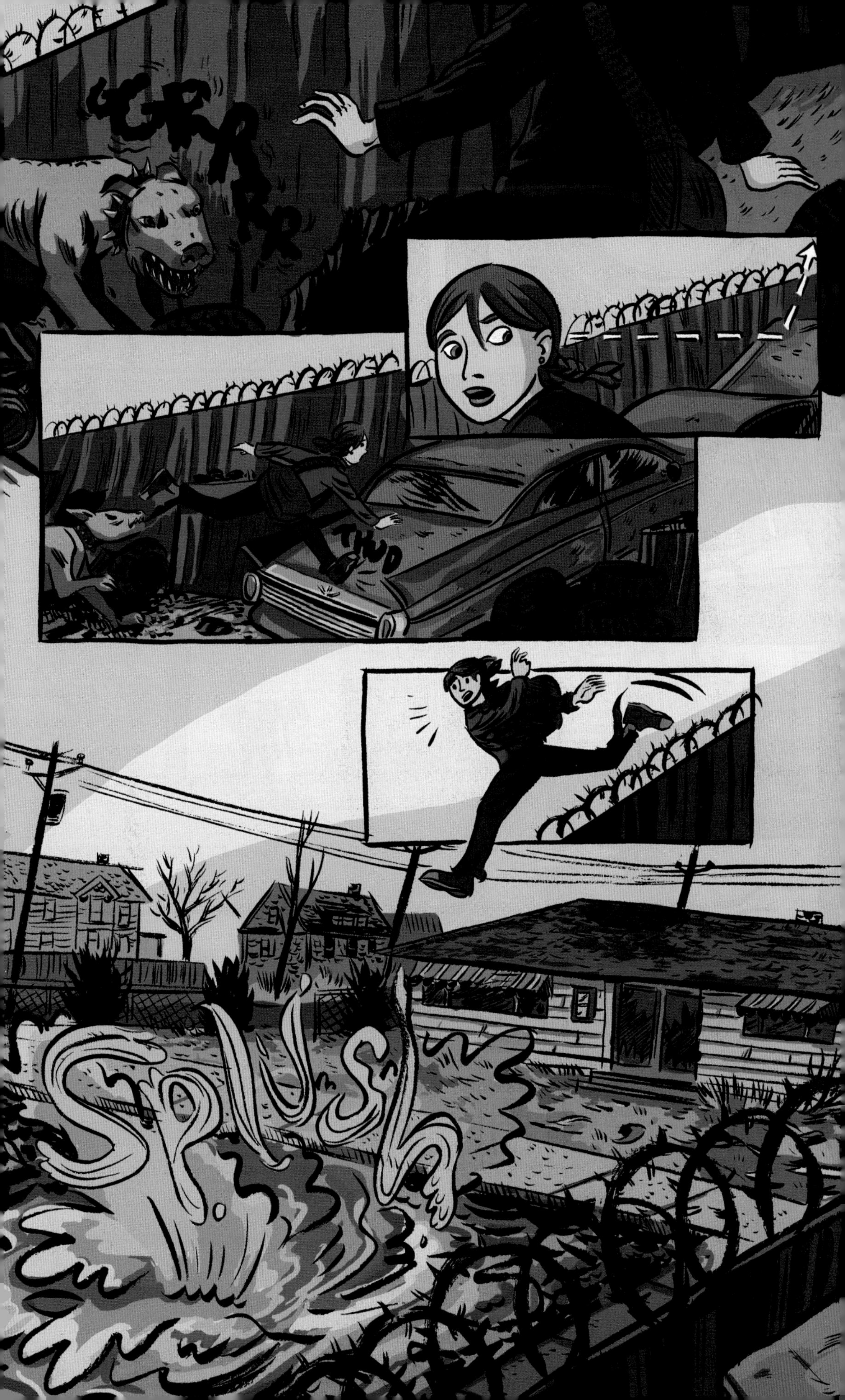
GRRRR
THUD
SPLUSH

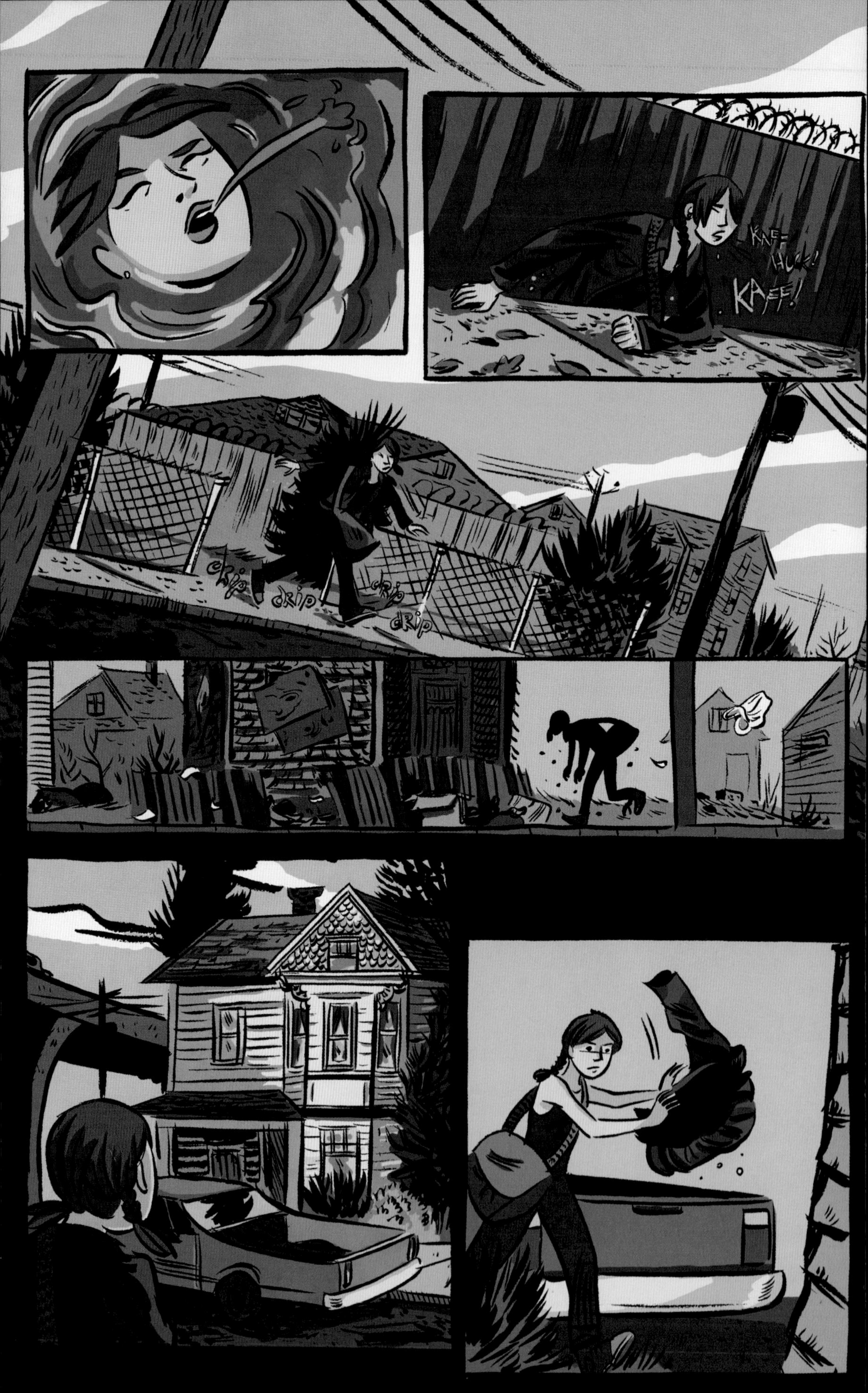
KAFF
HUCK!
KAFF!
drip
drip
drip
drip

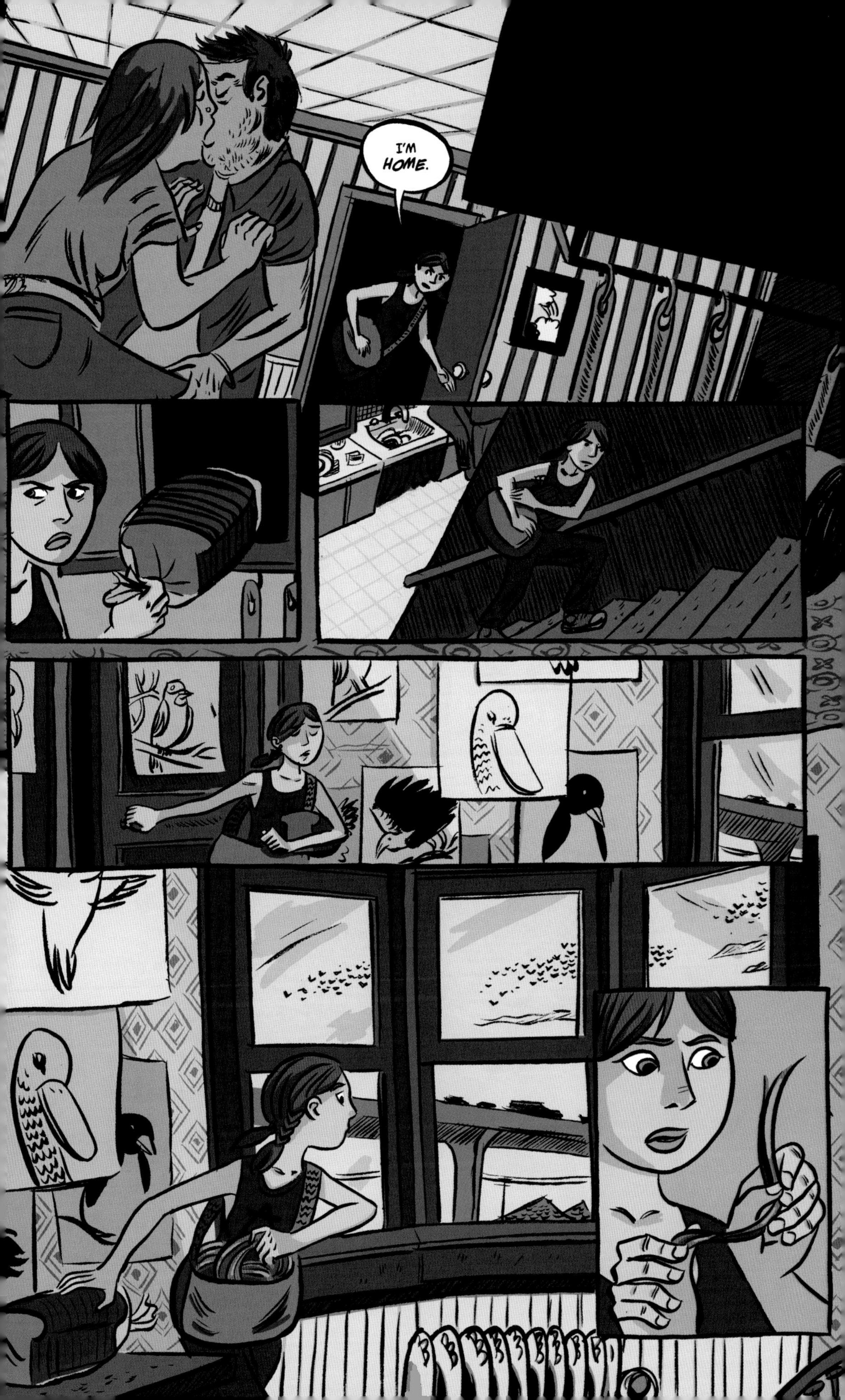
I'M HOME.

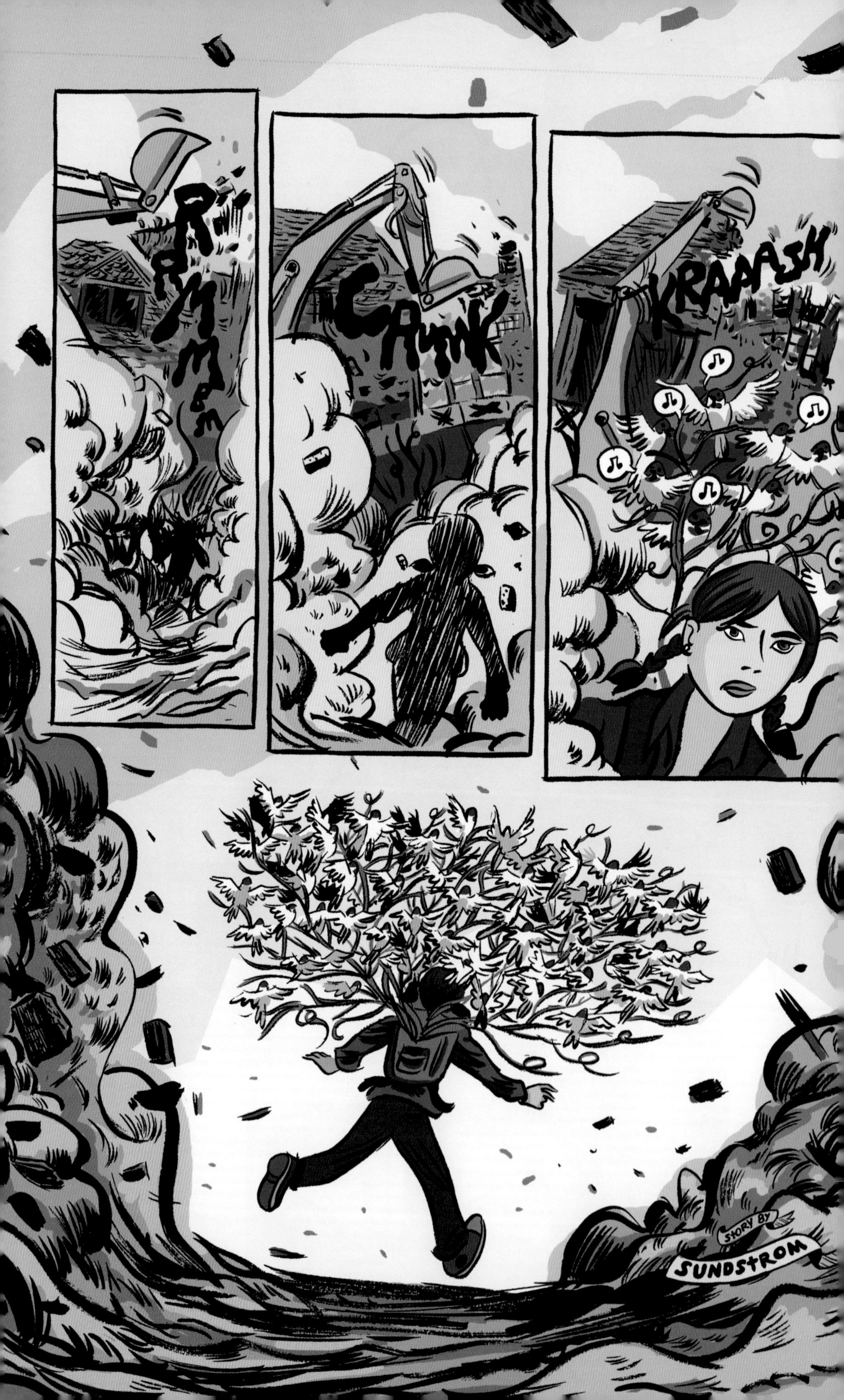
RRMMBM
CRUNK
KRAAASH
STORY BY
SUNDSTROM

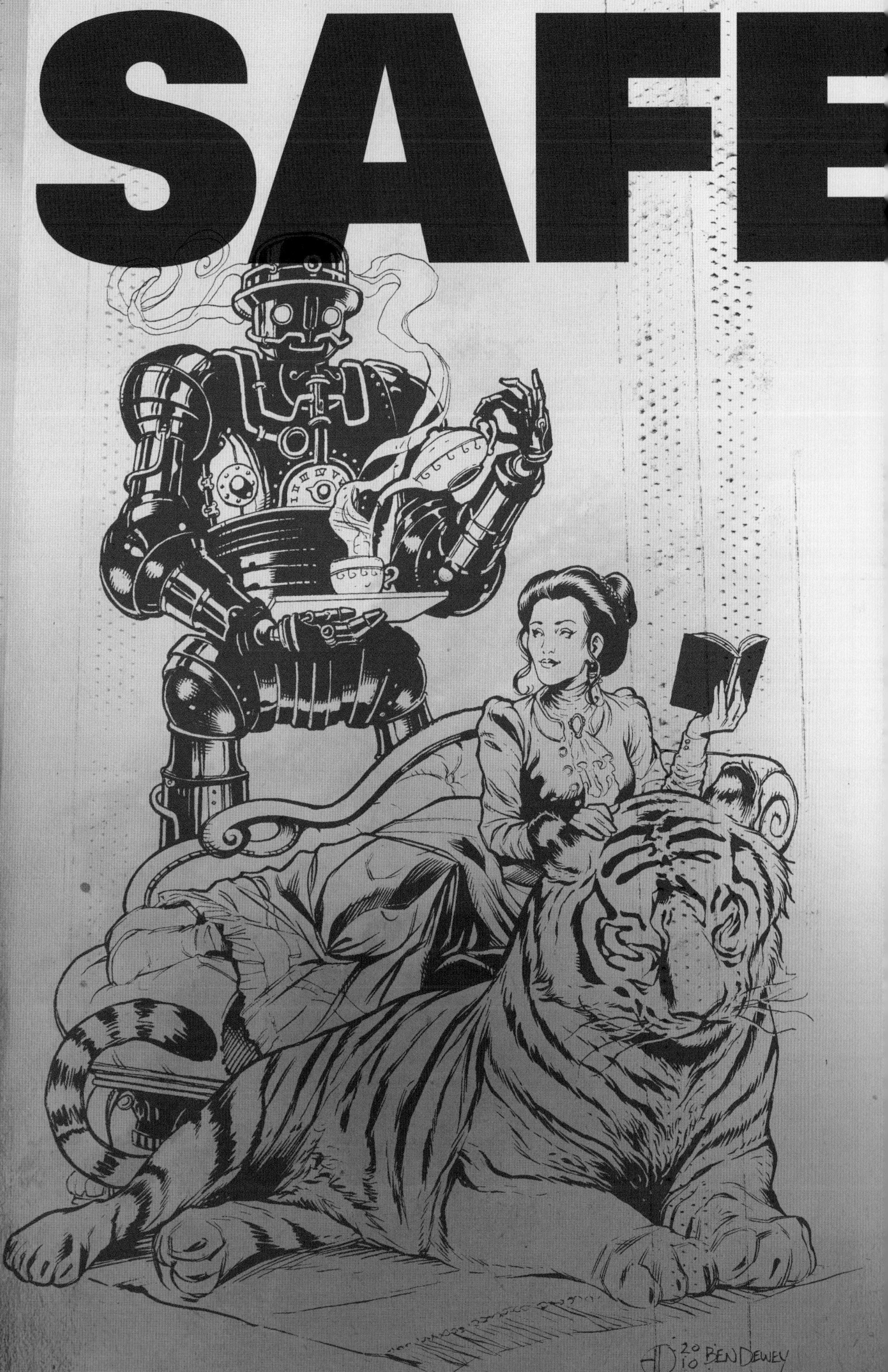
SAFE
2010 BEN DEWEY

OUR BOARDING HOUSE

RICK GEARY

THE NIGHT PASSED QUIETLY, BY ALL ACCOUNTS.

AT 6:15 AM, MRS. N. IN 1-B AROSE AND PREPARED COFFEE.

ITS AROMA, AS ALWAYS CALLED FORTH MEMORIES OF A LONG-AGO ACT OF BETRAYAL.

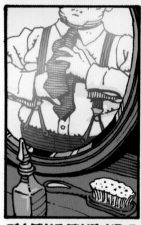

BY THIS TIME, MR. O. IN 3-B WAS DRESSING FOR THE OFFICE.

AN ELUSIVE CUFF LINK MADE HIM LATER THAN USUAL OUT THE DOOR.

FROM THE STAIRS, HE GLIMPSED A STOUT MAN LEAVING 2-C.

PERHAPS THE LADY THERE HAS TAKEN A LOVER, HE MUSED

TRUTH BE TOLD, HE LONGS FOR A SWEETHEART HIMSELF.

BY 7:30 AM, MRS. T. OF 2-A SAT IDLY SMOKING ON THE TERRACE.

THE MEDDLESOME WIDOW IN 1-D CAME OUT TO JOIN HER.

MRS. T. SOON MADE AN EXCUSE AND RETREATED TO HER ROOMS.

SO FAR AS SHE KNEW, THE WIDOW REMAINED ON THE TERRACE...

ALTHOUGH SHE WAS NOT SEEN THERE BY MR. W. OF 2·D AS HE LEFT FOR WORK AT 7:47 AM.

MRS. K. IN 3·E WATCHED HIS DEPARTURE FROM HER WINDOW...

AS SHE HAS EACH MORNING FOR THIRTEEN YEARS.

AT 8:13 AM, MR. H. OF 3·A CARRIED HIS REFUSE DOWN THE BACK STAIRS.

APPARENTLY HE WAS THE ONLY ONE TO HEAR A "GROANING OR WHINING" IN THE WALLS.

THE QUARREL, AT 8:25 AM, BETWEEN THE COUPLE IN 1·C IS A DAILY RITUAL.

THE HUSBAND BEAT A HASTY EXIT OUT THE FRONT DOOR...

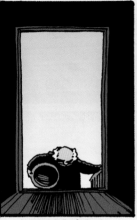

JUST AS MR. H. REENTERED VIA THE REAR, WITH HIS EMPTY REFUSE CONTAINER.

COULD HE HAVE FAILED TO NOTICE THE REMAINS OF MR. J. OF 2·E CRUMPLED BENEATH THE STEPS?

IT SEEMS THAT HIS IS THE ONLY KNIFE CADDY WITH AN EMPTY SLOT...

THAT PRECISELY FITS THE BLADE WITHDRAWN FROM MR. J.'S VITALS!

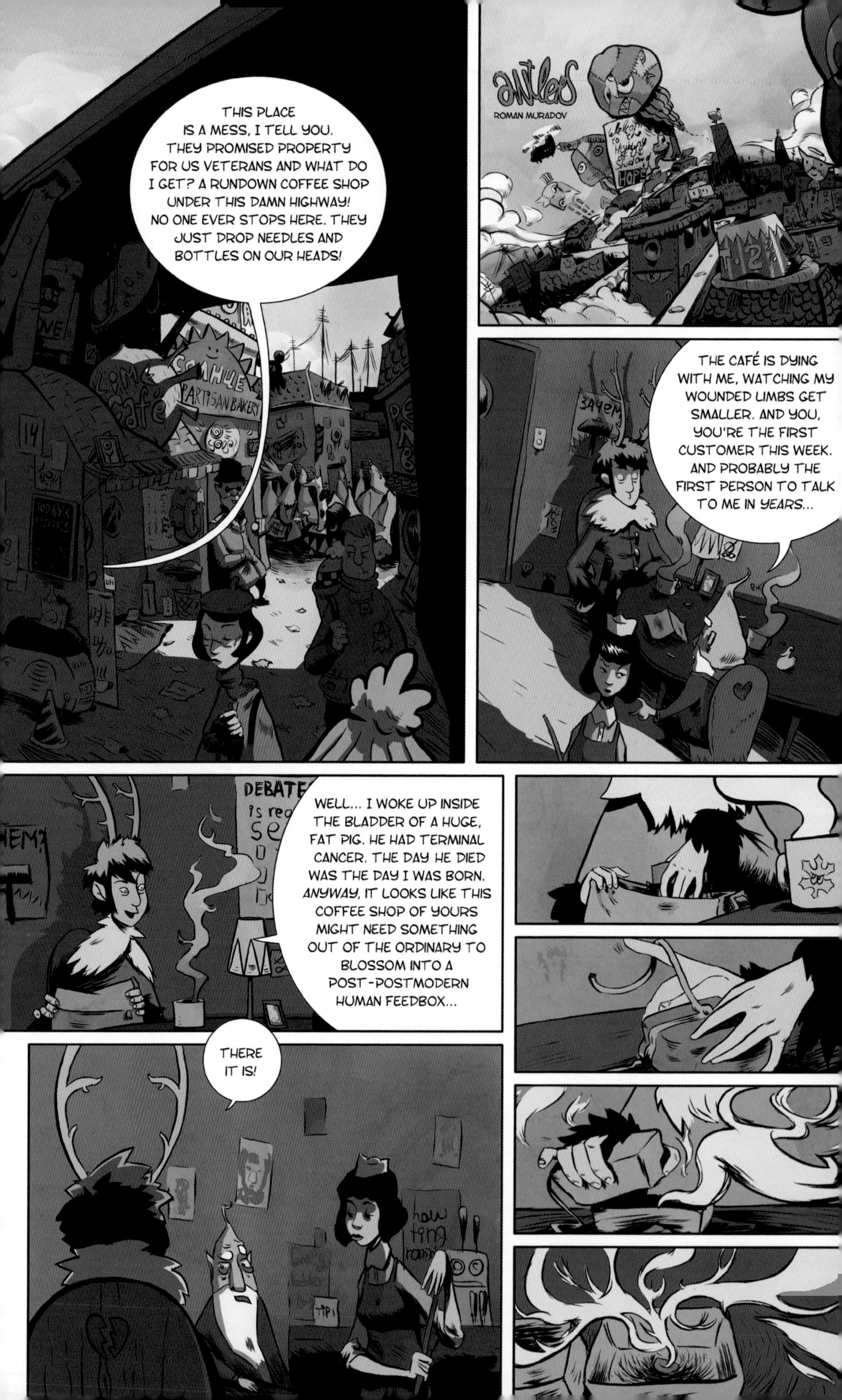
antlers
ROMAN MURADOV
THIS PLACE IS A MESS, I TELL YOU. THEY PROMISED PROPERTY FOR US VETERANS AND WHAT DO I GET? A RUNDOWN COFFEE SHOP UNDER THIS DAMN HIGHWAY! NO ONE EVER STOPS HERE. THEY JUST DROP NEEDLES AND BOTTLES ON OUR HEADS!
THE CAFÉ IS DYING WITH ME, WATCHING MY WOUNDED LIMBS GET SMALLER. AND YOU, YOU'RE THE FIRST CUSTOMER THIS WEEK. AND PROBABLY THE FIRST PERSON TO TALK TO ME IN YEARS...
WELL... I WOKE UP INSIDE THE BLADDER OF A HUGE, FAT PIG. HE HAD TERMINAL CANCER. THE DAY HE DIED WAS THE DAY I WAS BORN. *ANYWAY*, IT LOOKS LIKE THIS COFFEE SHOP OF YOURS MIGHT NEED SOMETHING OUT OF THE ORDINARY TO BLOSSOM INTO A POST-POSTMODERN HUMAN FEEDBOX...
THERE IT IS!

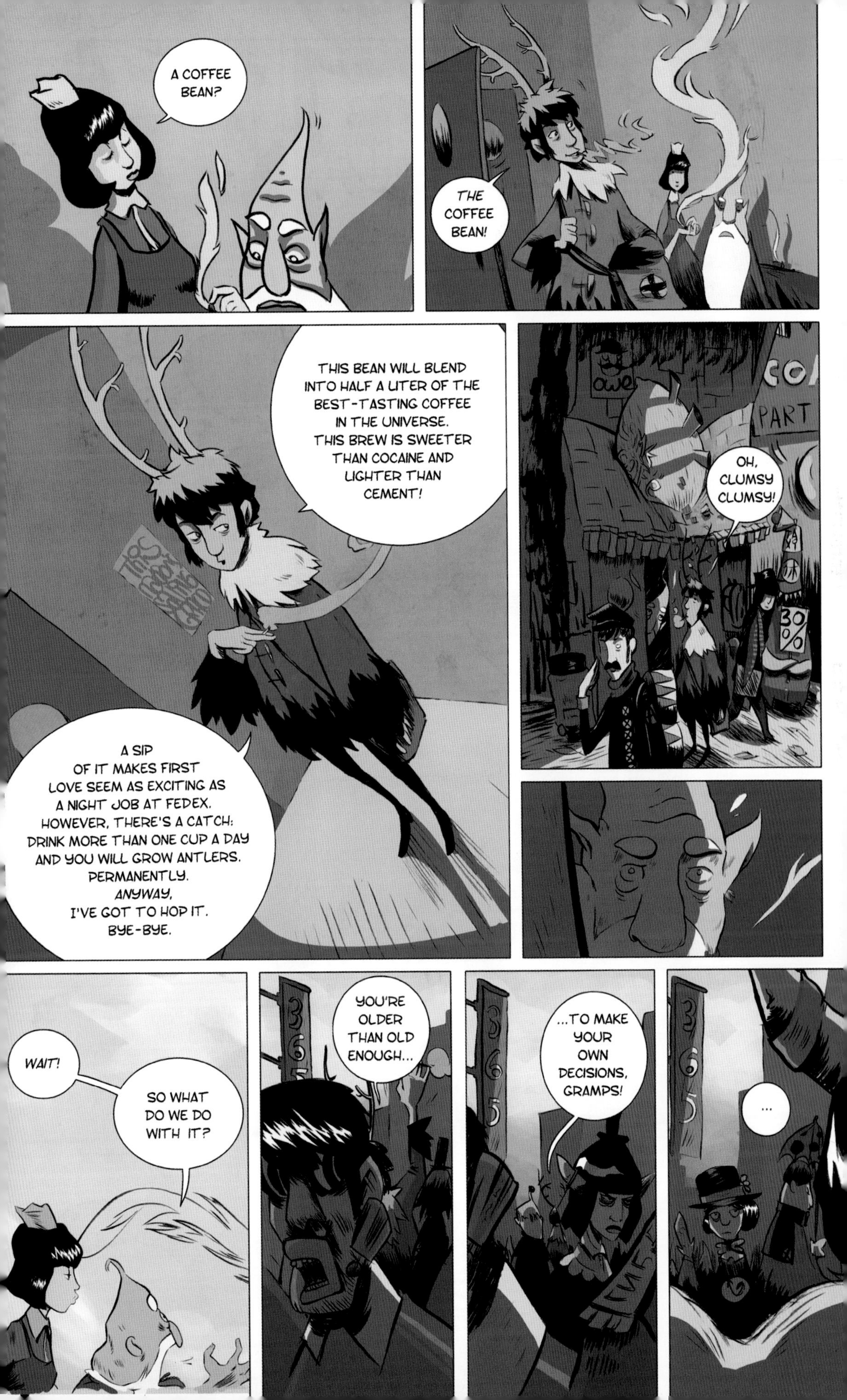
A COFFEE BEAN?
THE COFFEE BEAN!
THIS BEAN WILL BLEND INTO HALF A LITER OF THE BEST-TASTING COFFEE IN THE UNIVERSE. THIS BREW IS SWEETER THAN COCAINE AND LIGHTER THAN CEMENT!
A SIP OF IT MAKES FIRST LOVE SEEM AS EXCITING AS A NIGHT JOB AT FEDEX. HOWEVER, THERE'S A CATCH: DRINK MORE THAN ONE CUP A DAY AND YOU WILL GROW ANTLERS. PERMANENTLY. *ANYWAY,* I'VE GOT TO HOP IT. BYE-BYE.
OH, CLUMSY CLUMSY!
PART
30%
WAIT!
SO WHAT DO WE DO WITH IT?
YOU'RE OLDER THAN OLD ENOUGH...
...TO MAKE YOUR OWN DECISIONS, GRAMPS!
...

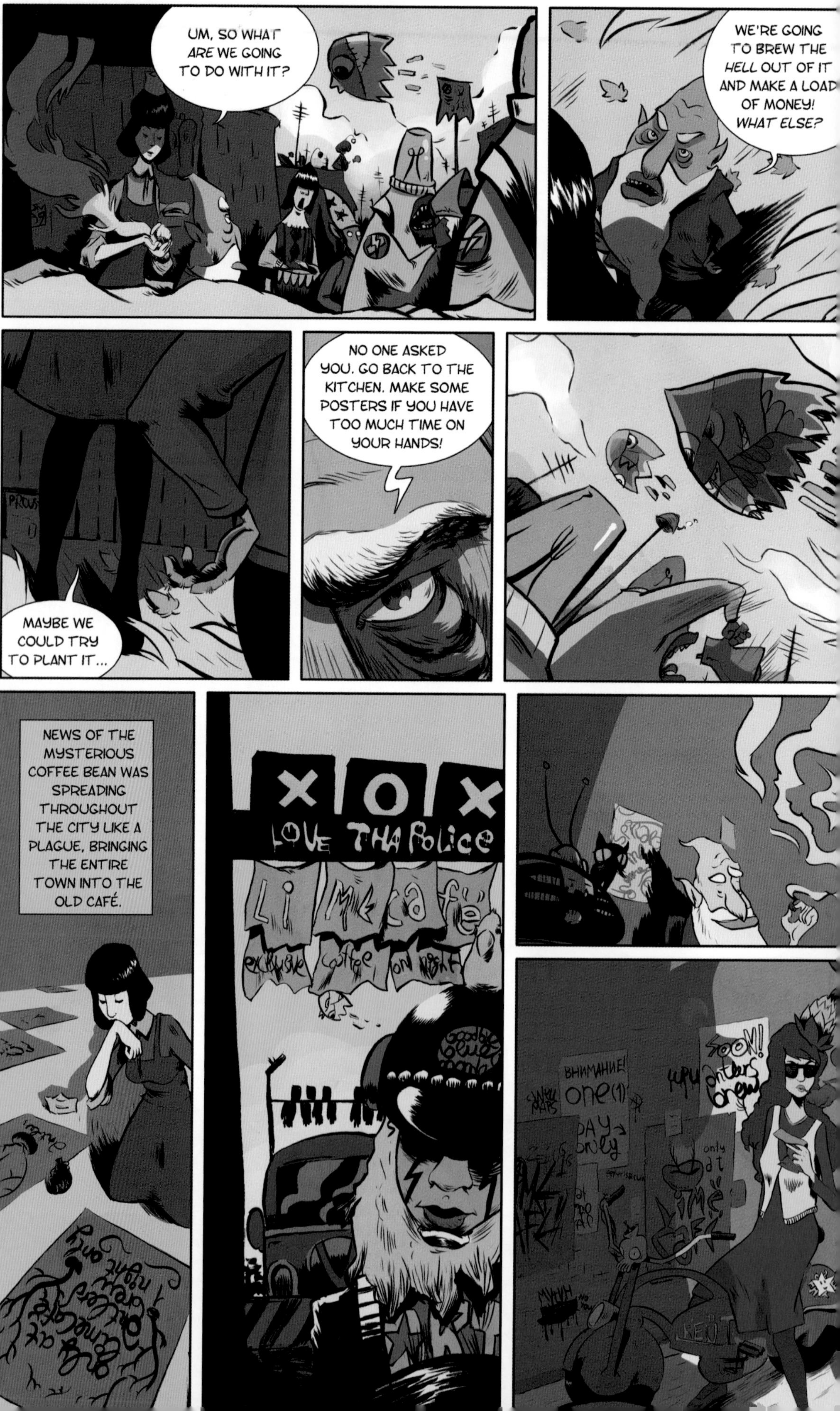

UM, SO WHAT ARE WE GOING TO DO WITH IT?
WE'RE GOING TO BREW THE HELL OUT OF IT AND MAKE A LOAD OF MONEY! WHAT ELSE?
MAYBE WE COULD TRY TO PLANT IT...
NO ONE ASKED YOU. GO BACK TO THE KITCHEN. MAKE SOME POSTERS IF YOU HAVE TOO MUCH TIME ON YOUR HANDS!
NEWS OF THE MYSTERIOUS COFFEE BEAN WAS SPREADING THROUGHOUT THE CITY LIKE A PLAGUE, BRINGING THE ENTIRE TOWN INTO THE OLD CAFÉ.
XOX
LOVE THA POLICE
LIME CAFÉ
exclusive coffee one night
ВНИМАНИЕ!
one (1)
only at lime café

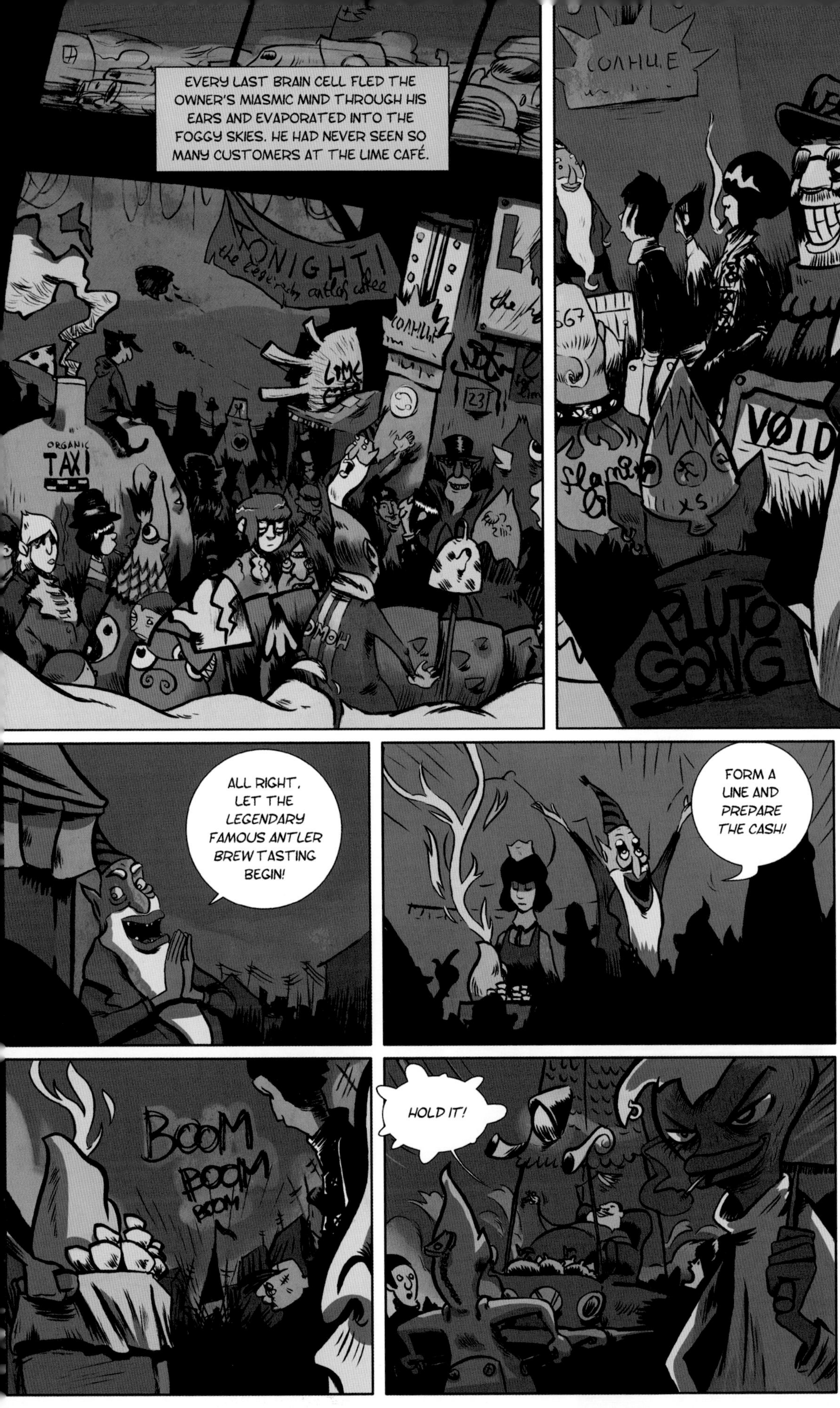
EVERY LAST BRAIN CELL FLED THE OWNER'S MIASMIC MIND THROUGH HIS EARS AND EVAPORATED INTO THE FOGGY SKIES. HE HAD NEVER SEEN SO MANY CUSTOMERS AT THE LIME CAFÉ.
TONIGHT!
ORGANIC
TAXI
23
VØID
PLUTO
GONG
ALL RIGHT, LET THE LEGENDARY FAMOUS ANTLER BREW TASTING BEGIN!
FORM A LINE AND PREPARE THE CASH!
BOOM
BOOM
BOOM
HOLD IT!

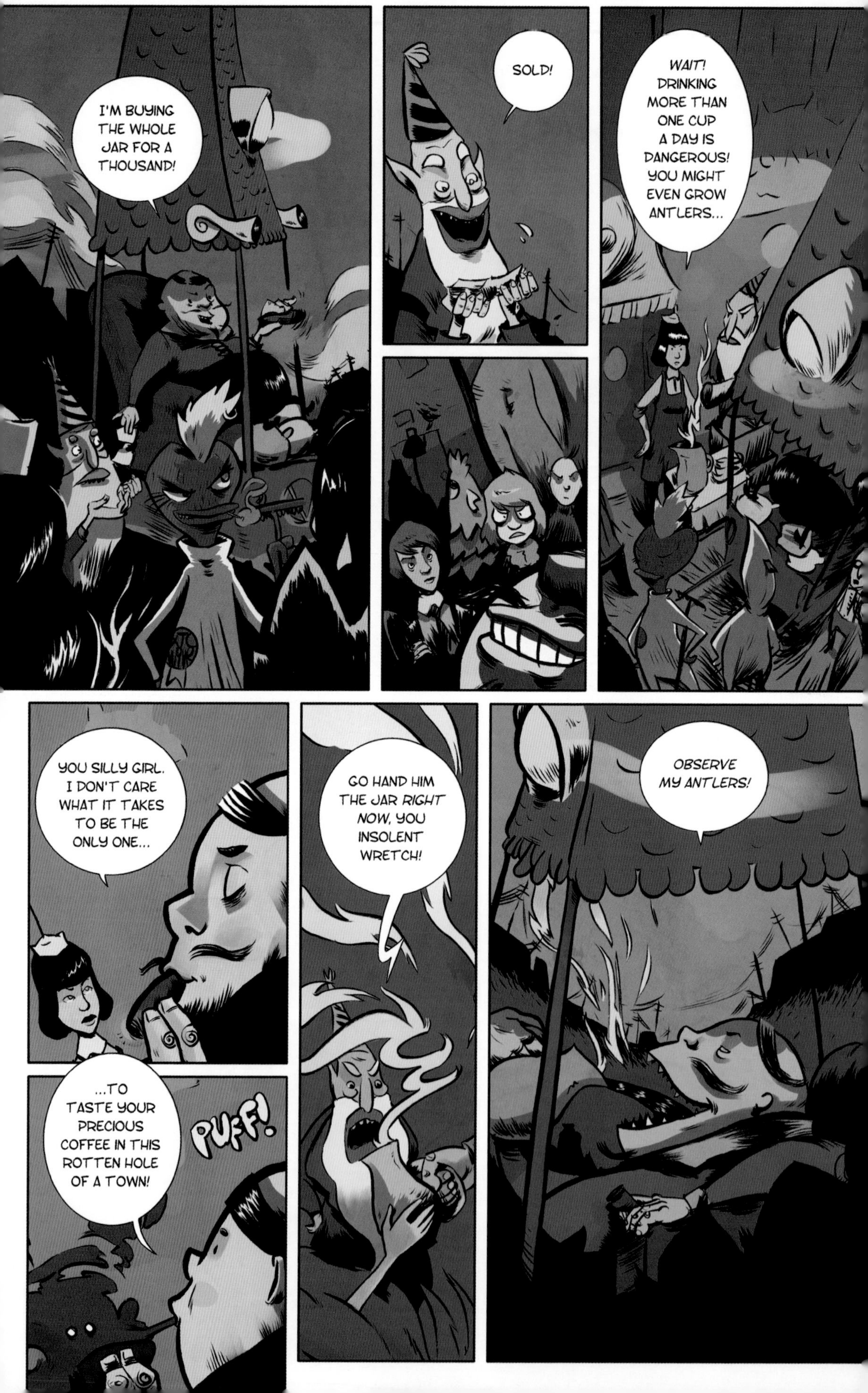
I'M BUYING THE WHOLE JAR FOR A THOUSAND!
SOLD!
WAIT! DRINKING MORE THAN ONE CUP A DAY IS DANGEROUS! YOU MIGHT EVEN GROW ANTLERS...
YOU SILLY GIRL. I DON'T CARE WHAT IT TAKES TO BE THE ONLY ONE...
...TO TASTE YOUR PRECIOUS COFFEE IN THIS ROTTEN HOLE OF A TOWN!
PUFF!
GO HAND HIM THE JAR RIGHT NOW, YOU INSOLENT WRETCH!
OBSERVE MY ANTLERS!

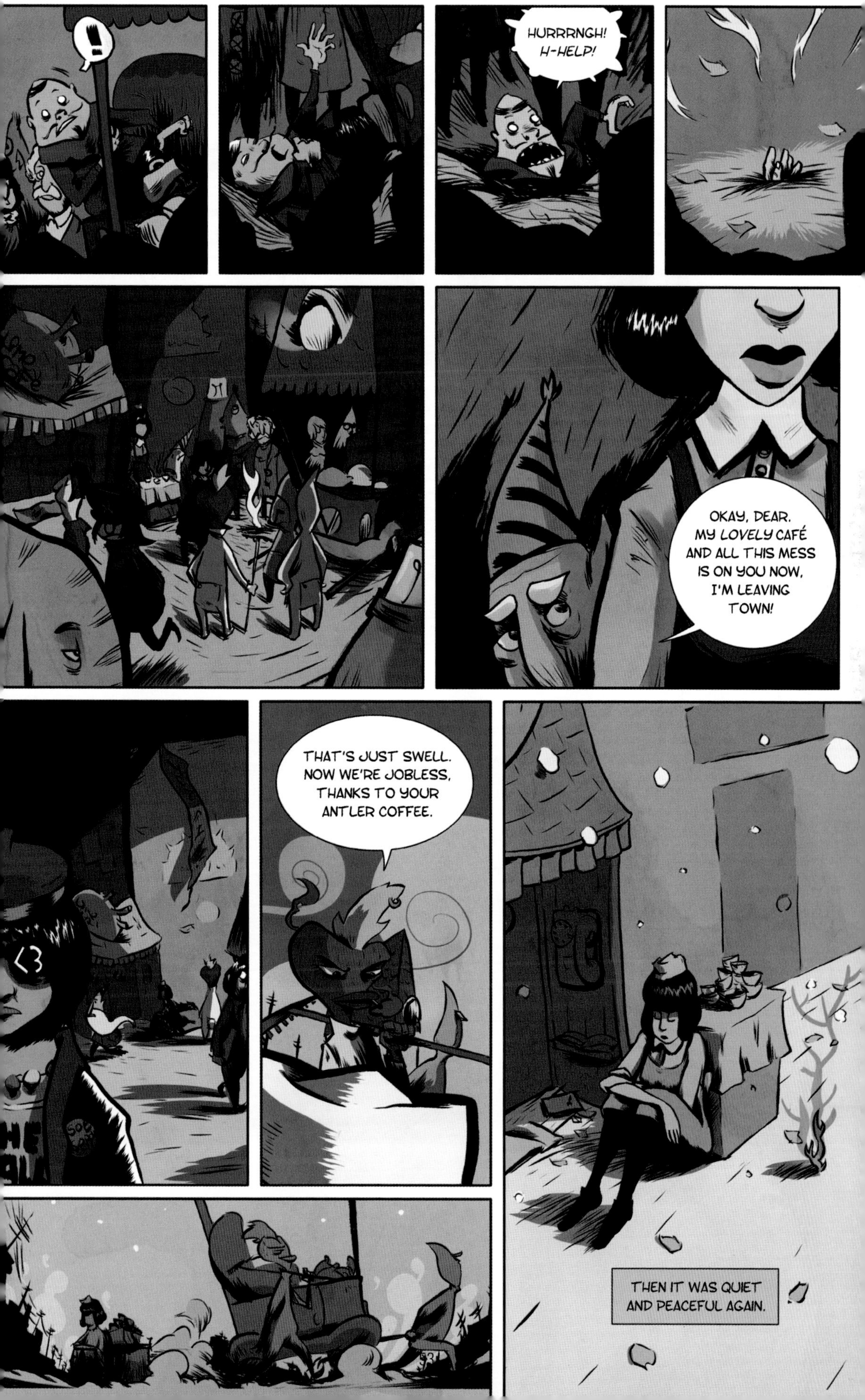
!
HURRRNGH! H-HELP!
OKAY, DEAR. MY LOVELY CAFÉ AND ALL THIS MESS IS ON YOU NOW, I'M LEAVING TOWN!
THAT'S JUST SWELL. NOW WE'RE JOBLESS, THANKS TO YOUR ANTLER COFFEE.
THEN IT WAS QUIET AND PEACEFUL AGAIN.

NEXT MORNING, A BEAUTIFUL AND PECULIAR TREE ROSE FROM THE GROUND, GENEROUSLY FERTILIZED BY THE TOWN'S LAST MILLIONAIRE.

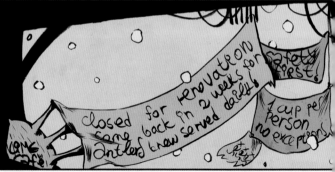

closed for renovation come back in 2 weeks for Antler brew served daily.

1 cup per person no exceptions

THAT DAY, WARM RAYS OF HOPE SHOWERED OVER THE RUNDOWN COFFEE SHOP, PAINTING ITS RUSTY SIGN IN BRIGHT, RADIANT SHADES.

AREN'T WE GRAND?

NOW YOU CAN HAVE IT TO GO

I'LL HAVE A CUP OF YOUR FAMOUS ANTLER BREW COFFEE.

ORDER HERE

OH... TO GO, PLEASE.

WELL, I SURE DIDN'T EXPECT THE OLD MAN TO ACT WISELY.

WHERE IS HE ANYWAY?

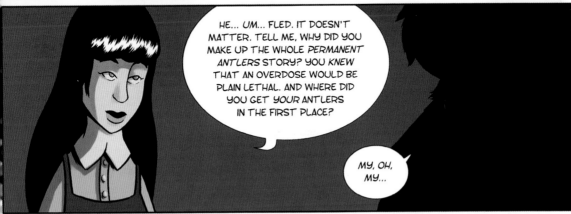

HE... UM... FLED. IT DOESN'T MATTER. TELL ME, WHY DID YOU MAKE UP THE WHOLE *PERMANENT ANTLERS* STORY? YOU KNEW THAT AN OVERDOSE WOULD BE PLAIN LETHAL. AND WHERE DID YOU GET *YOUR* ANTLERS IN THE FIRST PLACE?

MY, OH, MY...

THERE ARE THINGS THAT YOU FIND OUT ON YOUR OWN.

THERE ARE THINGS THAT YOU DON'T, BUT YOU BELIEVE IN THEM SOMEHOW.

AND THEN THERE'S GOOD COFFEE.

end.

MATT KINDT

THE SECRET FILES OF THE GIANT MAN IN EGYPT

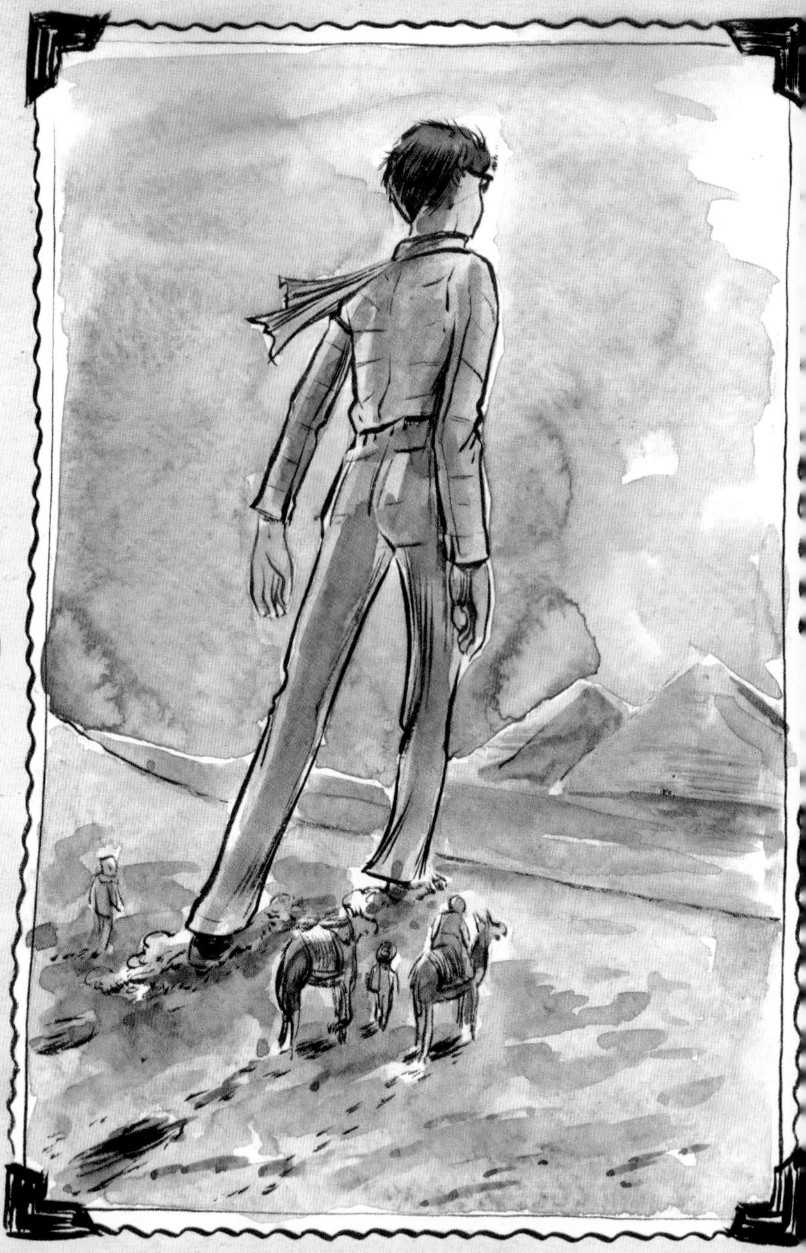

Craig Pressgang was born in 1945. By 1960 he was nearly three stories tall and one of the most famous individuals on the planet.

His entire life story can be found in the new book 3 Story: The Secret History of the Giant Man. This eyewitness account takes place during one of his many world tours...

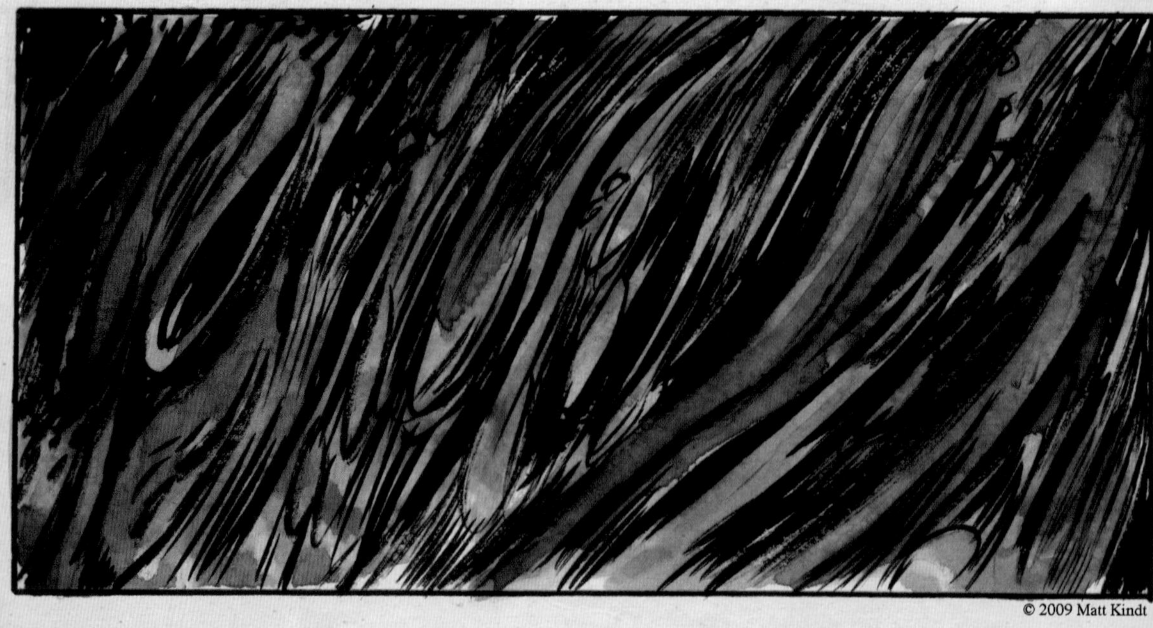

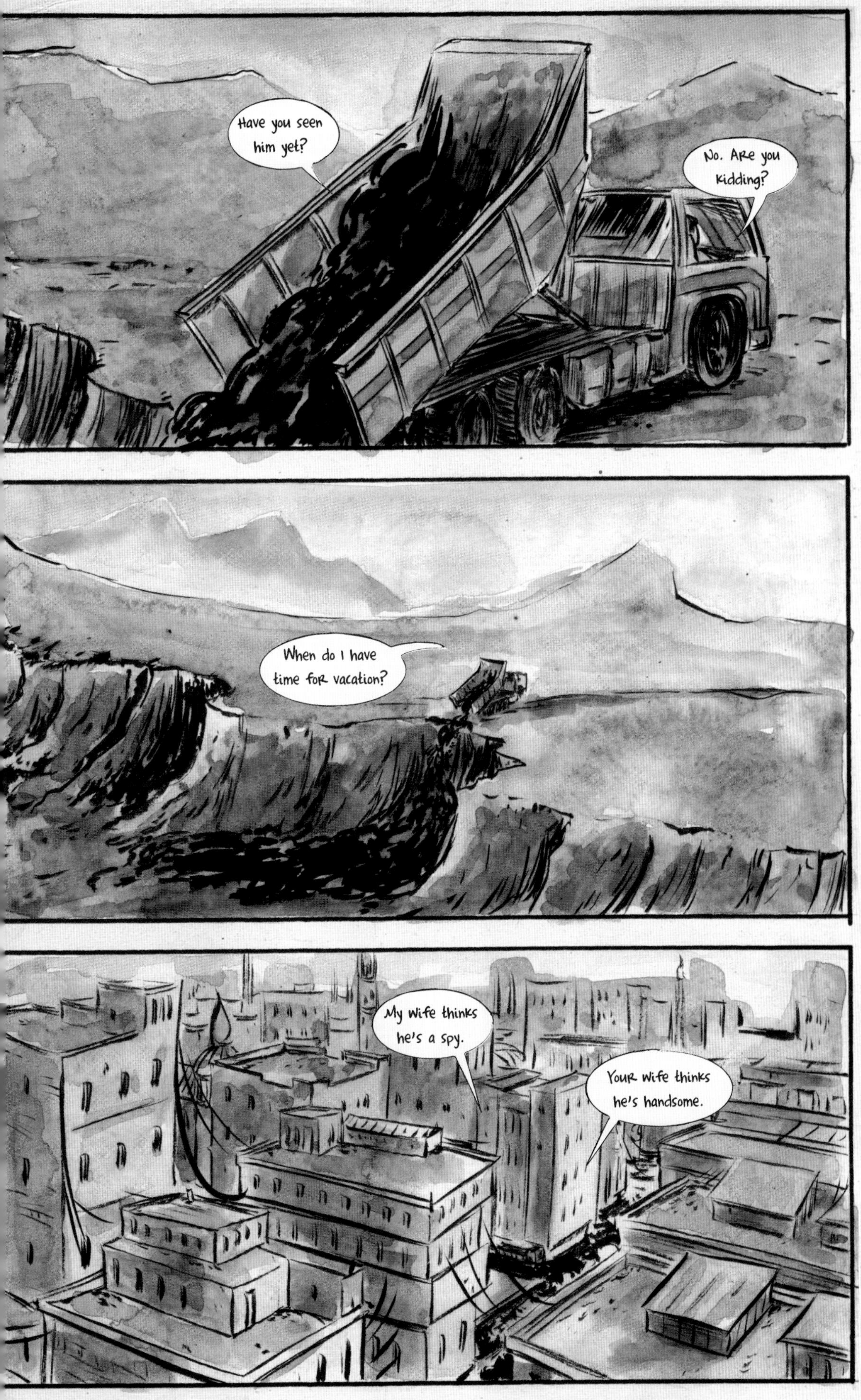

Have you seen him yet?
No. Are you kidding?
When do I have time for vacation?
My wife thinks he's a spy.
Your wife thinks he's handsome.

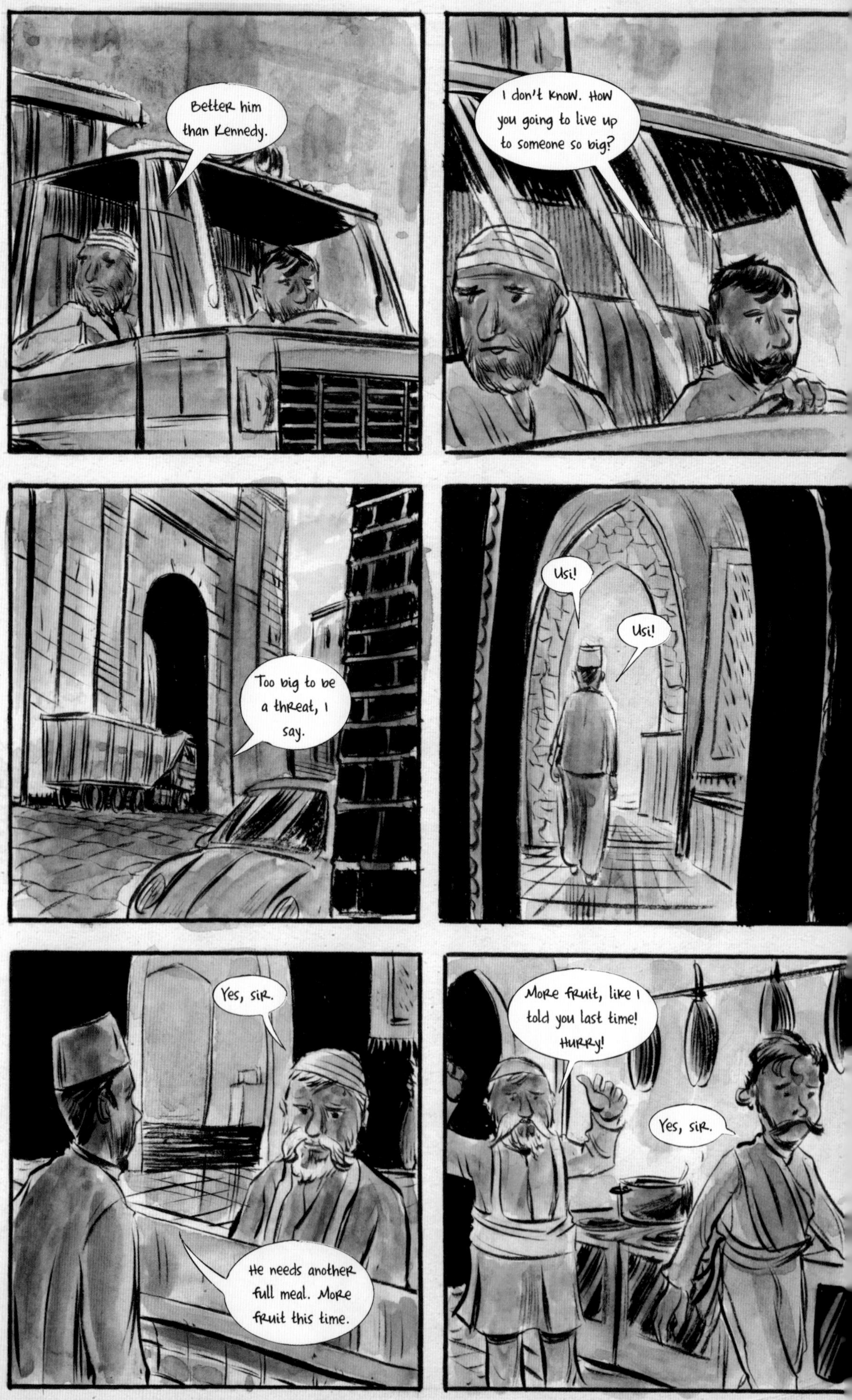
Better him than Kennedy.
I don't know. How you going to live up to someone so big?
Too big to be a threat, I say.
Usi!
Usi!
Yes, sir.
He needs another full meal. More fruit this time.
More fruit, like I told you last time! Hurry!
Yes, sir.

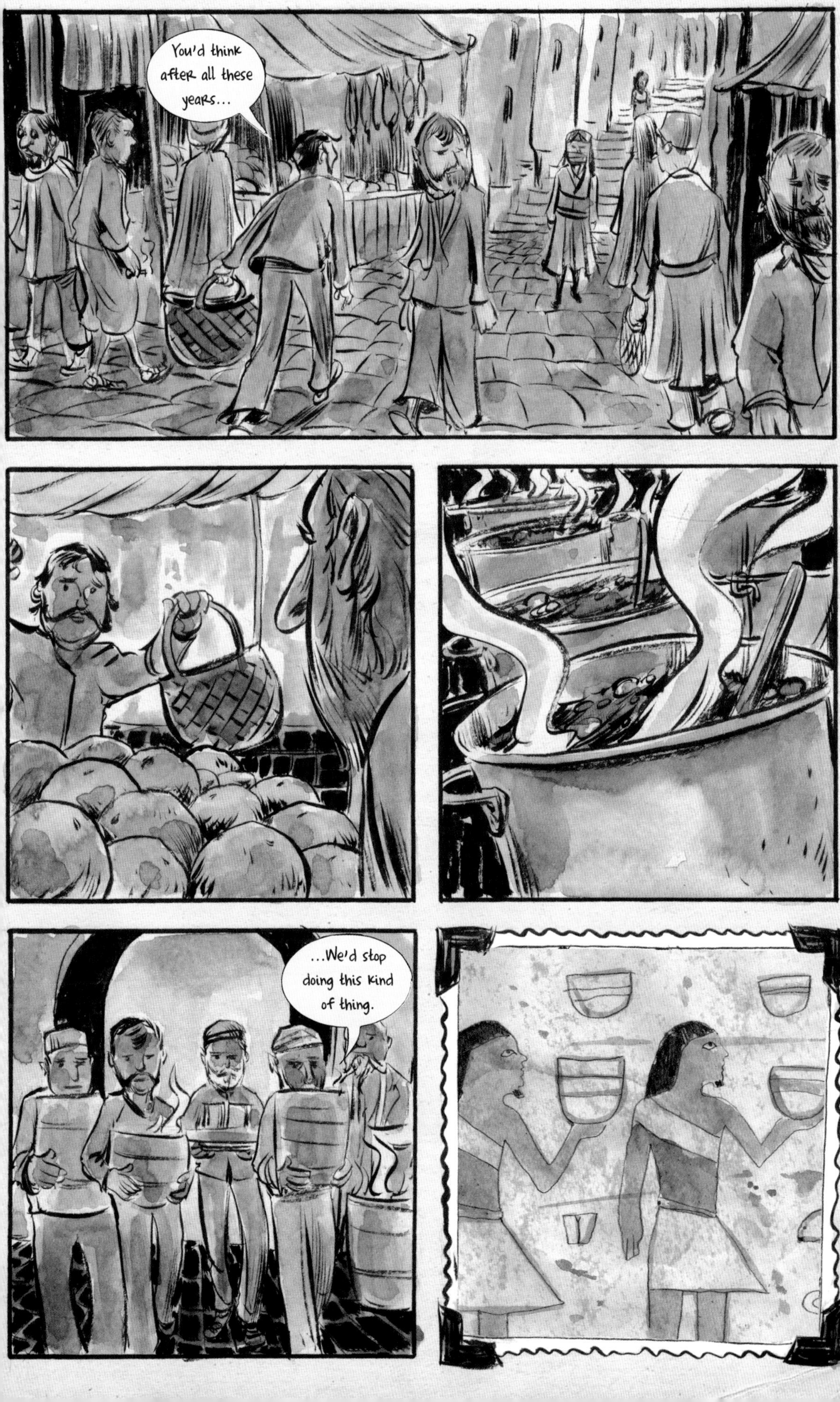
You'd think after all these years...
...We'd stop doing this kind of thing.

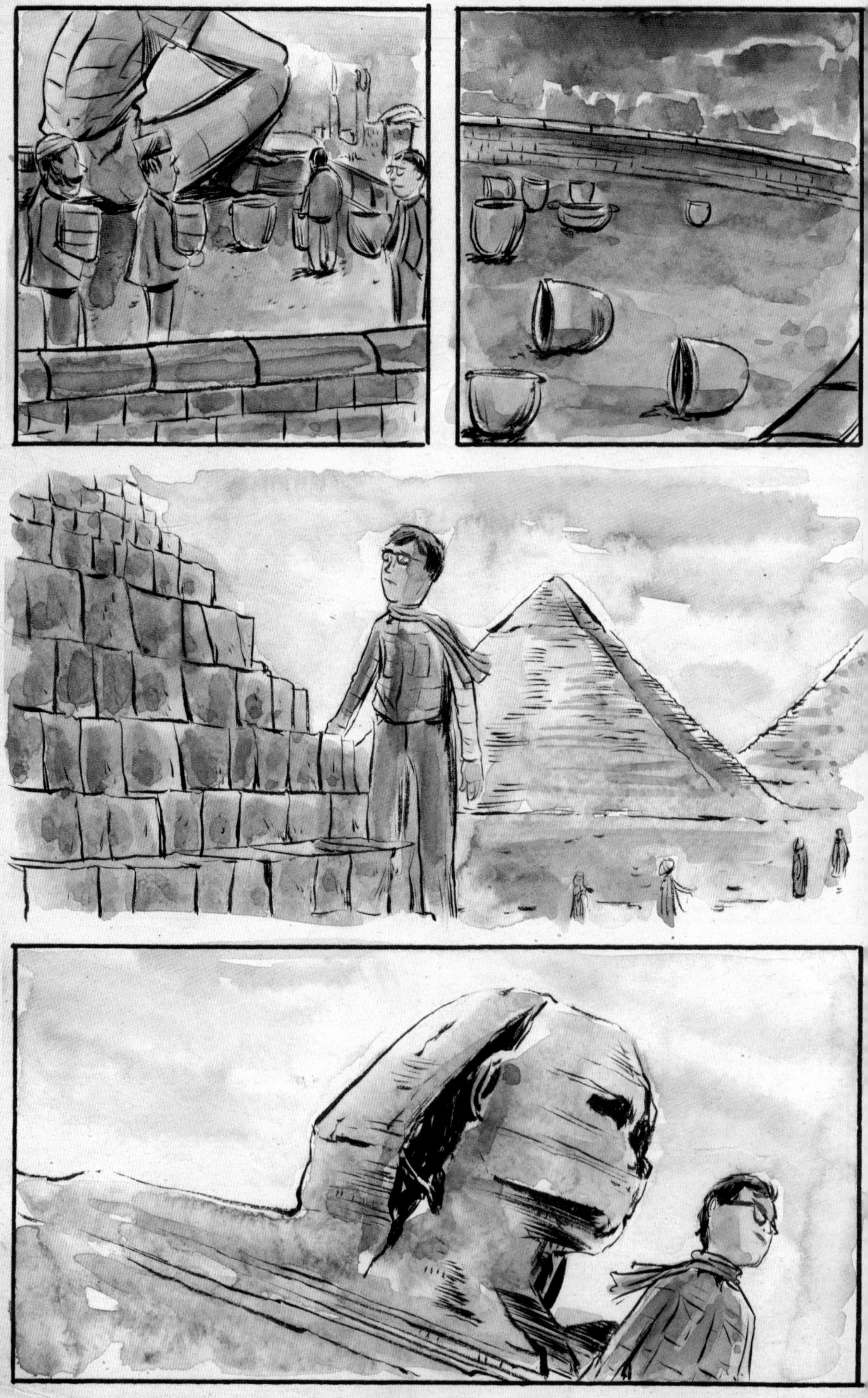

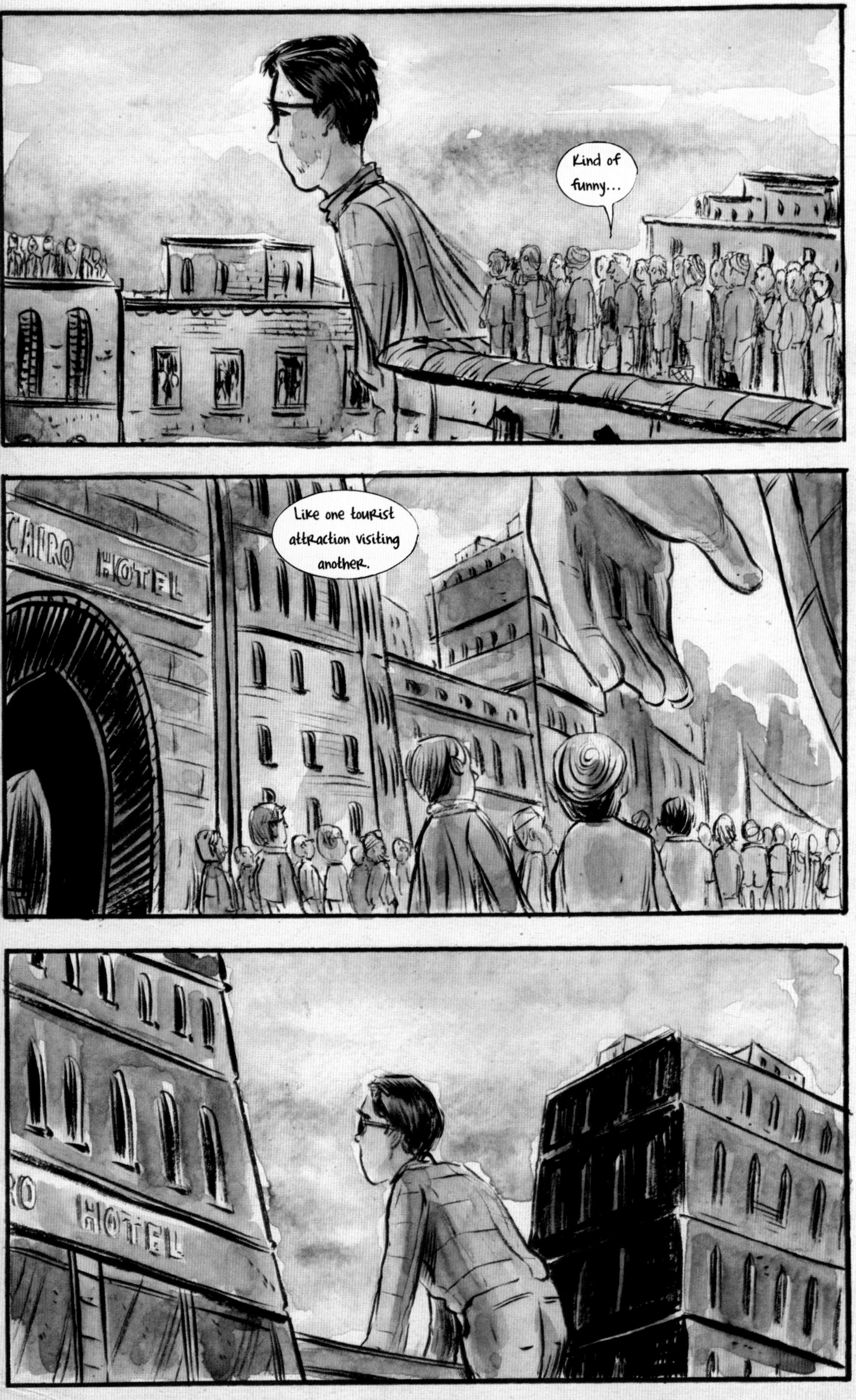
Kind of funny...
Like one tourist attraction visiting another.
CAIRO HOTEL
HOTEL

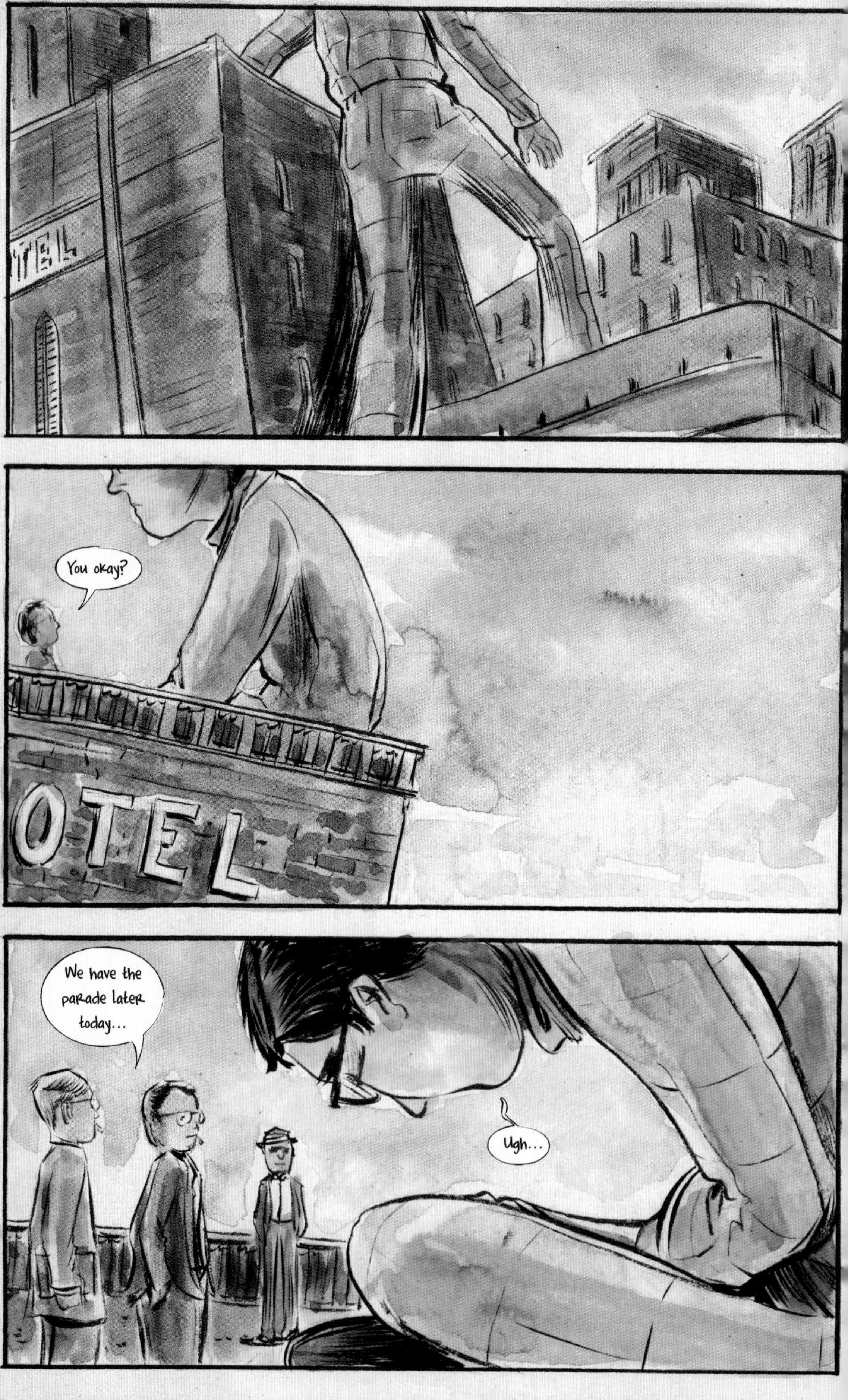
TEL
You okay?
OTEL
We have the parade later today...
Ugh...

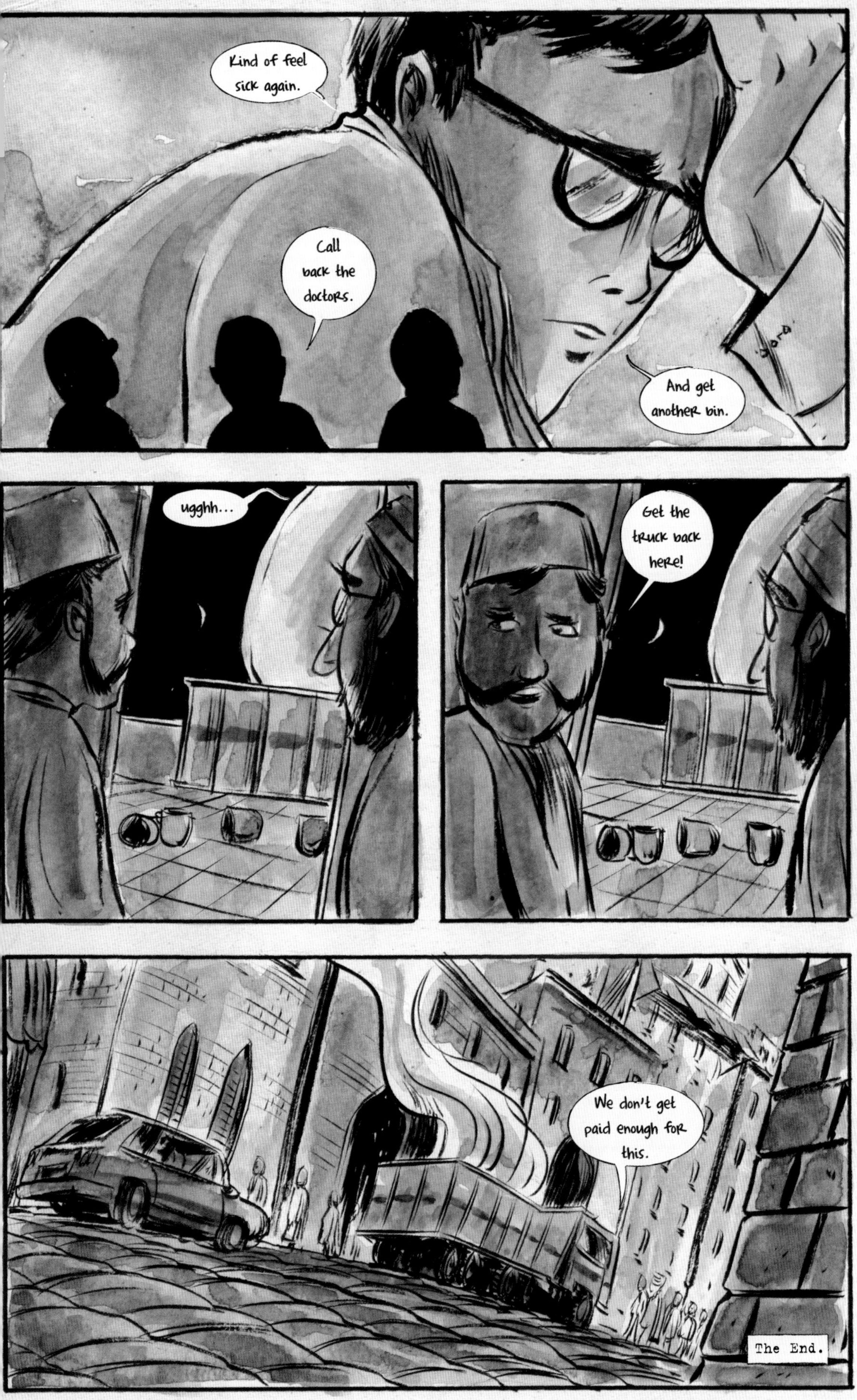
Kind of feel sick again.
Call back the doctors.
And get another bin.
ugghh...
Get the truck back here!
We don't get paid enough for this.
The End.

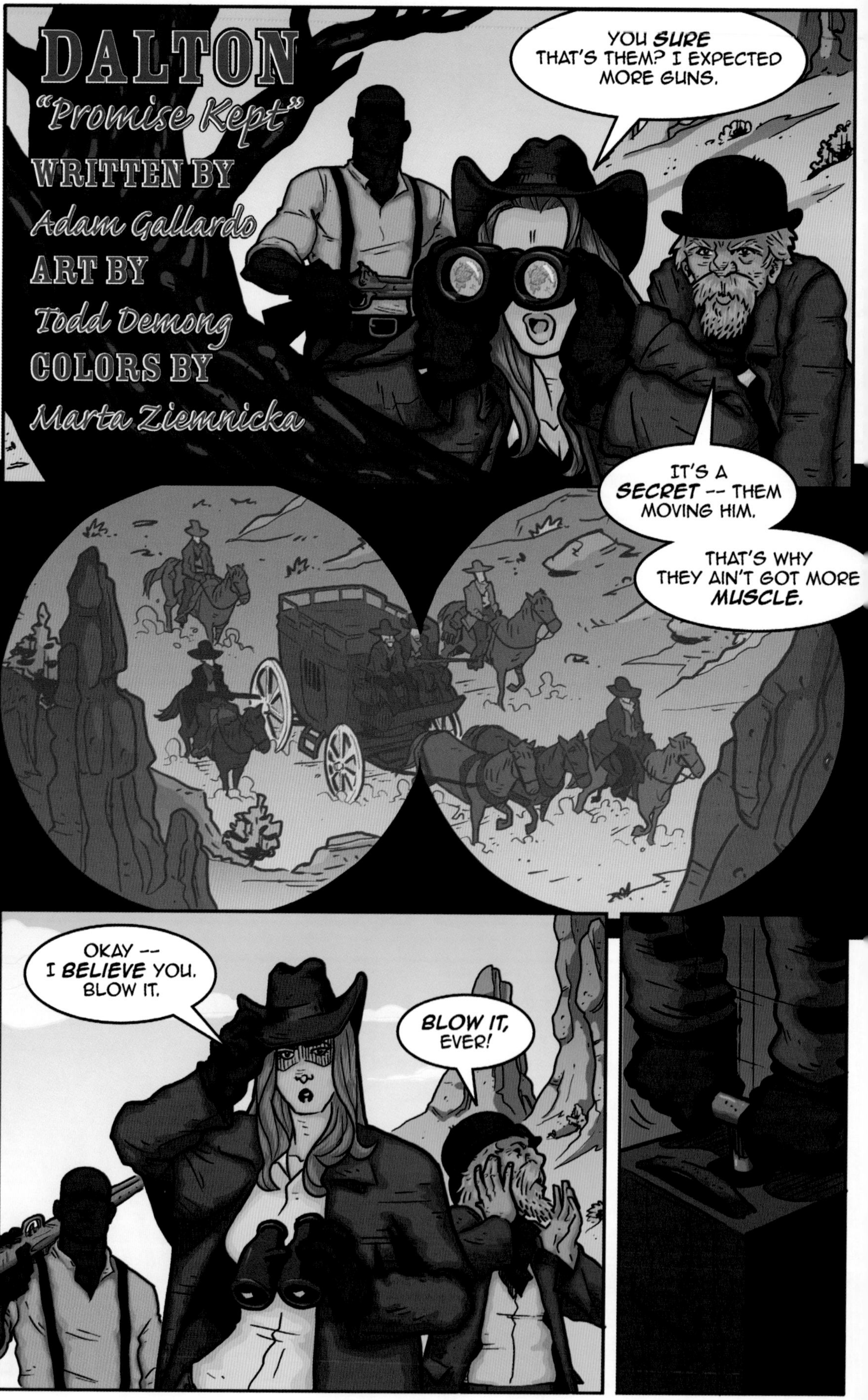
DALTON
"Promise Kept"
WRITTEN BY
Adam Gallardo
ART BY
Todd Demong
COLORS BY
Marta Ziemnicka
YOU SURE THAT'S THEM? I EXPECTED MORE GUNS.
IT'S A SECRET -- THEM MOVING HIM.
THAT'S WHY THEY AIN'T GOT MORE MUSCLE.
OKAY -- I BELIEVE YOU. BLOW IT.
BLOW IT, EVER!

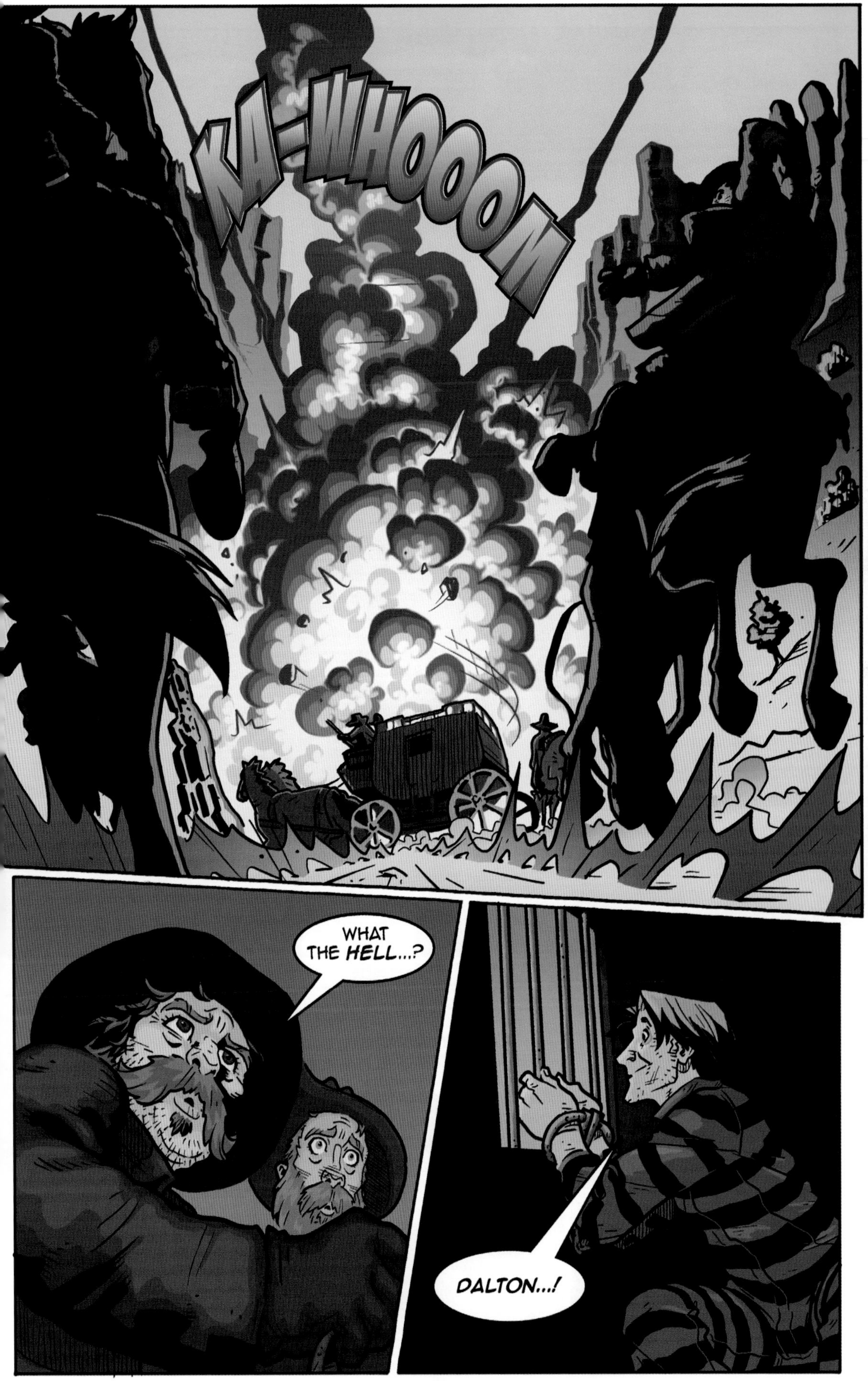
KA-WHOOOM
WHAT THE HELL...?
DALTON...!

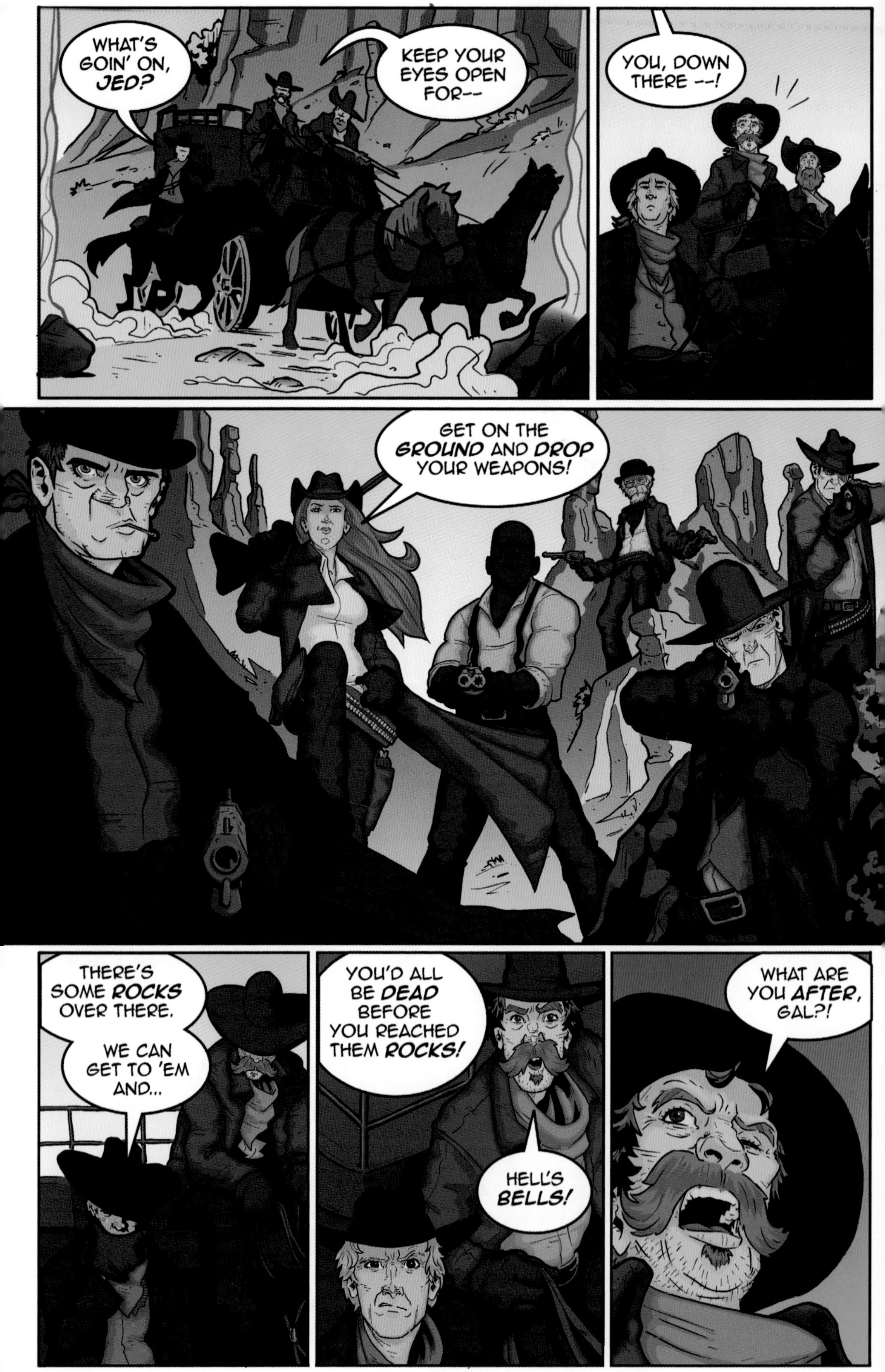
WHAT'S GOIN' ON, JED?
KEEP YOUR EYES OPEN FOR--
YOU, DOWN THERE --!
GET ON THE GROUND AND DROP YOUR WEAPONS!
THERE'S SOME ROCKS OVER THERE.
WE CAN GET TO 'EM AND...
YOU'D ALL BE DEAD BEFORE YOU REACHED THEM ROCKS!
HELL'S BELLS!
WHAT ARE YOU AFTER, GAL?!

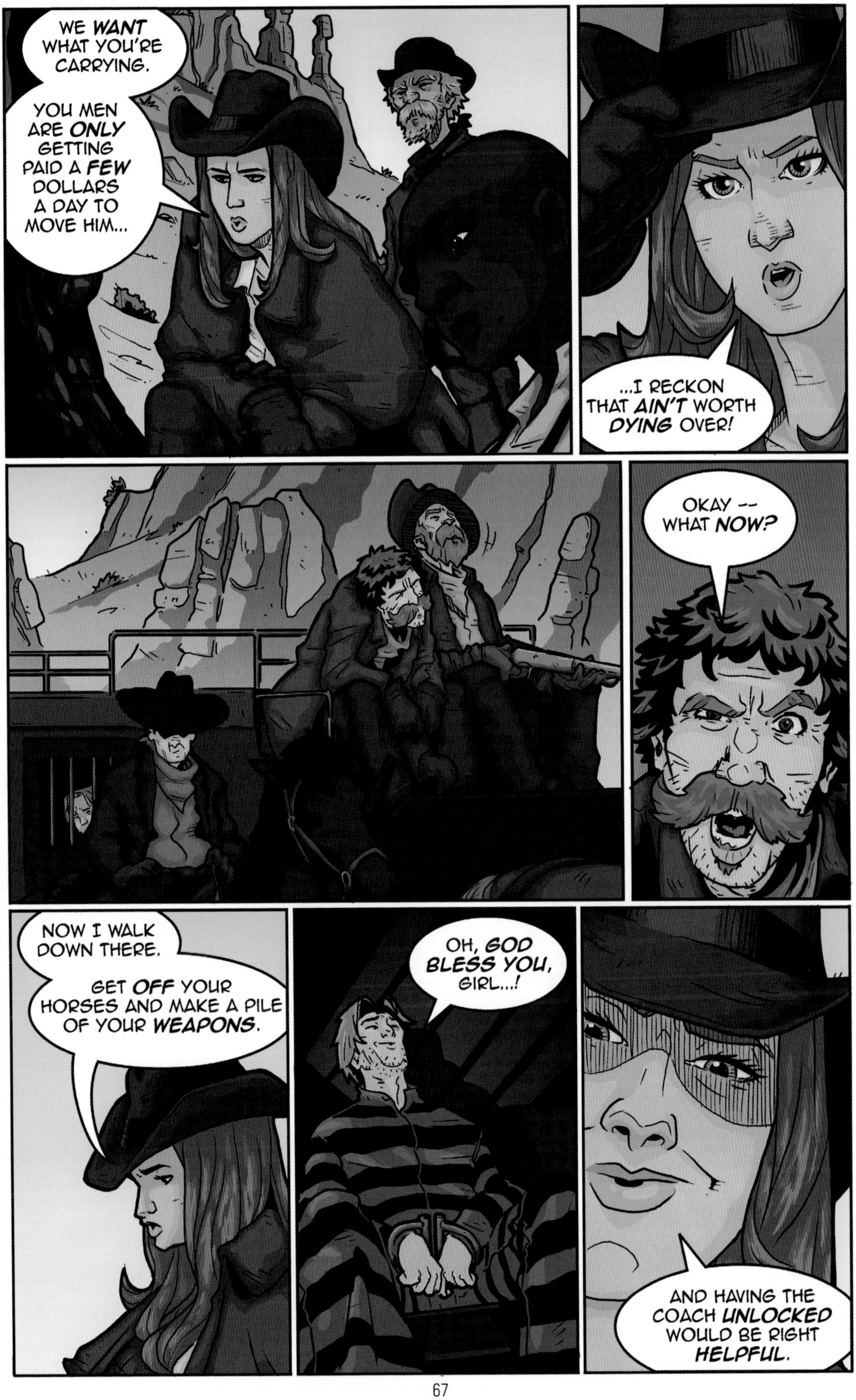
WE WANT WHAT YOU'RE CARRYING.
YOU MEN ARE ONLY GETTING PAID A FEW DOLLARS A DAY TO MOVE HIM...
...I RECKON THAT AIN'T WORTH DYING OVER!
OKAY -- WHAT NOW?
NOW I WALK DOWN THERE.
GET OFF YOUR HORSES AND MAKE A PILE OF YOUR WEAPONS.
OH, GOD BLESS YOU, GIRL...!
AND HAVING THE COACH UNLOCKED WOULD BE RIGHT HELPFUL.

WE'LL LEAVE THE *HORSES* AND *WEAPONS* AT THE MOUTH OF THE CANYON.

I *DON'T* THINK YOU SHOULD TRY AND *FOLLOW* US.

HERE...

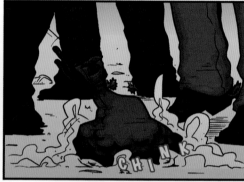

CHINK

HERE'S WHAT YOU WOULDA EARNED FOR THIS JOB... PLUS A *BONUS.*

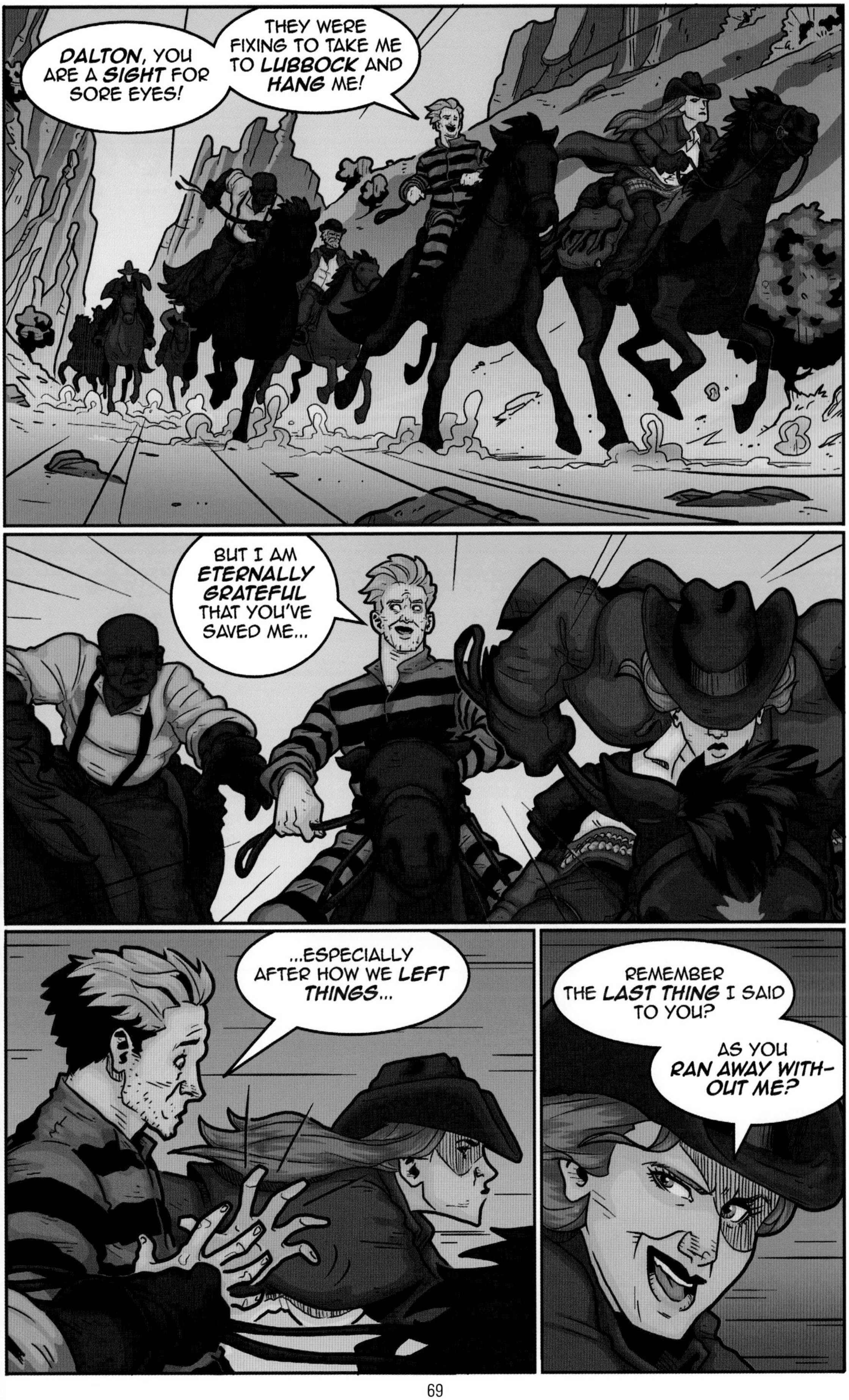
DALTON, YOU ARE A SIGHT FOR SORE EYES!
THEY WERE FIXING TO TAKE ME TO LUBBOCK AND HANG ME!
BUT I AM ETERNALLY GRATEFUL THAT YOU'VE SAVED ME...
...ESPECIALLY AFTER HOW WE LEFT THINGS...
REMEMBER THE LAST THING I SAID TO YOU?
AS YOU RAN AWAY WITH-OUT ME?

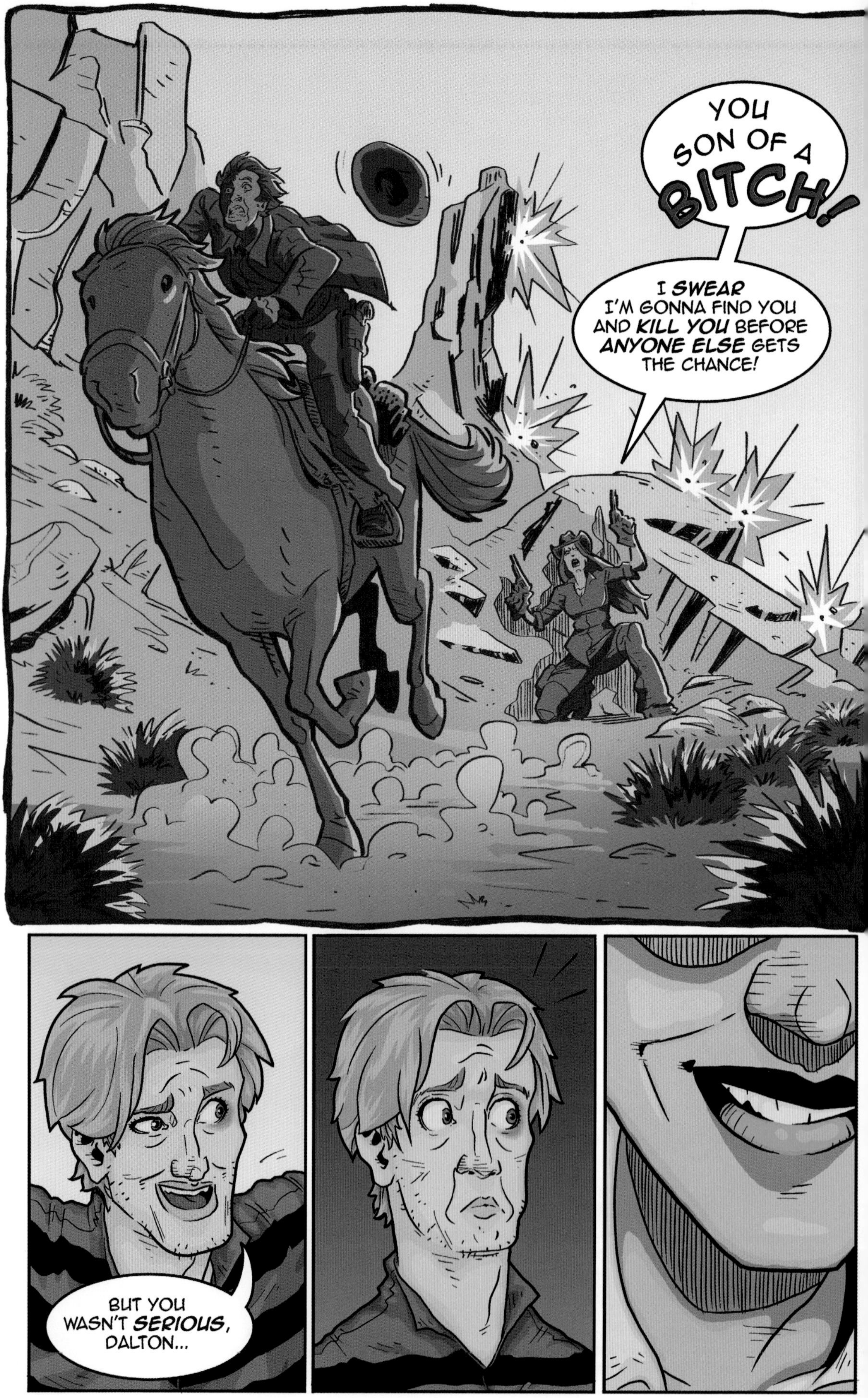
YOU SON OF A BITCH!
I SWEAR I'M GONNA FIND YOU AND KILL YOU BEFORE ANYONE ELSE GETS THE CHANCE!
BUT YOU WASN'T SERIOUS, DALTON...

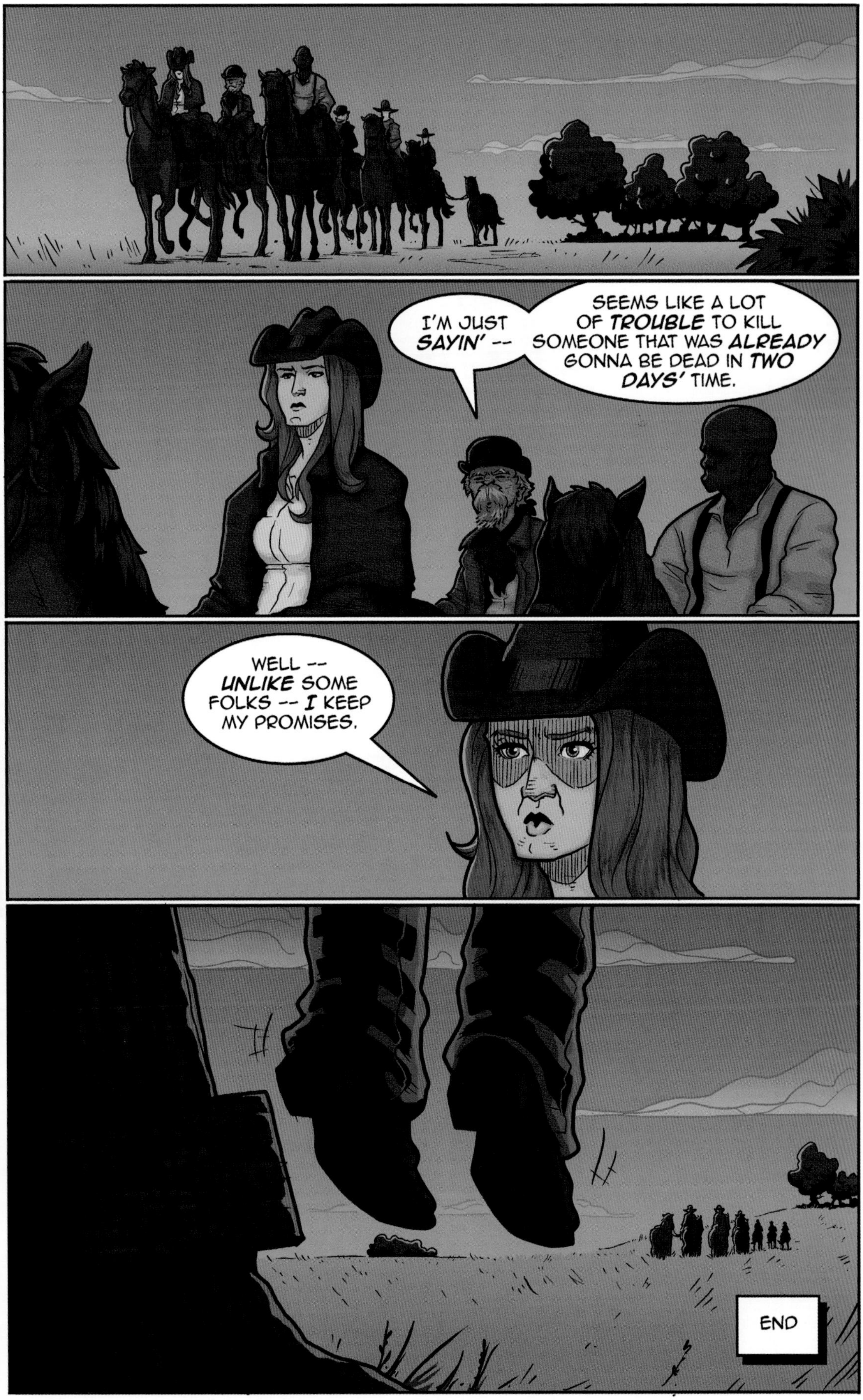
I'M JUST SAYIN' --
SEEMS LIKE A LOT OF TROUBLE TO KILL SOMEONE THAT WAS ALREADY GONNA BE DEAD IN TWO DAYS' TIME.
WELL -- UNLIKE SOME FOLKS -- I KEEP MY PROMISES.
END

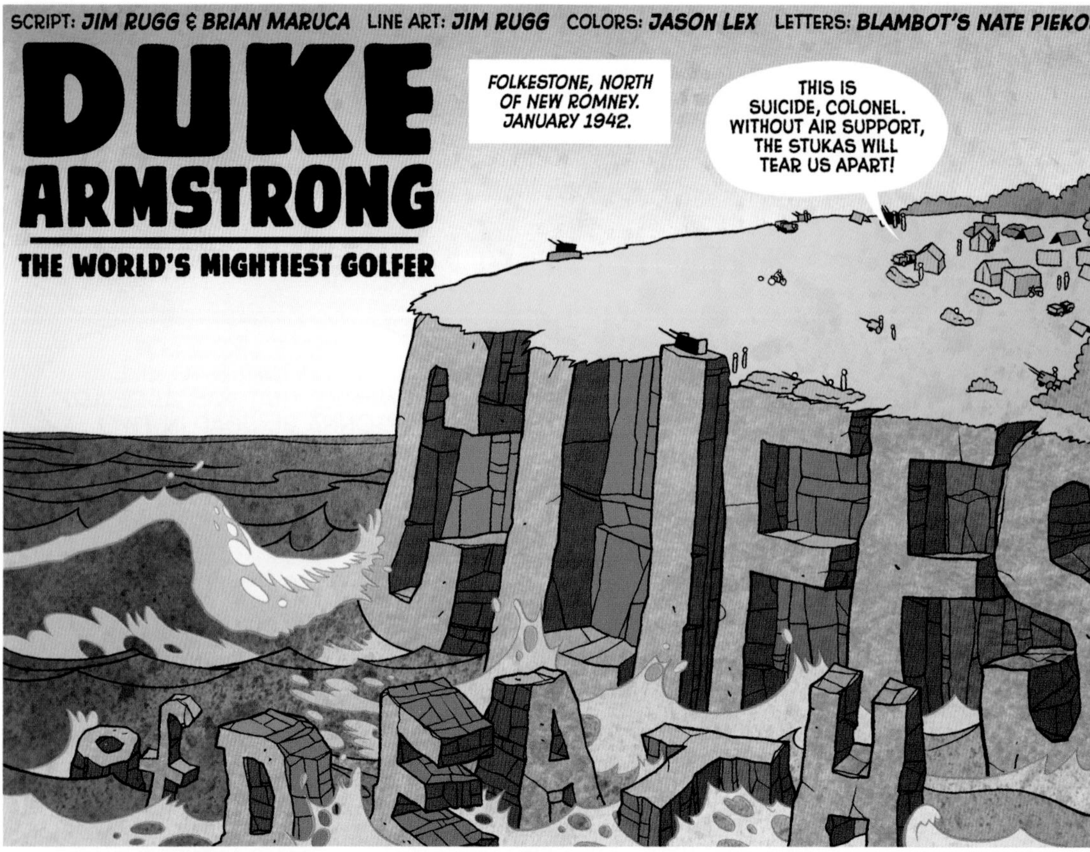
SCRIPT: JIM RUGG & BRIAN MARUCA LINE ART: JIM RUGG COLORS: JASON LEX LETTERS: BLAMBOT'S NATE PIEKOS
DUKE ARMSTRONG
THE WORLD'S MIGHTIEST GOLFER
FOLKESTONE, NORTH OF NEW ROMNEY. JANUARY 1942.
THIS IS SUICIDE, COLONEL. WITHOUT AIR SUPPORT, THE STUKAS WILL TEAR US APART!
CLIFFS of DEATH

SPECIAL THANKS TO ANDREAS MERGENTHALER.

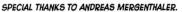

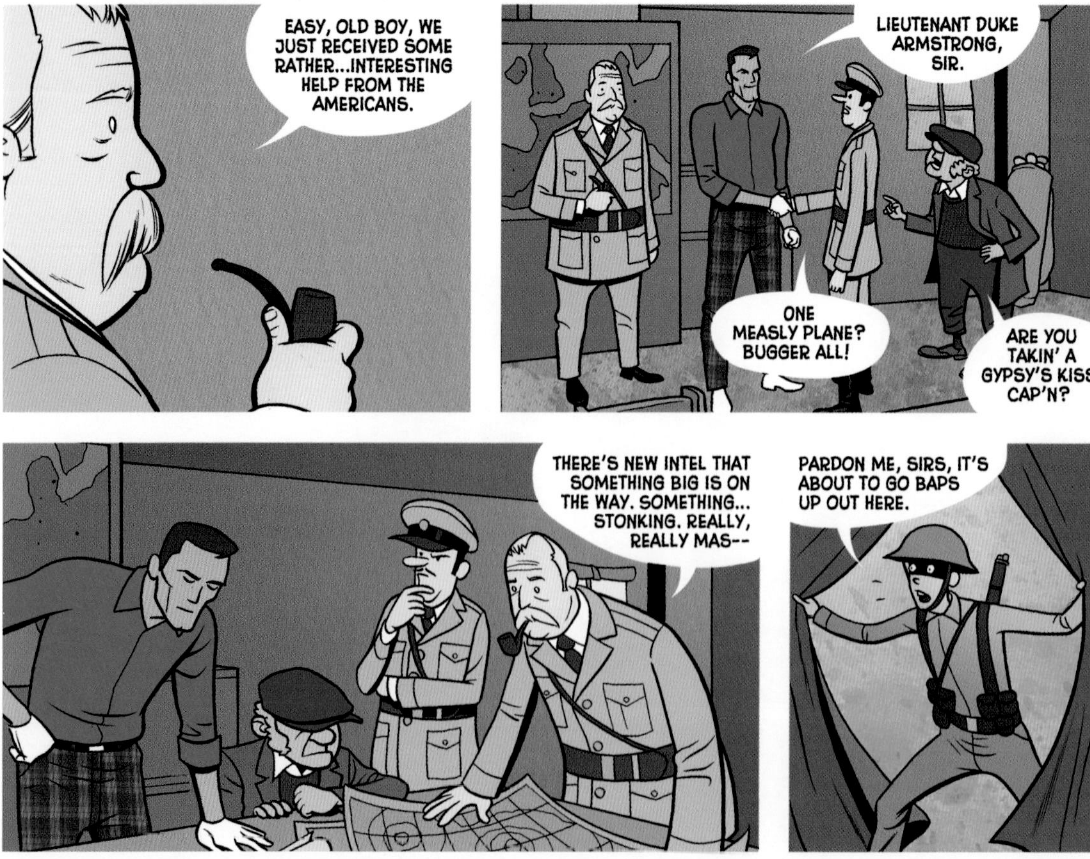
EASY, OLD BOY, WE JUST RECEIVED SOME RATHER...INTERESTING HELP FROM THE AMERICANS.
LIEUTENANT DUKE ARMSTRONG, SIR.
ONE MEASLY PLANE? BUGGER ALL!
ARE YOU TAKIN' A GYPSY'S KISS, CAP'N?
THERE'S NEW INTEL THAT SOMETHING BIG IS ON THE WAY. SOMETHING... STONKING. REALLY, REALLY MAS--
PARDON ME, SIRS, IT'S ABOUT TO GO BAPS UP OUT HERE.

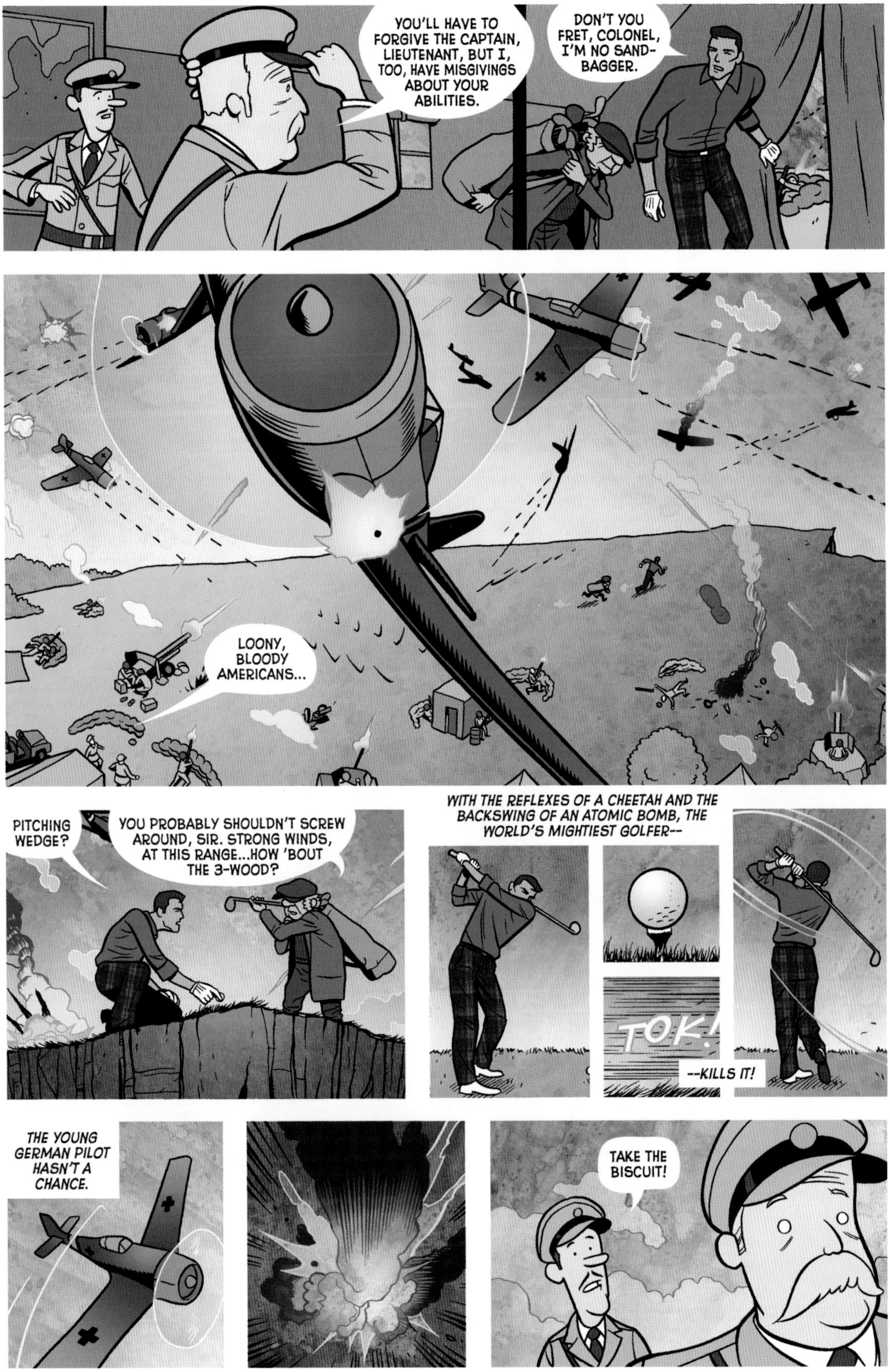
YOU'LL HAVE TO FORGIVE THE CAPTAIN, LIEUTENANT, BUT I, TOO, HAVE MISGIVINGS ABOUT YOUR ABILITIES.
DON'T YOU FRET, COLONEL, I'M NO SAND-BAGGER.
LOONY, BLOODY AMERICANS...
PITCHING WEDGE?
YOU PROBABLY SHOULDN'T SCREW AROUND, SIR. STRONG WINDS, AT THIS RANGE...HOW 'BOUT THE 3-WOOD?
WITH THE REFLEXES OF A CHEETAH AND THE BACKSWING OF AN ATOMIC BOMB, THE WORLD'S MIGHTIEST GOLFER--
TOK!
--KILLS IT!
THE YOUNG GERMAN PILOT HASN'T A CHANCE.
TAKE THE BISCUIT!

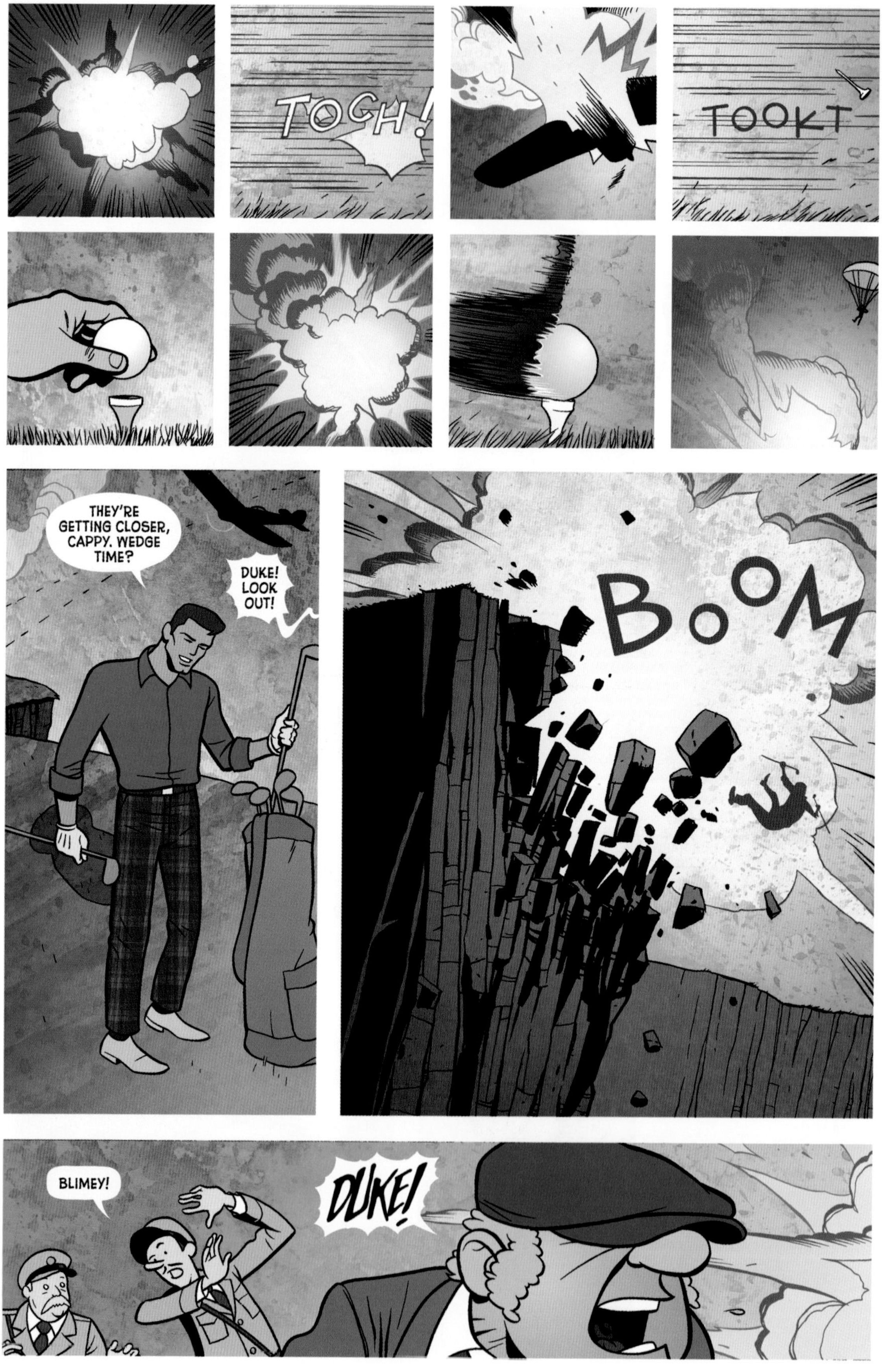
TOCH!
TOOKT
THEY'RE GETTING CLOSER, CAPPY. WEDGE TIME?
DUKE! LOOK OUT!
BOOOM
BLIMEY!
DUKE!

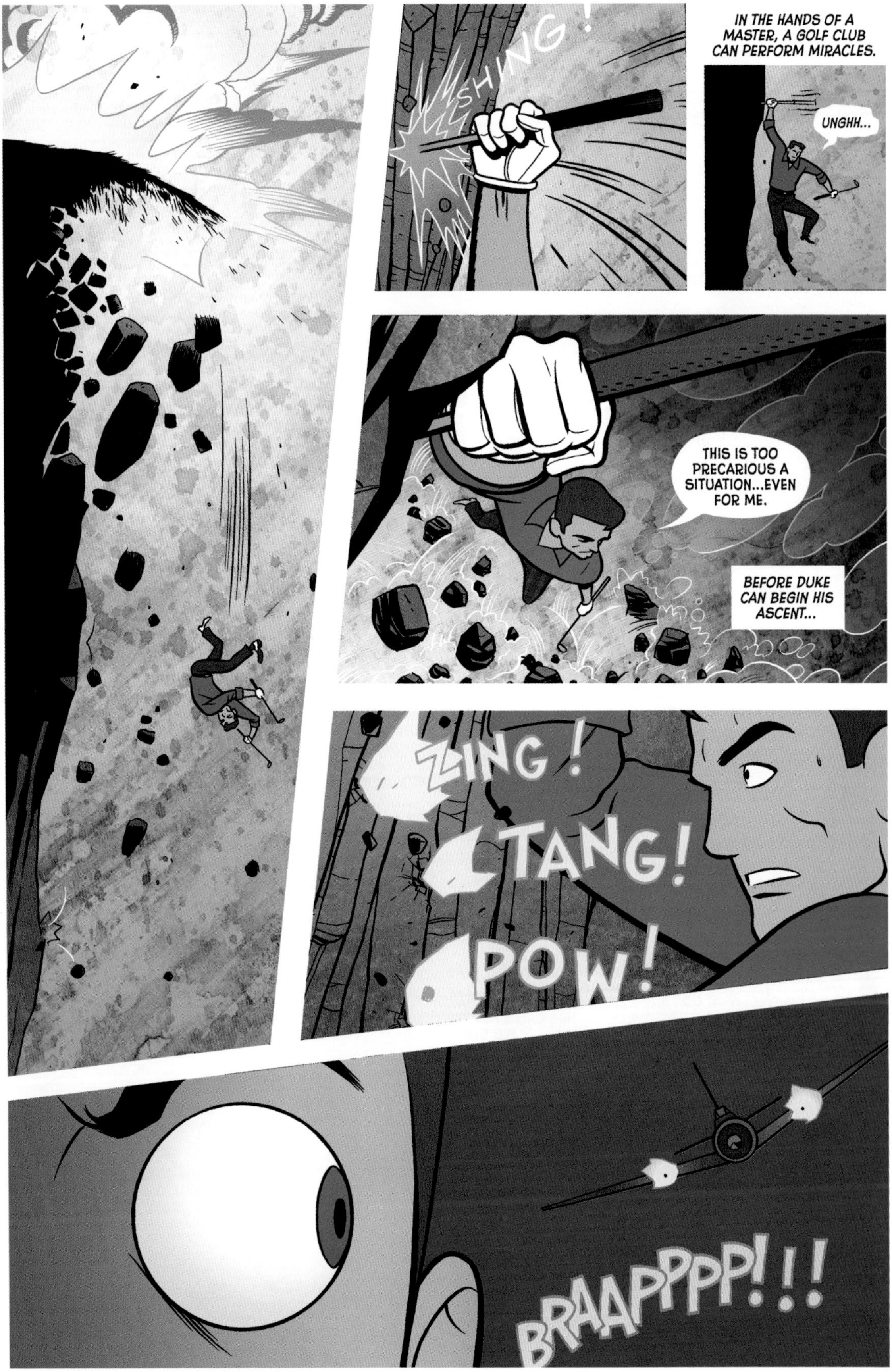
SHING!
IN THE HANDS OF A MASTER, A GOLF CLUB CAN PERFORM MIRACLES.
UNGHH...
THIS IS TOO PRECARIOUS A SITUATION...EVEN FOR ME.
BEFORE DUKE CAN BEGIN HIS ASCENT...
ZING!
TANG!
POW!
BRAAPPPP!!!

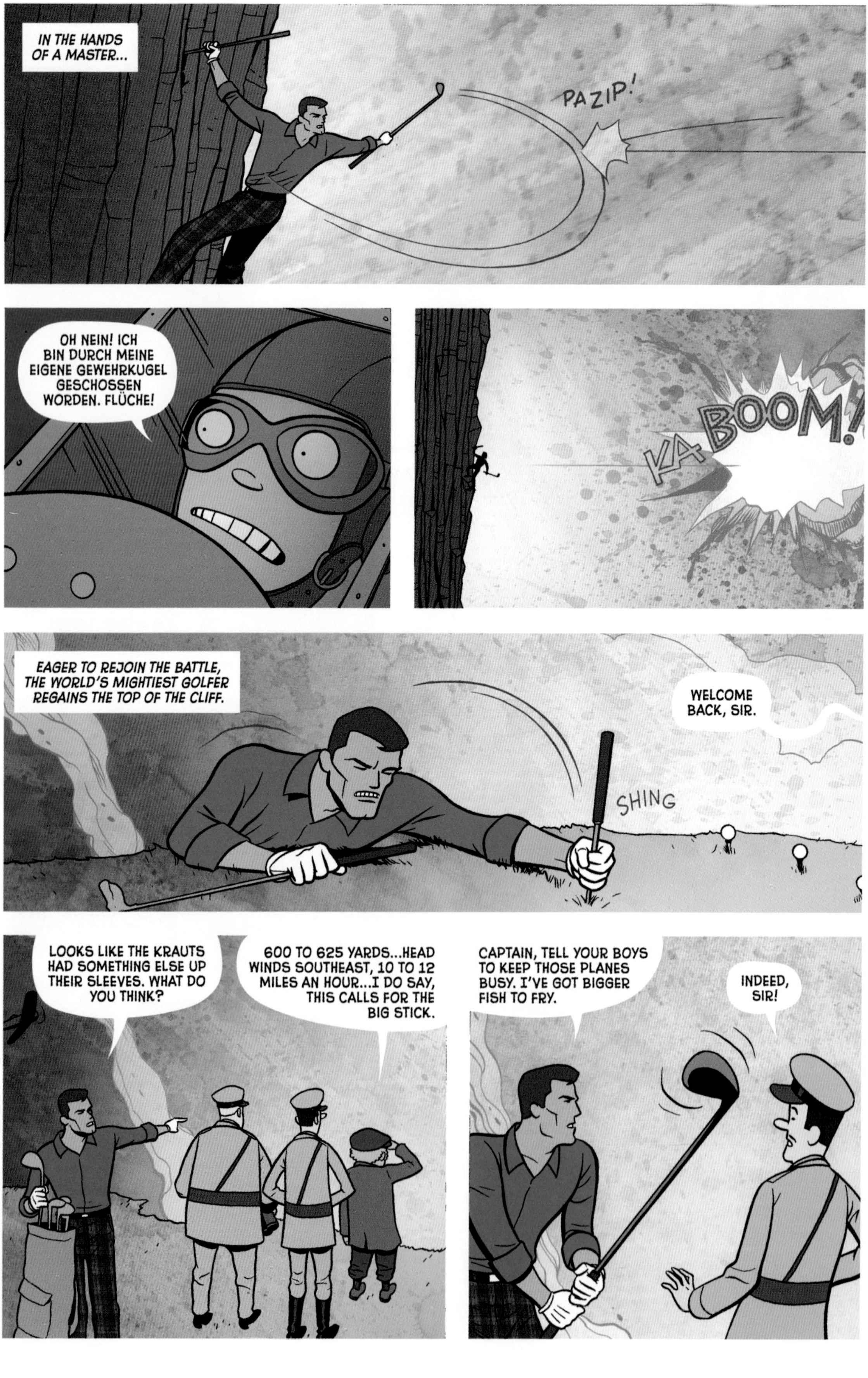
IN THE HANDS OF A MASTER...
PAZIP!
OH NEIN! ICH BIN DURCH MEINE EIGENE GEWEHRKUGEL GESCHOSSEN WORDEN. FLÜCHE!
KA BOOM!
EAGER TO REJOIN THE BATTLE, THE WORLD'S MIGHTIEST GOLFER REGAINS THE TOP OF THE CLIFF.
WELCOME BACK, SIR.
SHING
LOOKS LIKE THE KRAUTS HAD SOMETHING ELSE UP THEIR SLEEVES. WHAT DO YOU THINK?
600 TO 625 YARDS...HEAD WINDS SOUTHEAST, 10 TO 12 MILES AN HOUR...I DO SAY, THIS CALLS FOR THE BIG STICK.
CAPTAIN, TELL YOUR BOYS TO KEEP THOSE PLANES BUSY. I'VE GOT BIGGER FISH TO FRY.
INDEED, SIR!

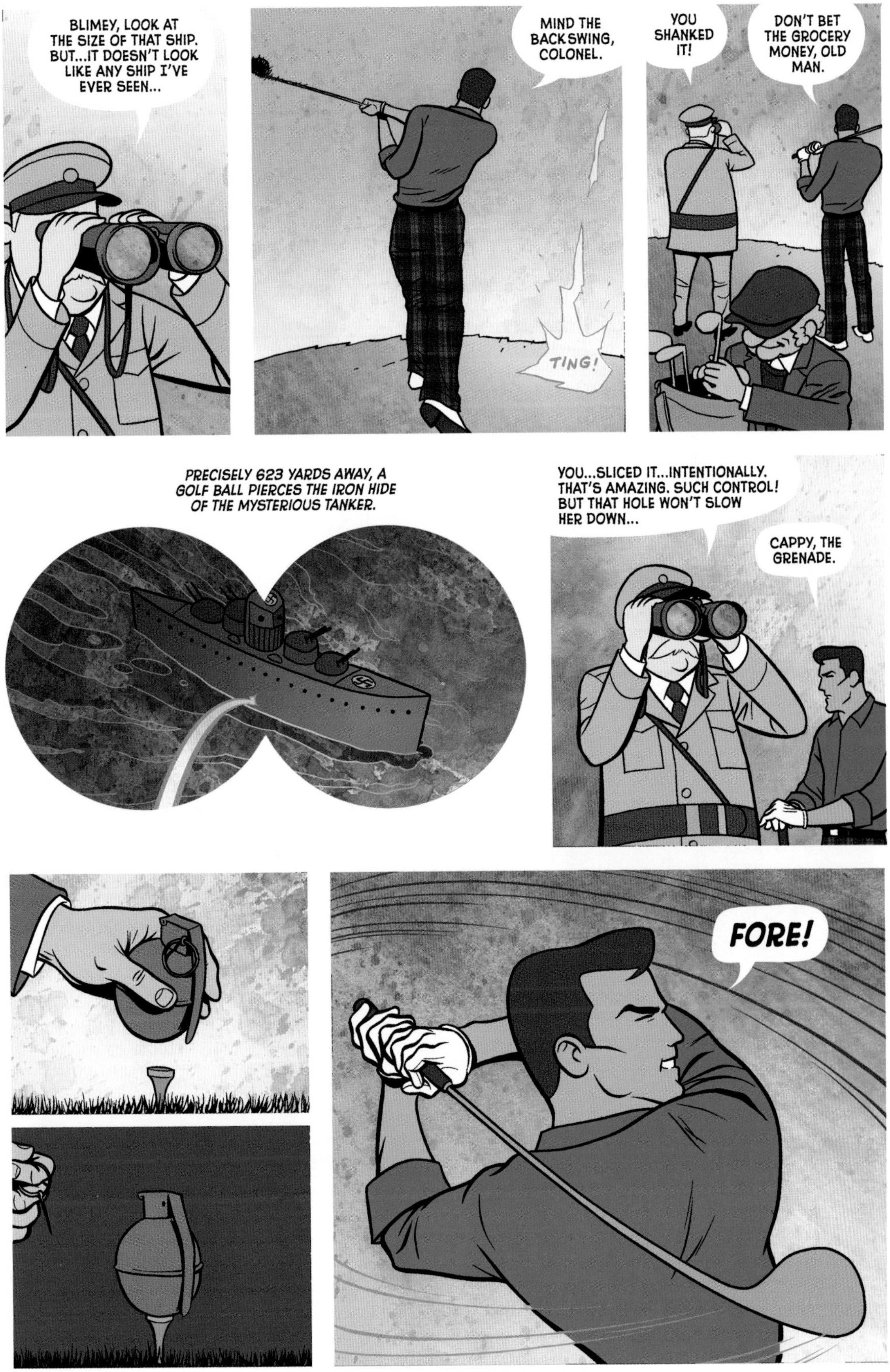

BLIMEY, LOOK AT THE SIZE OF THAT SHIP. BUT...IT DOESN'T LOOK LIKE ANY SHIP I'VE EVER SEEN...
MIND THE BACKSWING, COLONEL.
TING!
YOU SHANKED IT!
DON'T BET THE GROCERY MONEY, OLD MAN.
PRECISELY 623 YARDS AWAY, A GOLF BALL PIERCES THE IRON HIDE OF THE MYSTERIOUS TANKER.
YOU...SLICED IT...INTENTIONALLY. THAT'S AMAZING. SUCH CONTROL! BUT THAT HOLE WON'T SLOW HER DOWN...
CAPPY, THE GRENADE.
FORE!

WAS IST LOS?!

FEUER UND EXPLOSIONEN UNTER DEM ERSTEN DECK, KAPITÄN!

ALLE MANN VON BORD!

UNMÖGLICH, HANS! WIR SIND NICHT GETROFFEN WORDEN!

ROBOTER

"LOOK! SHE'S GOING DOWN!"

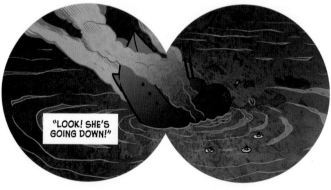

CALL COMMAND, SIR, AND GET A DIVE TEAM OVER THERE...MAYBE WE CAN SALVAGE SOMETHING.

GOOD IDEA, CHAP.

WITH THE BATTLE DECIDED...THE REMAINING PLANES RETREAT.

BLOODY HELL...WHO IS THAT MAN?

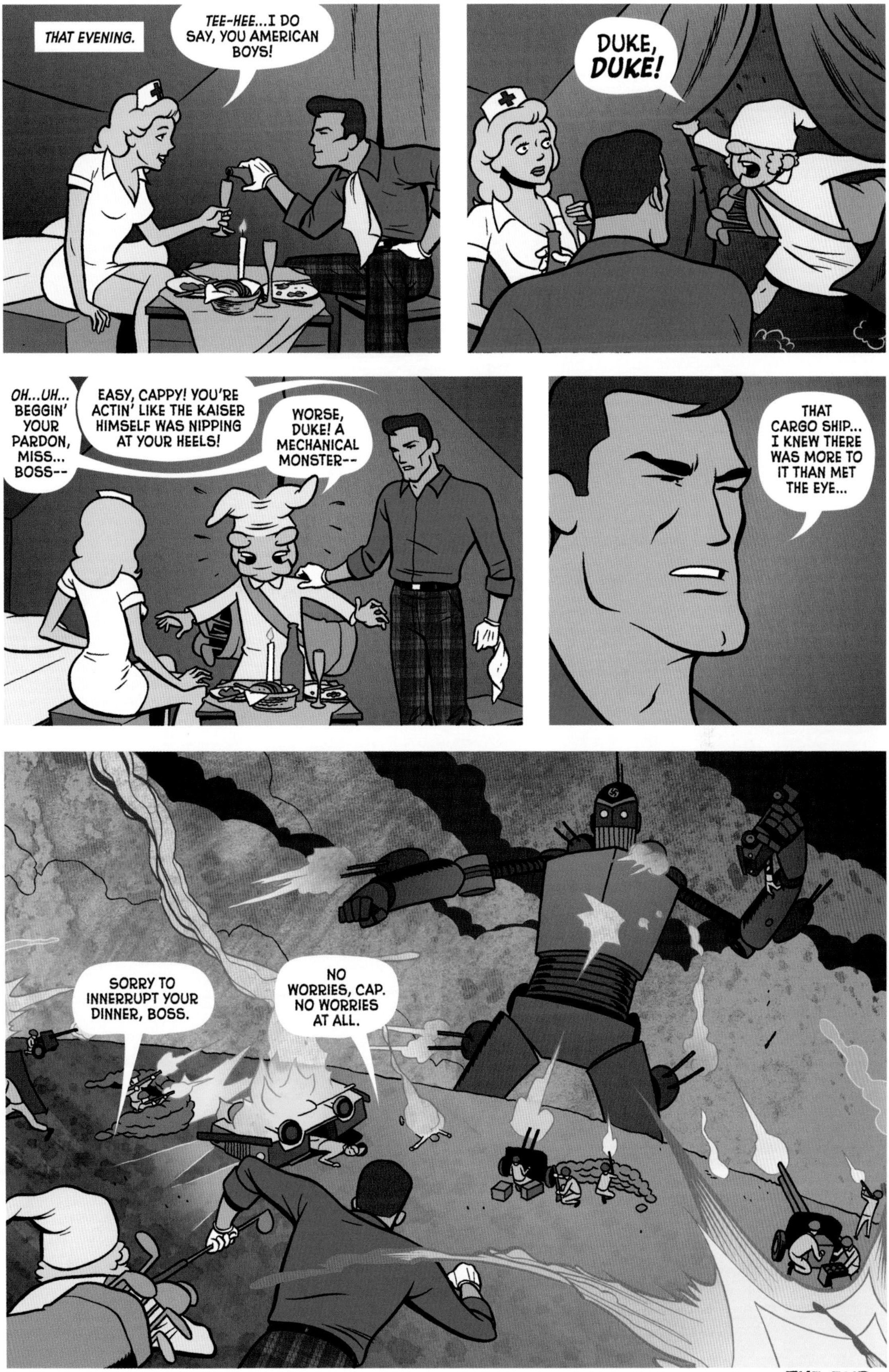
THAT EVENING.
TEE-HEE...I DO SAY, YOU AMERICAN BOYS!
DUKE, DUKE!
OH...UH... BEGGIN' YOUR PARDON, MISS... BOSS--
EASY, CAPPY! YOU'RE ACTIN' LIKE THE KAISER HIMSELF WAS NIPPING AT YOUR HEELS!
WORSE, DUKE! A MECHANICAL MONSTER--
THAT CARGO SHIP... I KNEW THERE WAS MORE TO IT THAN MET THE EYE...
SORRY TO INNERRUPT YOUR DINNER, BOSS.
NO WORRIES, CAP. NO WORRIES AT ALL.

THE END

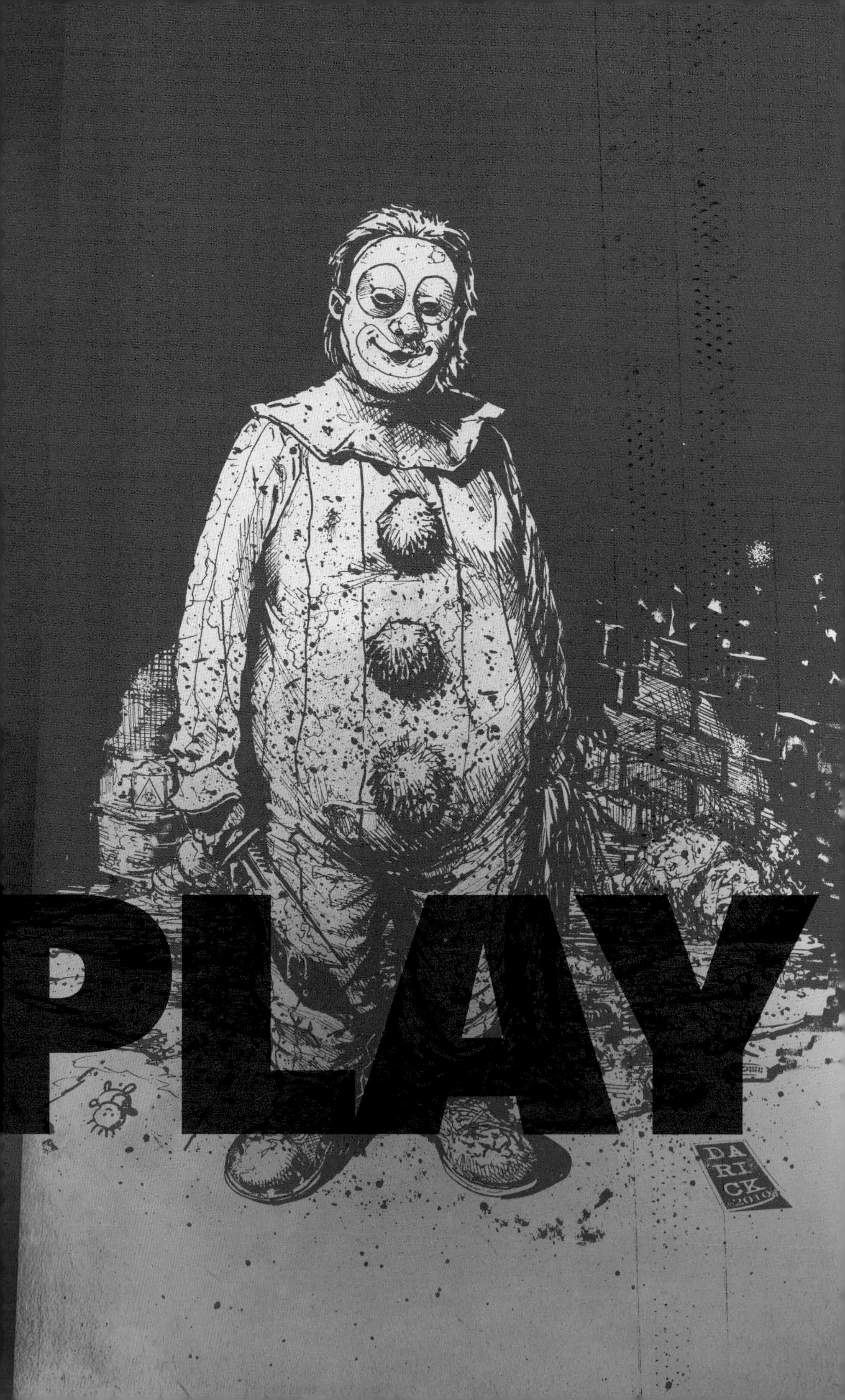
PLAY
DA RI CK 2010

WRITTEN BY
DAMON GENTRY

ART BY
AARON CONLEY

LEGENDS HAVE BEEN BORN FROM THE FEARS OF MAN.

:rustle:

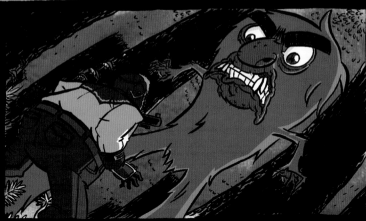

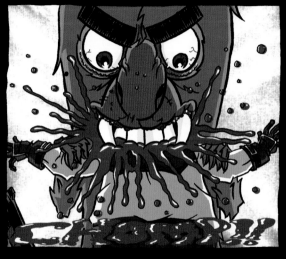

:rustle:

BUT WHAT HORROR HAS BEEN BORN FROM THE FEARS OF LEGENDS?

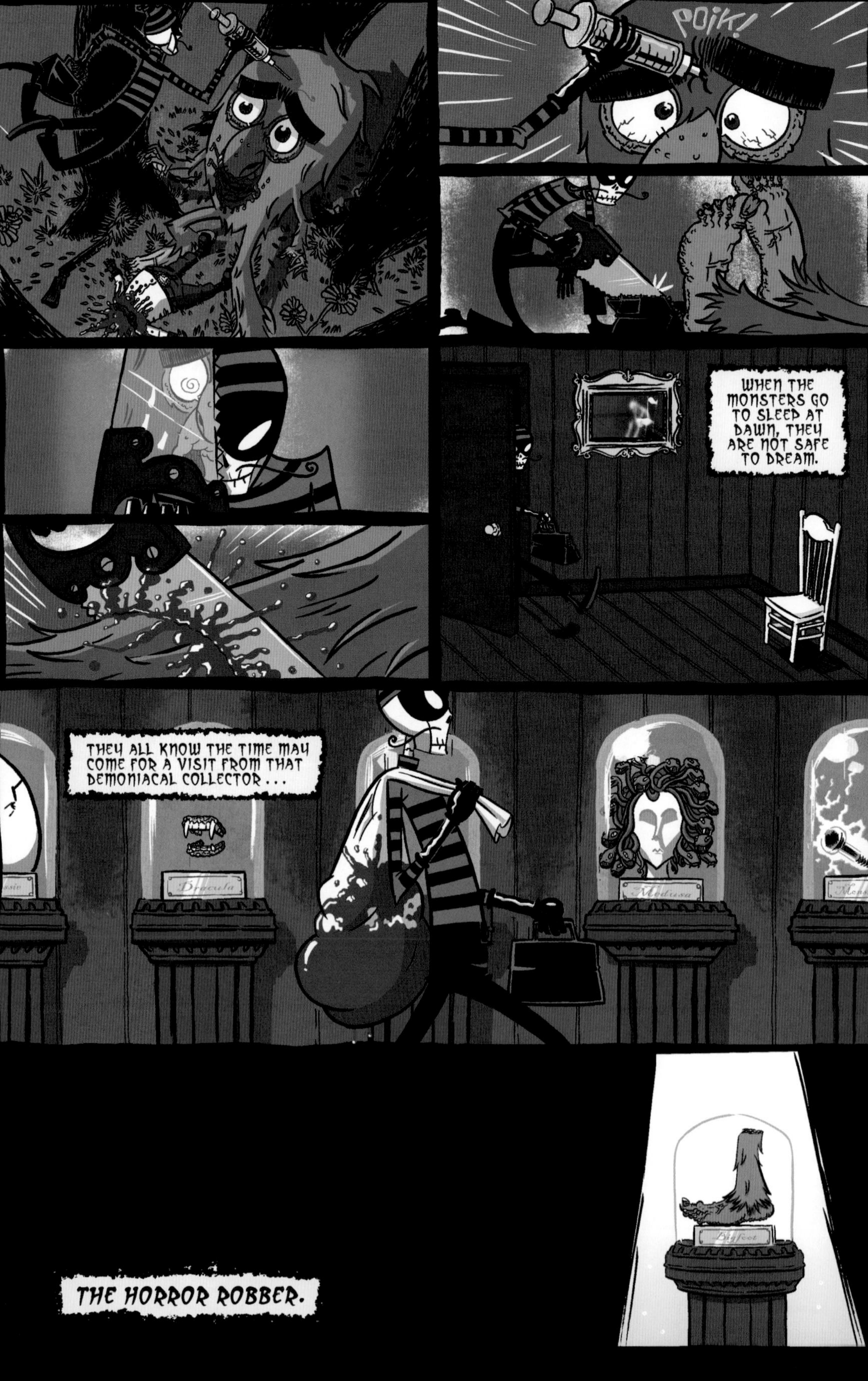
POIK!
WHEN THE MONSTERS GO TO SLEEP AT DAWN, THEY ARE NOT SAFE TO DREAM.
THEY ALL KNOW THE TIME MAY COME FOR A VISIT FROM THAT DEMONIACAL COLLECTOR . . .
Dracula
Medusa
Bigfoot
THE HORROR ROBBER.

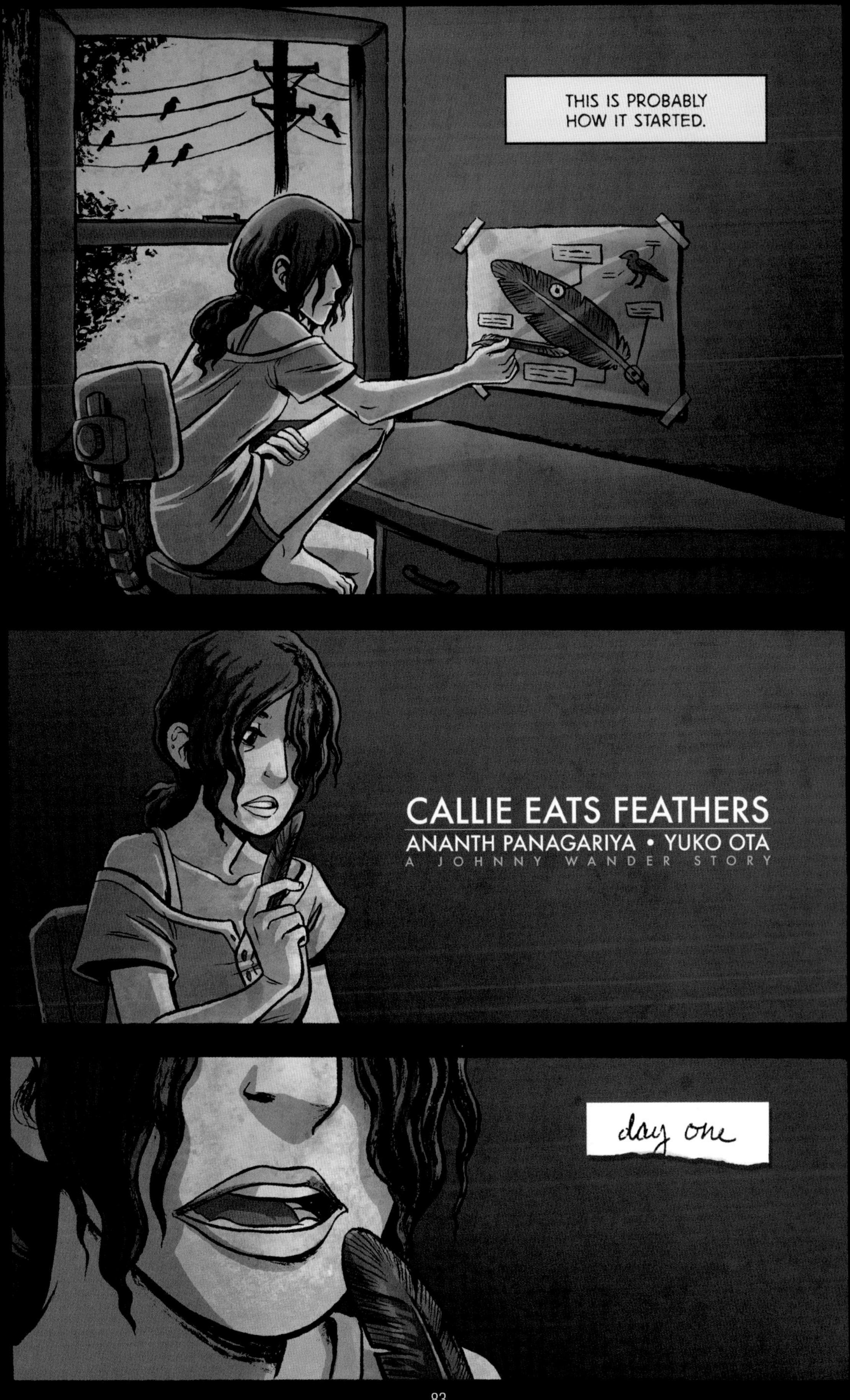
THIS IS PROBABLY HOW IT STARTED.
CALLIE EATS FEATHERS
ANANTH PANAGARIYA • YUKO OTA
A JOHNNY WANDER STORY
day one

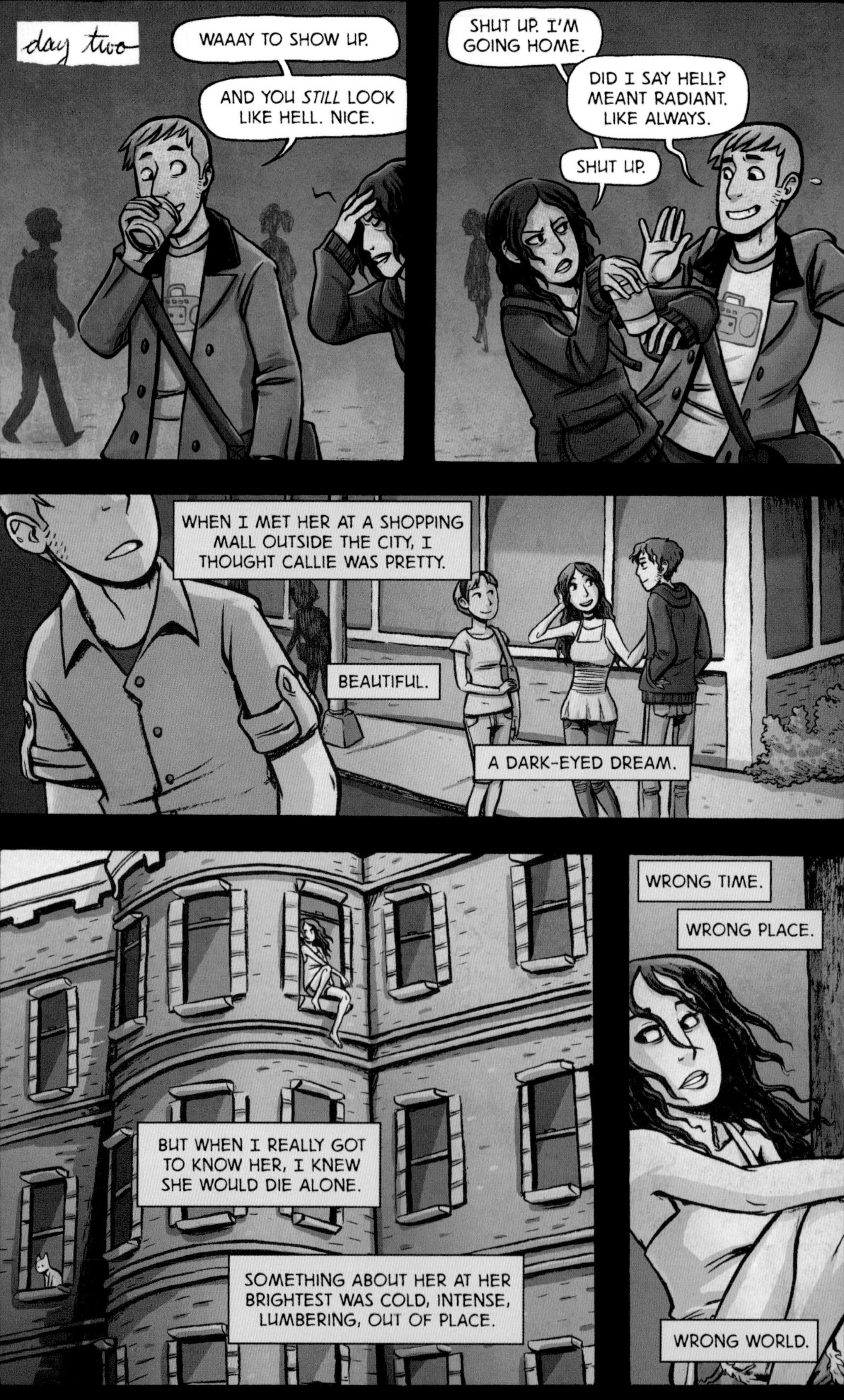
day two
WAAAY TO SHOW UP.
AND YOU STILL LOOK LIKE HELL. NICE.
SHUT UP. I'M GOING HOME.
DID I SAY HELL? MEANT RADIANT. LIKE ALWAYS.
SHUT UP.
WHEN I MET HER AT A SHOPPING MALL OUTSIDE THE CITY, I THOUGHT CALLIE WAS PRETTY.
BEAUTIFUL.
A DARK-EYED DREAM.
BUT WHEN I REALLY GOT TO KNOW HER, I KNEW SHE WOULD DIE ALONE.
SOMETHING ABOUT HER AT HER BRIGHTEST WAS COLD, INTENSE, LUMBERING, OUT OF PLACE.
WRONG TIME.
WRONG PLACE.
WRONG WORLD.

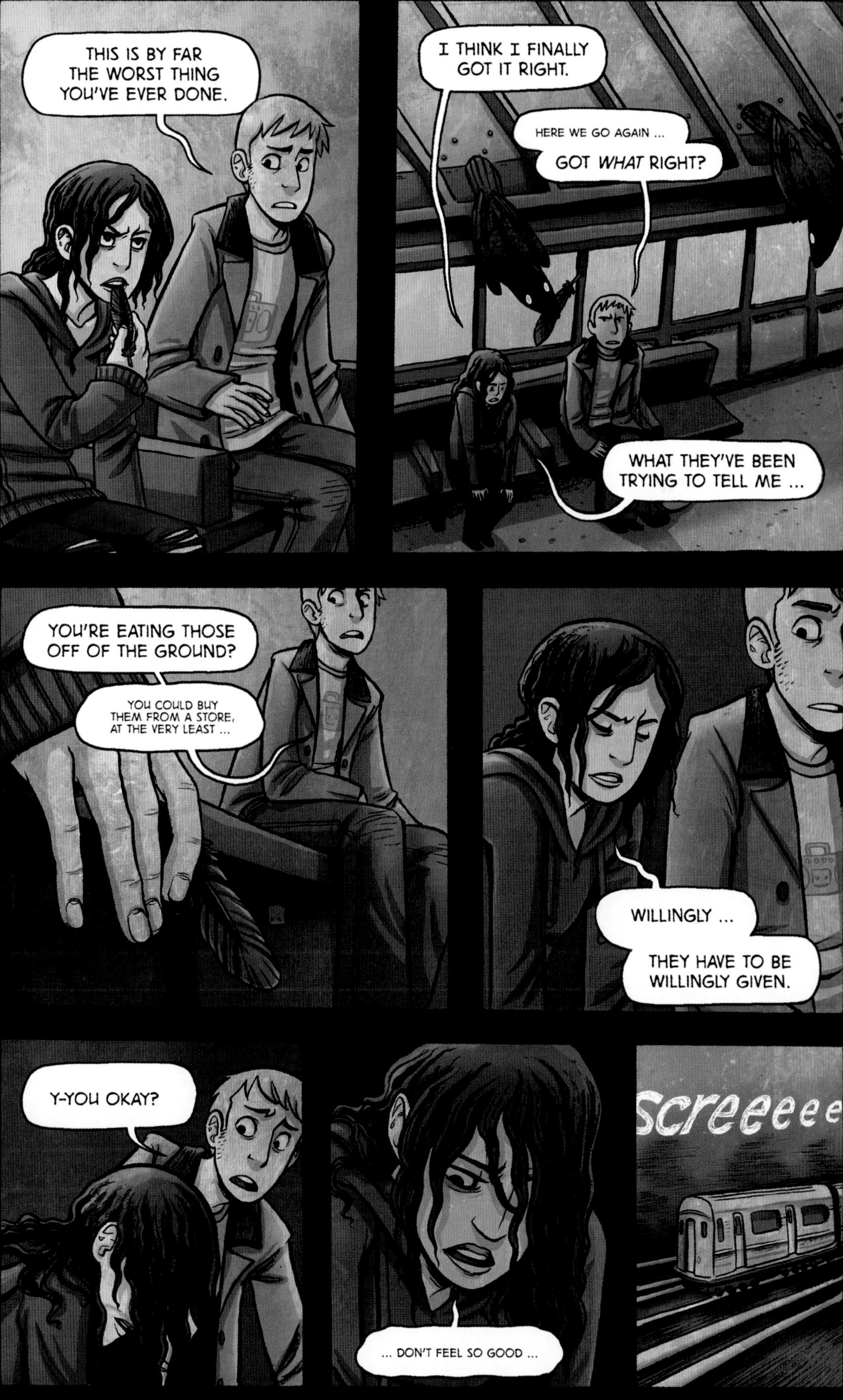
THIS IS BY FAR THE WORST THING YOU'VE EVER DONE.
I THINK I FINALLY GOT IT RIGHT.
HERE WE GO AGAIN ...
GOT *WHAT* RIGHT?
WHAT THEY'VE BEEN TRYING TO TELL ME ...
YOU'RE EATING THOSE OFF OF THE GROUND?
YOU COULD BUY THEM FROM A STORE, AT THE VERY LEAST ...
WILLINGLY ...
THEY HAVE TO BE WILLINGLY GIVEN.
Y-YOU OKAY?
... DON'T FEEL SO GOOD ...
SCREEEEE

day three

HEYYY, WHAT DO YOU THINK?

DIDN'T EVEN KNOW YOU *HAD* DRESSES.

I SUPPOSE IT'S NOT A SECRET ANYMORE.

YOU'RE AWFUL FRIENDLY TODAY ... FEELING BETTER?

I'M *NEVER* FRIENDLY. YOU JUST LIKE ME ENOUGH TO PUT UP WITH MY SHIT ...

... AWFUL FORWARD, TOO ...

YOU QUIETLY LIT THIS CANDLE FOR ME ...

... IT'S MORE LIKE A BLOWTORCH ...

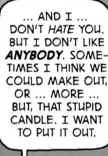

... AND I ... DON'T *HATE* YOU. BUT I DON'T LIKE *ANYBODY*. SOMETIMES I THINK WE COULD MAKE OUT, OR ... MORE ... BUT, THAT STUPID CANDLE. I WANT TO PUT IT OUT.

WHAT, SO FRIENDS WITH BENEFITS IS OKAY AS LONG AS I DON'T *CARE* ABOUT YOU?

ARE WE FRIENDS?

CALLIE WAS CLUMSY ENOUGH THAT EVERY CONVERSATION WAS HONEST ...

CAN I *HAVE* FRIENDS?

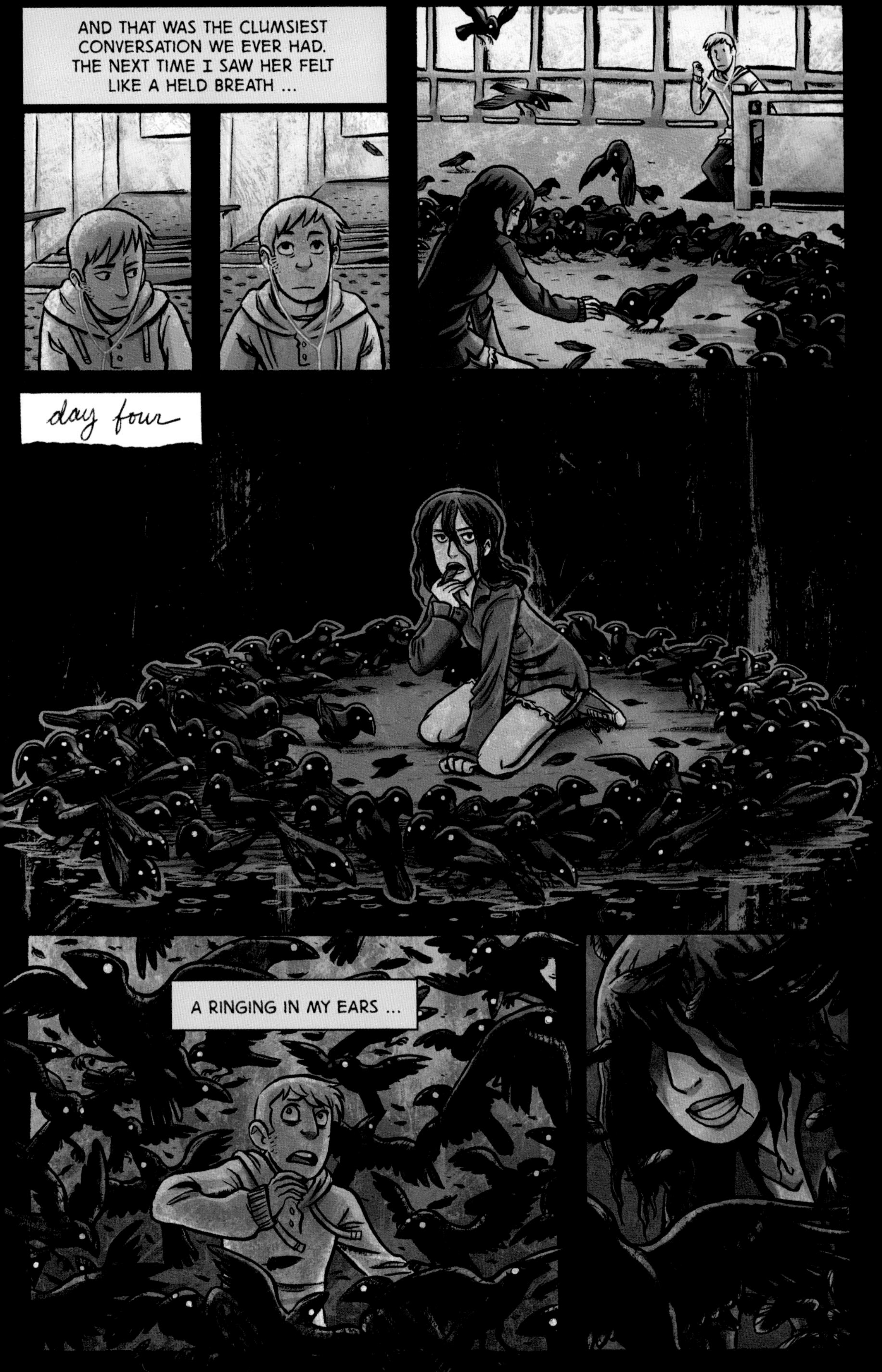
AND THAT WAS THE CLUMSIEST CONVERSATION WE EVER HAD. THE NEXT TIME I SAW HER FELT LIKE A HELD BREATH ...
day four
A RINGING IN MY EARS ...

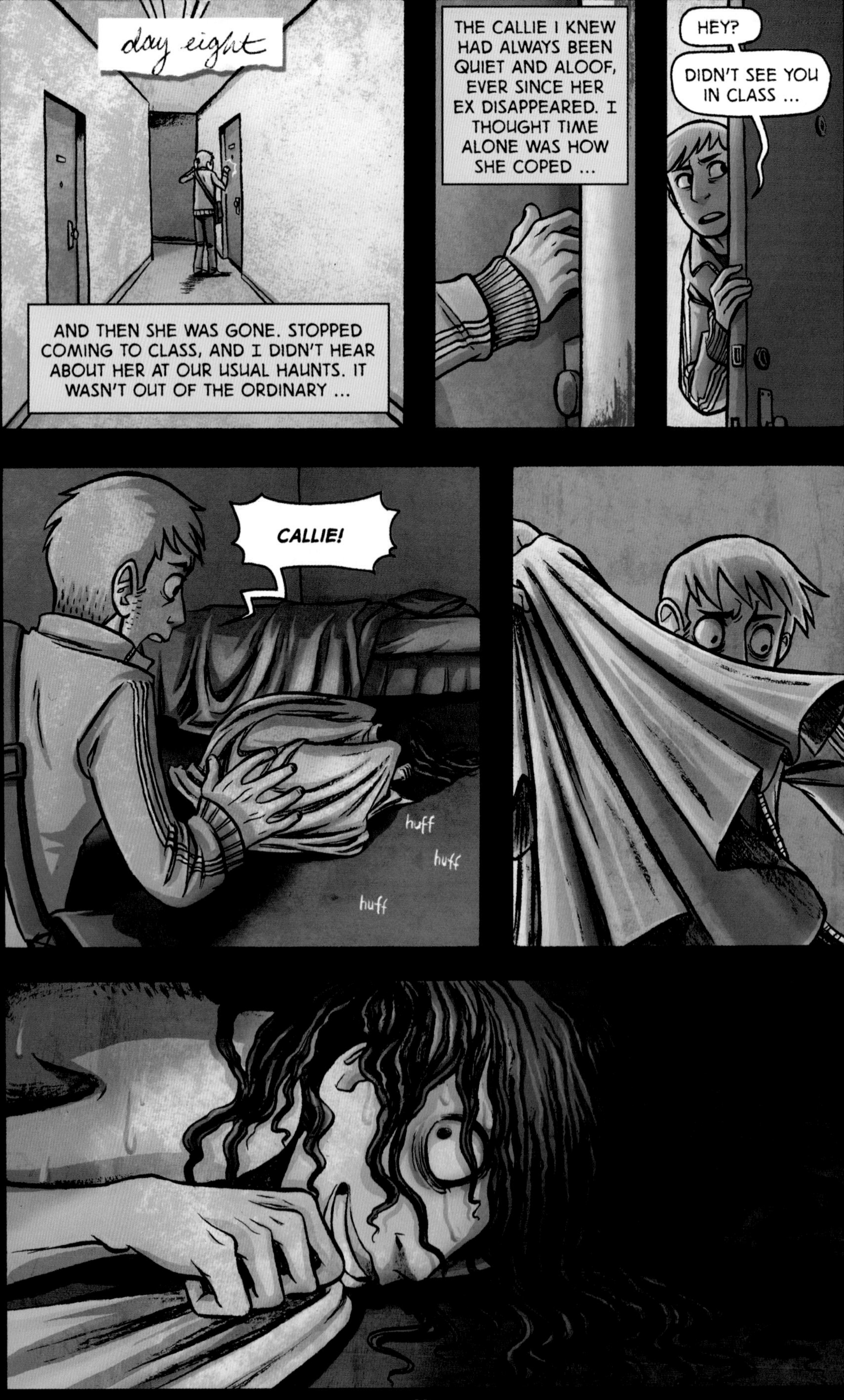
day eight
AND THEN SHE WAS GONE. STOPPED COMING TO CLASS, AND I DIDN'T HEAR ABOUT HER AT OUR USUAL HAUNTS. IT WASN'T OUT OF THE ORDINARY ...
THE CALLIE I KNEW HAD ALWAYS BEEN QUIET AND ALOOF, EVER SINCE HER EX DISAPPEARED. I THOUGHT TIME ALONE WAS HOW SHE COPED ...
HEY?
DIDN'T SEE YOU IN CLASS ...
CALLIE!
huff
huff
huff

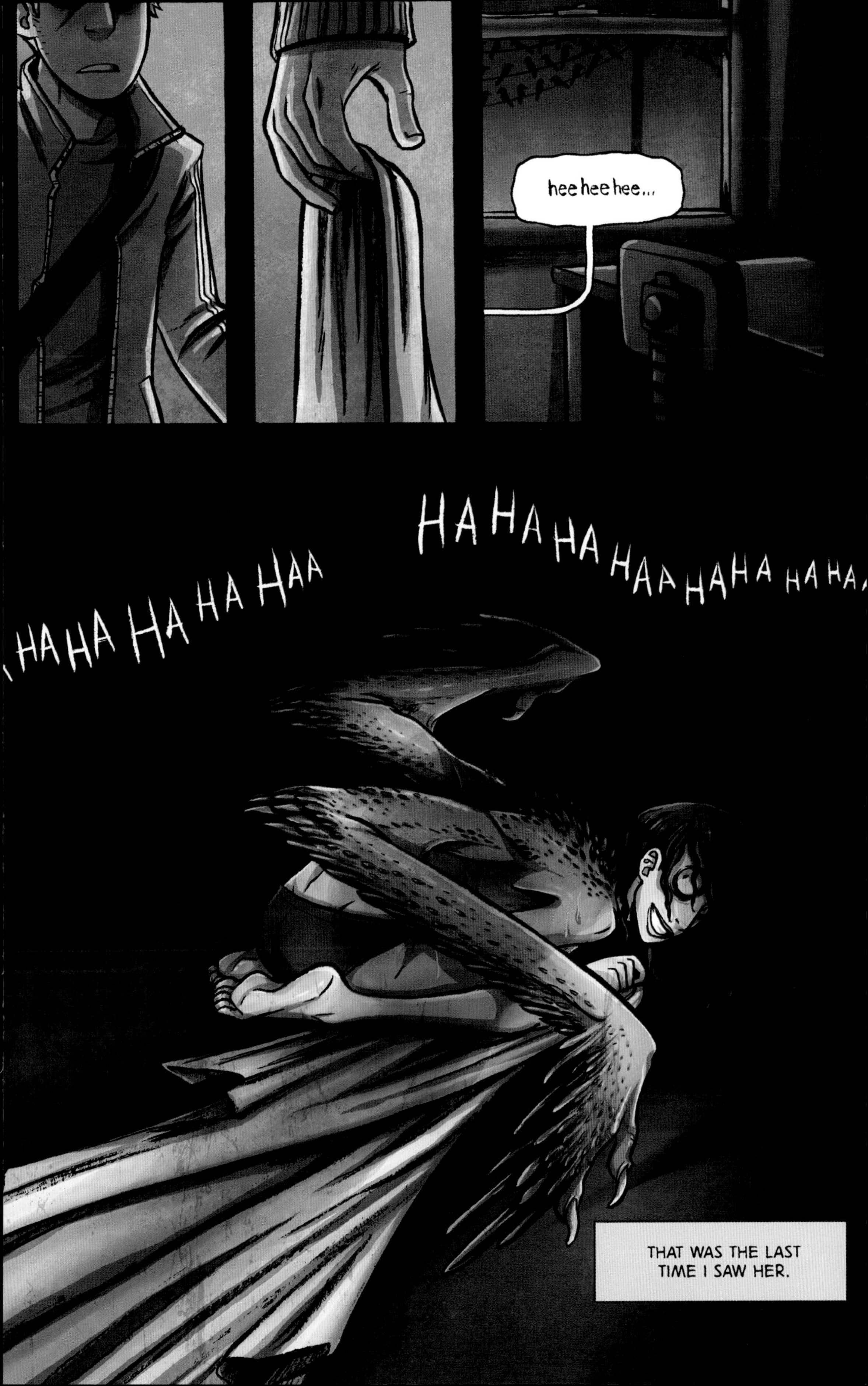
heeheehee...
HA HA HA HA HAA HAHA HA HA...
HA HA HA HA HA HAA
THAT WAS THE LAST TIME I SAW HER.

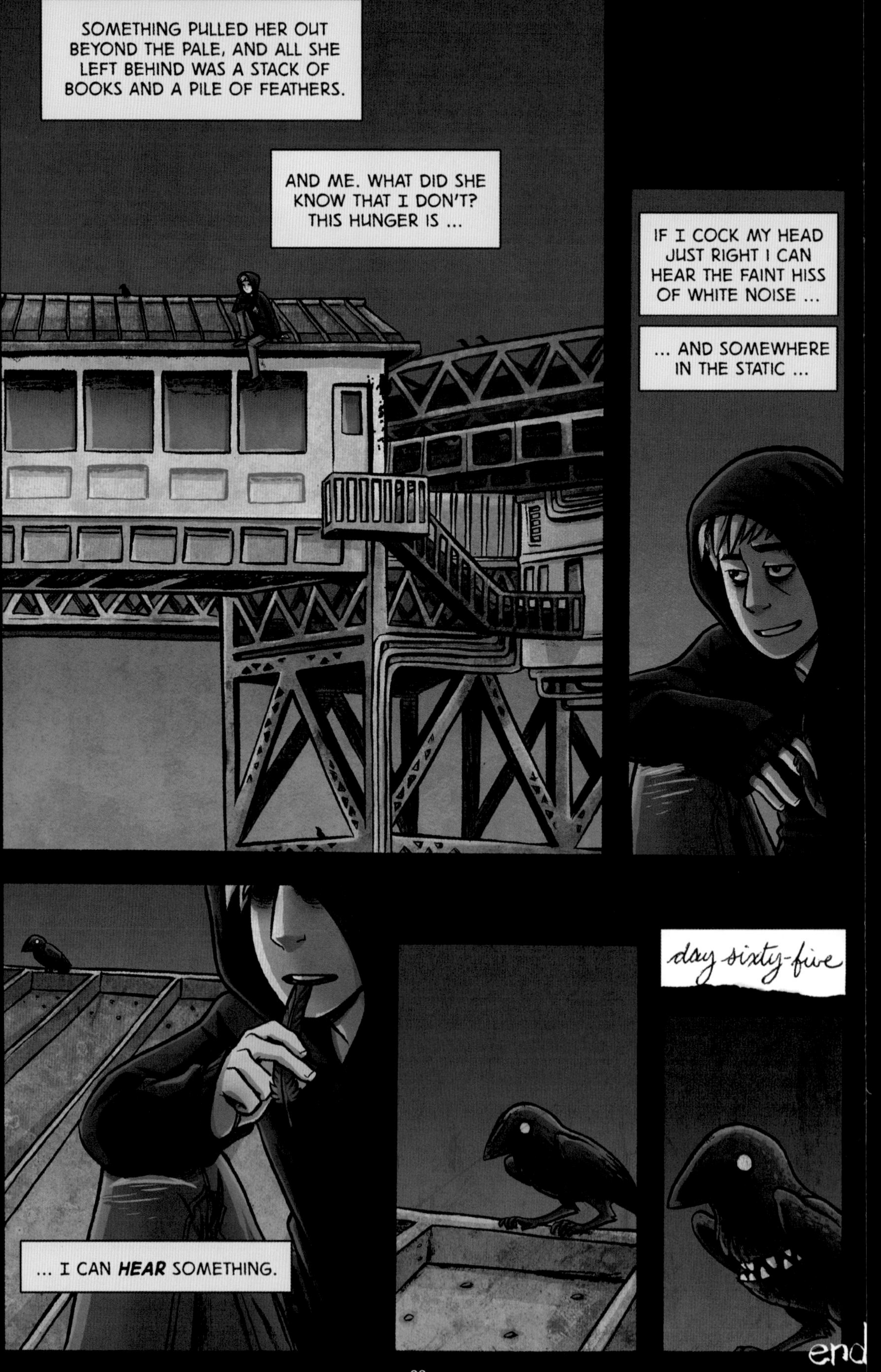
SOMETHING PULLED HER OUT BEYOND THE PALE, AND ALL SHE LEFT BEHIND WAS A STACK OF BOOKS AND A PILE OF FEATHERS.
AND ME. WHAT DID SHE KNOW THAT I DON'T? THIS HUNGER IS ...
IF I COCK MY HEAD JUST RIGHT I CAN HEAR THE FAINT HISS OF WHITE NOISE ...
... AND SOMEWHERE IN THE STATIC ...
... I CAN *HEAR* SOMETHING.
day sixty-five
end

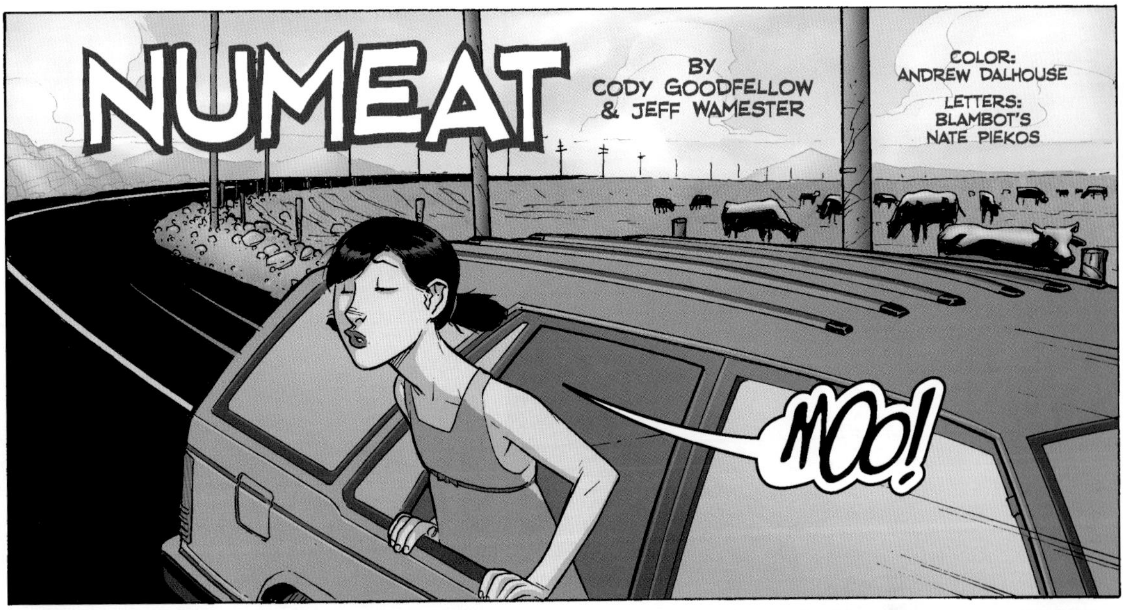
NUMEAT
BY CODY GOODFELLOW & JEFF WAMESTER
COLOR: ANDREW DALHOUSE
LETTERS: BLAMBOT'S NATE PIEKOS
MOO!

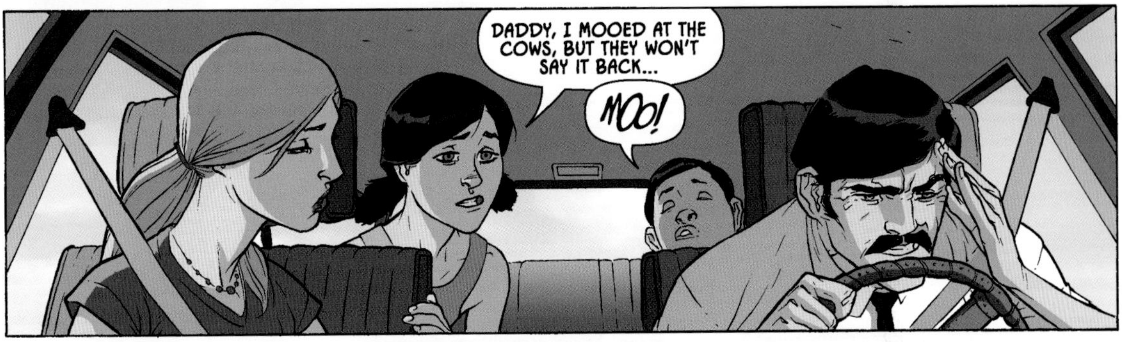
DADDY, I MOOED AT THE COWS, BUT THEY WON'T SAY IT BACK...
MOO!

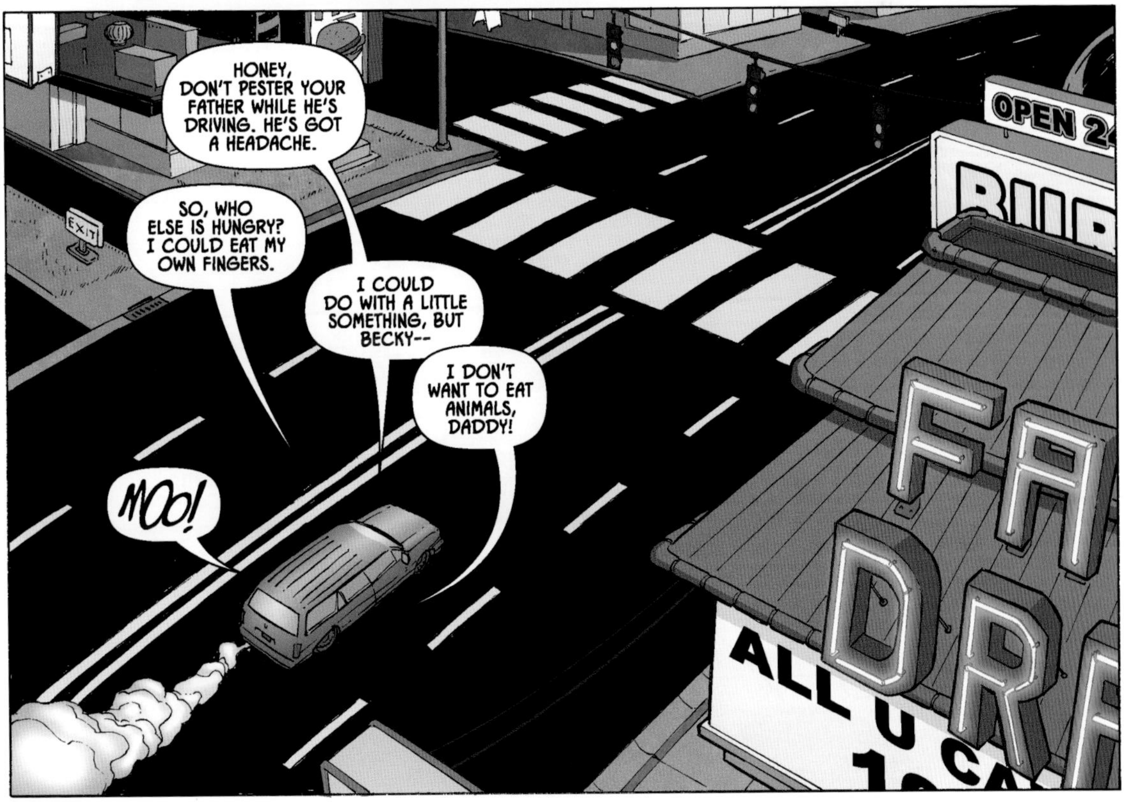
HONEY, DON'T PESTER YOUR FATHER WHILE HE'S DRIVING. HE'S GOT A HEADACHE.
SO, WHO ELSE IS HUNGRY? I COULD EAT MY OWN FINGERS.
I COULD DO WITH A LITTLE SOMETHING, BUT BECKY--
I DON'T WANT TO EAT ANIMALS, DADDY!
MOO!
EXIT
OPEN 24
ALL U CA

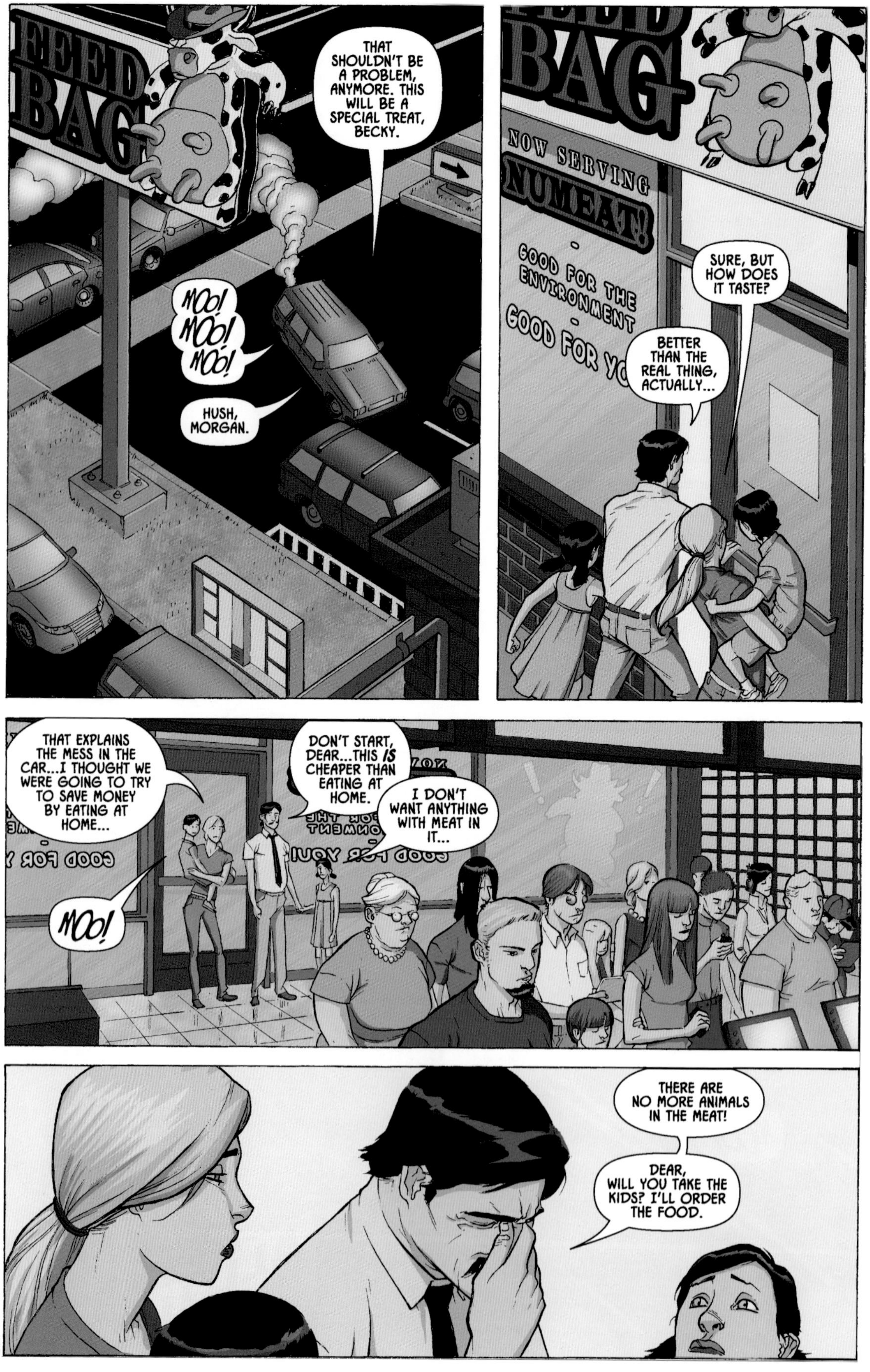
FEED BAG
THAT SHOULDN'T BE A PROBLEM, ANYMORE. THIS WILL BE A SPECIAL TREAT, BECKY.
MOO! MOO! MOO!
HUSH, MORGAN.
NOW SERVING NUMEAT! - GOOD FOR THE ENVIRONMENT - GOOD FOR YO
SURE, BUT HOW DOES IT TASTE?
BETTER THAN THE REAL THING, ACTUALLY...
THAT EXPLAINS THE MESS IN THE CAR...I THOUGHT WE WERE GOING TO TRY TO SAVE MONEY BY EATING AT HOME...
DON'T START, DEAR...THIS *IS* CHEAPER THAN EATING AT HOME.
I DON'T WANT ANYTHING WITH MEAT IN IT...
MOO!
THERE ARE NO MORE ANIMALS IN THE MEAT!
DEAR, WILL YOU TAKE THE KIDS? I'LL ORDER THE FOOD.

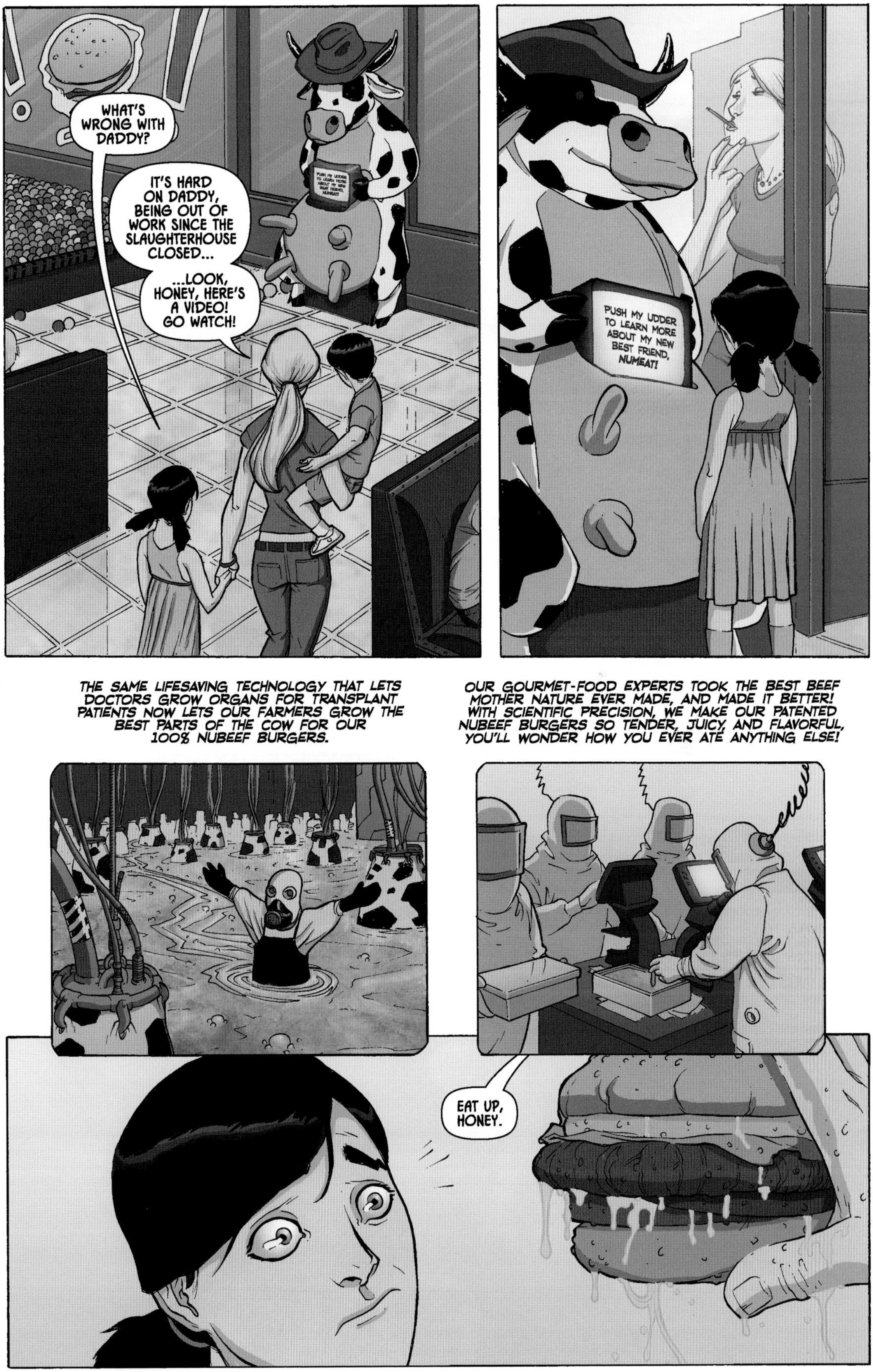
WHAT'S WRONG WITH DADDY?
IT'S HARD ON DADDY, BEING OUT OF WORK SINCE THE SLAUGHTERHOUSE CLOSED...
...LOOK, HONEY, HERE'S A VIDEO! GO WATCH!
PUSH MY UDDER TO LEARN MORE ABOUT MY NEW BEST FRIEND, NUMEAT!
THE SAME LIFESAVING TECHNOLOGY THAT LETS DOCTORS GROW ORGANS FOR TRANSPLANT PATIENTS NOW LETS OUR FARMERS GROW THE BEST PARTS OF THE COW FOR OUR 100% NUBEEF BURGERS.
OUR GOURMET-FOOD EXPERTS TOOK THE BEST BEEF MOTHER NATURE EVER MADE, AND MADE IT BETTER! WITH SCIENTIFIC PRECISION, WE MAKE OUR PATENTED NUBEEF BURGERS SO TENDER, JUICY, AND FLAVORFUL, YOU'LL WONDER HOW YOU EVER ATE ANYTHING ELSE!
EAT UP, HONEY.

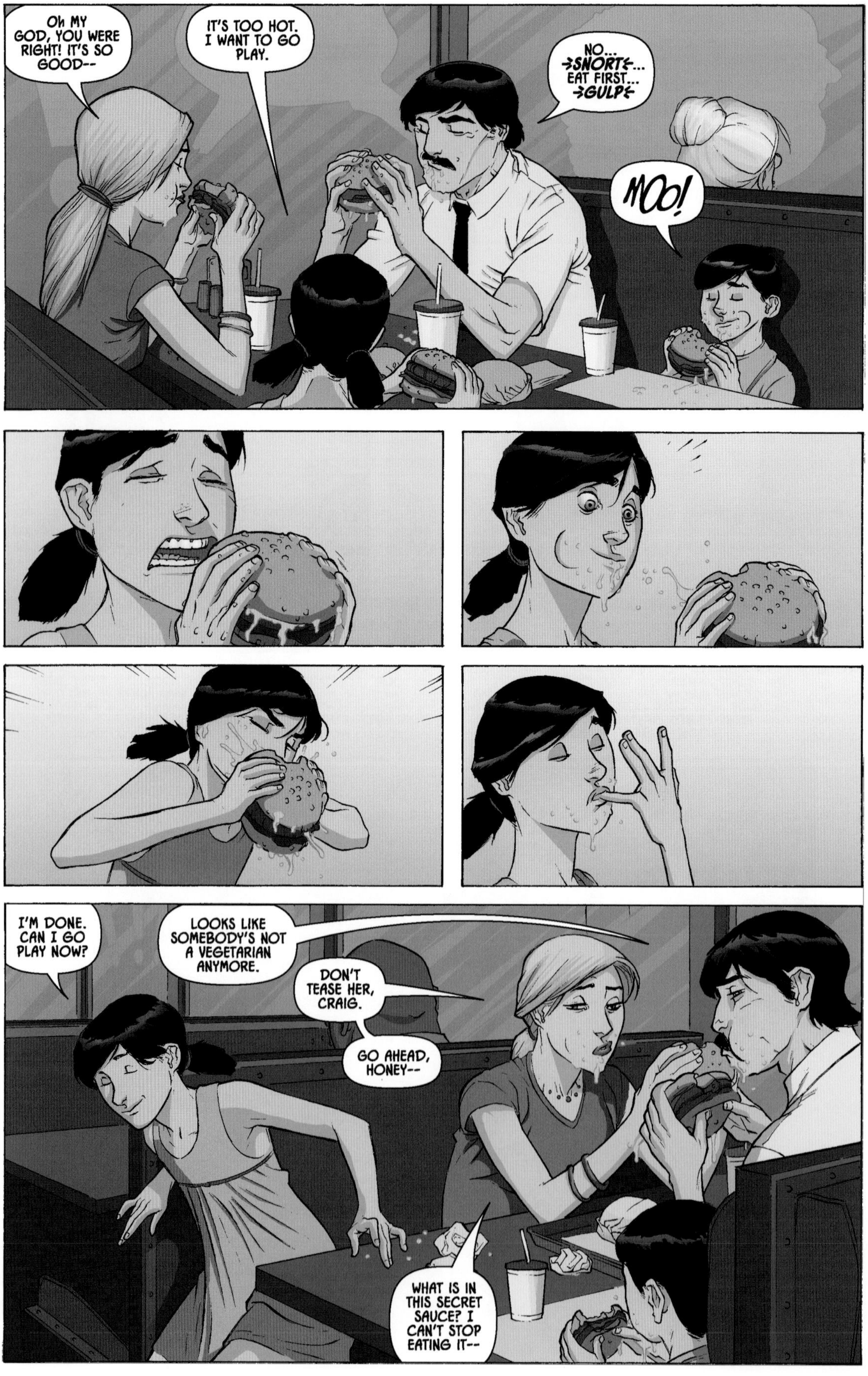
Oh MY GOD, YOU WERE RIGHT! IT'S SO GOOD--
IT'S TOO HOT. I WANT TO GO PLAY.
NO... SNORT... EAT FIRST... GULP
MOO!
I'M DONE. CAN I GO PLAY NOW?
LOOKS LIKE SOMEBODY'S NOT A VEGETARIAN ANYMORE.
DON'T TEASE HER, CRAIG.
GO AHEAD, HONEY--
WHAT IS IN THIS SECRET SAUCE? I CAN'T STOP EATING IT--

HEY, YOU GUYS...WANNA PLAY?
HIDE AND SEEK?
MOMMY! HELLLP MEEE!!!

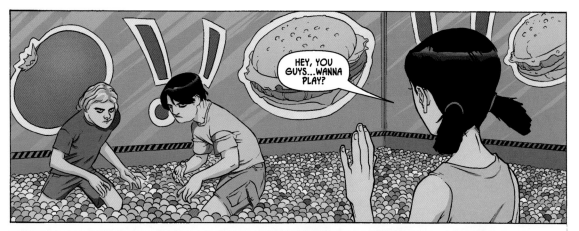

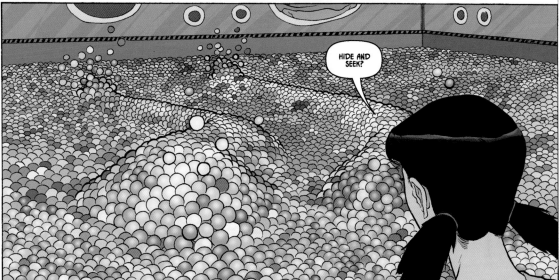

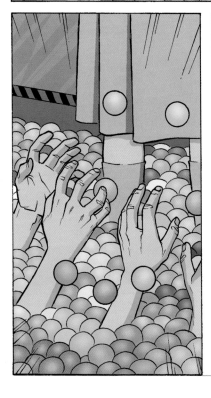

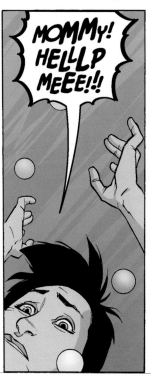

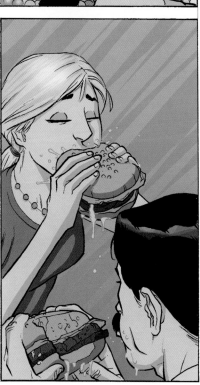

EEEEE EEE!

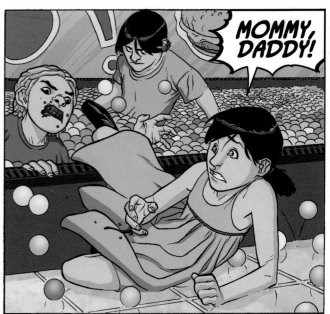

MOMMY, DADDY!

THOSE BOYS HURT ME, AND I--

--I DON'T FEEL--

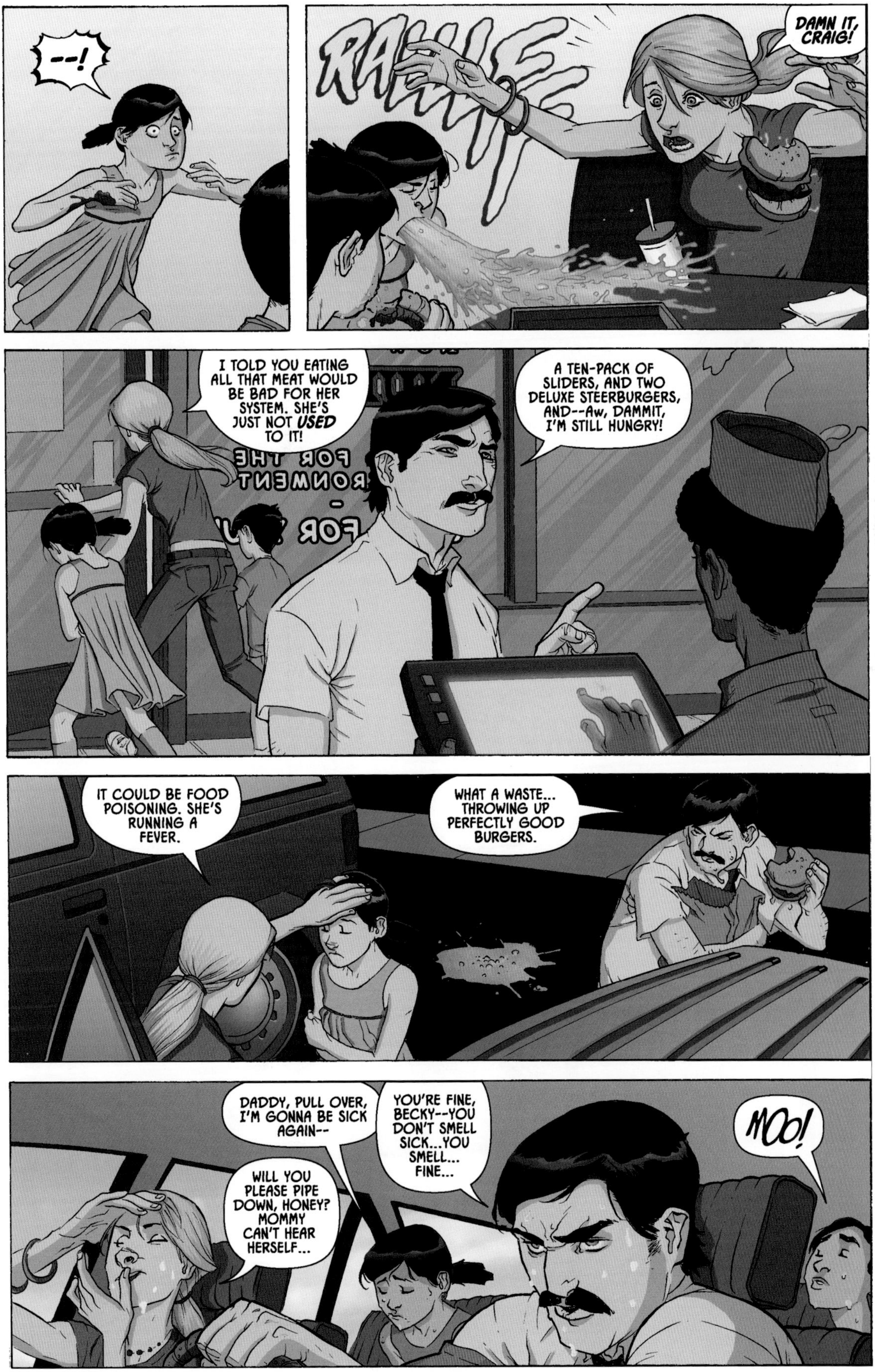
--!
DAMN IT, CRAIG!
I TOLD YOU EATING ALL THAT MEAT WOULD BE BAD FOR HER SYSTEM. SHE'S JUST NOT *USED* TO IT!
A TEN-PACK OF SLIDERS, AND TWO DELUXE STEERBURGERS, AND--Aw, DAMMIT, I'M STILL HUNGRY!
IT COULD BE FOOD POISONING. SHE'S RUNNING A FEVER.
WHAT A WASTE... THROWING UP PERFECTLY GOOD BURGERS.
DADDY, PULL OVER, I'M GONNA BE SICK AGAIN--
YOU'RE FINE, BECKY--YOU DON'T SMELL SICK...YOU SMELL... FINE...
WILL YOU PLEASE PIPE DOWN, HONEY? MOMMY CAN'T HEAR HERSELF...
MOO!

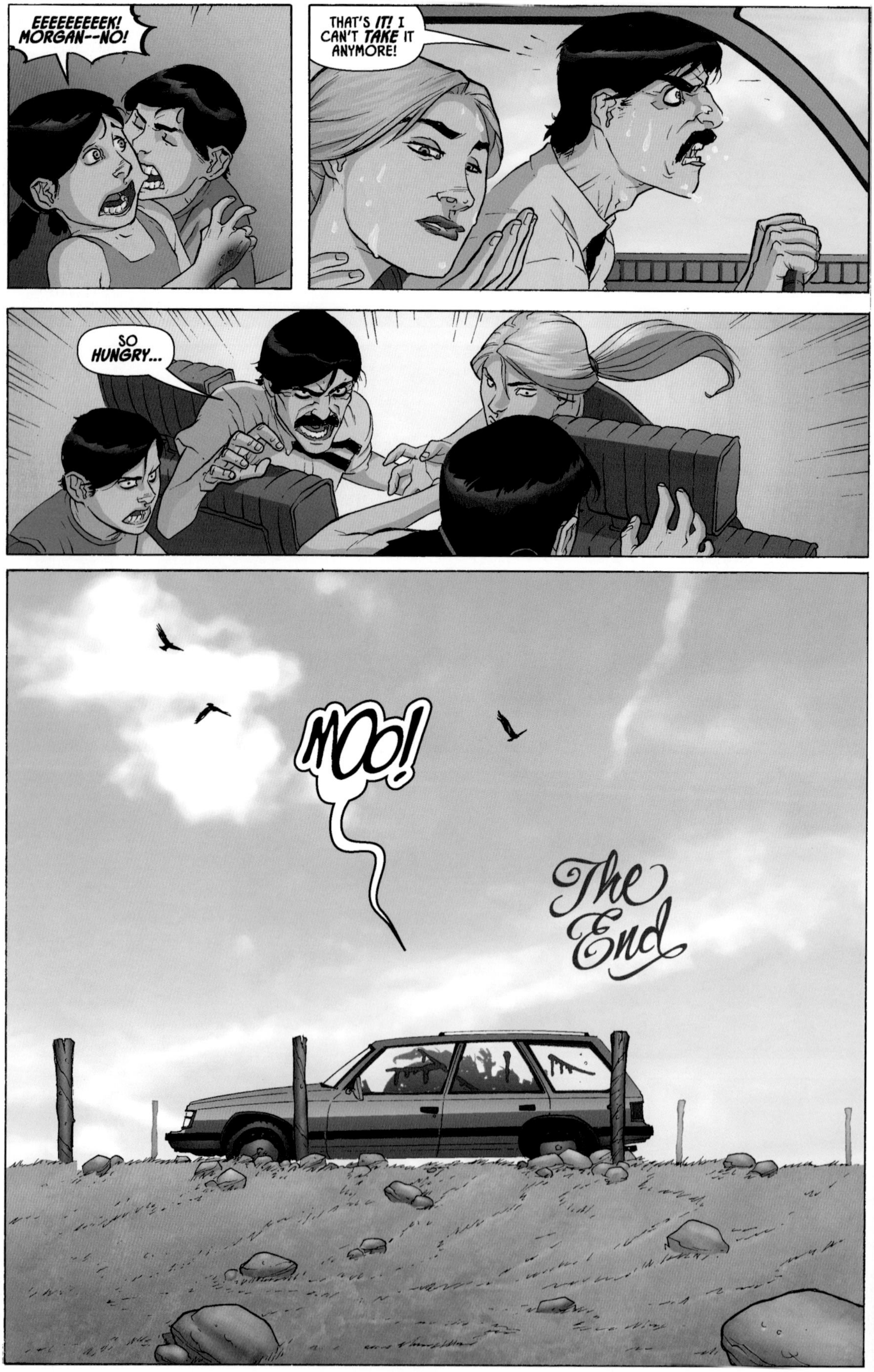
EEEEEEEEEK! MORGAN--NO!
THAT'S IT! I CAN'T TAKE IT ANYMORE!
SO HUNGRY...
MOO!
The End

CUISINE

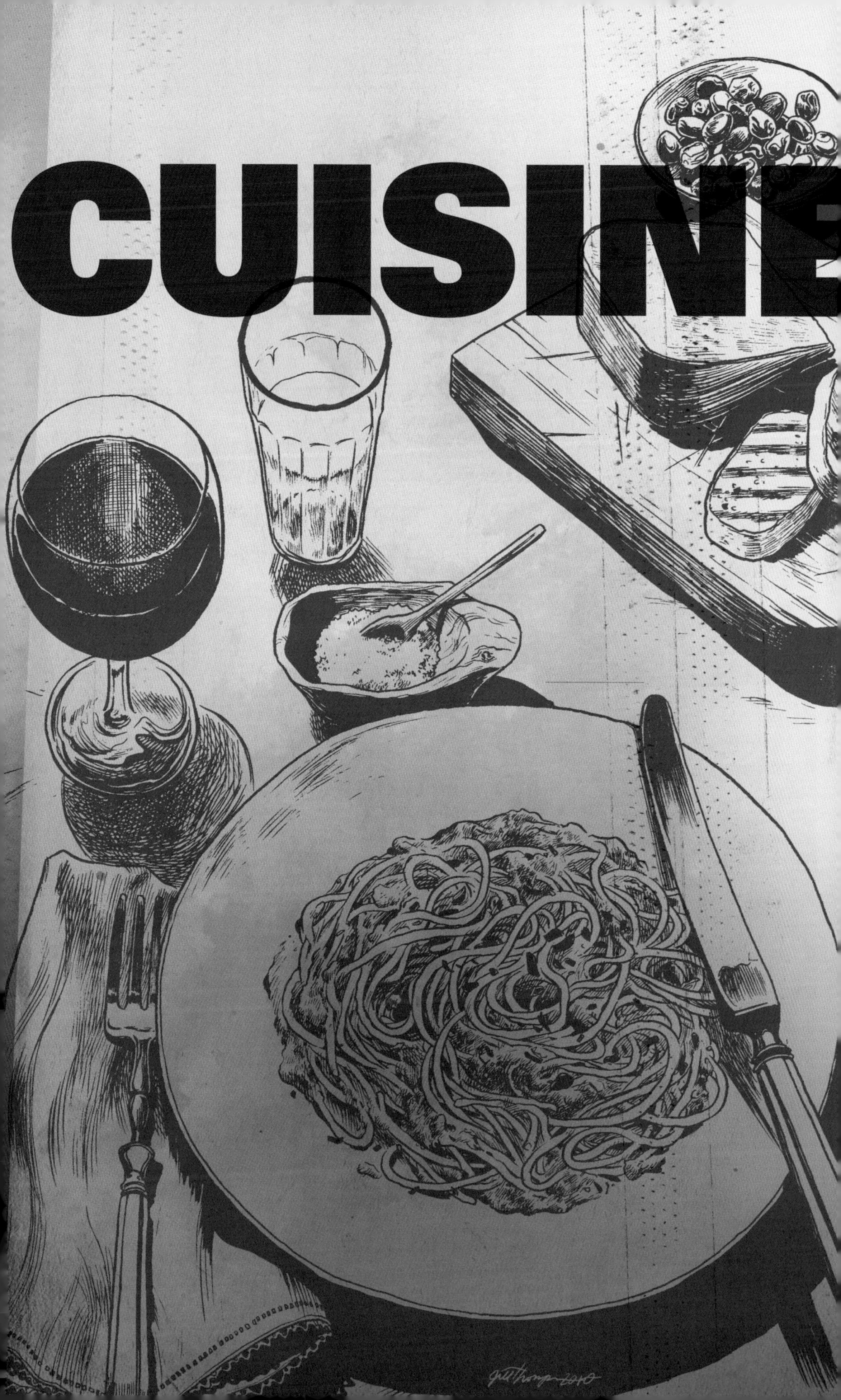

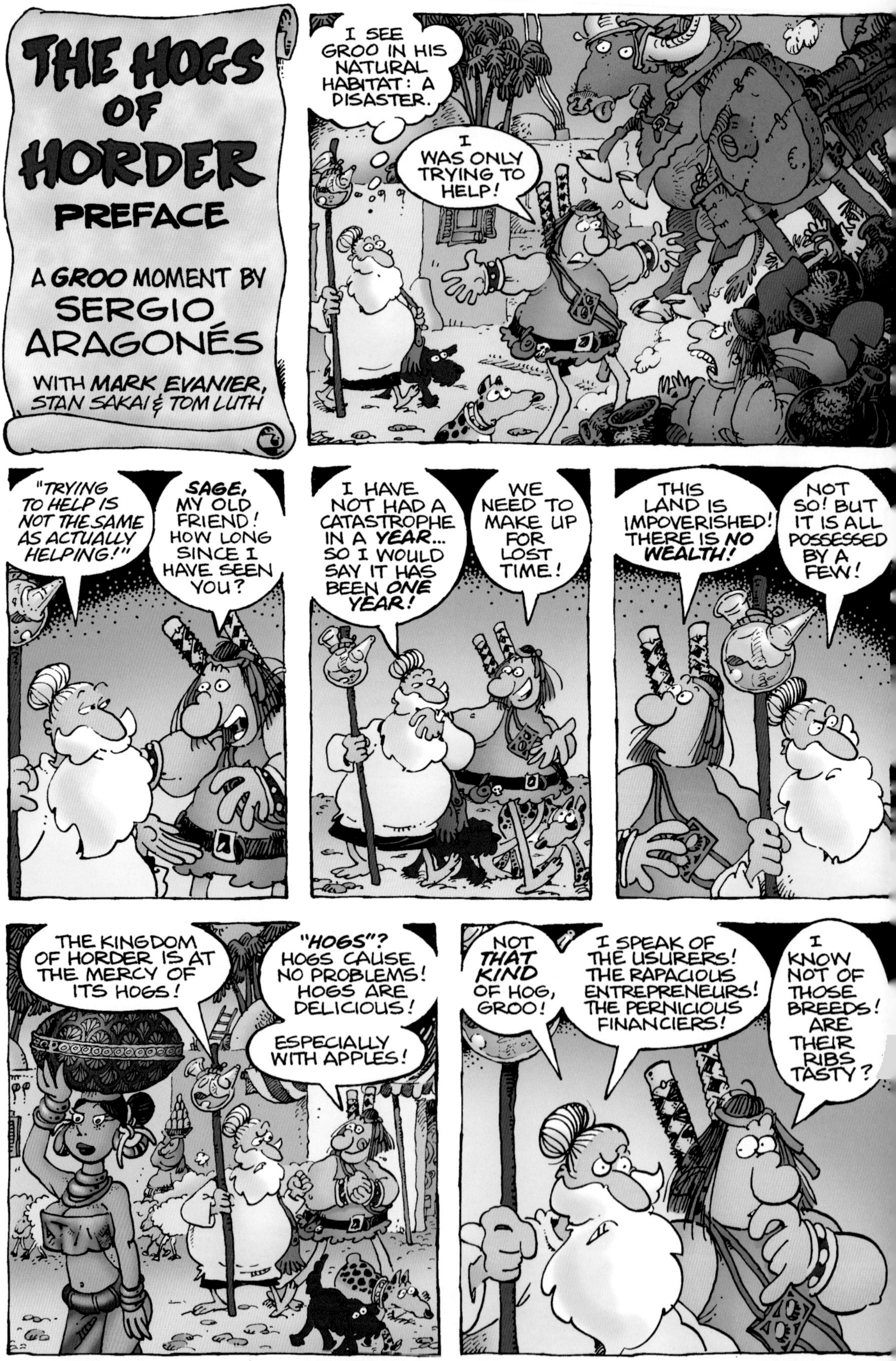
THE HOGS OF HORDER
PREFACE
A GROO MOMENT BY
SERGIO ARAGONÉS
WITH MARK EVANIER, STAN SAKAI & TOM LUTH
I SEE GROO IN HIS NATURAL HABITAT: A DISASTER.
I WAS ONLY TRYING TO HELP!
"TRYING TO HELP IS NOT THE SAME AS ACTUALLY HELPING!"
SAGE, MY OLD FRIEND! HOW LONG SINCE I HAVE SEEN YOU?
I HAVE NOT HAD A CATASTROPHE IN A YEAR... SO I WOULD SAY IT HAS BEEN ONE YEAR!
WE NEED TO MAKE UP FOR LOST TIME!
THIS LAND IS IMPOVERISHED! THERE IS NO WEALTH!
NOT SO! BUT IT IS ALL POSSESSED BY A FEW!
THE KINGDOM OF HORDER IS AT THE MERCY OF ITS HOGS!
"HOGS"? HOGS CAUSE NO PROBLEMS! HOGS ARE DELICIOUS!
ESPECIALLY WITH APPLES!
NOT THAT KIND OF HOG, GROO!
I SPEAK OF THE USURERS! THE RAPACIOUS ENTREPRENEURS! THE PERNICIOUS FINANCIERS!
I KNOW NOT OF THOSE BREEDS! ARE THEIR RIBS TASTY?

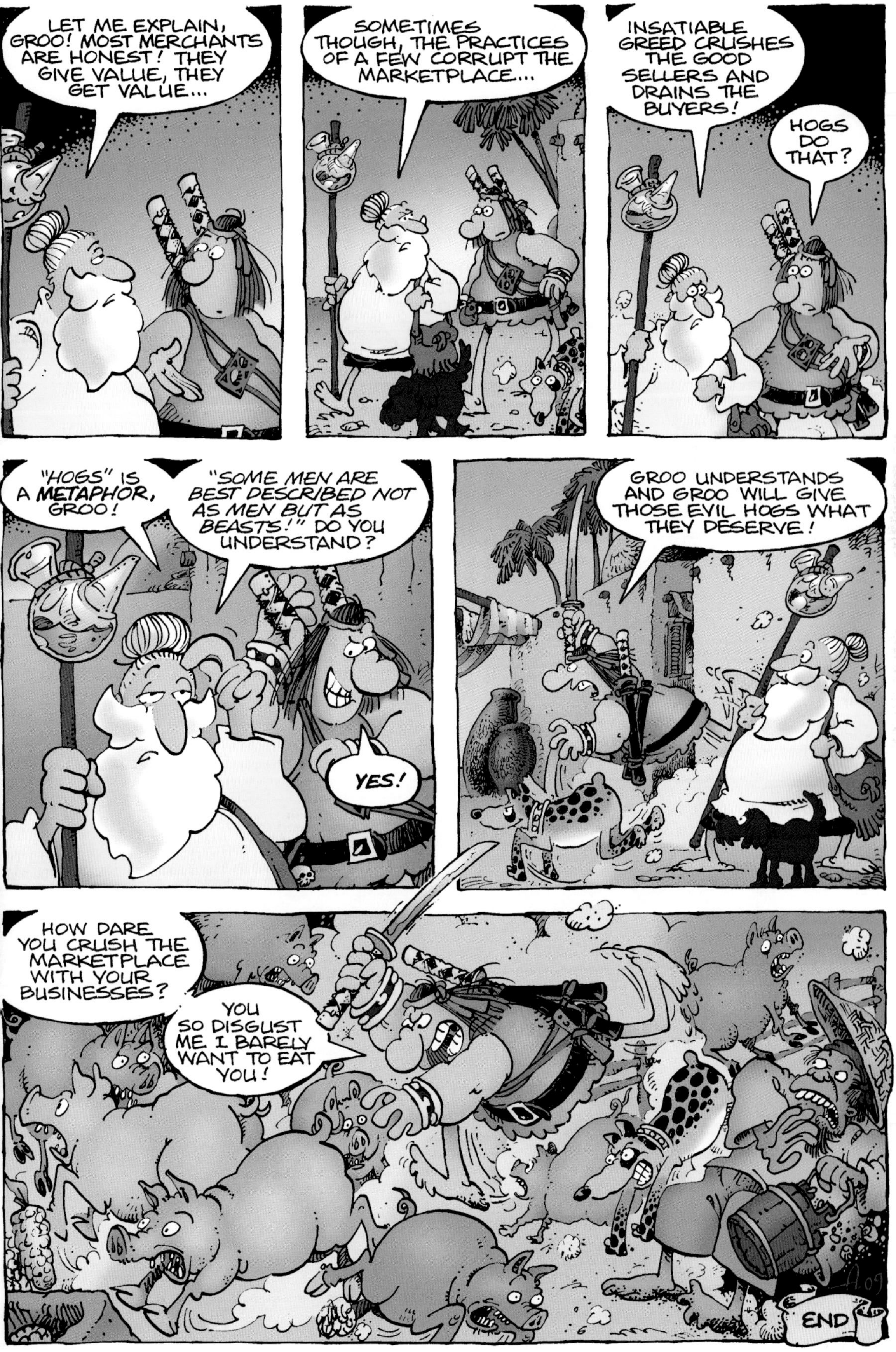
LET ME EXPLAIN, GROO! MOST MERCHANTS ARE HONEST! THEY GIVE VALUE, THEY GET VALUE...
SOMETIMES THOUGH, THE PRACTICES OF A FEW CORRUPT THE MARKETPLACE...
INSATIABLE GREED CRUSHES THE GOOD SELLERS AND DRAINS THE BUYERS!
HOGS DO THAT?
"HOGS" IS A METAPHOR, GROO!
"SOME MEN ARE BEST DESCRIBED NOT AS MEN BUT AS BEASTS!" DO YOU UNDERSTAND?
YES!
GROO UNDERSTANDS AND GROO WILL GIVE THOSE EVIL HOGS WHAT THEY DESERVE!
HOW DARE YOU CRUSH THE MARKETPLACE WITH YOUR BUSINESSES?
YOU SO DISGUST ME I BARELY WANT TO EAT YOU!
END

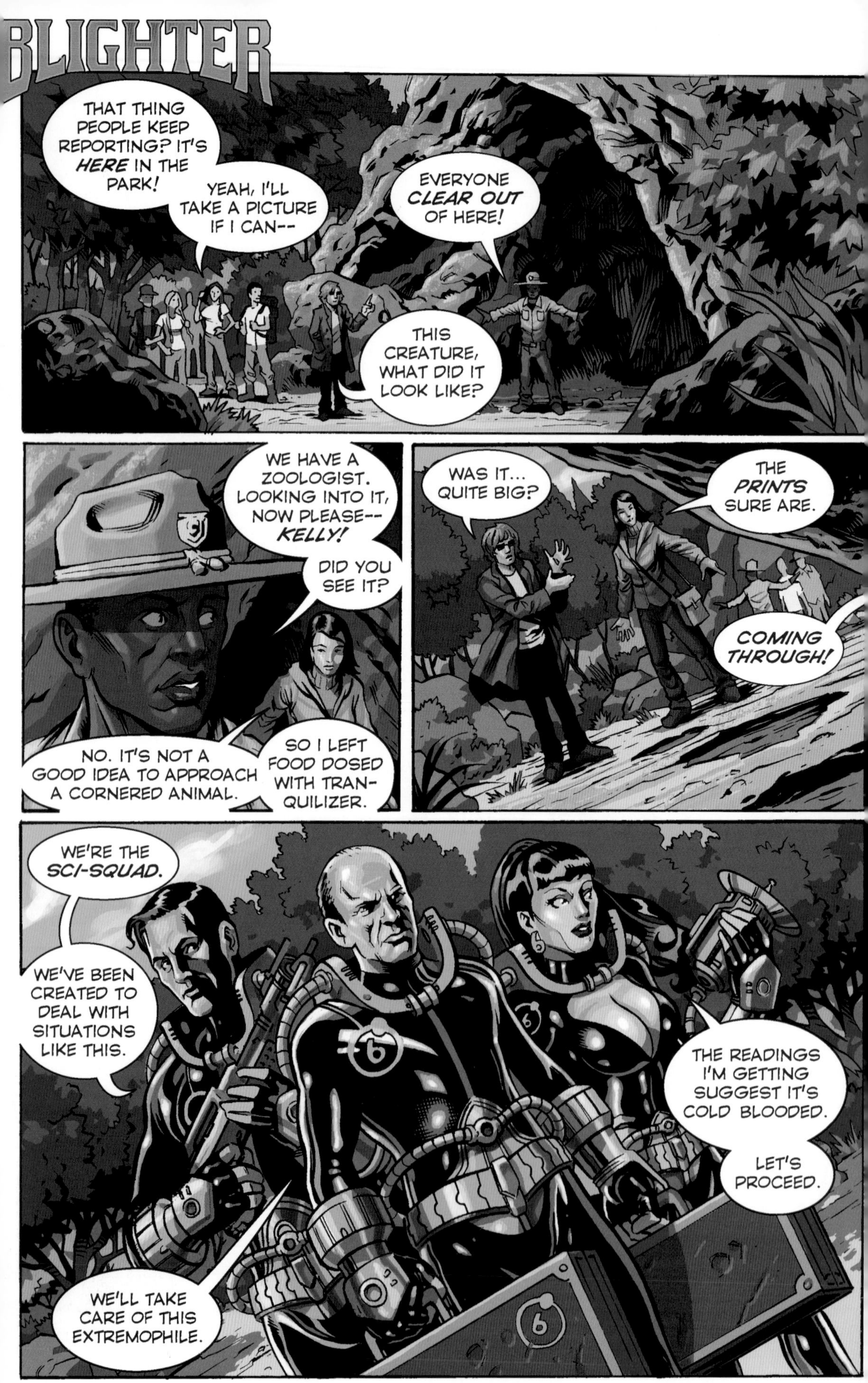
BLIGHTER
THAT THING PEOPLE KEEP REPORTING? IT'S HERE IN THE PARK!
YEAH, I'LL TAKE A PICTURE IF I CAN--
EVERYONE CLEAR OUT OF HERE!
THIS CREATURE, WHAT DID IT LOOK LIKE?
WE HAVE A ZOOLOGIST. LOOKING INTO IT, NOW PLEASE-- KELLY!
DID YOU SEE IT?
NO. IT'S NOT A GOOD IDEA TO APPROACH A CORNERED ANIMAL.
SO I LEFT FOOD DOSED WITH TRAN-QUILIZER.
WAS IT... QUITE BIG?
THE PRINTS SURE ARE.
COMING THROUGH!
WE'RE THE SCI-SQUAD.
WE'VE BEEN CREATED TO DEAL WITH SITUATIONS LIKE THIS.
WE'LL TAKE CARE OF THIS EXTREMOPHILE.
THE READINGS I'M GETTING SUGGEST IT'S COLD BLOODED.
LET'S PROCEED.

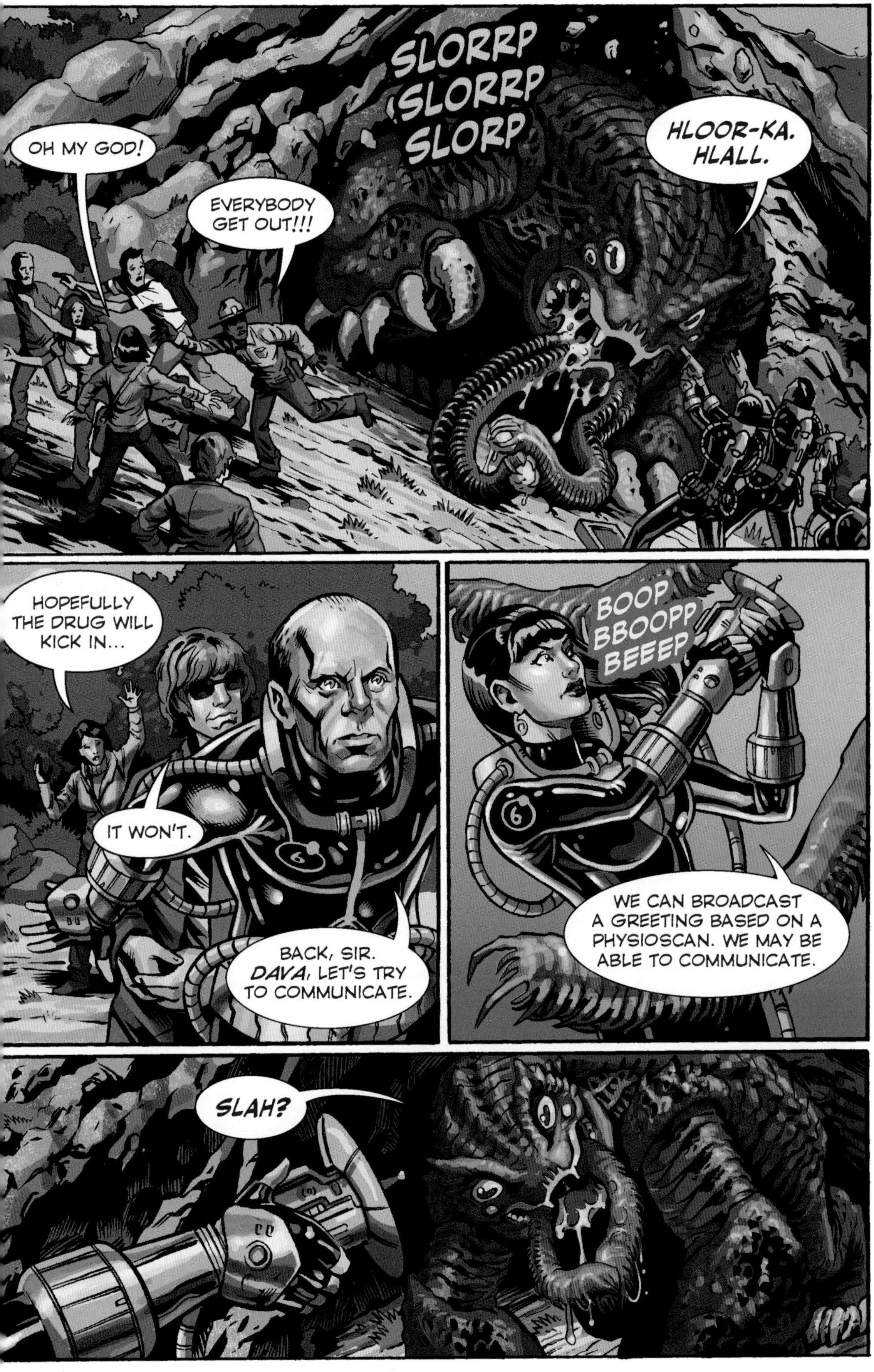
SLORRP SLORRP SLORP
OH MY GOD!
EVERYBODY GET OUT!!!
HLOOR-KA. HLALL.
HOPEFULLY THE DRUG WILL KICK IN...
IT WON'T.
BACK, SIR. *DAVA*, LET'S TRY TO COMMUNICATE.
BOOP BBOOPP BEEEP
WE CAN BROADCAST A GREETING BASED ON A PHYSIOSCAN. WE MAY BE ABLE TO COMMUNICATE.
SLAH?

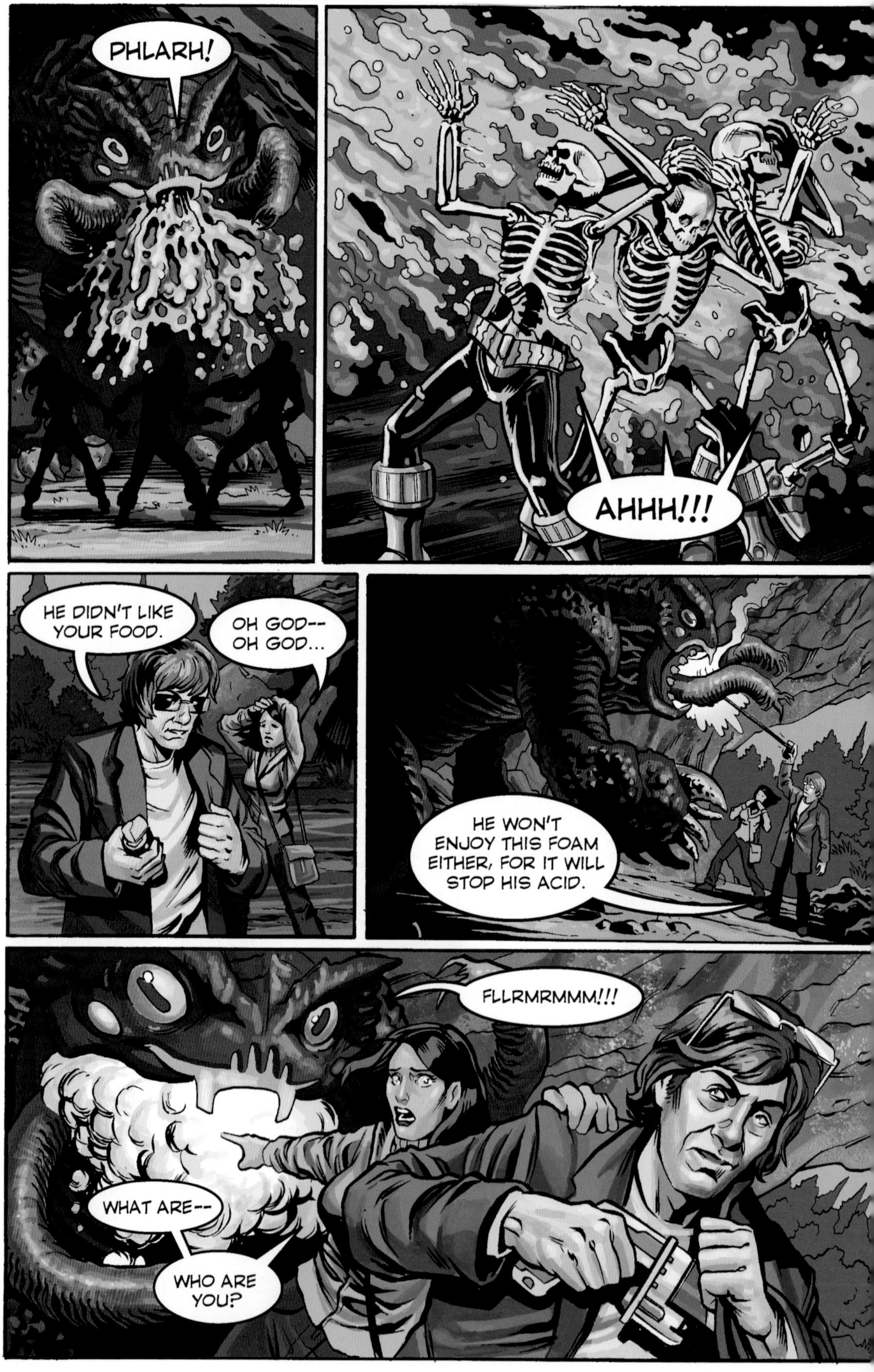
PHLARH!
AHHH!!!
HE DIDN'T LIKE YOUR FOOD.
OH GOD-- OH GOD...
HE WON'T ENJOY THIS FOAM EITHER, FOR IT WILL STOP HIS ACID.
FLLRMRMMM!!!
WHAT ARE--
WHO ARE YOU?

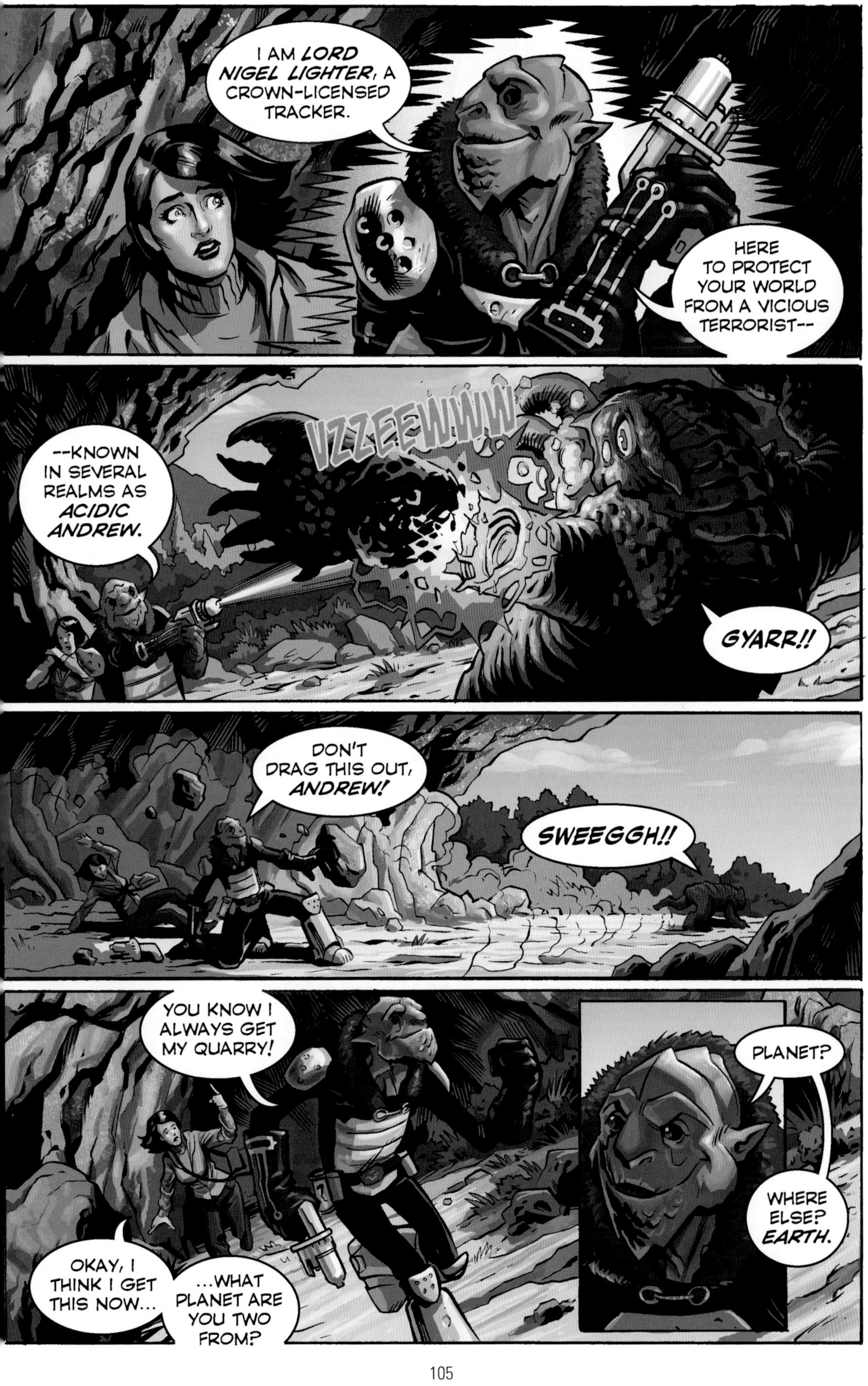
I AM LORD NIGEL LIGHTER, A CROWN-LICENSED TRACKER.
HERE TO PROTECT YOUR WORLD FROM A VICIOUS TERRORIST--
VZZEEWWW
--KNOWN IN SEVERAL REALMS AS ACIDIC ANDREW.
GYARR!!
DON'T DRAG THIS OUT, ANDREW!
SWEEGGH!!
YOU KNOW I ALWAYS GET MY QUARRY!
OKAY, I THINK I GET THIS NOW...
...WHAT PLANET ARE YOU TWO FROM?
PLANET?
WHERE ELSE? EARTH.

I'VE NEVER SEEN-- --ANY SPECIES LIKE EITHER OF YOU--

A *DIVERGENT* EARTH, GIRL.

WELL, THE TRUE EARTH-- YOURS AND THESE OTHERS ARE PALE COPIES.

THESE FIENDS HIDE ON THE MIRROR WORLDS AS IF I CAN'T FIND THEM, THE FOOLS.

THERE'S MORE LIKE THAT?

A PLETHORA! ONCE LATERAL TIME TRAVEL BECAME POSSIBLE...

OUR ROYAL PENITENTIARY *BANISHED* OUR MOST DANGEROUS FELONS.

LATER, SOME ACTIVISTS DECIDED YOUR WORLDS "COUNT." HERE, LOOK AT SOME OF YOUR NEW INHABITANTS.

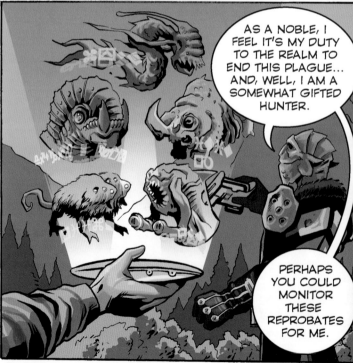

AS A NOBLE, I FEEL IT'S MY DUTY TO THE REALM TO END THIS PLAGUE... AND, WELL, I AM A SOMEWHAT GIFTED HUNTER.

PERHAPS YOU COULD MONITOR THESE REPROBATES FOR ME.

I'M A *ZOOLOGIST*, NOT--

A TRAPPER? NO, NO, NO.

THESE PEOPLE HAVE TO BE KILLED.

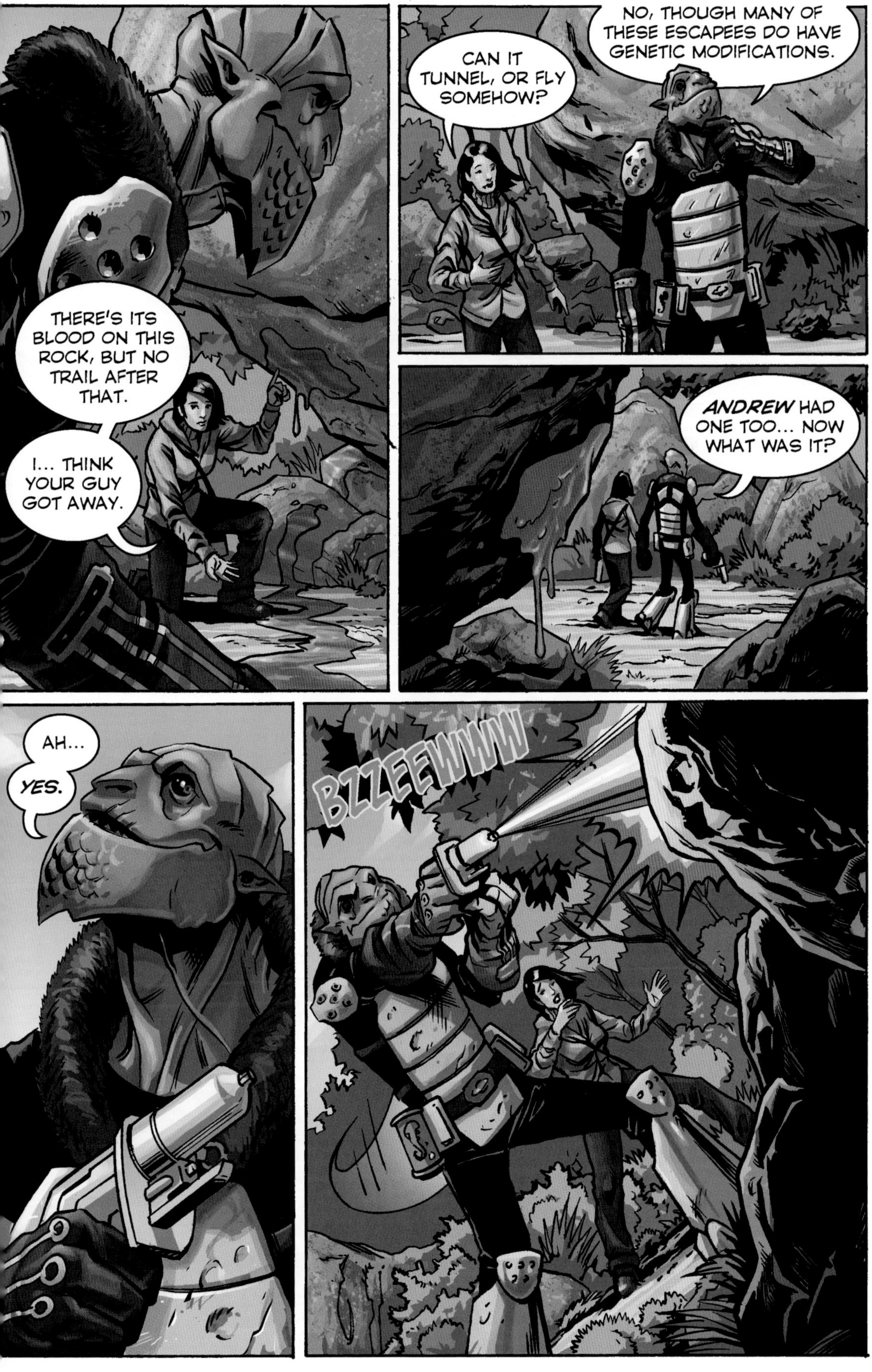
THERE'S ITS BLOOD ON THIS ROCK, BUT NO TRAIL AFTER THAT.
I... THINK YOUR GUY GOT AWAY.
CAN IT TUNNEL, OR FLY SOMEHOW?
NO, THOUGH MANY OF THESE ESCAPEES DO HAVE GENETIC MODIFICATIONS.
ANDREW HAD ONE TOO... NOW WHAT WAS IT?
AH...
YES.
BZZEEWWW

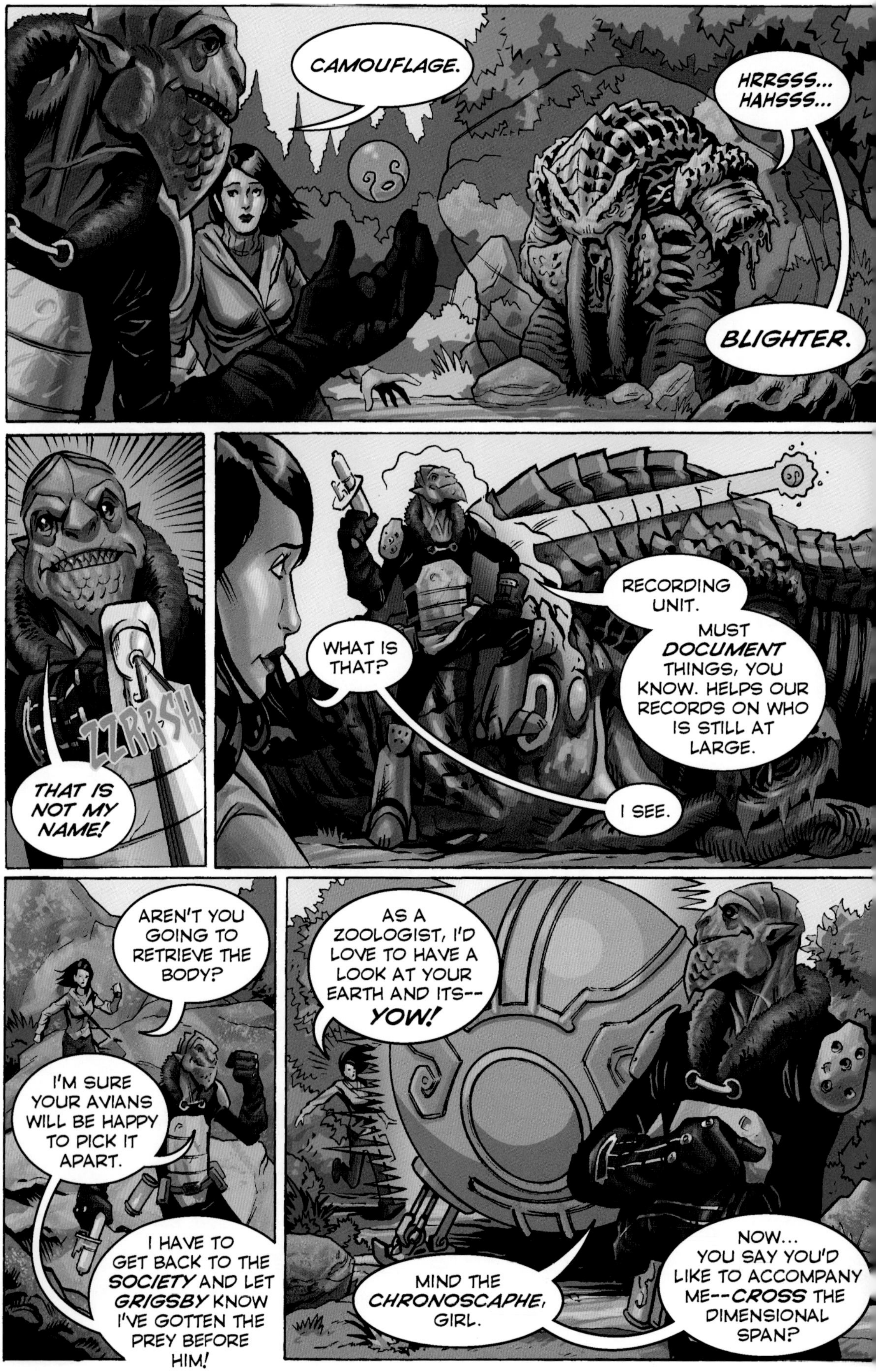
CAMOUFLAGE.
HRRSSS... HAHSSS...
BLIGHTER.
ZZRRSH
THAT IS NOT MY NAME!
WHAT IS THAT?
RECORDING UNIT.
MUST DOCUMENT THINGS, YOU KNOW. HELPS OUR RECORDS ON WHO IS STILL AT LARGE.
I SEE.
AREN'T YOU GOING TO RETRIEVE THE BODY?
I'M SURE YOUR AVIANS WILL BE HAPPY TO PICK IT APART.
I HAVE TO GET BACK TO THE SOCIETY AND LET GRIGSBY KNOW I'VE GOTTEN THE PREY BEFORE HIM!
AS A ZOOLOGIST, I'D LOVE TO HAVE A LOOK AT YOUR EARTH AND ITS-- YOW!
MIND THE CHRONOSCAPHE, GIRL.
NOW... YOU SAY YOU'D LIKE TO ACCOMPANY ME--CROSS THE DIMENSIONAL SPAN?

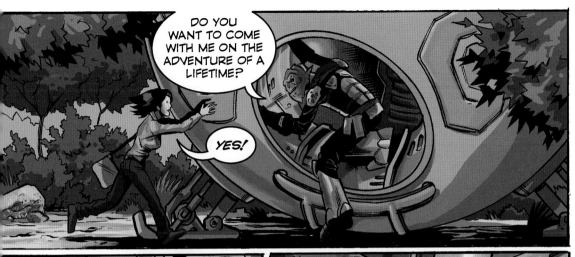

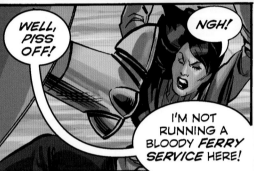

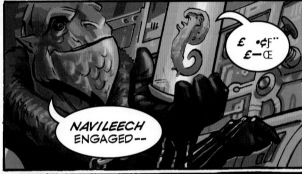

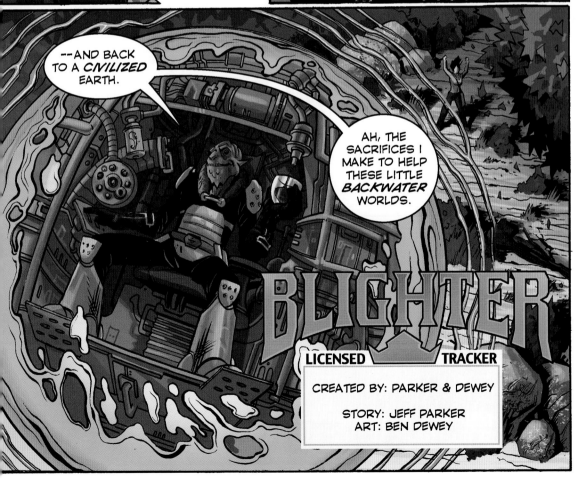

DO YOU WANT TO COME WITH ME ON THE ADVENTURE OF A LIFETIME?
YES!
WELL, PISS OFF!
NGH!
I'M NOT RUNNING A BLOODY FERRY SERVICE HERE!
£ •¢F¨ £—Œ
NAVILEECH ENGAGED--
--AND BACK TO A CIVILIZED EARTH.
AH, THE SACRIFICES I MAKE TO HELP THESE LITTLE BACKWATER WORLDS.
BLIGHTER
LICENSED TRACKER
CREATED BY: PARKER & DEWEY
STORY: JEFF PARKER
ART: BEN DEWEY

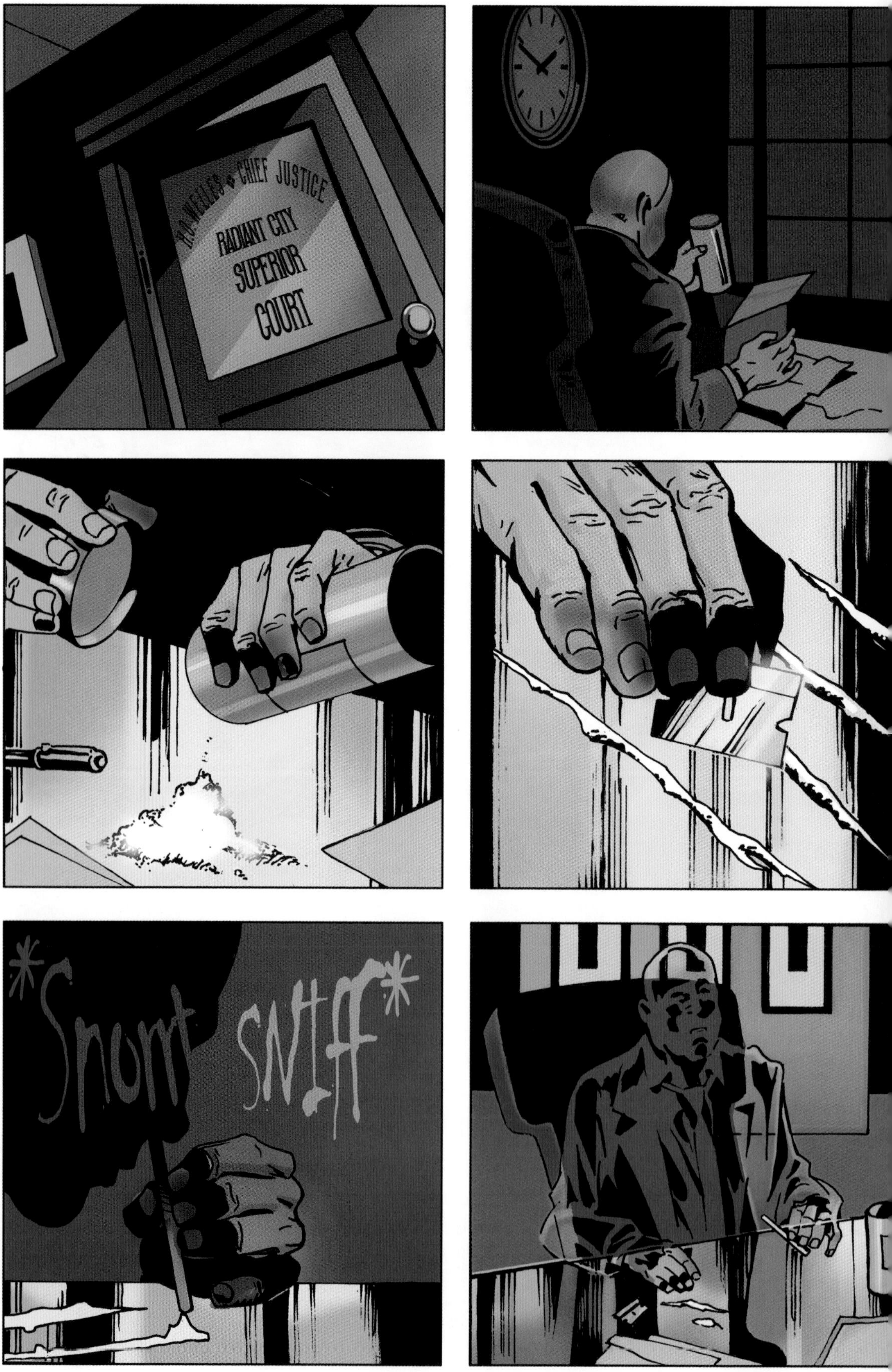
H.O. WELLES ◆ CHIEF JUSTICE
RADIANT CITY
SUPERIOR
COURT
Snort SNIFF

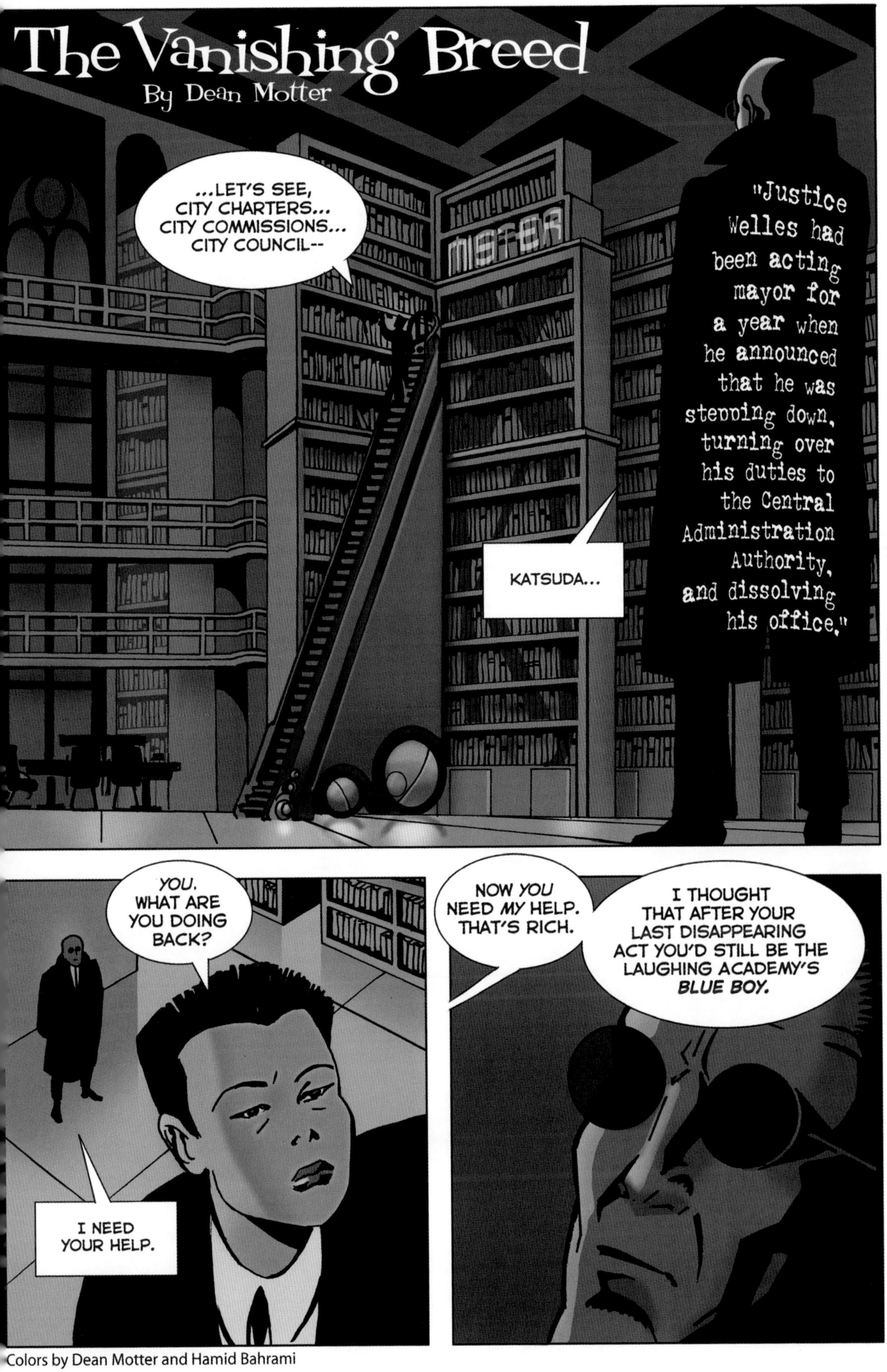
The Vanishing Breed
By Dean Motter
"Justice Welles had been acting mayor for a year when he announced that he was stepping down, turning over his duties to the Central Administration Authority, and dissolving his office."
...LET'S SEE, CITY CHARTERS... CITY COMMISSIONS... CITY COUNCIL--
KATSUDA...
YOU. WHAT ARE YOU DOING BACK?
I NEED YOUR HELP.
NOW *YOU* NEED *MY* HELP. THAT'S RICH.
I THOUGHT THAT AFTER YOUR LAST DISAPPEARING ACT YOU'D STILL BE THE LAUGHING ACADEMY'S *BLUE BOY.*

Colors by Dean Motter and Hamid Bahrami

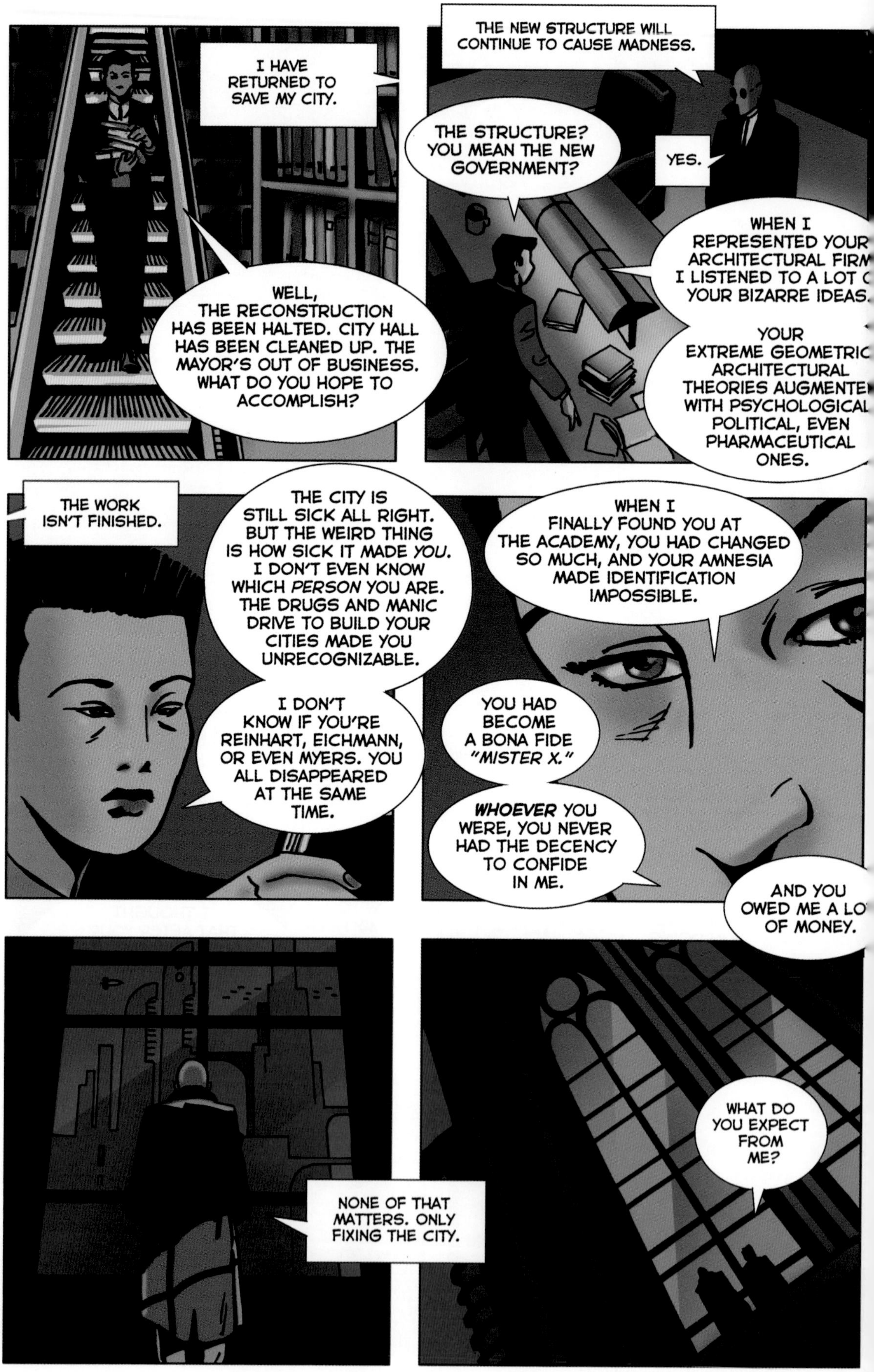
I HAVE RETURNED TO SAVE MY CITY.
WELL, THE RECONSTRUCTION HAS BEEN HALTED. CITY HALL HAS BEEN CLEANED UP. THE MAYOR'S OUT OF BUSINESS. WHAT DO YOU HOPE TO ACCOMPLISH?
THE NEW STRUCTURE WILL CONTINUE TO CAUSE MADNESS.
THE STRUCTURE? YOU MEAN THE NEW GOVERNMENT?
YES.
WHEN I REPRESENTED YOUR ARCHITECTURAL FIRM I LISTENED TO A LOT OF YOUR BIZARRE IDEAS.
YOUR EXTREME GEOMETRIC ARCHITECTURAL THEORIES AUGMENTED WITH PSYCHOLOGICAL, POLITICAL, EVEN PHARMACEUTICAL ONES.
THE WORK ISN'T FINISHED.
THE CITY IS STILL SICK ALL RIGHT. BUT THE WEIRD THING IS HOW SICK IT MADE *YOU*. I DON'T EVEN KNOW WHICH *PERSON* YOU ARE. THE DRUGS AND MANIC DRIVE TO BUILD YOUR CITIES MADE YOU UNRECOGNIZABLE.
I DON'T KNOW IF YOU'RE REINHART, EICHMANN, OR EVEN MYERS. YOU ALL DISAPPEARED AT THE SAME TIME.
WHEN I FINALLY FOUND YOU AT THE ACADEMY, YOU HAD CHANGED SO MUCH, AND YOUR AMNESIA MADE IDENTIFICATION IMPOSSIBLE.
YOU HAD BECOME A BONA FIDE *"MISTER X."*
WHOEVER YOU WERE, YOU NEVER HAD THE DECENCY TO CONFIDE IN ME.
AND YOU OWED ME A LOT OF MONEY.
NONE OF THAT MATTERS. ONLY FIXING THE CITY.
WHAT DO YOU EXPECT FROM ME?

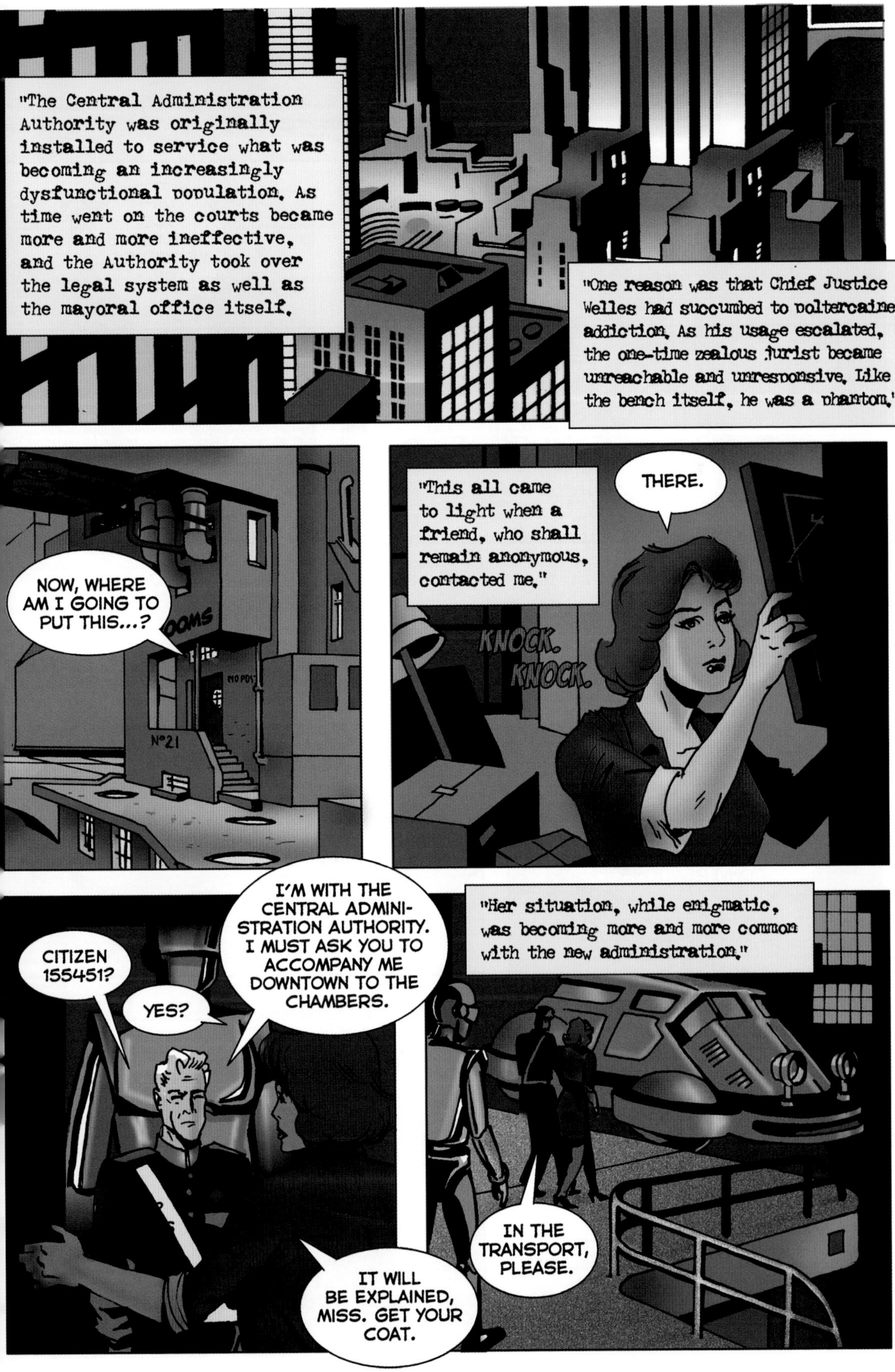
"The Central Administration Authority was originally installed to service what was becoming an increasingly dysfunctional population. As time went on the courts became more and more ineffective, and the Authority took over the legal system as well as the mayoral office itself.
"One reason was that Chief Justice Welles had succumbed to poltercaine addiction. As his usage escalated, the one-time zealous jurist became unreachable and unresponsive. Like the bench itself, he was a phantom."
NOW, WHERE AM I GOING TO PUT THIS...?
N°21
"This all came to light when a friend, who shall remain anonymous, contacted me."
THERE.
KNOCK. KNOCK.
CITIZEN 155451?
YES?
I'M WITH THE CENTRAL ADMINI-STRATION AUTHORITY. I MUST ASK YOU TO ACCOMPANY ME DOWNTOWN TO THE CHAMBERS.
IT WILL BE EXPLAINED, MISS. GET YOUR COAT.
"Her situation, while enigmatic, was becoming more and more common with the new administration."
IN THE TRANSPORT, PLEASE.

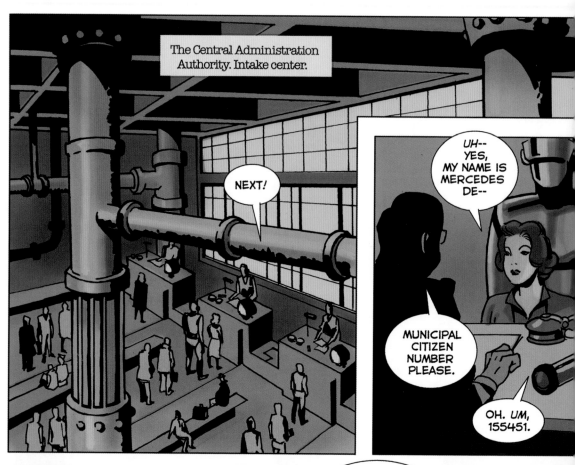

The Central Administration Authority. Intake center.

NEXT!

UH-- YES, MY NAME IS MERCEDES DE--

MUNICIPAL CITIZEN NUMBER PLEASE.

OH. UM, 155451.

AH YES. YOU'RE WANTED IN PERSONAL ASSOCIATIONS AND RECORDS. A MATTER CONCERNING PRIVATE ASSEMBLY AND CONVERSATIONS.

I DON'T UNDERSTAND--

FILL OUT THIS FORM. HAVE A SEAT AND SOMEONE WILL BE WITH YOU PRESENTLY.

HOW LONG WILL THIS TAKE?

NEXT!

DAMN CITY...

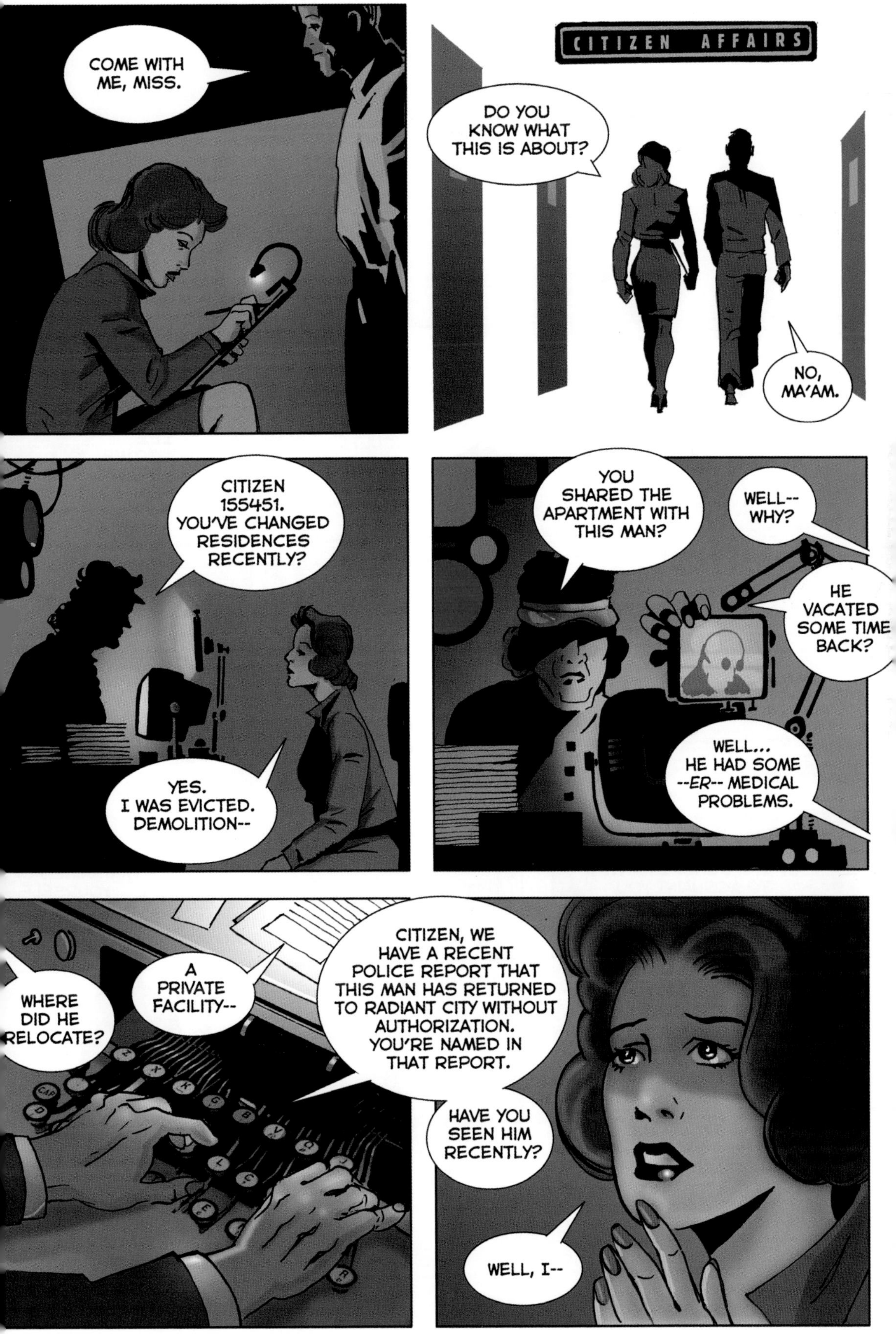
COME WITH ME, MISS.
CITIZEN AFFAIRS
DO YOU KNOW WHAT THIS IS ABOUT?
NO, MA'AM.
CITIZEN 155451. YOU'VE CHANGED RESIDENCES RECENTLY?
YES. I WAS EVICTED. DEMOLITION--
YOU SHARED THE APARTMENT WITH THIS MAN?
WELL-- WHY?
HE VACATED SOME TIME BACK?
WELL... HE HAD SOME --*ER*-- MEDICAL PROBLEMS.
WHERE DID HE RELOCATE?
A PRIVATE FACILITY--
CITIZEN, WE HAVE A RECENT POLICE REPORT THAT THIS MAN HAS RETURNED TO RADIANT CITY WITHOUT AUTHORIZATION. YOU'RE NAMED IN THAT REPORT.
HAVE YOU SEEN HIM RECENTLY?
WELL, I--

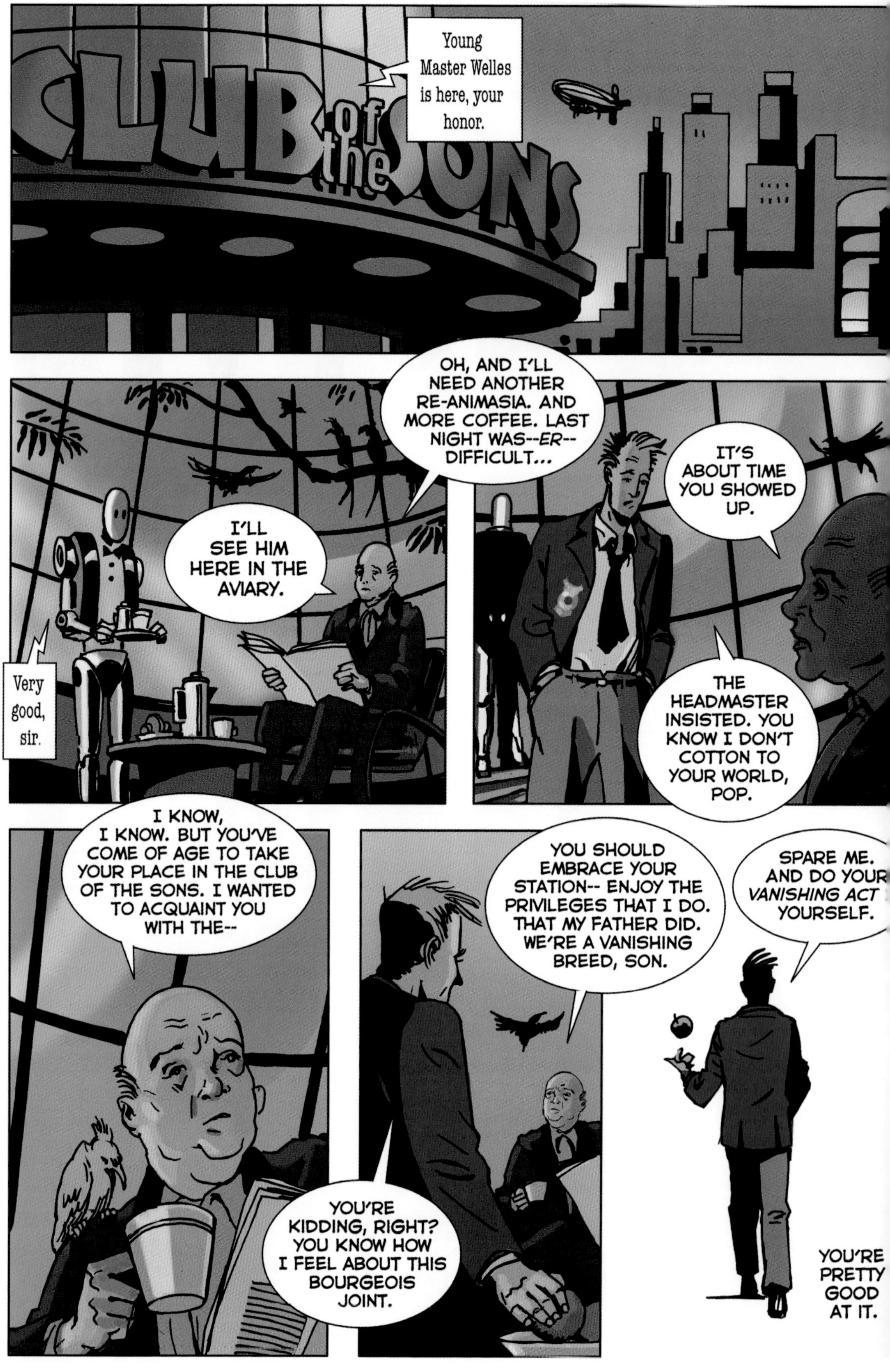

CLUB of the SONS
Young Master Welles is here, your honor.
I'LL SEE HIM HERE IN THE AVIARY.
Very good, sir.
OH, AND I'LL NEED ANOTHER RE-ANIMASIA. AND MORE COFFEE. LAST NIGHT WAS--*ER*--DIFFICULT...
IT'S ABOUT TIME YOU SHOWED UP.
THE HEADMASTER INSISTED. YOU KNOW I DON'T COTTON TO YOUR WORLD, POP.
I KNOW, I KNOW. BUT YOU'VE COME OF AGE TO TAKE YOUR PLACE IN THE CLUB OF THE SONS. I WANTED TO ACQUAINT YOU WITH THE--
YOU'RE KIDDING, RIGHT? YOU KNOW HOW I FEEL ABOUT THIS BOURGEOIS JOINT.
YOU SHOULD EMBRACE YOUR STATION-- ENJOY THE PRIVILEGES THAT I DO. THAT MY FATHER DID. WE'RE A VANISHING BREED, SON.
SPARE ME. AND DO YOUR *VANISHING ACT* YOURSELF.
YOU'RE PRETTY GOOD AT IT.

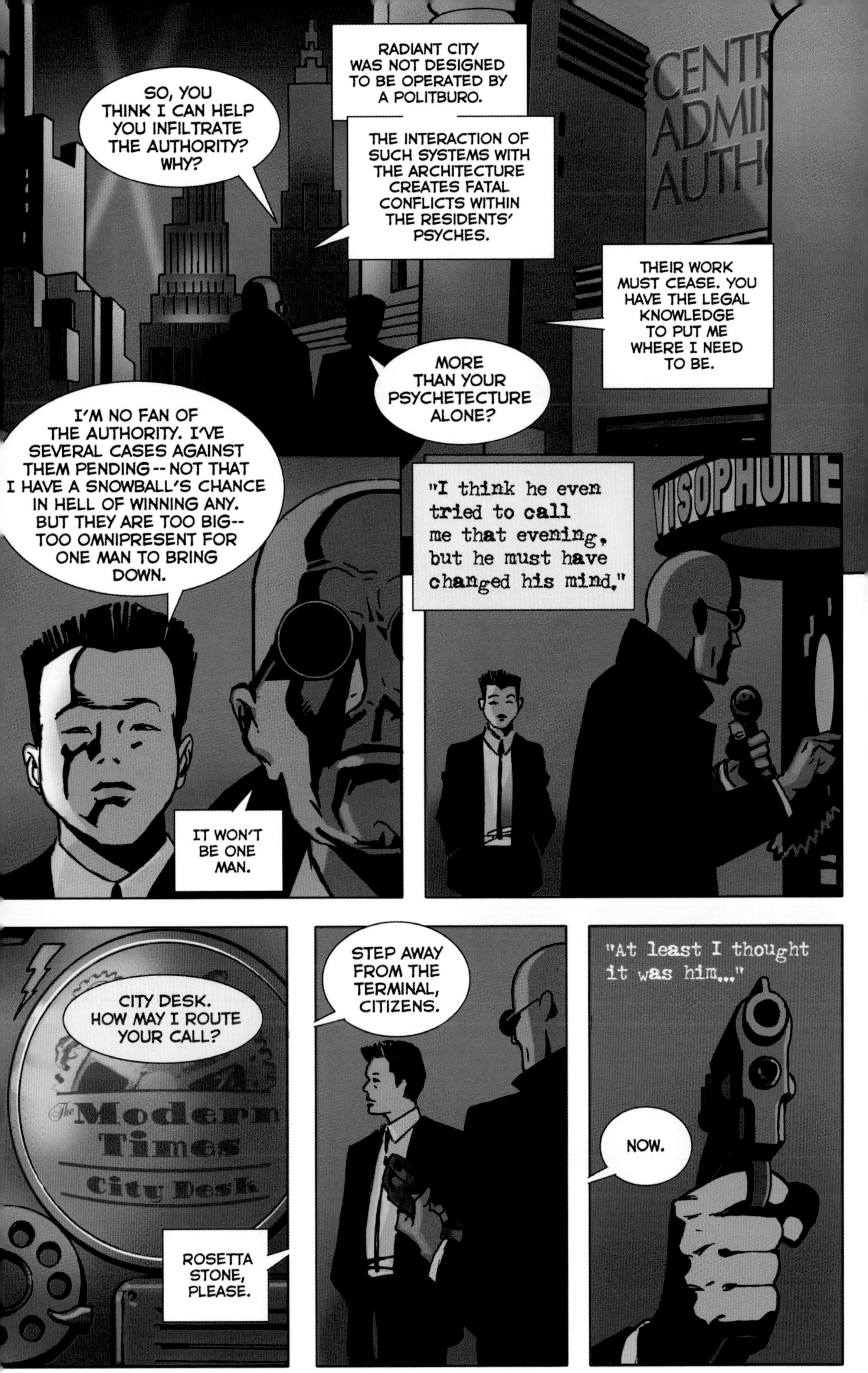
SO, YOU THINK I CAN HELP YOU INFILTRATE THE AUTHORITY? WHY?
RADIANT CITY WAS NOT DESIGNED TO BE OPERATED BY A POLITBURO.
THE INTERACTION OF SUCH SYSTEMS WITH THE ARCHITECTURE CREATES FATAL CONFLICTS WITHIN THE RESIDENTS' PSYCHES.
THEIR WORK MUST CEASE. YOU HAVE THE LEGAL KNOWLEDGE TO PUT ME WHERE I NEED TO BE.
MORE THAN YOUR PSYCHETECTURE ALONE?
I'M NO FAN OF THE AUTHORITY. I'VE SEVERAL CASES AGAINST THEM PENDING -- NOT THAT I HAVE A SNOWBALL'S CHANCE IN HELL OF WINNING ANY. BUT THEY ARE TOO BIG-- TOO OMNIPRESENT FOR ONE MAN TO BRING DOWN.
IT WON'T BE ONE MAN.
"I think he even tried to call me that evening, but he must have changed his mind."
CITY DESK. HOW MAY I ROUTE YOUR CALL?
The Modern Times
City Desk
ROSETTA STONE, PLEASE.
STEP AWAY FROM THE TERMINAL, CITIZENS.
"At least I thought it was him..."
NOW.

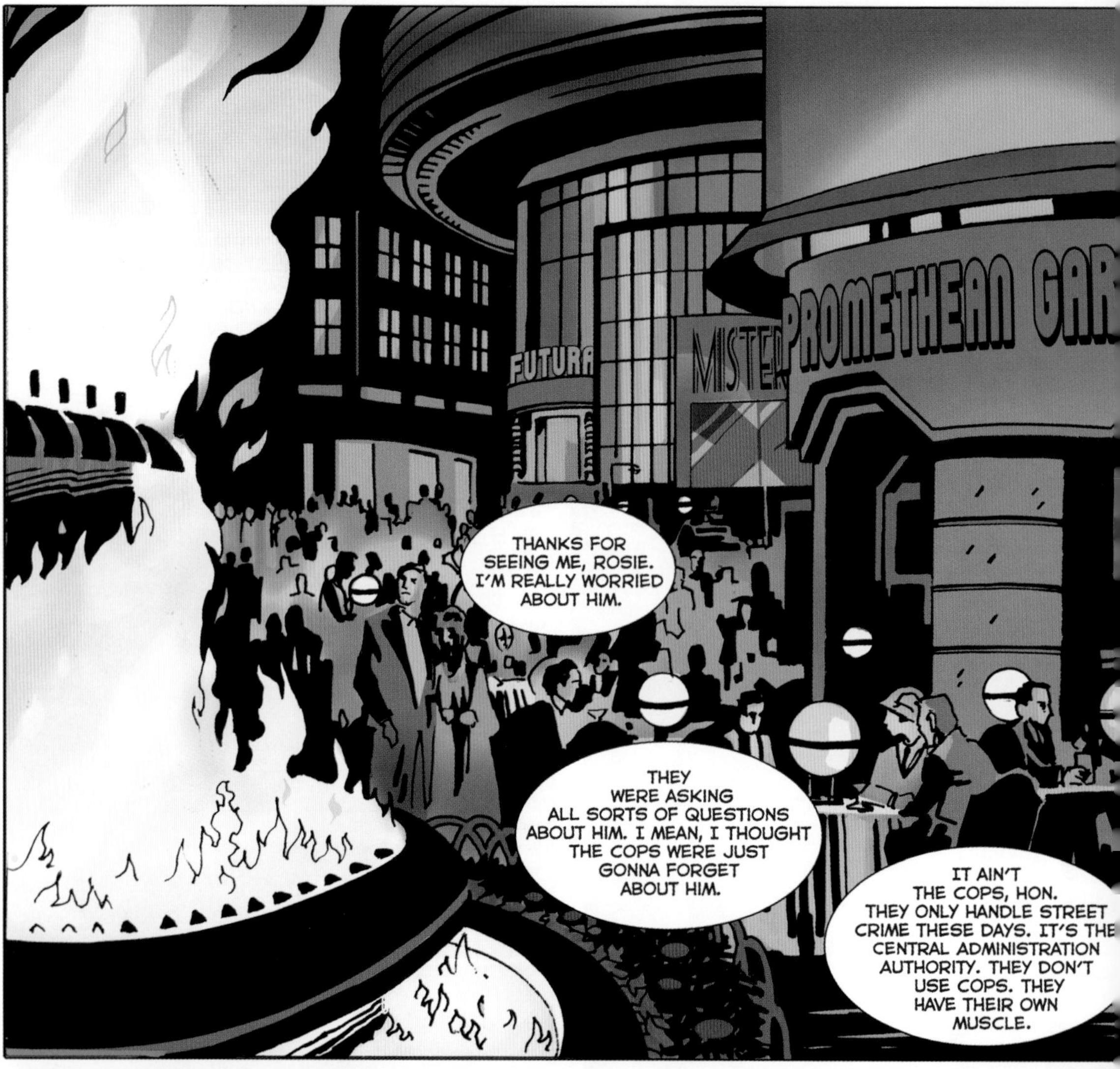
PROMETHEAN GAR
FUTURA
MISTER
THANKS FOR SEEING ME, ROSIE. I'M REALLY WORRIED ABOUT HIM.
THEY WERE ASKING ALL SORTS OF QUESTIONS ABOUT HIM. I MEAN, I THOUGHT THE COPS WERE JUST GONNA FORGET ABOUT HIM.
IT AIN'T THE COPS, HON. THEY ONLY HANDLE STREET CRIME THESE DAYS. IT'S THE CENTRAL ADMINISTRATION AUTHORITY. THEY DON'T USE COPS. THEY HAVE THEIR OWN MUSCLE.

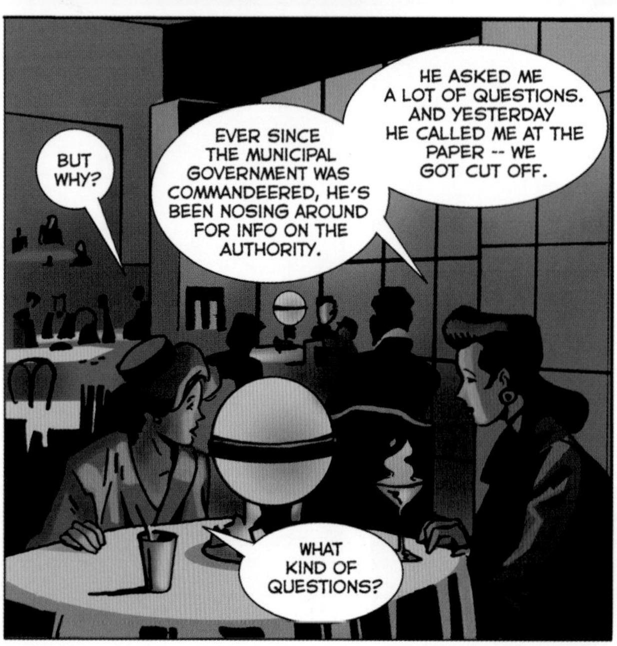
BUT WHY?
EVER SINCE THE MUNICIPAL GOVERNMENT WAS COMMANDEERED, HE'S BEEN NOSING AROUND FOR INFO ON THE AUTHORITY.
HE ASKED ME A LOT OF QUESTIONS. AND YESTERDAY HE CALLED ME AT THE PAPER -- WE GOT CUT OFF.
WHAT KIND OF QUESTIONS?

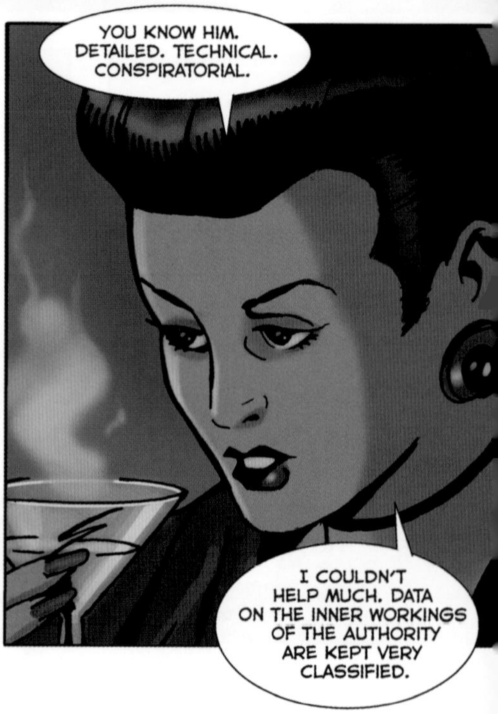
YOU KNOW HIM. DETAILED. TECHNICAL. CONSPIRATORIAL.
I COULDN'T HELP MUCH. DATA ON THE INNER WORKINGS OF THE AUTHORITY ARE KEPT VERY CLASSIFIED.

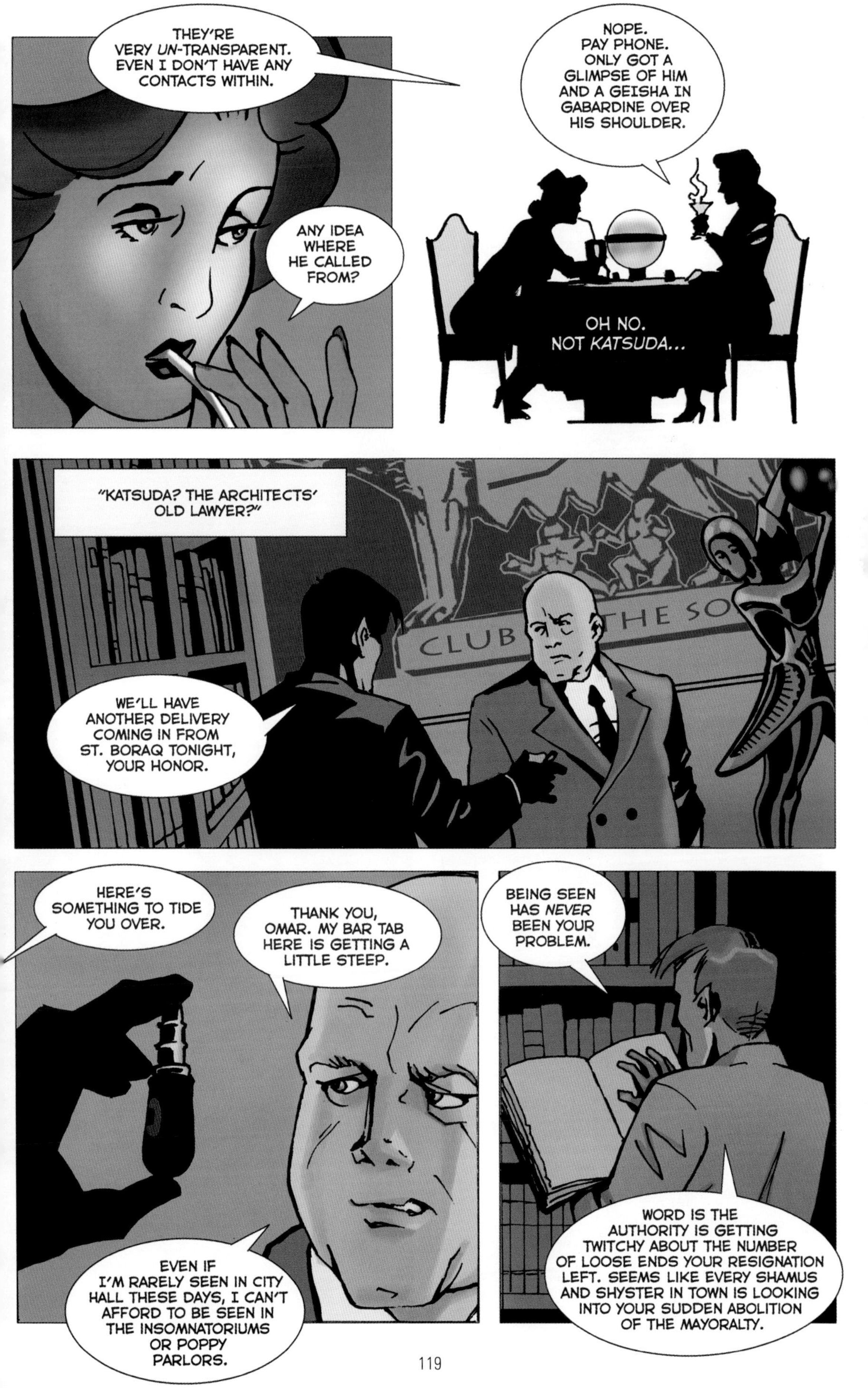

THEY'RE VERY *UN*-TRANSPARENT. EVEN I DON'T HAVE ANY CONTACTS WITHIN.
ANY IDEA WHERE HE CALLED FROM?
NOPE. PAY PHONE. ONLY GOT A GLIMPSE OF HIM AND A GEISHA IN GABARDINE OVER HIS SHOULDER.
OH NO. NOT *KATSUDA*...
"KATSUDA? THE ARCHITECTS' OLD LAWYER?"
CLUB THE SO
WE'LL HAVE ANOTHER DELIVERY COMING IN FROM ST. BORAQ TONIGHT, YOUR HONOR.
HERE'S SOMETHING TO TIDE YOU OVER.
THANK *YOU*, OMAR. MY BAR TAB HERE IS GETTING A LITTLE STEEP.
EVEN IF I'M RARELY SEEN IN CITY HALL THESE DAYS, I CAN'T AFFORD TO BE SEEN IN THE INSOMNATORIUMS OR POPPY PARLORS.
BEING SEEN HAS *NEVER* BEEN YOUR PROBLEM.
WORD IS THE AUTHORITY IS GETTING TWITCHY ABOUT THE NUMBER OF LOOSE ENDS YOUR RESIGNATION LEFT. SEEMS LIKE EVERY SHAMUS AND SHYSTER IN TOWN IS LOOKING INTO YOUR SUDDEN ABOLITION OF THE MAYORALTY.

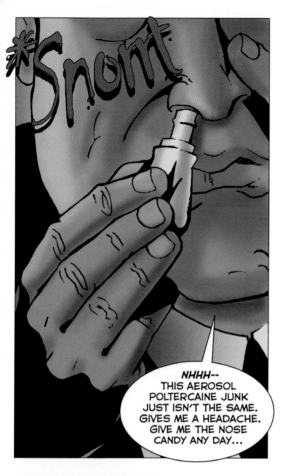

NHHH-- THIS AEROSOL POLTERCAINE JUNK JUST ISN'T THE SAME. GIVES ME A HEADACHE. GIVE ME THE NOSE CANDY ANY DAY...

IT'S ONLY A MATTER OF TIME BEFORE YOU'RE FOUND AND THE NATURE OF YOUR ARRANGEMENT BECOMES OBVIOUS.

WHAT DO THEY--SNIFF--EXPECT ME TO DO ABOUT IT? I'M RETIRED.

YOU'RE THE WEAK LINK, WELLES, OLD FRIEND.

SNIFF...

THEY'D LIKE YOU TO DISAPPEAR... ONCE AND FOR ALL.

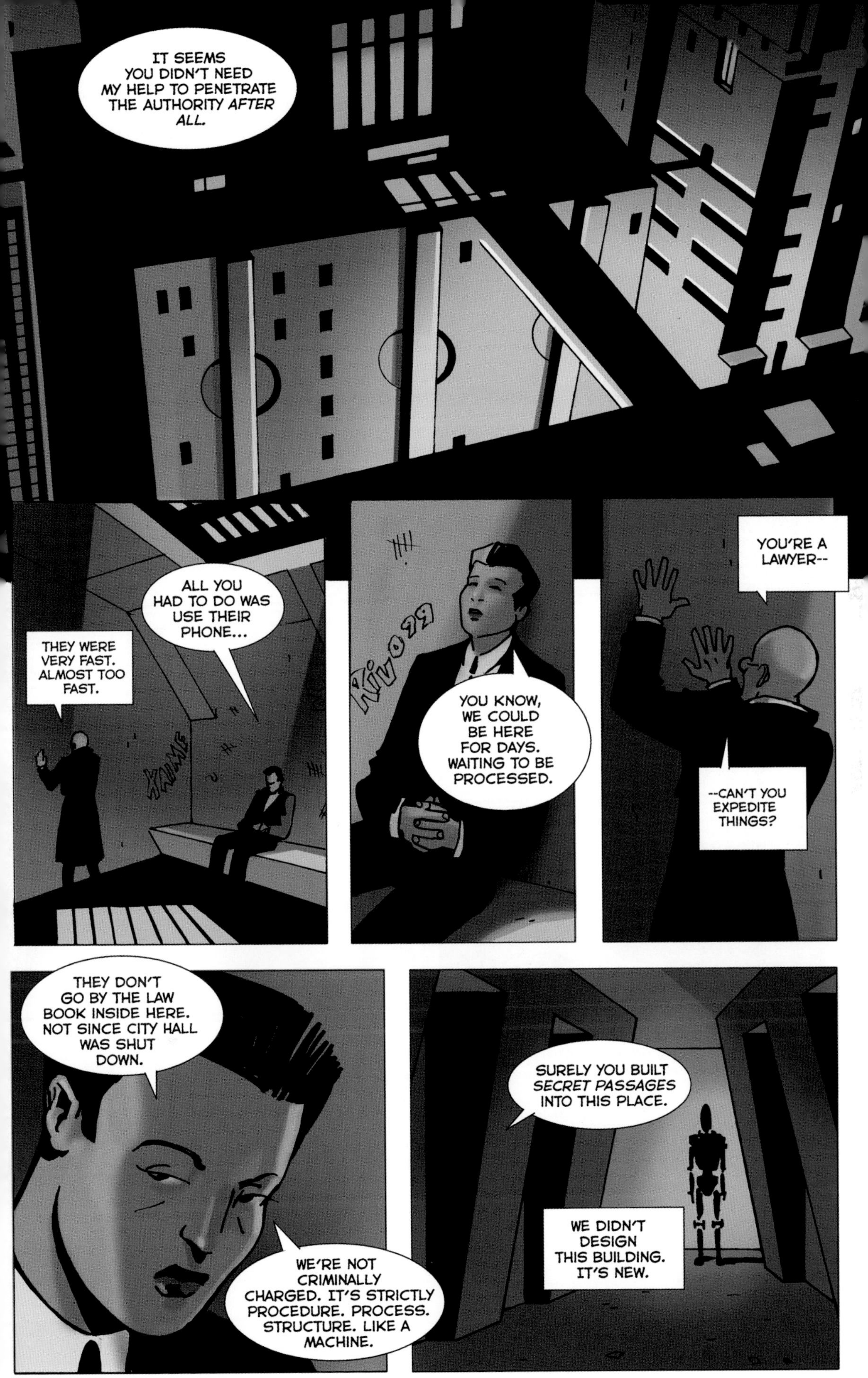
IT SEEMS YOU DIDN'T NEED MY HELP TO PENETRATE THE AUTHORITY AFTER ALL.
THEY WERE VERY FAST. ALMOST TOO FAST.
ALL YOU HAD TO DO WAS USE THEIR PHONE...
YOU KNOW, WE COULD BE HERE FOR DAYS. WAITING TO BE PROCESSED.
YOU'RE A LAWYER--
--CAN'T YOU EXPEDITE THINGS?
THEY DON'T GO BY THE LAW BOOK INSIDE HERE. NOT SINCE CITY HALL WAS SHUT DOWN.
WE'RE NOT CRIMINALLY CHARGED. IT'S STRICTLY PROCEDURE. PROCESS. STRUCTURE. LIKE A MACHINE.
SURELY YOU BUILT SECRET PASSAGES INTO THIS PLACE.
WE DIDN'T DESIGN THIS BUILDING. IT'S NEW.

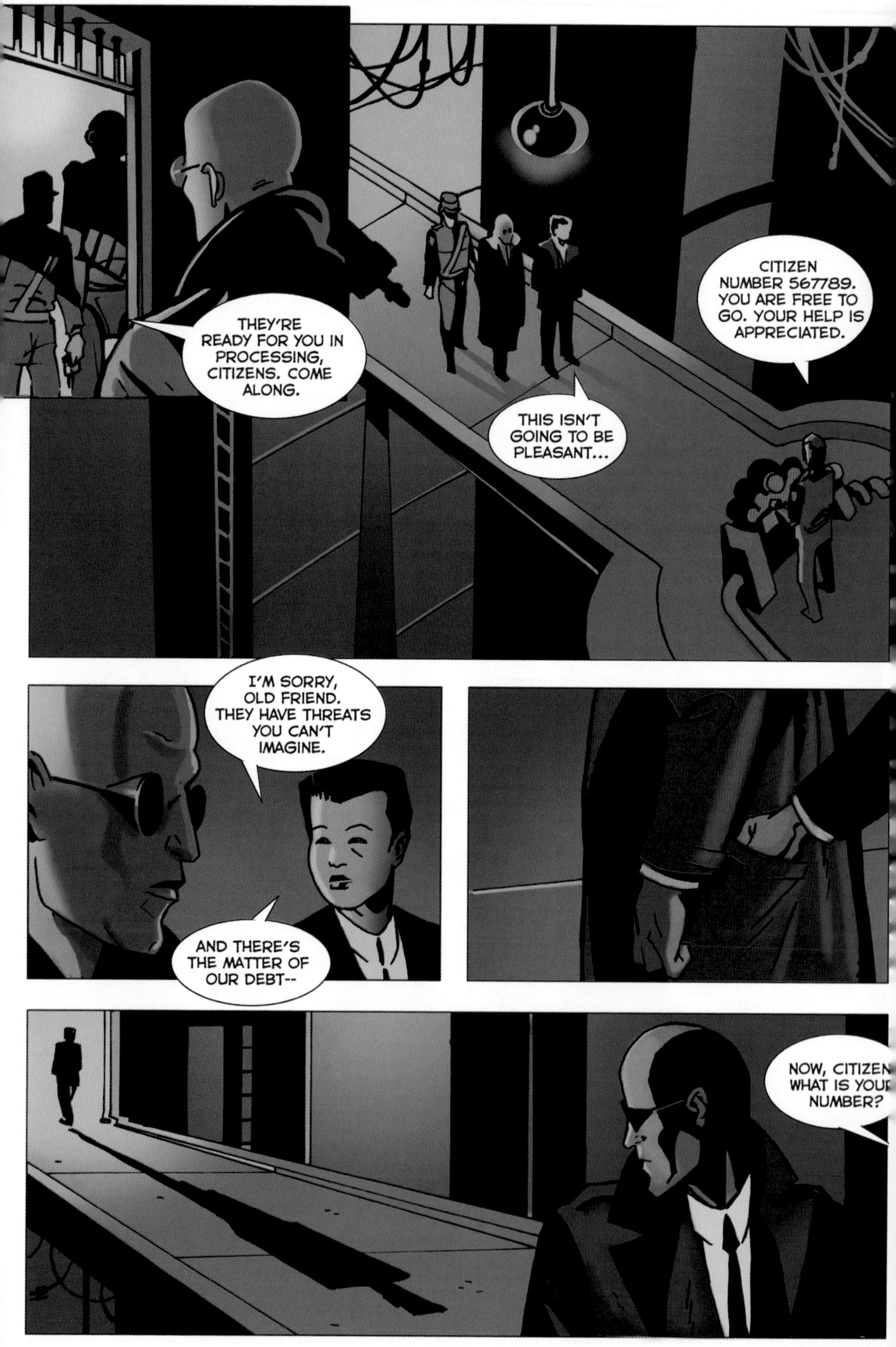
THEY'RE READY FOR YOU IN PROCESSING, CITIZENS. COME ALONG.
THIS ISN'T GOING TO BE PLEASANT...
CITIZEN NUMBER 567789. YOU ARE FREE TO GO. YOUR HELP IS APPRECIATED.
I'M SORRY, OLD FRIEND. THEY HAVE THREATS YOU CAN'T IMAGINE.
AND THERE'S THE MATTER OF OUR DEBT--
NOW, CITIZEN WHAT IS YOUR NUMBER?

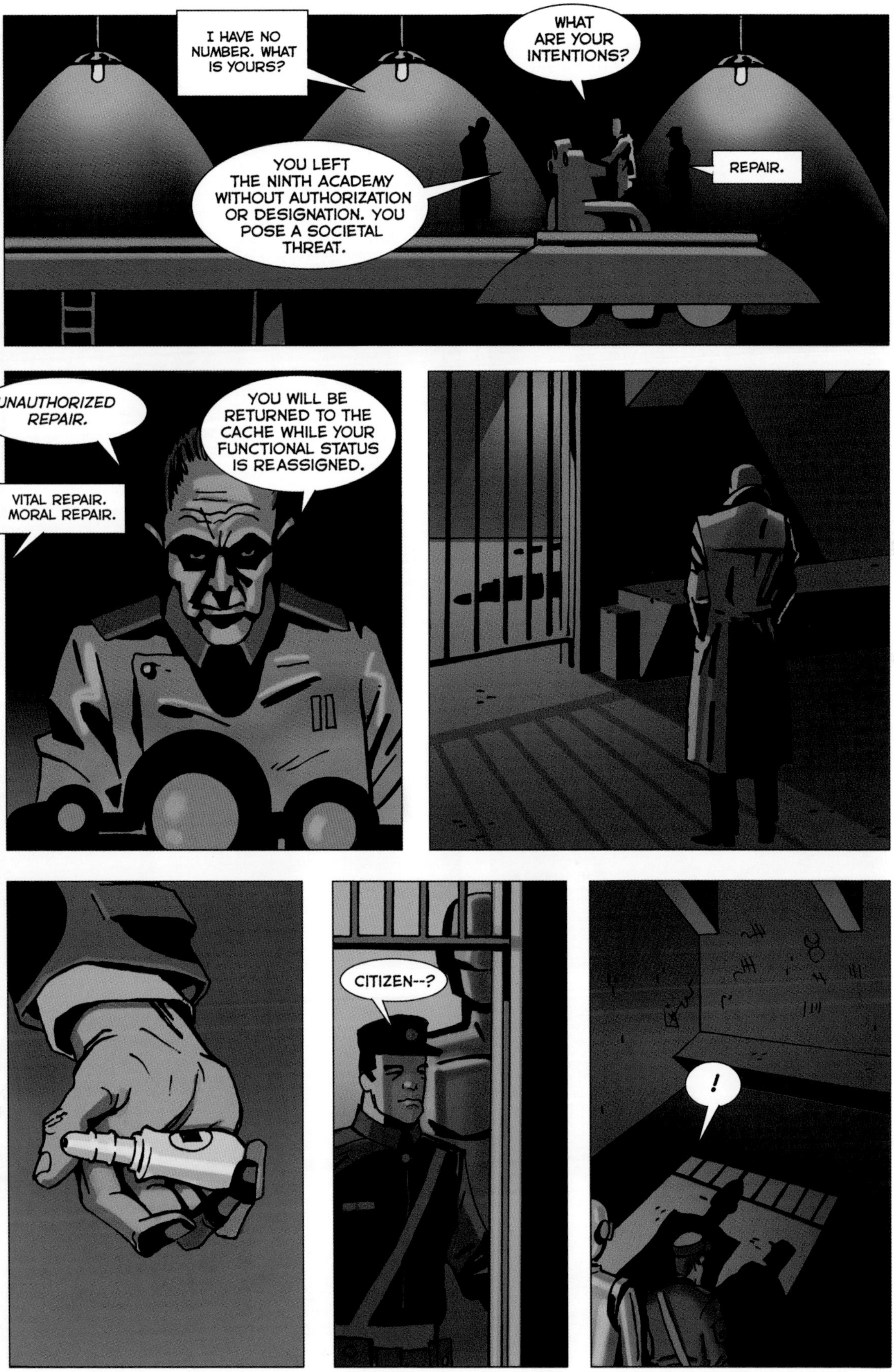
I HAVE NO NUMBER. WHAT IS YOURS?
WHAT ARE YOUR INTENTIONS?
YOU LEFT THE NINTH ACADEMY WITHOUT AUTHORIZATION OR DESIGNATION. YOU POSE A SOCIETAL THREAT.
REPAIR.
UNAUTHORIZED REPAIR.
VITAL REPAIR. MORAL REPAIR.
YOU WILL BE RETURNED TO THE CACHE WHILE YOUR FUNCTIONAL STATUS IS REASSIGNED.
CITIZEN--?
!

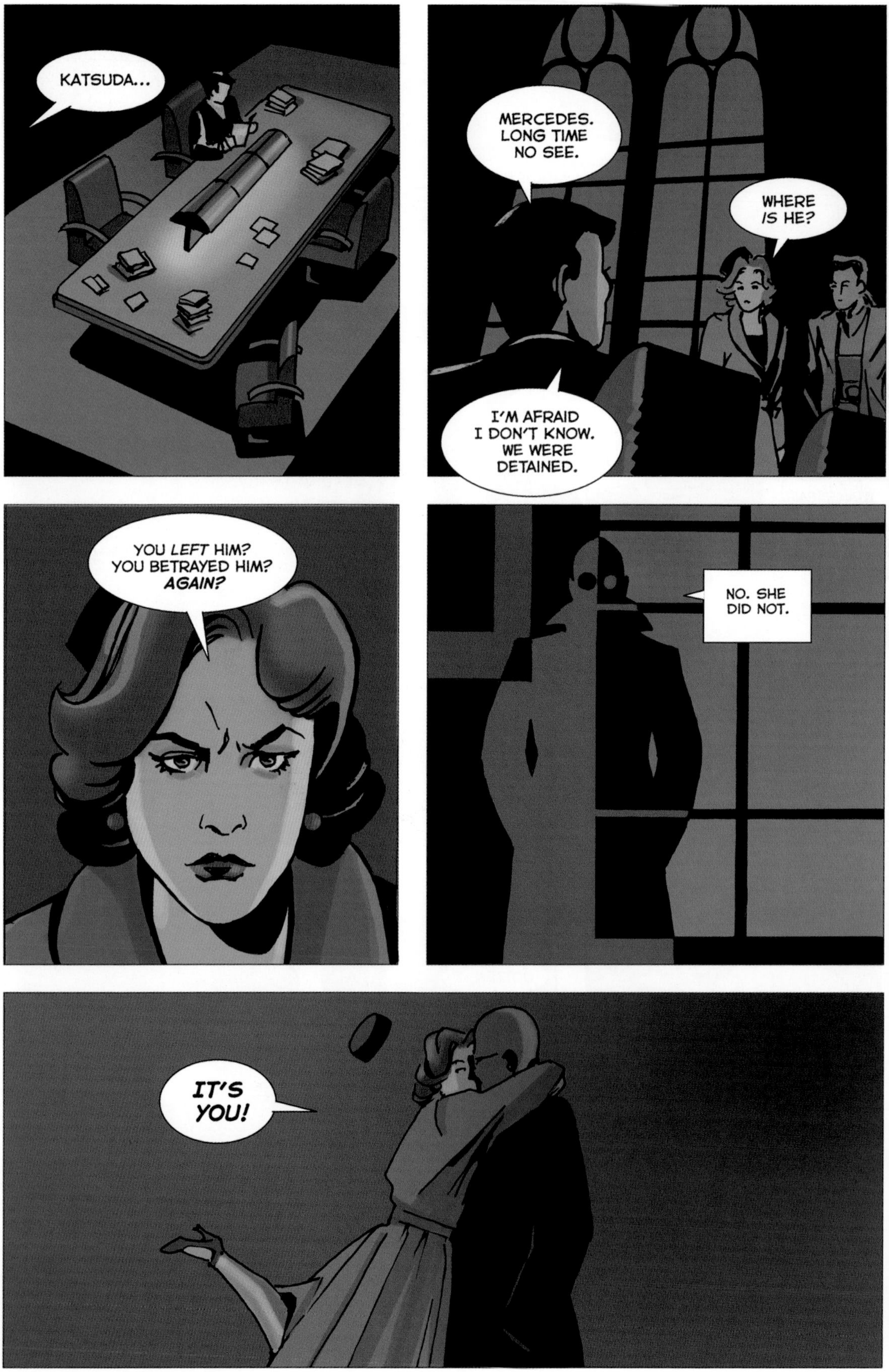
KATSUDA...
MERCEDES. LONG TIME NO SEE.
WHERE IS HE?
I'M AFRAID I DON'T KNOW. WE WERE DETAINED.
YOU *LEFT* HIM? YOU BETRAYED HIM? ***AGAIN?***
NO. SHE DID NOT.
IT'S YOU!

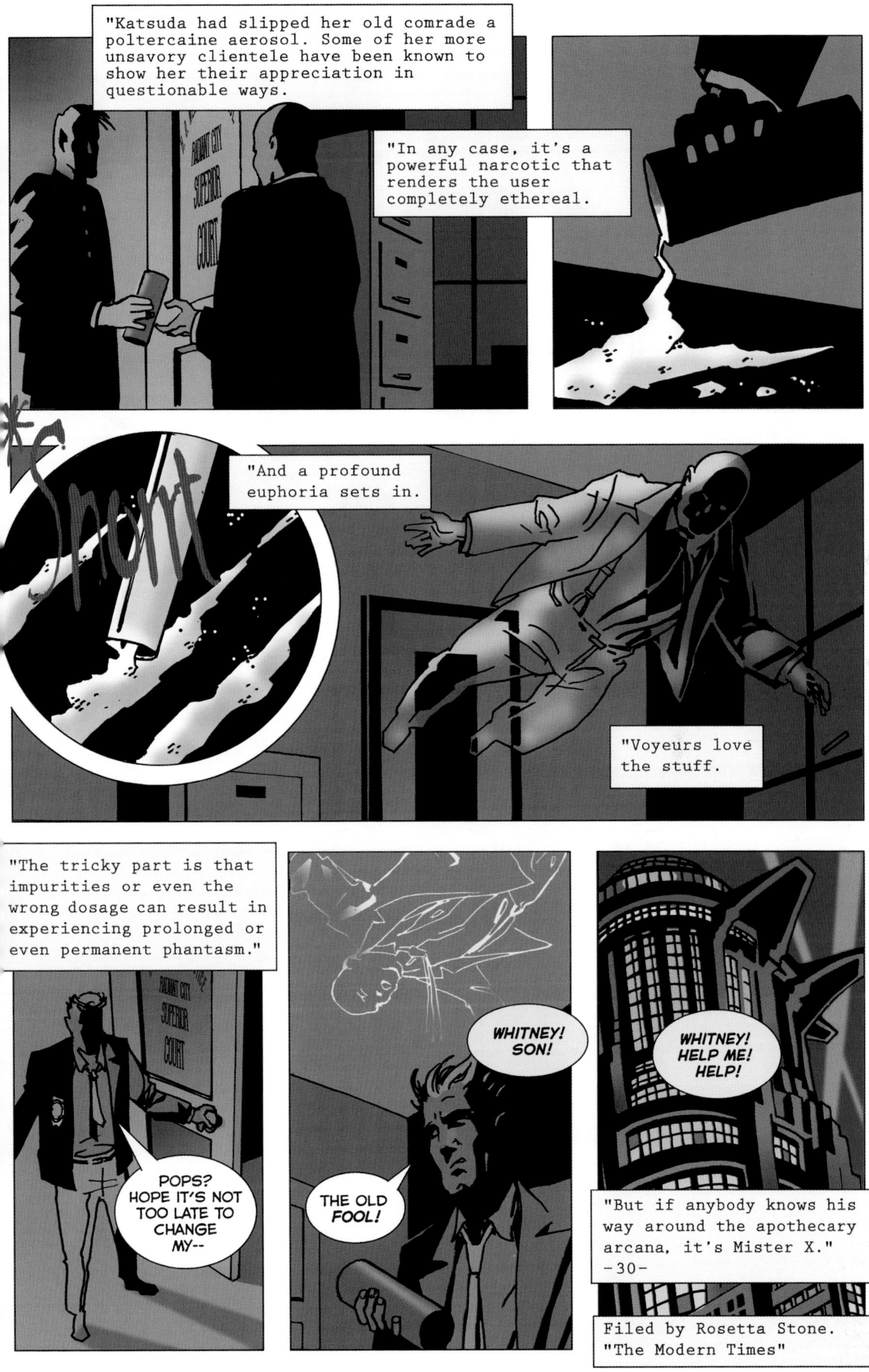
"Katsuda had slipped her old comrade a poltercaine aerosol. Some of her more unsavory clientele have been known to show her their appreciation in questionable ways.
RADIANT CITY SUPERIOR COURT
"In any case, it's a powerful narcotic that renders the user completely ethereal.
"And a profound euphoria sets in.
"Voyeurs love the stuff.
"The tricky part is that impurities or even the wrong dosage can result in experiencing prolonged or even permanent phantasm."
RADIANT CITY SUPERIOR COURT
POPS? HOPE IT'S NOT TOO LATE TO CHANGE MY--
WHITNEY! SON!
THE OLD FOOL!
WHITNEY! HELP ME! HELP!
"But if anybody knows his way around the apothecary arcana, it's Mister X."
-30-
Filed by Rosetta Stone.
"The Modern Times"

HEALTH

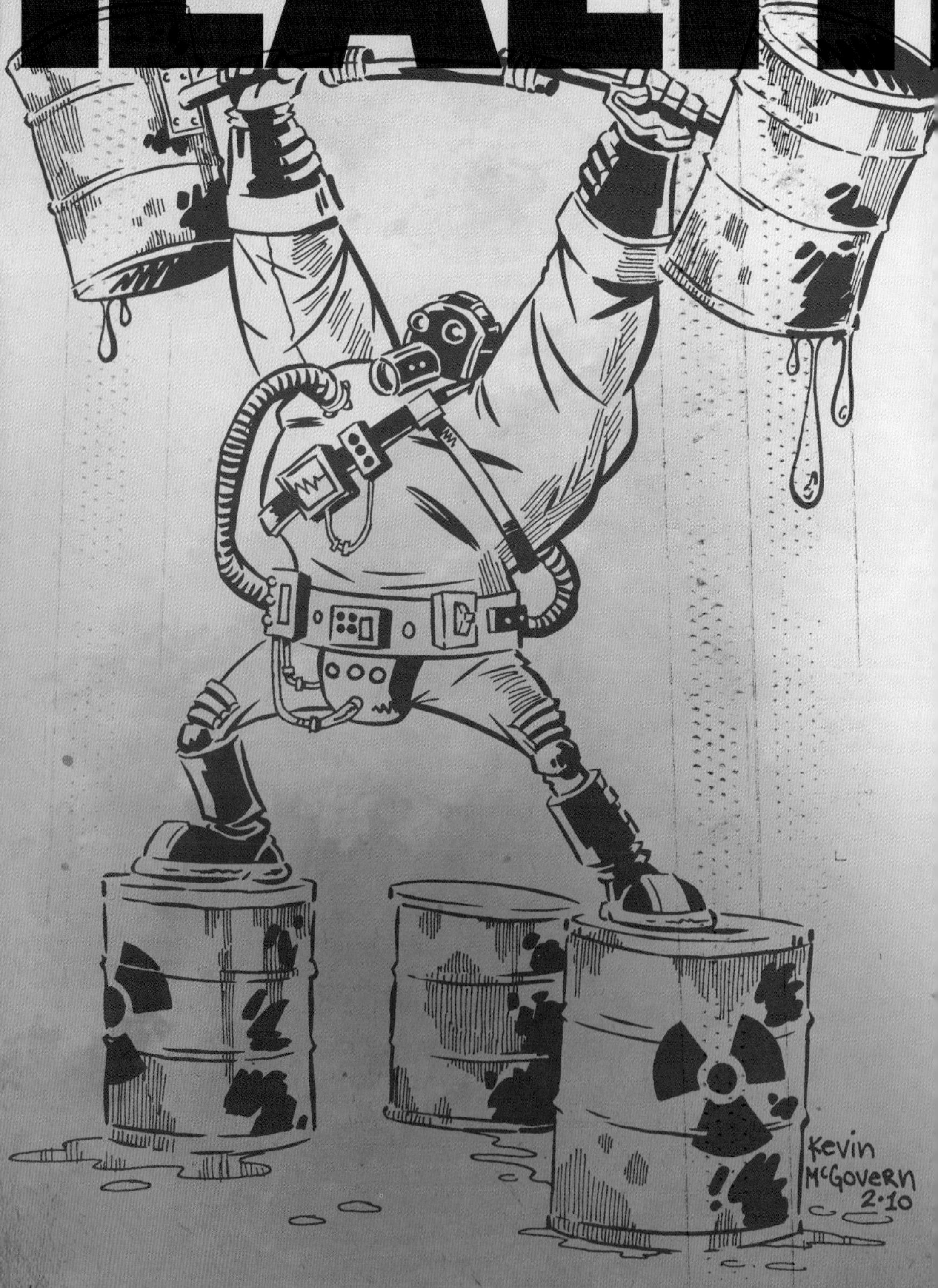
Kevin
McGovern
2·10

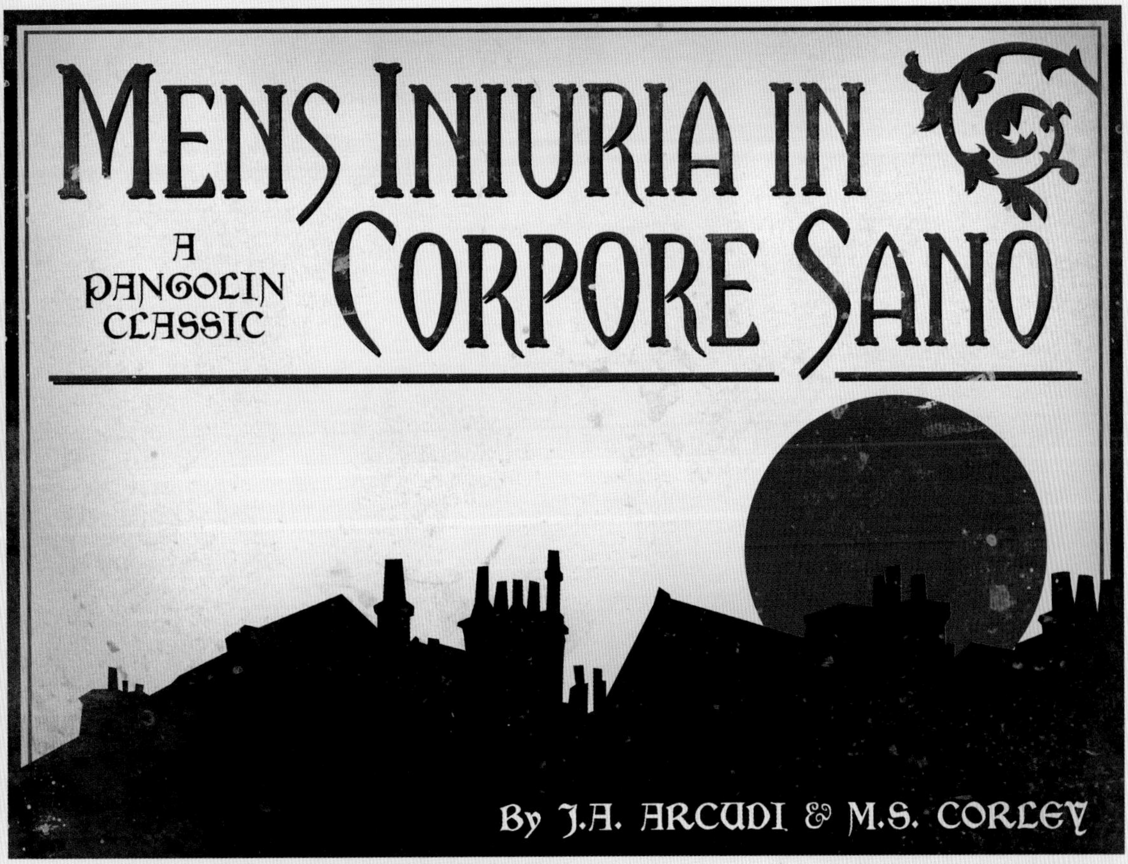
MENS INIURIA IN CORPORE SANO
A PANGOLIN CLASSIC
By J.A. ARCUDI & M.S. CORLEY

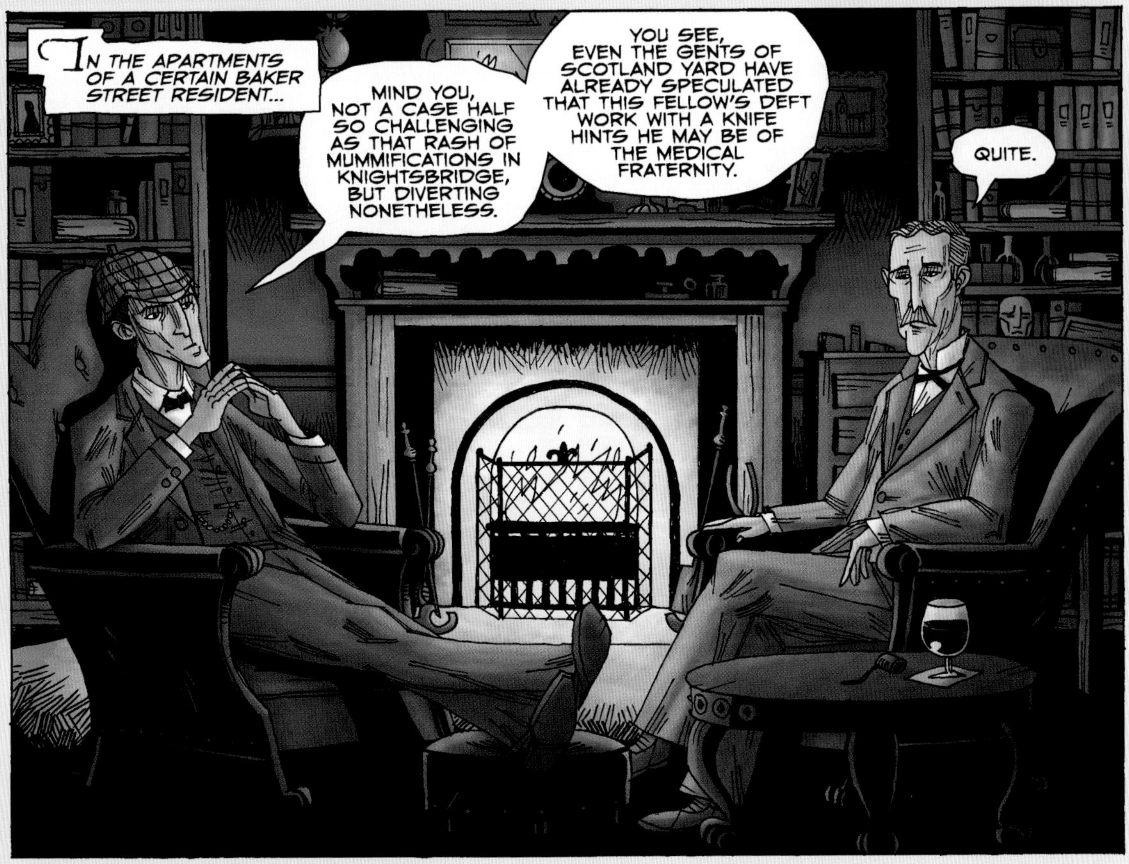
IN THE APARTMENTS OF A CERTAIN BAKER STREET RESIDENT...
MIND YOU, NOT A CASE HALF SO CHALLENGING AS THAT RASH OF MUMMIFICATIONS IN KNIGHTSBRIDGE, BUT DIVERTING NONETHELESS.
YOU SEE, EVEN THE GENTS OF SCOTLAND YARD HAVE ALREADY SPECULATED THAT THIS FELLOW'S DEFT WORK WITH A KNIFE HINTS HE MAY BE OF THE MEDICAL FRATERNITY.
QUITE.

LETTERING BY BLAMBOT'S NATE PIEKOS

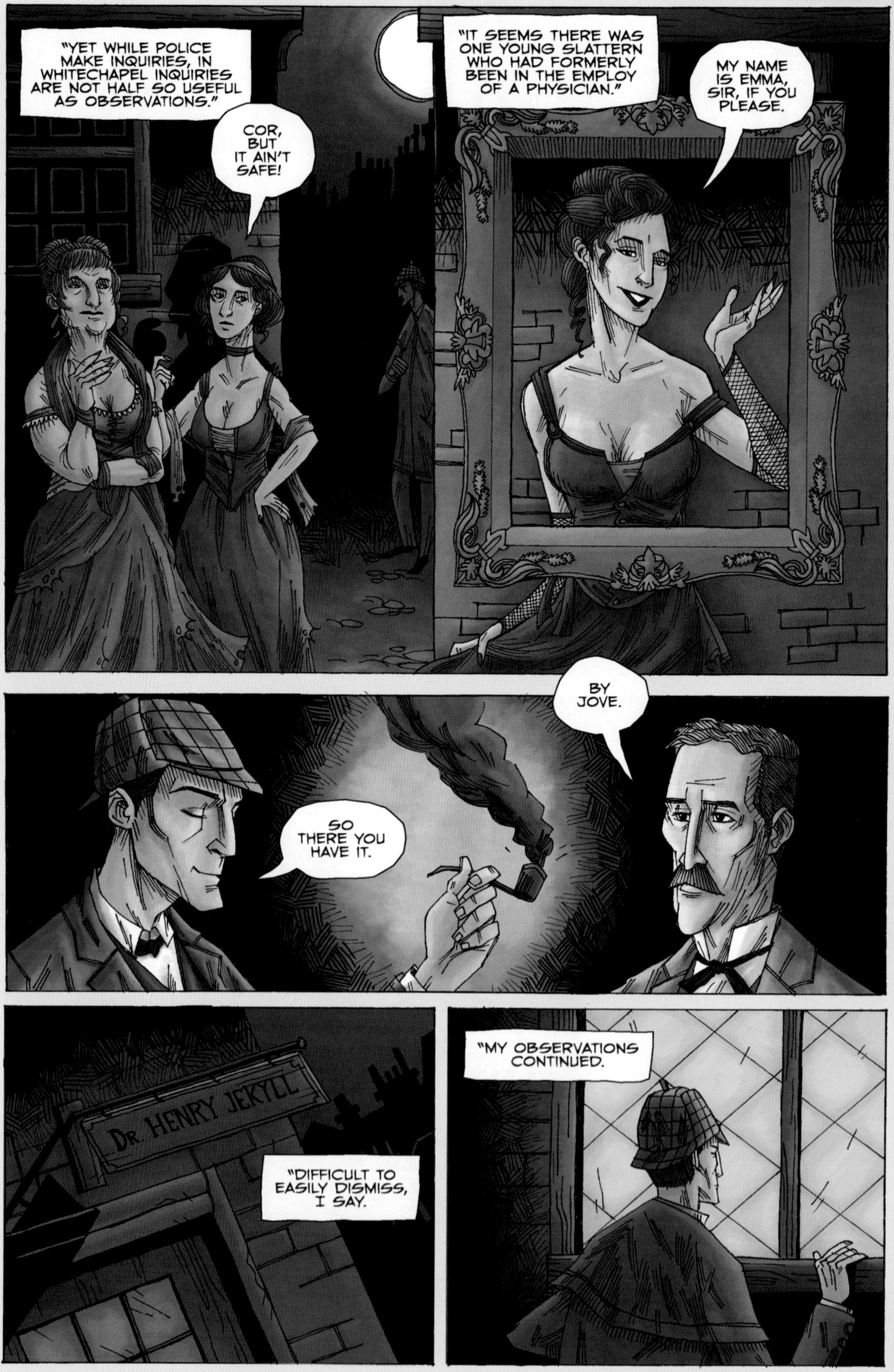
"YET WHILE POLICE MAKE INQUIRIES, IN WHITECHAPEL INQUIRIES ARE NOT HALF SO USEFUL AS OBSERVATIONS."
COR, BUT IT AIN'T SAFE!
"IT SEEMS THERE WAS ONE YOUNG SLATTERN WHO HAD FORMERLY BEEN IN THE EMPLOY OF A PHYSICIAN."
MY NAME IS EMMA, SIR, IF YOU PLEASE.
SO THERE YOU HAVE IT.
BY JOVE.
DR. HENRY JEKYLL
"DIFFICULT TO EASILY DISMISS, I SAY.
"MY OBSERVATIONS CONTINUED.

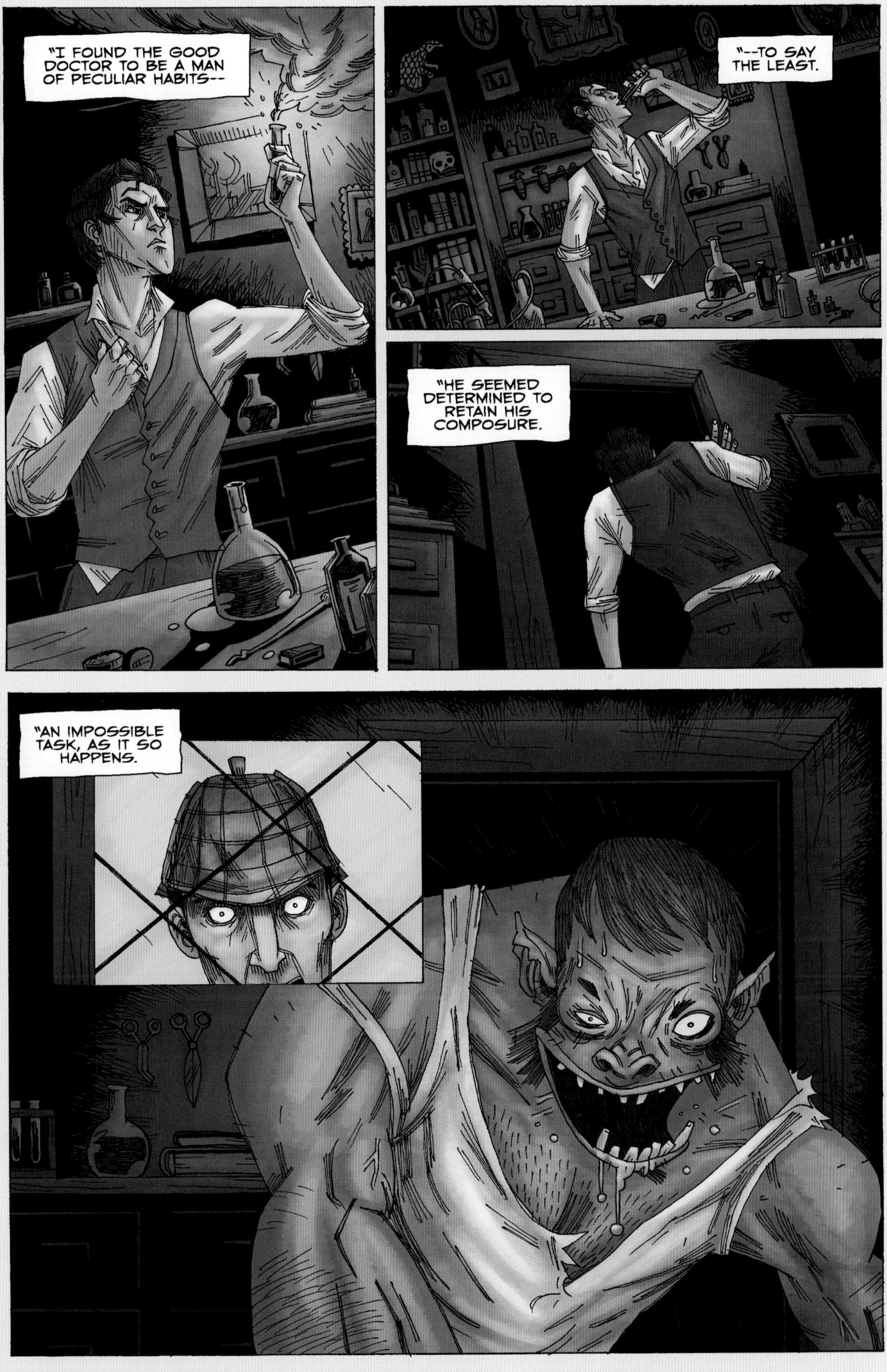
"I FOUND THE GOOD DOCTOR TO BE A MAN OF PECULIAR HABITS--
"--TO SAY THE LEAST.
"HE SEEMED DETERMINED TO RETAIN HIS COMPOSURE.
"AN IMPOSSIBLE TASK, AS IT SO HAPPENS.

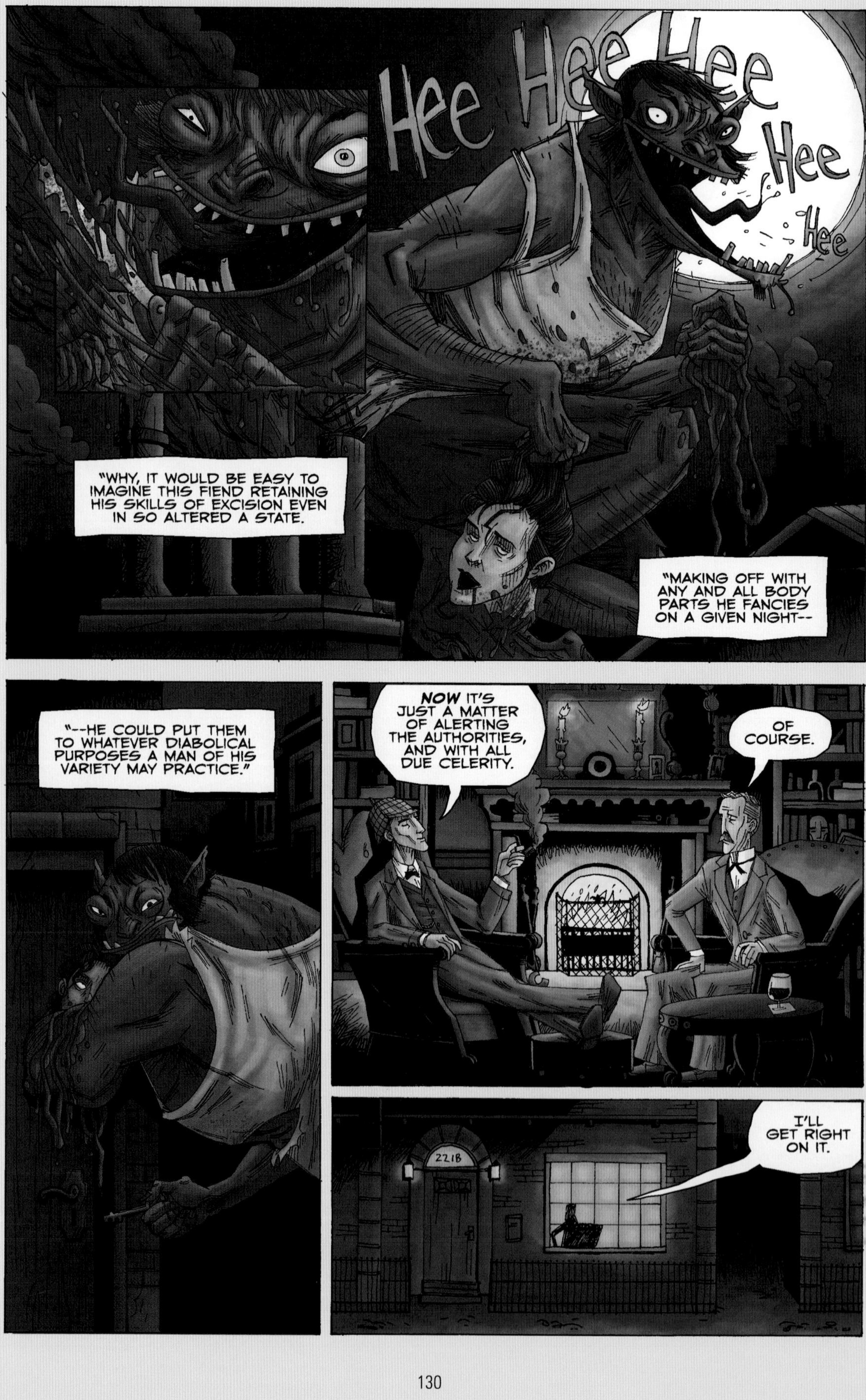
Hee Hee Hee Hee Hee Hee
"WHY, IT WOULD BE EASY TO IMAGINE THIS FIEND RETAINING HIS SKILLS OF EXCISION EVEN IN SO ALTERED A STATE.
"MAKING OFF WITH ANY AND ALL BODY PARTS HE FANCIES ON A GIVEN NIGHT--
"--HE COULD PUT THEM TO WHATEVER DIABOLICAL PURPOSES A MAN OF HIS VARIETY MAY PRACTICE."
NOW IT'S JUST A MATTER OF ALERTING THE AUTHORITIES, AND WITH ALL DUE CELERITY.
OF COURSE.
221B
I'LL GET RIGHT ON IT.

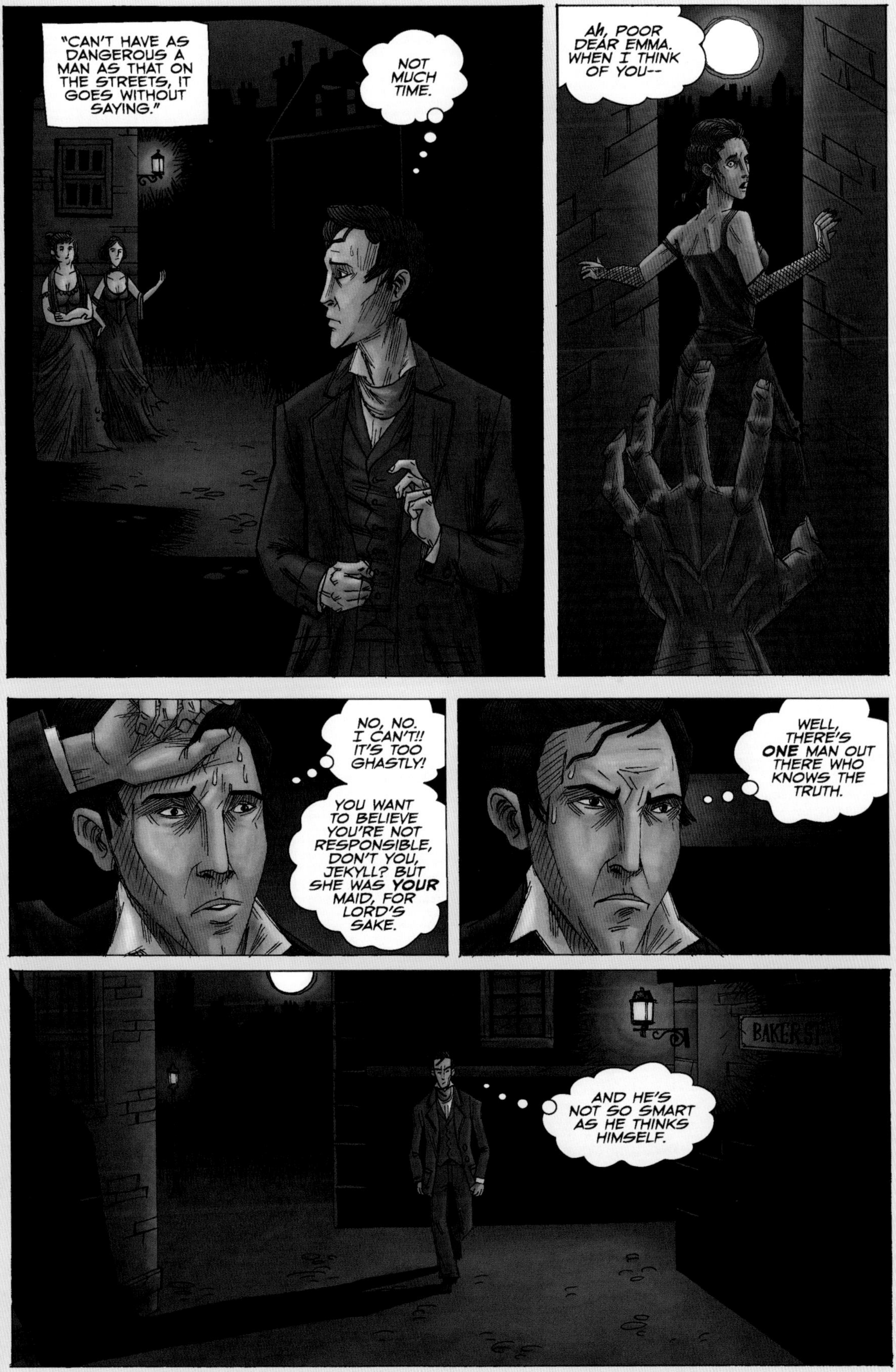
"CAN'T HAVE AS DANGEROUS A MAN AS THAT ON THE STREETS, IT GOES WITHOUT SAYING."
NOT MUCH TIME.
AH, POOR DEAR EMMA. WHEN I THINK OF YOU--
NO, NO. I CAN'T!! IT'S TOO GHASTLY!
YOU WANT TO BELIEVE YOU'RE NOT RESPONSIBLE, DON'T YOU, JEKYLL? BUT SHE WAS YOUR MAID, FOR LORD'S SAKE.
WELL, THERE'S ONE MAN OUT THERE WHO KNOWS THE TRUTH.
BAKER ST
AND HE'S NOT SO SMART AS HE THINKS HIMSELF.

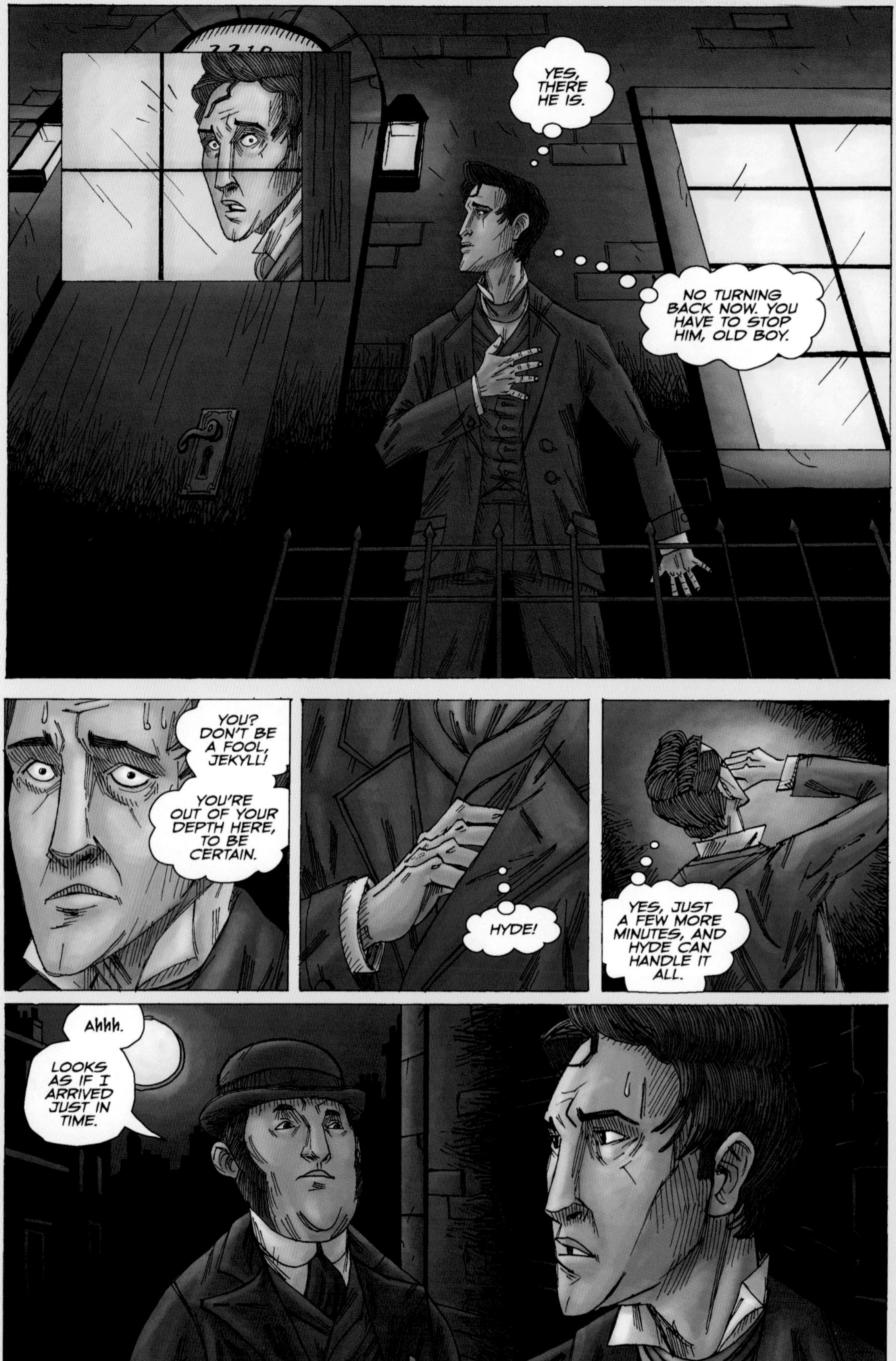
YES, THERE HE IS.
NO TURNING BACK NOW. YOU HAVE TO STOP HIM, OLD BOY.
YOU? DON'T BE A FOOL, JEKYLL!
YOU'RE OUT OF YOUR DEPTH HERE, TO BE CERTAIN.
HYDE!
YES, JUST A FEW MORE MINUTES, AND HYDE CAN HANDLE IT ALL.
Ahhh.
LOOKS AS IF I ARRIVED JUST IN TIME.

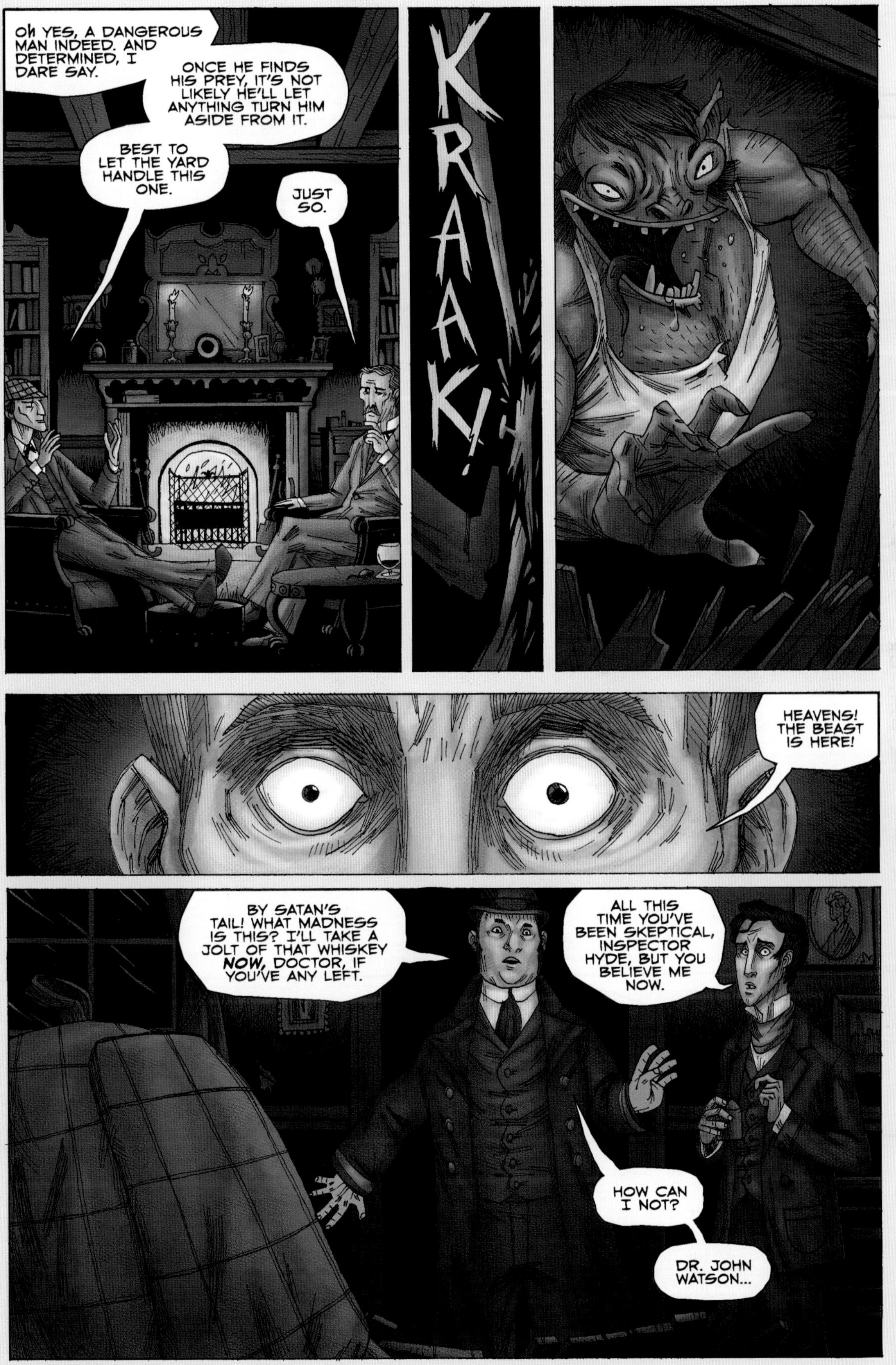

Oh YES, A DANGEROUS MAN INDEED. AND DETERMINED, I DARE SAY.
ONCE HE FINDS HIS PREY, IT'S NOT LIKELY HE'LL LET ANYTHING TURN HIM ASIDE FROM IT.
BEST TO LET THE YARD HANDLE THIS ONE.
JUST SO.
KRAAK!
HEAVENS! THE BEAST IS HERE!
BY SATAN'S TAIL! WHAT MADNESS IS THIS? I'LL TAKE A JOLT OF THAT WHISKEY **NOW,** DOCTOR, IF YOU'VE ANY LEFT.
ALL THIS TIME YOU'VE BEEN SKEPTICAL, INSPECTOR HYDE, BUT YOU BELIEVE ME NOW.
HOW CAN I NOT?
DR. JOHN WATSON...

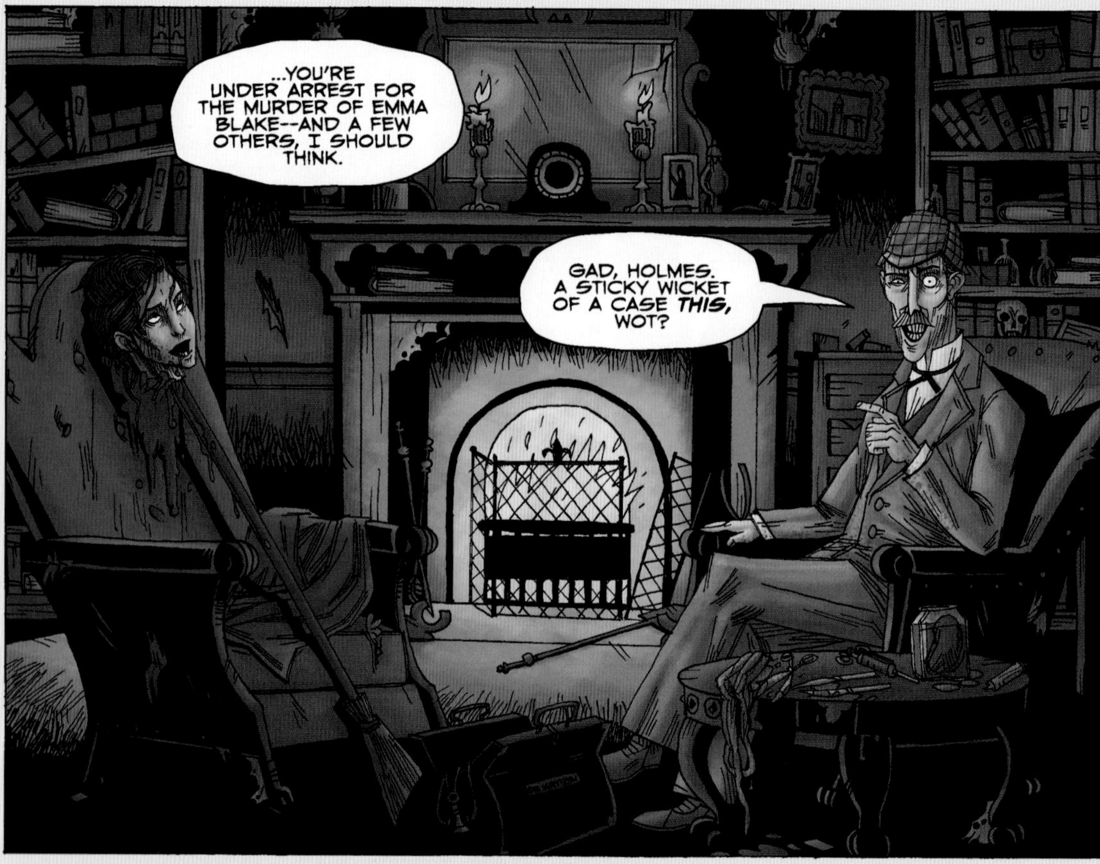
...YOU'RE UNDER ARREST FOR THE MURDER OF EMMA BLAKE--AND A FEW OTHERS, I SHOULD THINK.
GAD, HOLMES. A STICKY WICKET OF A CASE *THIS*, WOT?

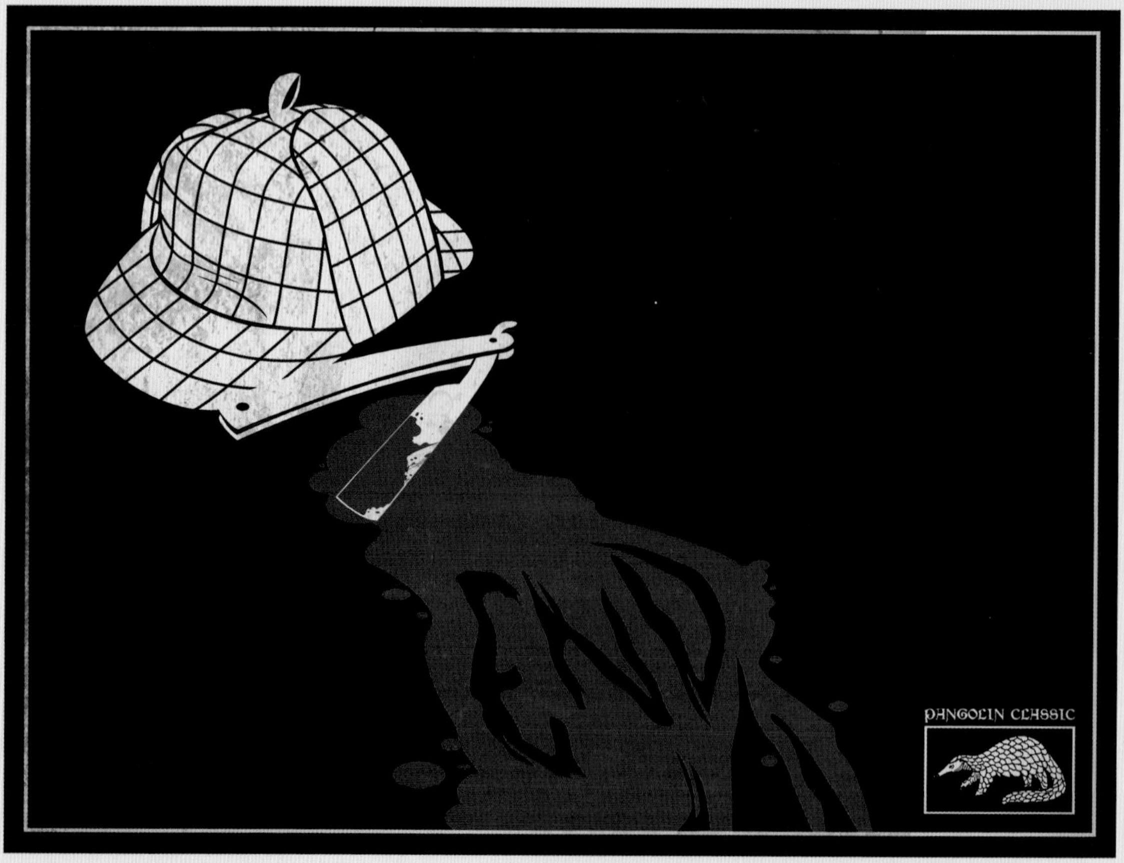
END
PANGOLIN CLASSIC

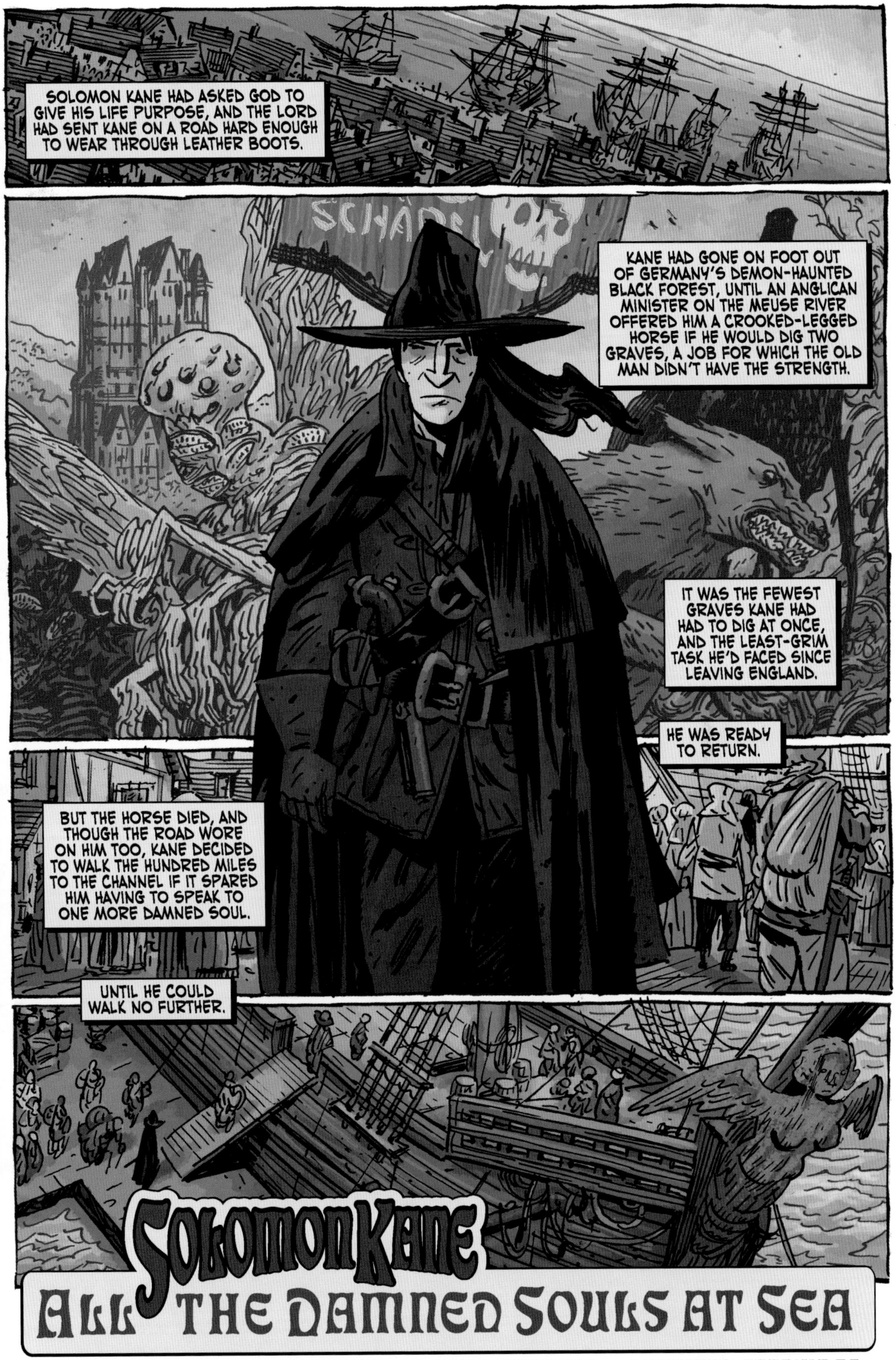
SOLOMON KANE HAD ASKED GOD TO GIVE HIS LIFE PURPOSE, AND THE LORD HAD SENT KANE ON A ROAD HARD ENOUGH TO WEAR THROUGH LEATHER BOOTS.
KANE HAD GONE ON FOOT OUT OF GERMANY'S DEMON-HAUNTED BLACK FOREST, UNTIL AN ANGLICAN MINISTER ON THE MEUSE RIVER OFFERED HIM A CROOKED-LEGGED HORSE IF HE WOULD DIG TWO GRAVES, A JOB FOR WHICH THE OLD MAN DIDN'T HAVE THE STRENGTH.
IT WAS THE FEWEST GRAVES KANE HAD HAD TO DIG AT ONCE, AND THE LEAST-GRIM TASK HE'D FACED SINCE LEAVING ENGLAND.
HE WAS READY TO RETURN.
BUT THE HORSE DIED, AND THOUGH THE ROAD WORE ON HIM TOO, KANE DECIDED TO WALK THE HUNDRED MILES TO THE CHANNEL IF IT SPARED HIM HAVING TO SPEAK TO ONE MORE DAMNED SOUL.
UNTIL HE COULD WALK NO FURTHER.
SOLOMON KANE
ALL THE DAMNED SOULS AT SEA

By SCOTT ALLIE and GUY DAVIS with DAVE STEWART and RICHARD STARKINGS

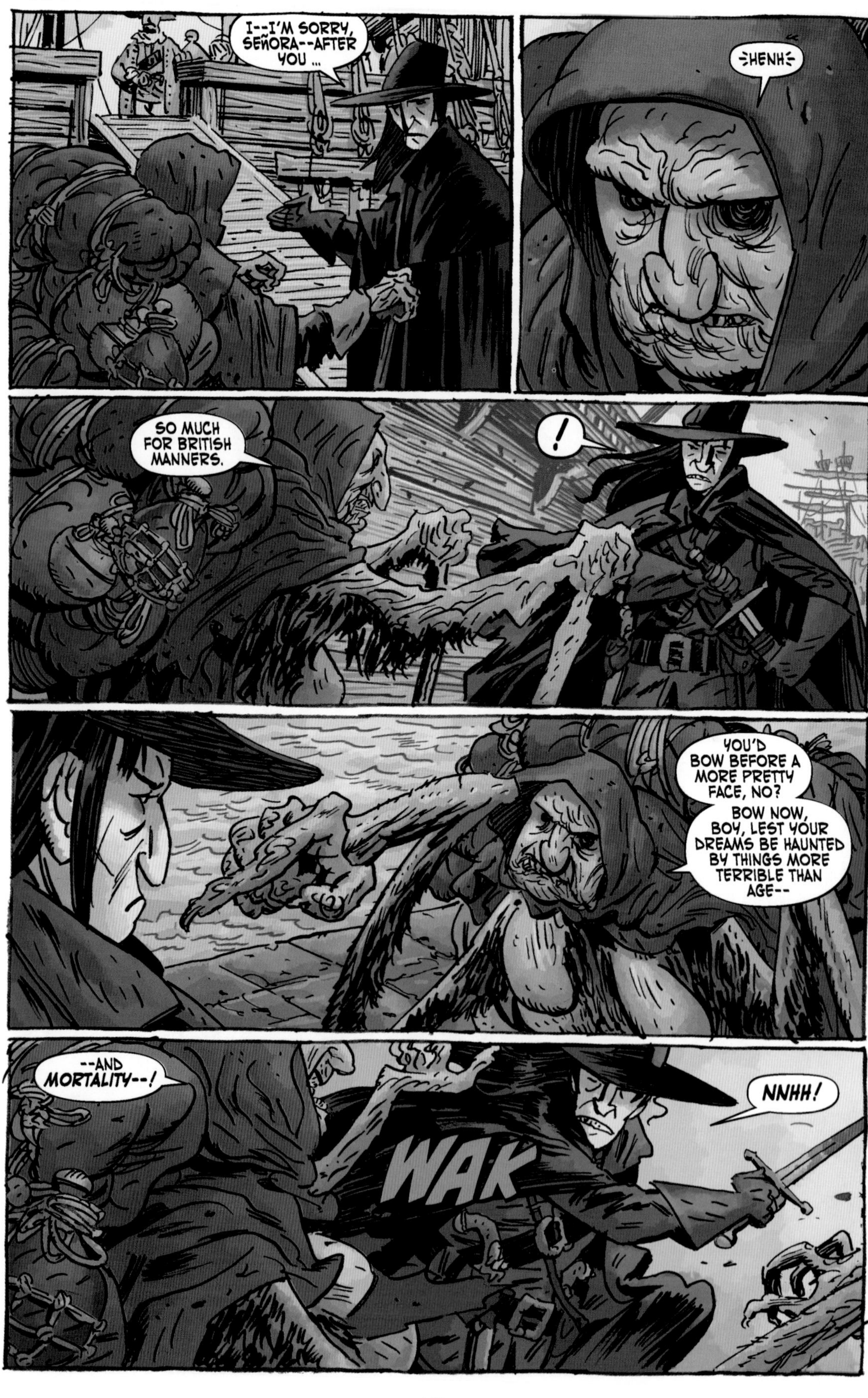
I--I'M SORRY, SEÑORA--AFTER YOU ...
HENH
SO MUCH FOR BRITISH MANNERS.
!
YOU'D BOW BEFORE A MORE PRETTY FACE, NO?
BOW NOW, BOY, LEST YOUR DREAMS BE HAUNTED BY THINGS MORE TERRIBLE THAN AGE--
--AND MORTALITY--!
WAK
NNHH!

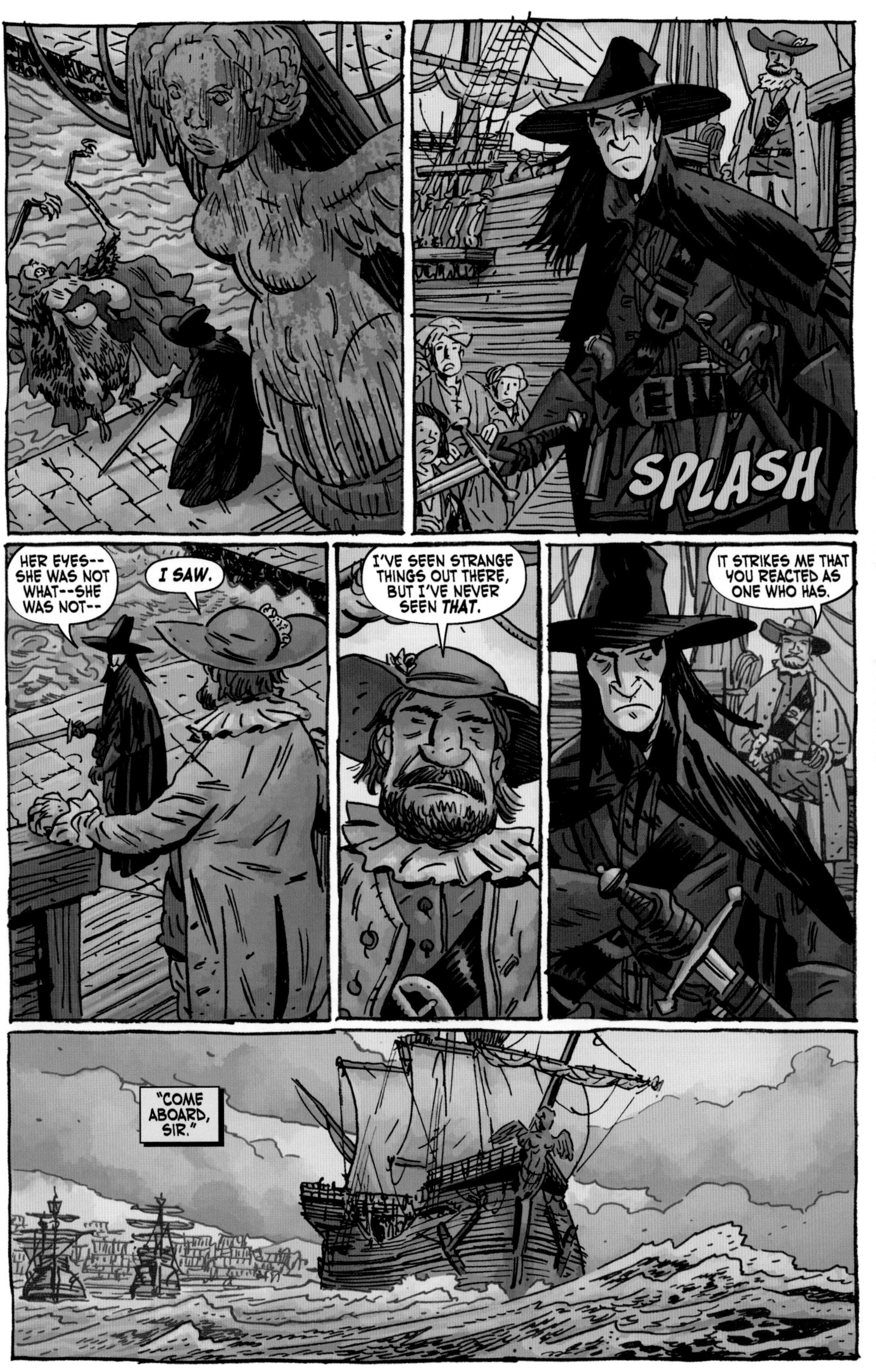
SPLASH
HER EYES--SHE WAS NOT WHAT--SHE WAS NOT--
I SAW.
I'VE SEEN STRANGE THINGS OUT THERE, BUT I'VE NEVER SEEN THAT.
IT STRIKES ME THAT YOU REACTED AS ONE WHO HAS.
"COME ABOARD, SIR."

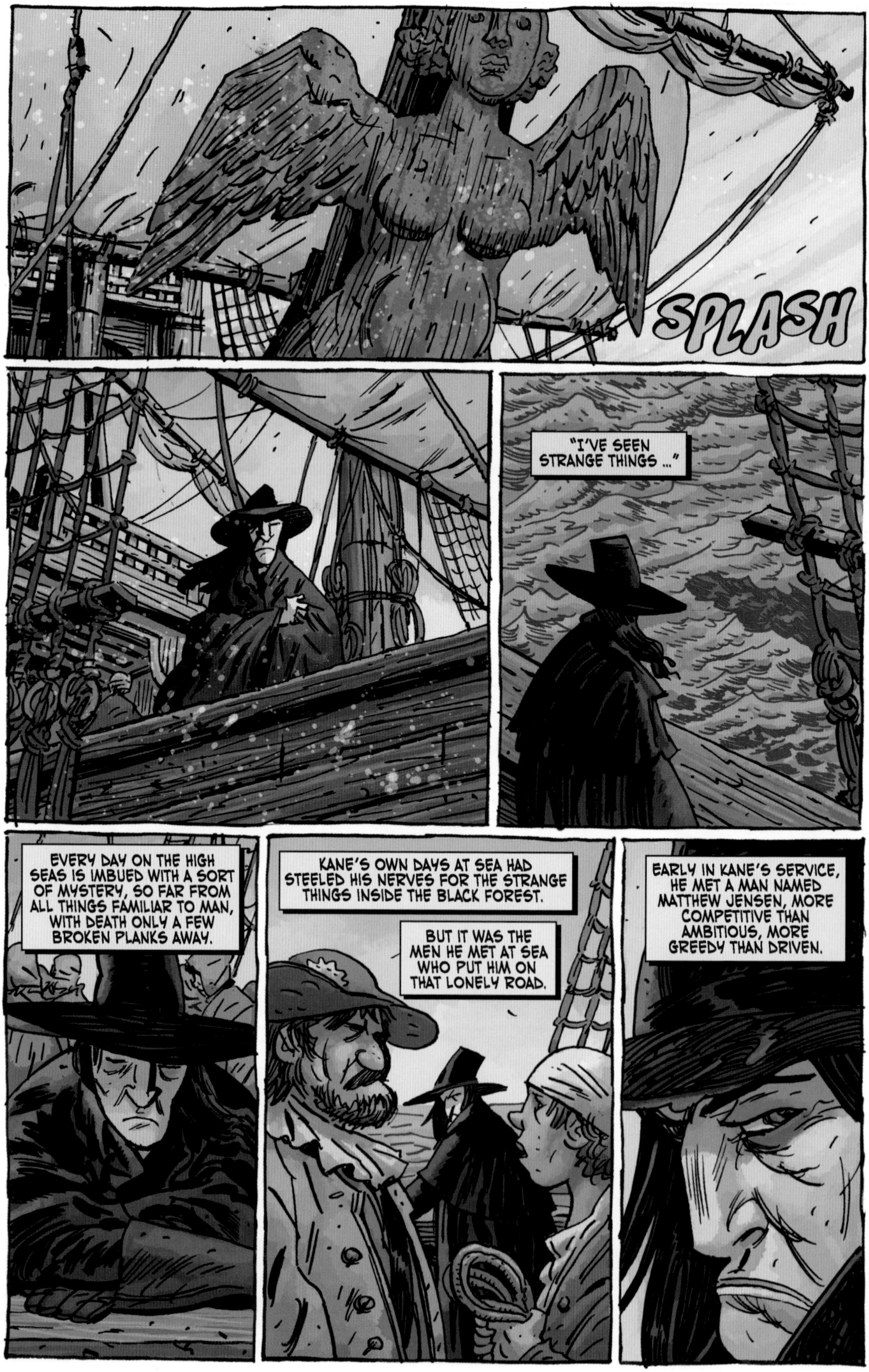
SPLASH
"I'VE SEEN STRANGE THINGS ..."
EVERY DAY ON THE HIGH SEAS IS IMBUED WITH A SORT OF MYSTERY, SO FAR FROM ALL THINGS FAMILIAR TO MAN, WITH DEATH ONLY A FEW BROKEN PLANKS AWAY.
KANE'S OWN DAYS AT SEA HAD STEELED HIS NERVES FOR THE STRANGE THINGS INSIDE THE BLACK FOREST.
BUT IT WAS THE MEN HE MET AT SEA WHO PUT HIM ON THAT LONELY ROAD.
EARLY IN KANE'S SERVICE, HE MET A MAN NAMED MATTHEW JENSEN, MORE COMPETITIVE THAN AMBITIOUS, MORE GREEDY THAN DRIVEN.

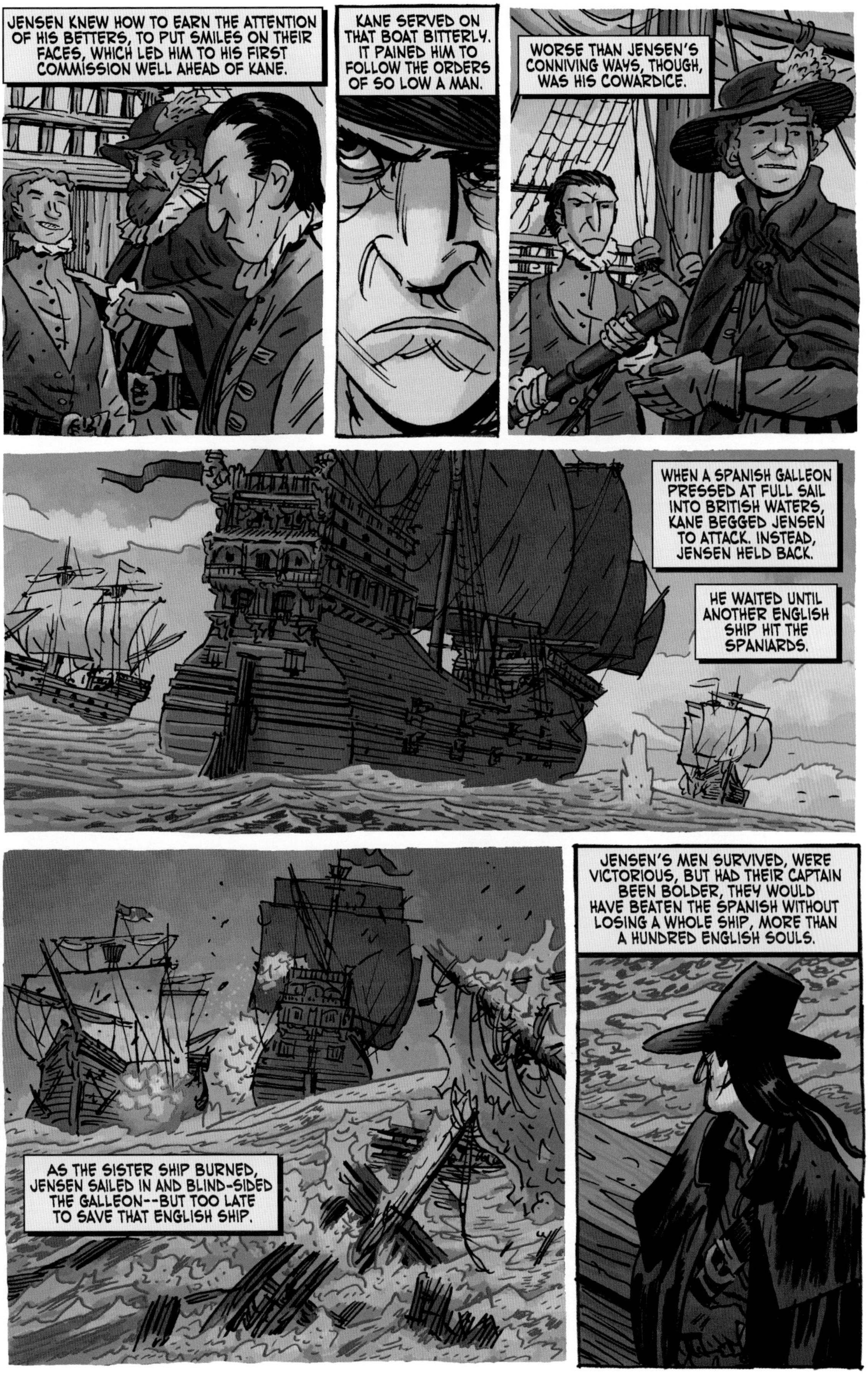
JENSEN KNEW HOW TO EARN THE ATTENTION OF HIS BETTERS, TO PUT SMILES ON THEIR FACES, WHICH LED HIM TO HIS FIRST COMMISSION WELL AHEAD OF KANE.
KANE SERVED ON THAT BOAT BITTERLY. IT PAINED HIM TO FOLLOW THE ORDERS OF SO LOW A MAN.
WORSE THAN JENSEN'S CONNIVING WAYS, THOUGH, WAS HIS COWARDICE.
WHEN A SPANISH GALLEON PRESSED AT FULL SAIL INTO BRITISH WATERS, KANE BEGGED JENSEN TO ATTACK. INSTEAD, JENSEN HELD BACK.
HE WAITED UNTIL ANOTHER ENGLISH SHIP HIT THE SPANIARDS.
AS THE SISTER SHIP BURNED, JENSEN SAILED IN AND BLIND-SIDED THE GALLEON--BUT TOO LATE TO SAVE THAT ENGLISH SHIP.
JENSEN'S MEN SURVIVED, WERE VICTORIOUS, BUT HAD THEIR CAPTAIN BEEN BOLDER, THEY WOULD HAVE BEATEN THE SPANISH WITHOUT LOSING A WHOLE SHIP, MORE THAN A HUNDRED ENGLISH SOULS.

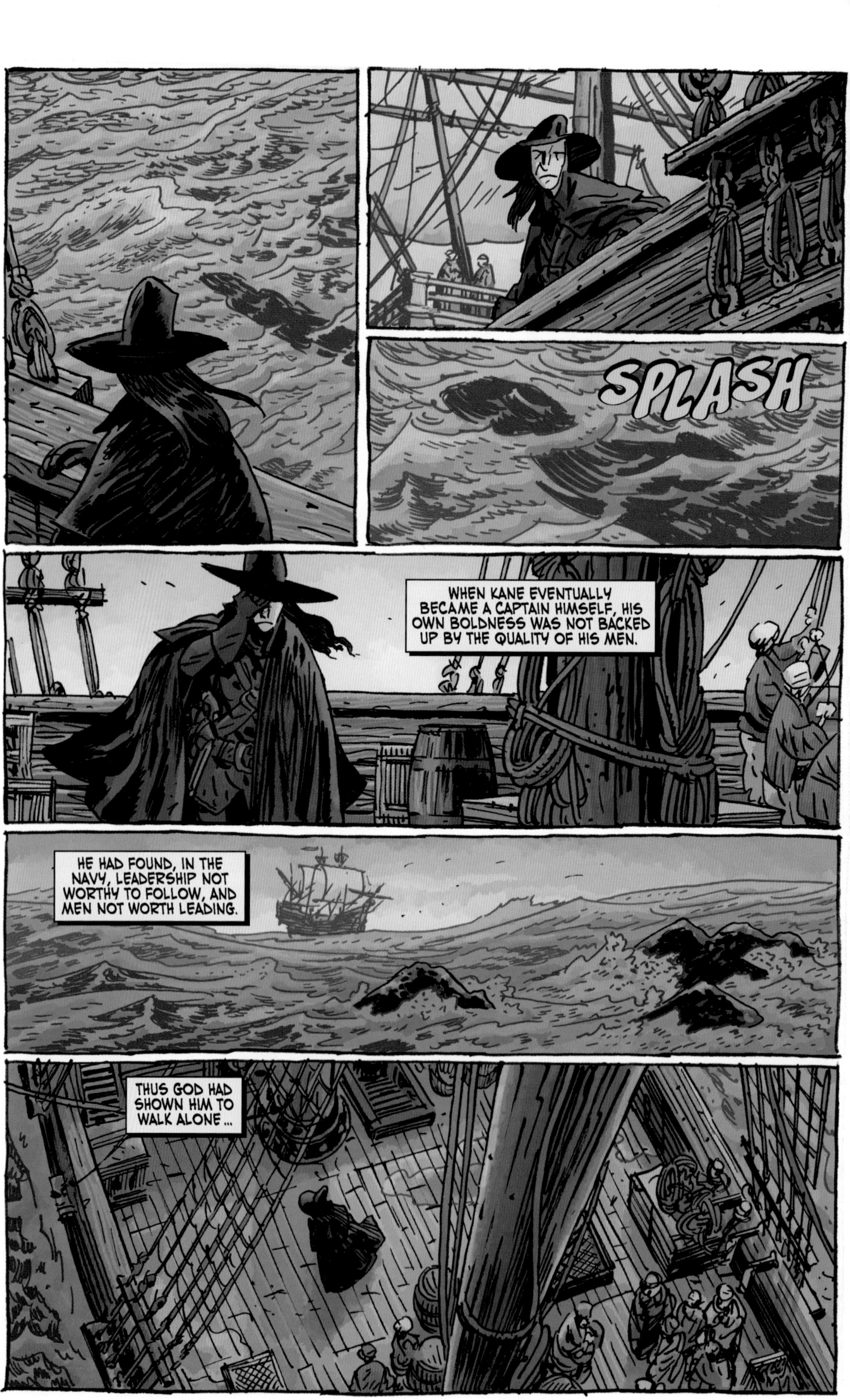
SPLASH
WHEN KANE EVENTUALLY BECAME A CAPTAIN HIMSELF, HIS OWN BOLDNESS WAS NOT BACKED UP BY THE QUALITY OF HIS MEN.
HE HAD FOUND, IN THE NAVY, LEADERSHIP NOT WORTHY TO FOLLOW, AND MEN NOT WORTH LEADING.
THUS GOD HAD SHOWN HIM TO WALK ALONE...

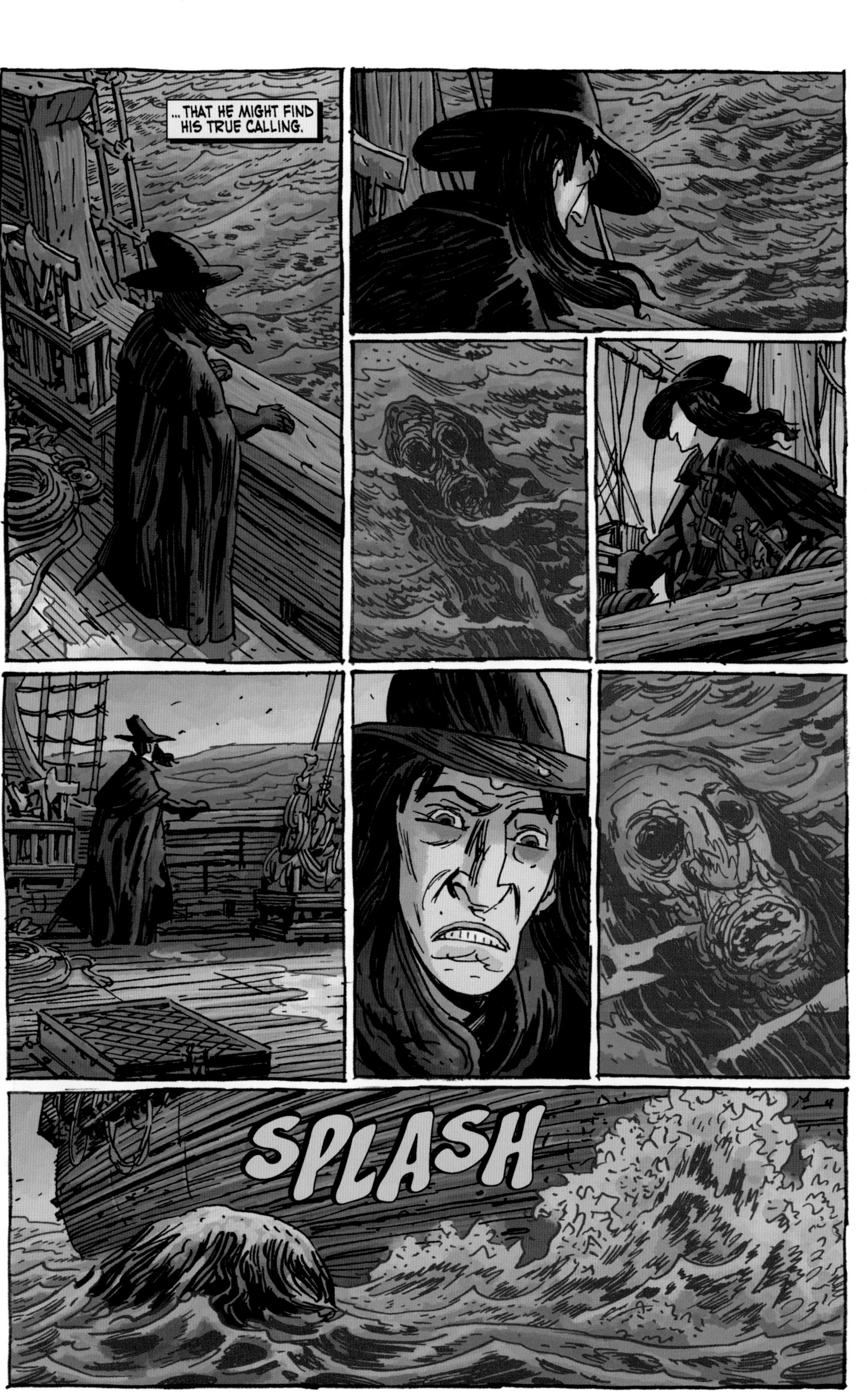
...THAT HE MIGHT FIND HIS TRUE CALLING.
SPLASH

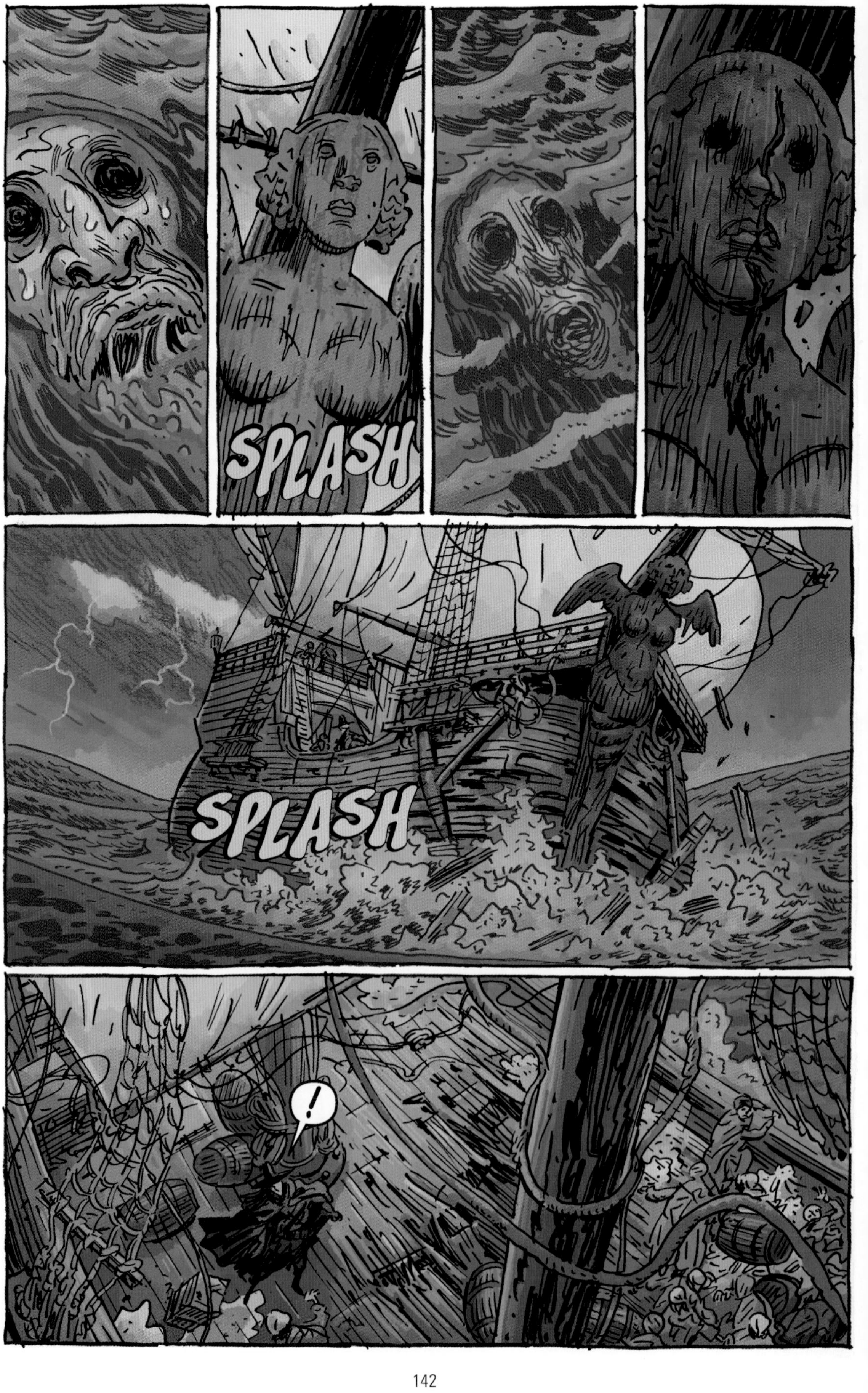
SPLASH
SPLASH
!

--BUT THE WIND CAME FROM WITHIN.

THE BOAT BEGAN TO COME APART AS IF BY SOME TERRIBLE WIND--

SPLASH

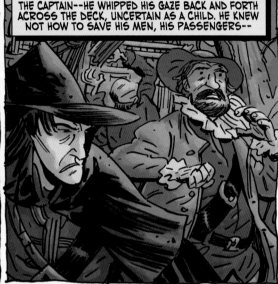

THE CAPTAIN--HE WHIPPED HIS GAZE BACK AND FORTH ACROSS THE DECK, UNCERTAIN AS A CHILD. HE KNEW NOT HOW TO SAVE HIS MEN, HIS PASSENGERS--

--NO IDEA AT ALL--TERROR ONLY. THOUGH EVEN KANE HAD TO ADMIT--

SPLASH

SPLASH

--THE SITUATION WAS DISMAL.

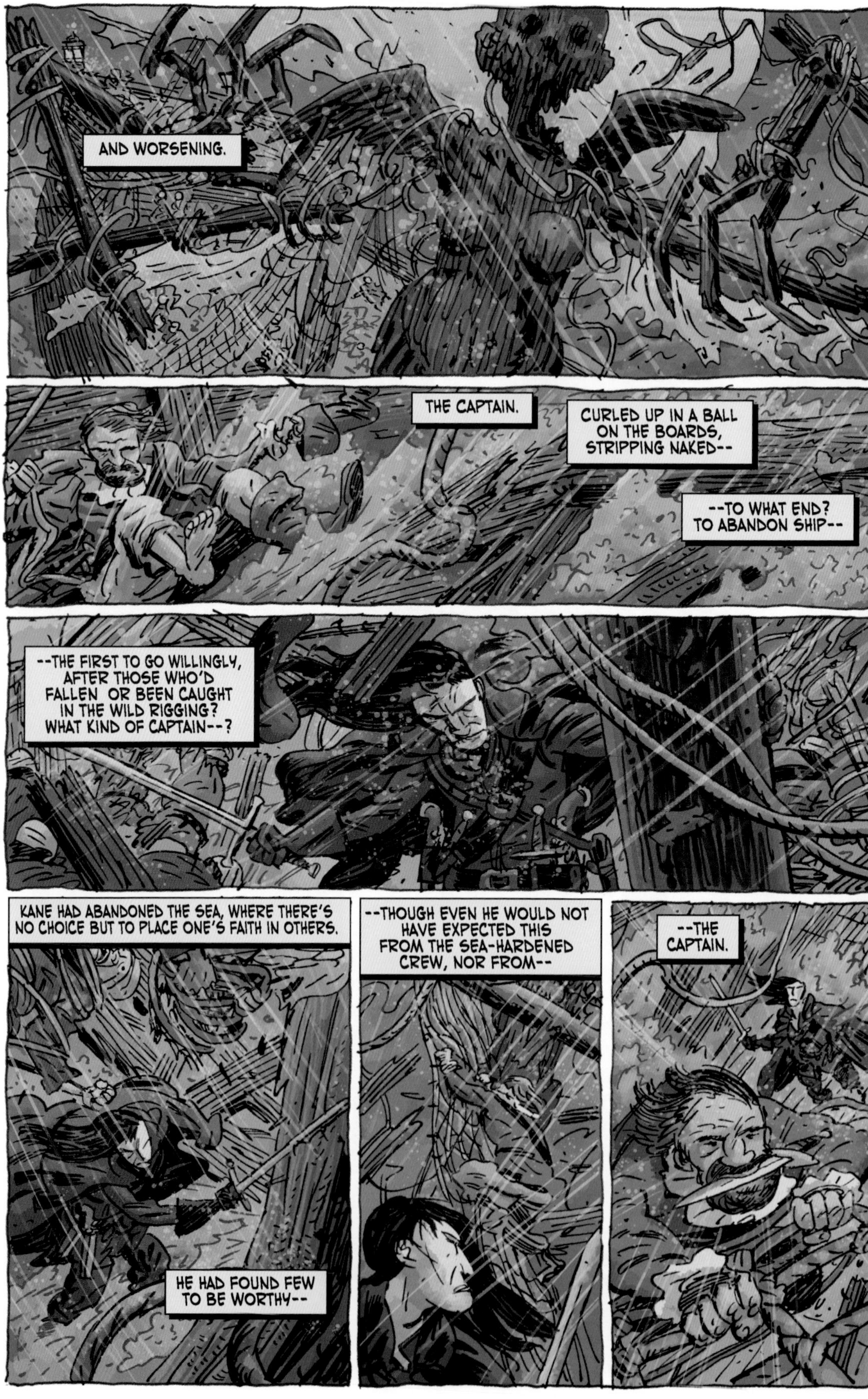
AND WORSENING.
THE CAPTAIN.
CURLED UP IN A BALL ON THE BOARDS, STRIPPING NAKED--
--TO WHAT END? TO ABANDON SHIP--
--THE FIRST TO GO WILLINGLY, AFTER THOSE WHO'D FALLEN OR BEEN CAUGHT IN THE WILD RIGGING? WHAT KIND OF CAPTAIN--?
KANE HAD ABANDONED THE SEA, WHERE THERE'S NO CHOICE BUT TO PLACE ONE'S FAITH IN OTHERS.
HE HAD FOUND FEW TO BE WORTHY--
--THOUGH EVEN HE WOULD NOT HAVE EXPECTED THIS FROM THE SEA-HARDENED CREW, NOR FROM--
--THE CAPTAIN.

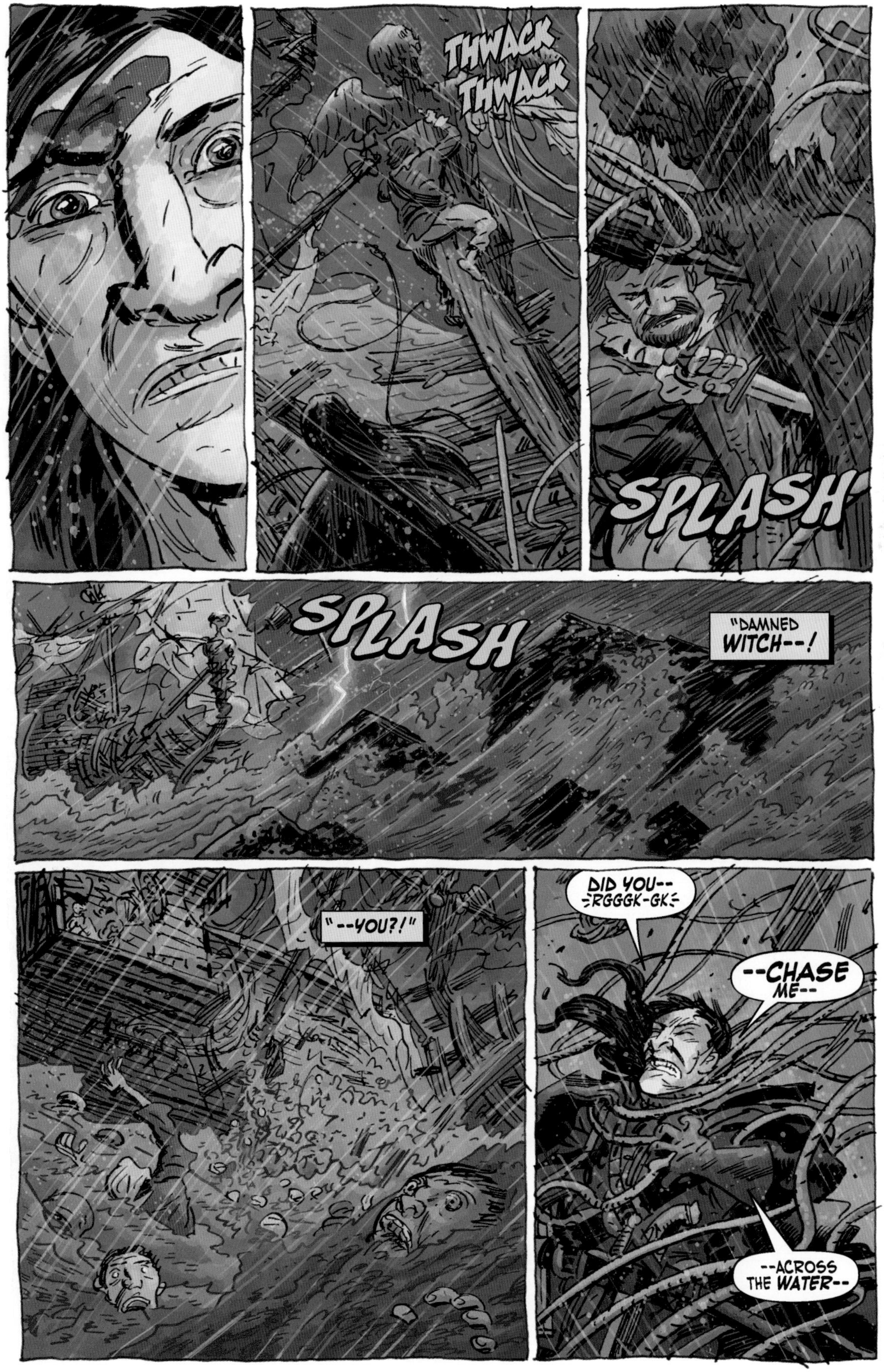
THWACK
THWACK
SPLASH
SPLASH
"DAMNED WITCH--!
"--YOU?!"
DID YOU-- -RGGGK-GK-
--CHASE ME--
--ACROSS THE WATER--

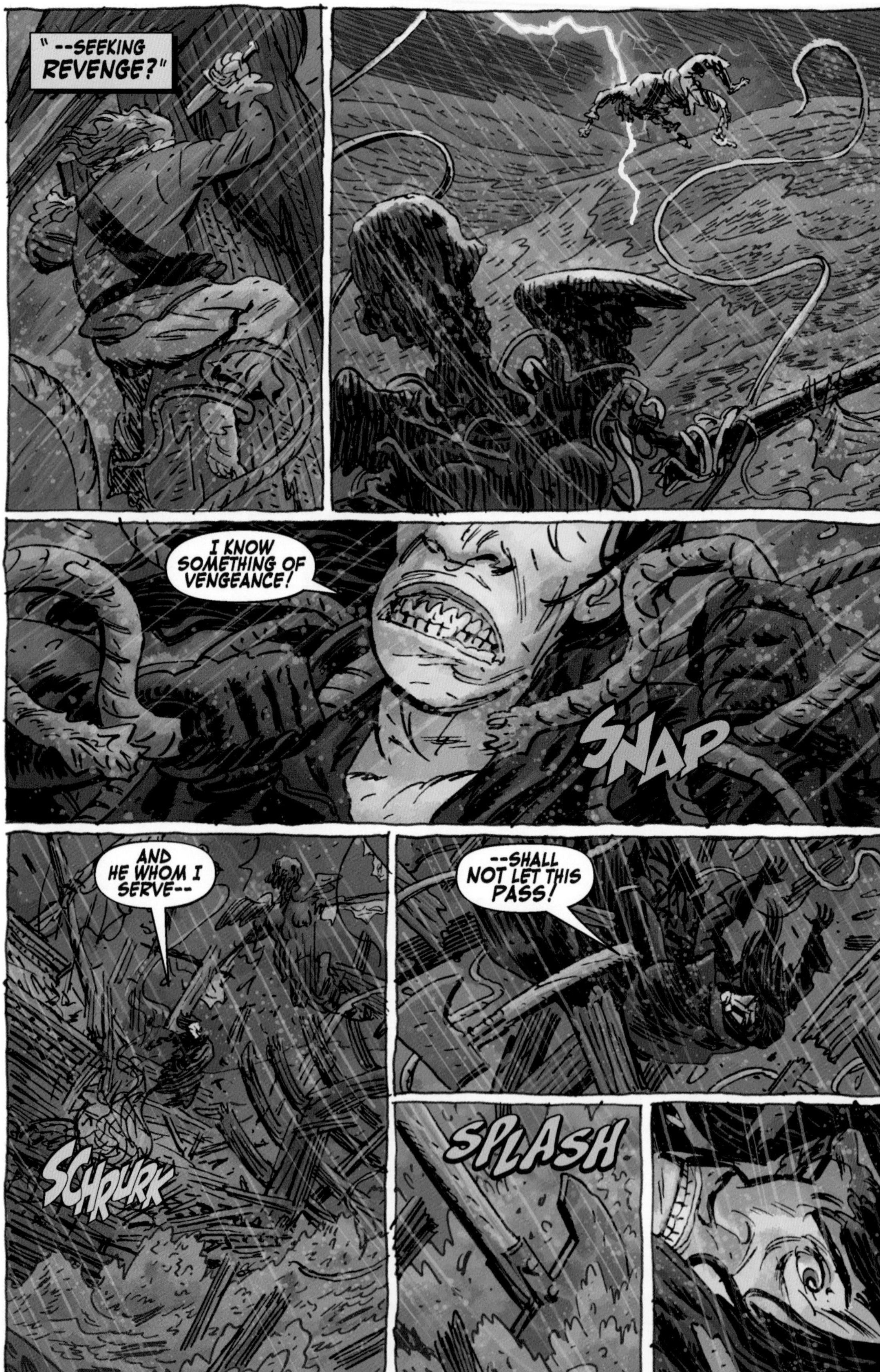
"--SEEKING REVENGE?"
I KNOW SOMETHING OF VENGEANCE!
SNAP
AND HE WHOM I SERVE--
SCHRURK
--SHALL NOT LET THIS PASS!
SPLASH

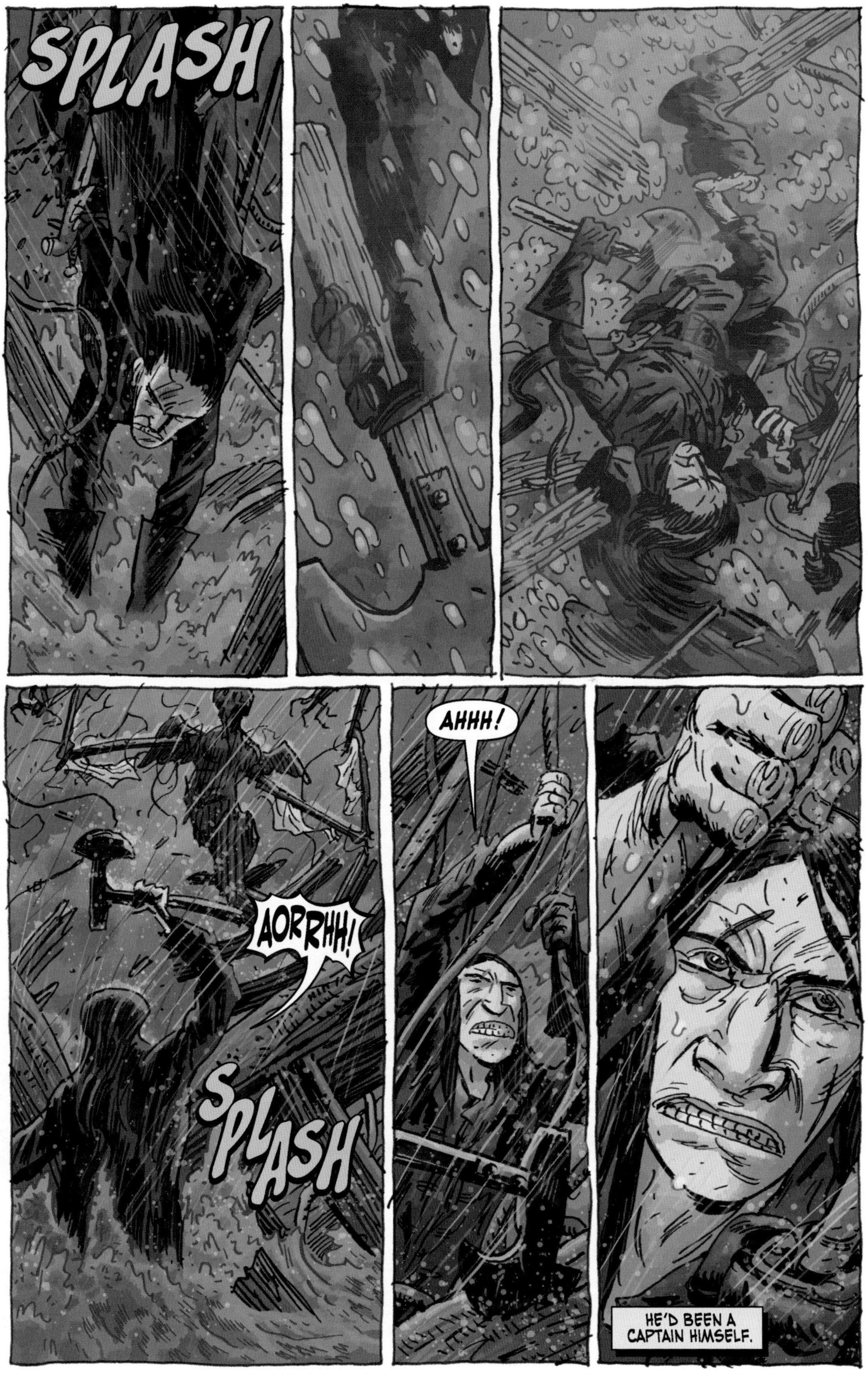
SPLASH
AORRHH!
SPLASH
AHHH!
HE'D BEEN A CAPTAIN HIMSELF.

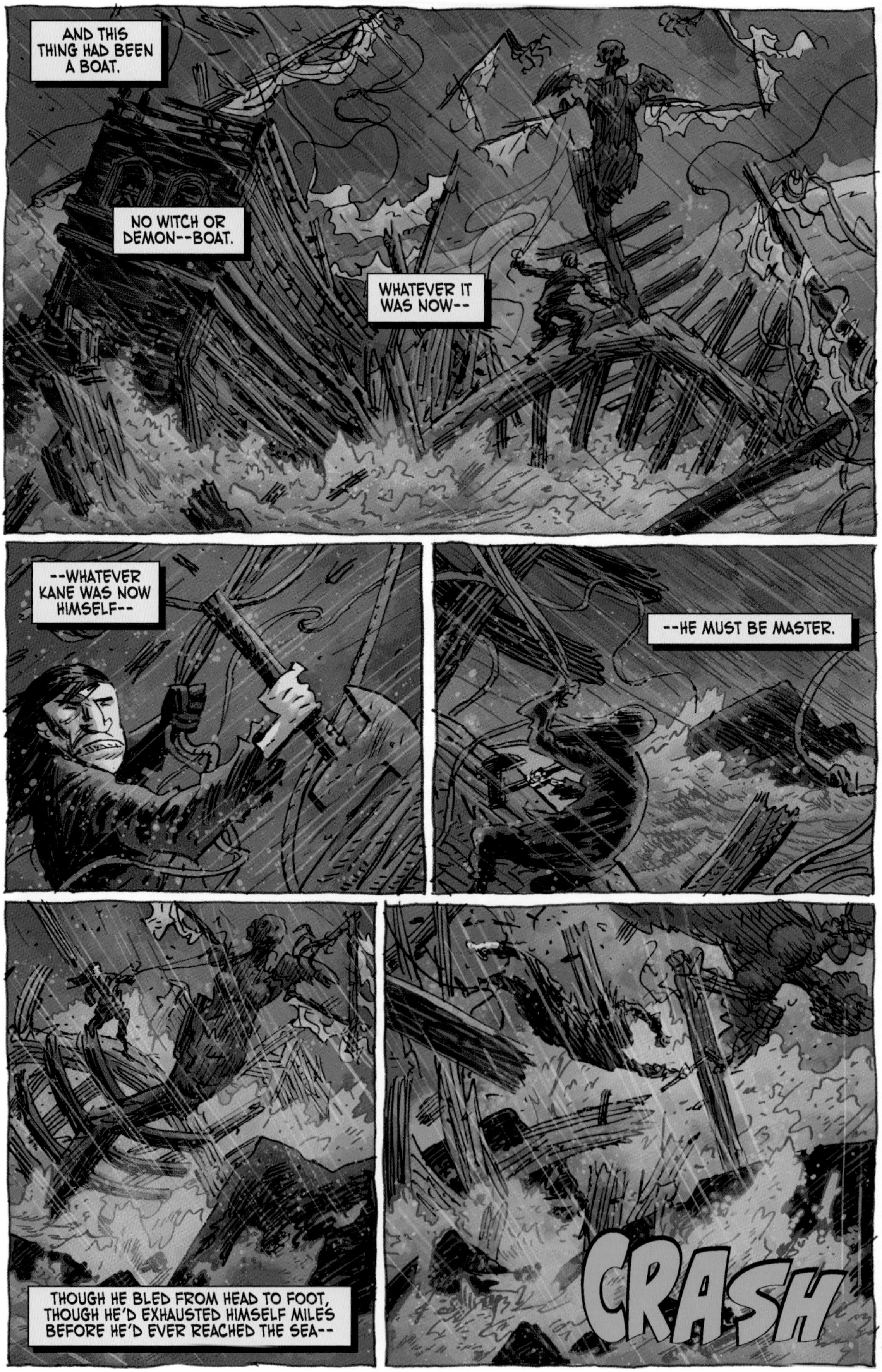
AND THIS THING HAD BEEN A BOAT.
NO WITCH OR DEMON--BOAT.
WHATEVER IT WAS NOW--
--WHATEVER KANE WAS NOW HIMSELF--
--HE MUST BE MASTER.
THOUGH HE BLED FROM HEAD TO FOOT, THOUGH HE'D EXHAUSTED HIMSELF MILES BEFORE HE'D EVER REACHED THE SEA--
CRASH

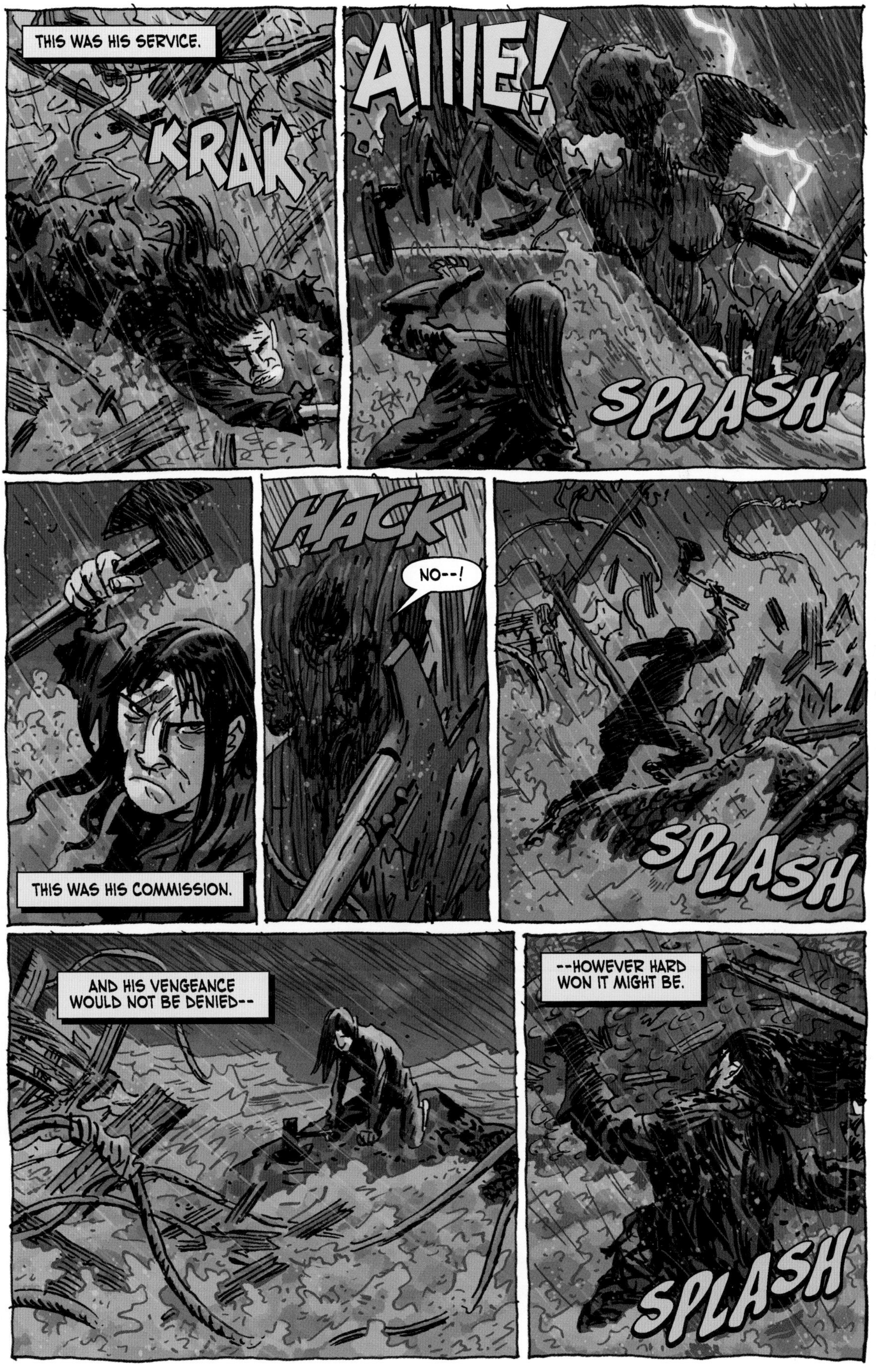
THIS WAS HIS SERVICE.
KRAK
AIIIE!
SPLASH
HACK
NO--!
THIS WAS HIS COMMISSION.
SPLASH
AND HIS VENGEANCE WOULD NOT BE DENIED--
--HOWEVER HARD WON IT MIGHT BE.
SPLASH

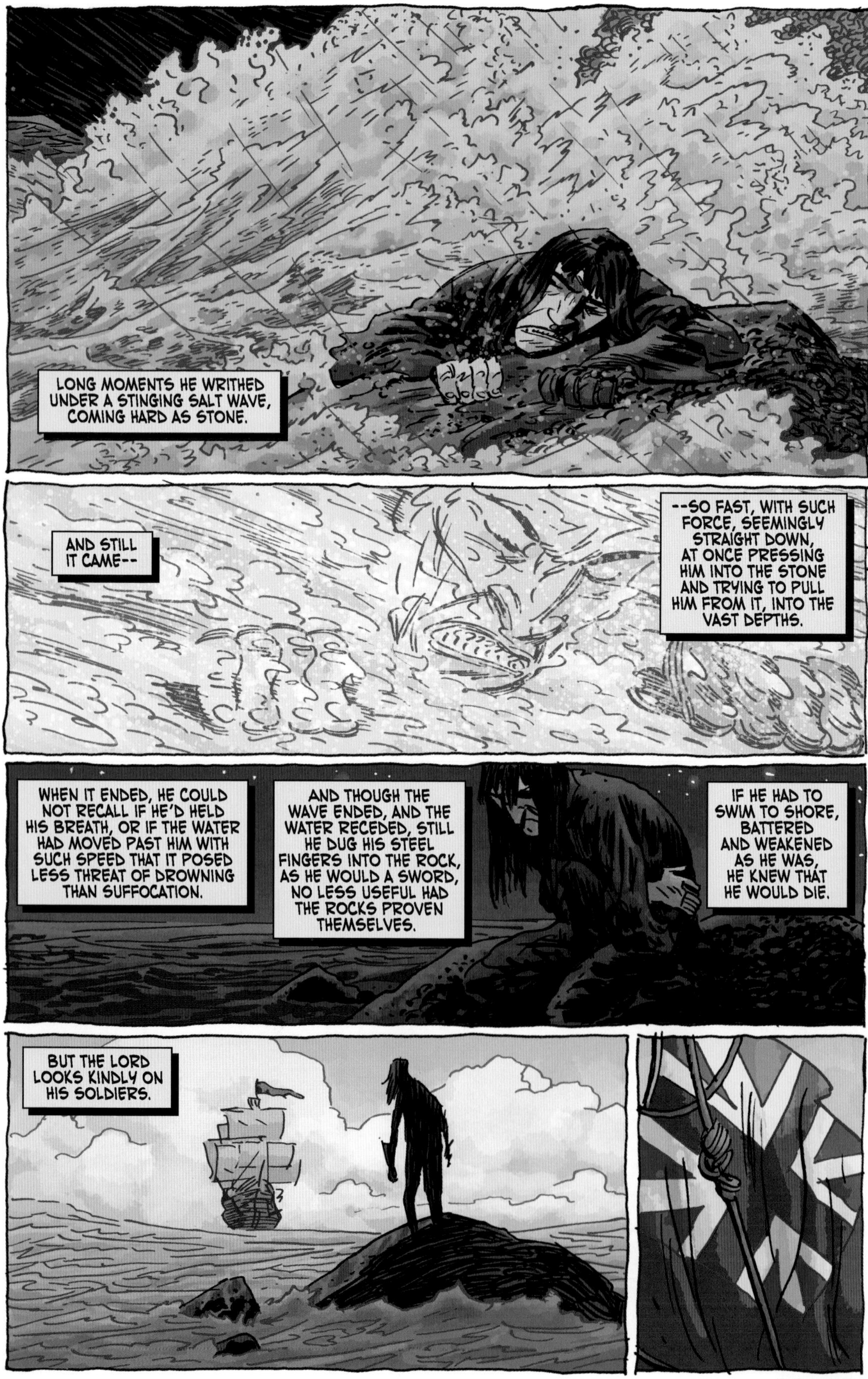
LONG MOMENTS HE WRITHED UNDER A STINGING SALT WAVE, COMING HARD AS STONE.
AND STILL IT CAME--
--SO FAST, WITH SUCH FORCE, SEEMINGLY STRAIGHT DOWN, AT ONCE PRESSING HIM INTO THE STONE AND TRYING TO PULL HIM FROM IT, INTO THE VAST DEPTHS.
WHEN IT ENDED, HE COULD NOT RECALL IF HE'D HELD HIS BREATH, OR IF THE WATER HAD MOVED PAST HIM WITH SUCH SPEED THAT IT POSED LESS THREAT OF DROWNING THAN SUFFOCATION.
AND THOUGH THE WAVE ENDED, AND THE WATER RECEDED, STILL HE DUG HIS STEEL FINGERS INTO THE ROCK, AS HE WOULD A SWORD, NO LESS USEFUL HAD THE ROCKS PROVEN THEMSELVES.
IF HE HAD TO SWIM TO SHORE, BATTERED AND WEAKENED AS HE WAS, HE KNEW THAT HE WOULD DIE.
BUT THE LORD LOOKS KINDLY ON HIS SOLDIERS.

THE END

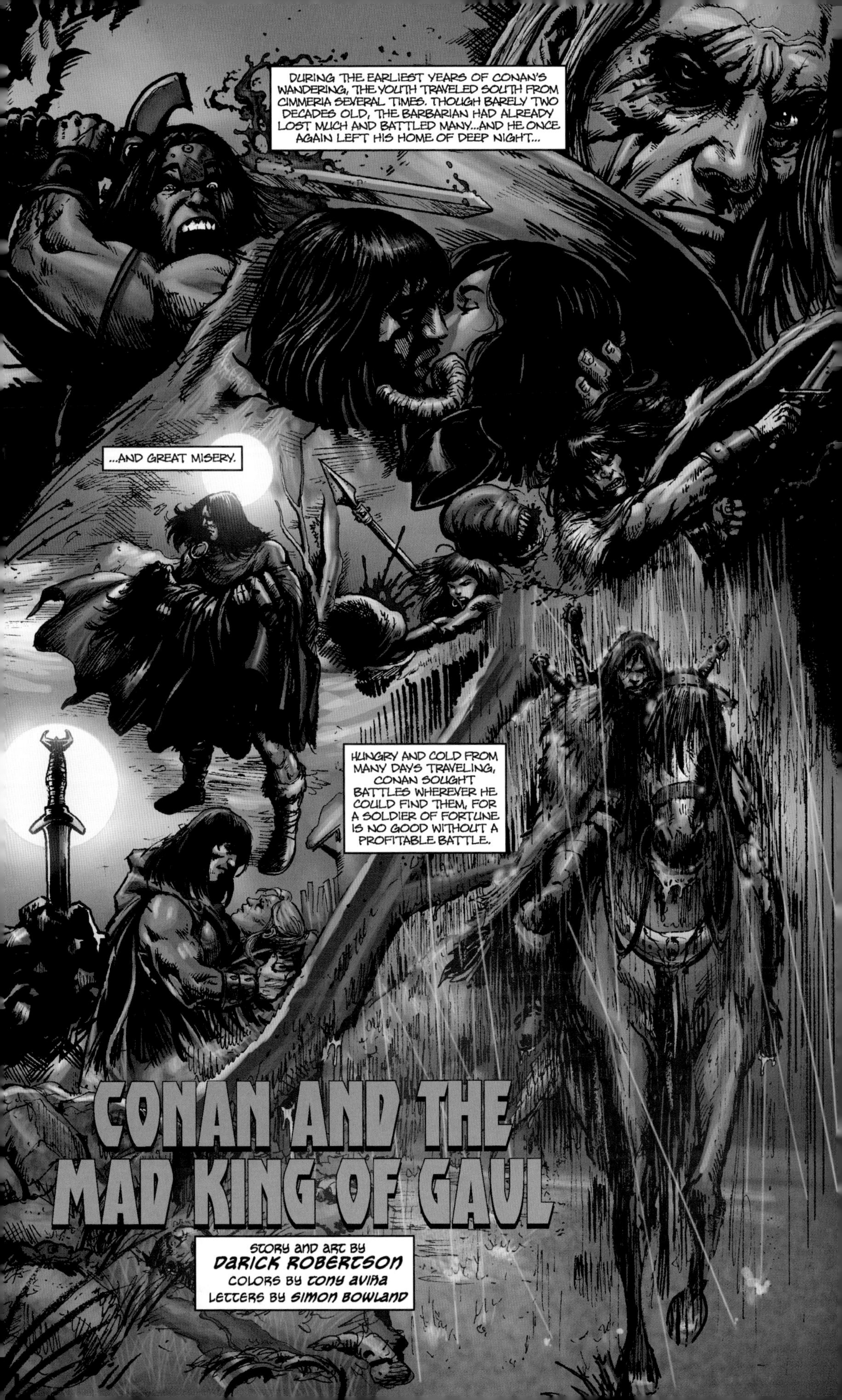
DURING THE EARLIEST YEARS OF CONAN'S WANDERING, THE YOUTH TRAVELED SOUTH FROM CIMMERIA SEVERAL TIMES. THOUGH BARELY TWO DECADES OLD, THE BARBARIAN HAD ALREADY LOST MUCH AND BATTLED MANY...AND HE ONCE AGAIN LEFT HIS HOME OF DEEP NIGHT...
...AND GREAT MISERY.
HUNGRY AND COLD FROM MANY DAYS TRAVELING, CONAN SOUGHT BATTLES WHEREVER HE COULD FIND THEM, FOR A SOLDIER OF FORTUNE IS NO GOOD WITHOUT A PROFITABLE BATTLE.
CONAN AND THE MAD KING OF GAUL
STORY AND ART BY DARICK ROBERTSON
COLORS BY TONY AVIÑA
LETTERS BY SIMON BOWLAND

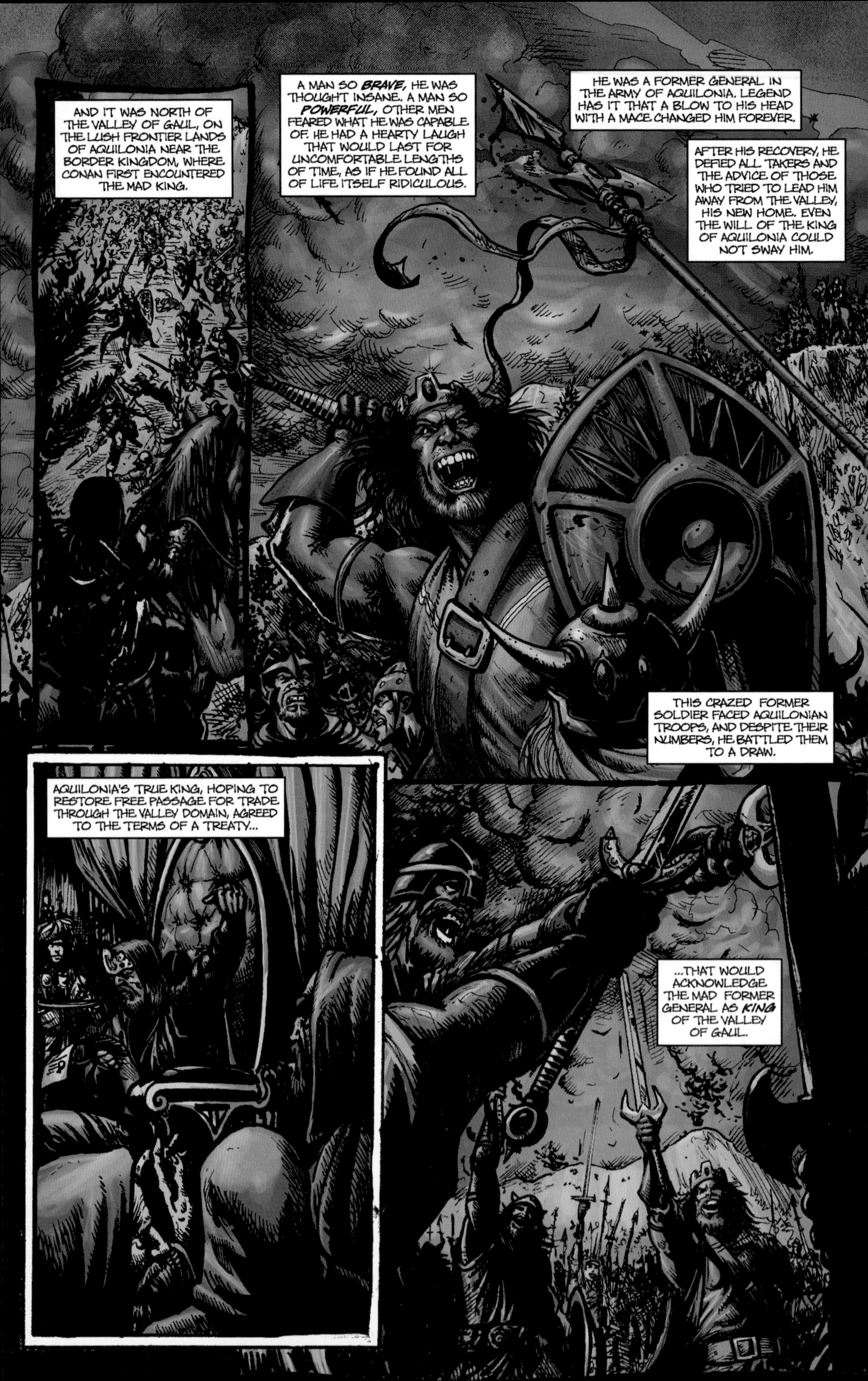
AND IT WAS NORTH OF THE VALLEY OF GAUL, ON THE LUSH FRONTIER LANDS OF AQUILONIA NEAR THE BORDER KINGDOM, WHERE CONAN FIRST ENCOUNTERED THE MAD KING.
A MAN SO BRAVE, HE WAS THOUGHT INSANE. A MAN SO POWERFUL, OTHER MEN FEARED WHAT HE WAS CAPABLE OF. HE HAD A HEARTY LAUGH THAT WOULD LAST FOR UNCOMFORTABLE LENGTHS OF TIME, AS IF HE FOUND ALL OF LIFE ITSELF RIDICULOUS.
HE WAS A FORMER GENERAL IN THE ARMY OF AQUILONIA. LEGEND HAS IT THAT A BLOW TO HIS HEAD WITH A MACE CHANGED HIM FOREVER.
AFTER HIS RECOVERY, HE DEFIED ALL TAKERS AND THE ADVICE OF THOSE WHO TRIED TO LEAD HIM AWAY FROM THE VALLEY, HIS NEW HOME. EVEN THE WILL OF THE KING OF AQUILONIA COULD NOT SWAY HIM.
THIS CRAZED FORMER SOLDIER FACED AQUILONIAN TROOPS, AND DESPITE THEIR NUMBERS, HE BATTLED THEM TO A DRAW.
AQUILONIA'S TRUE KING, HOPING TO RESTORE FREE PASSAGE FOR TRADE THROUGH THE VALLEY DOMAIN, AGREED TO THE TERMS OF A TREATY...
...THAT WOULD ACKNOWLEDGE THE MAD FORMER GENERAL AS KING OF THE VALLEY OF GAUL.

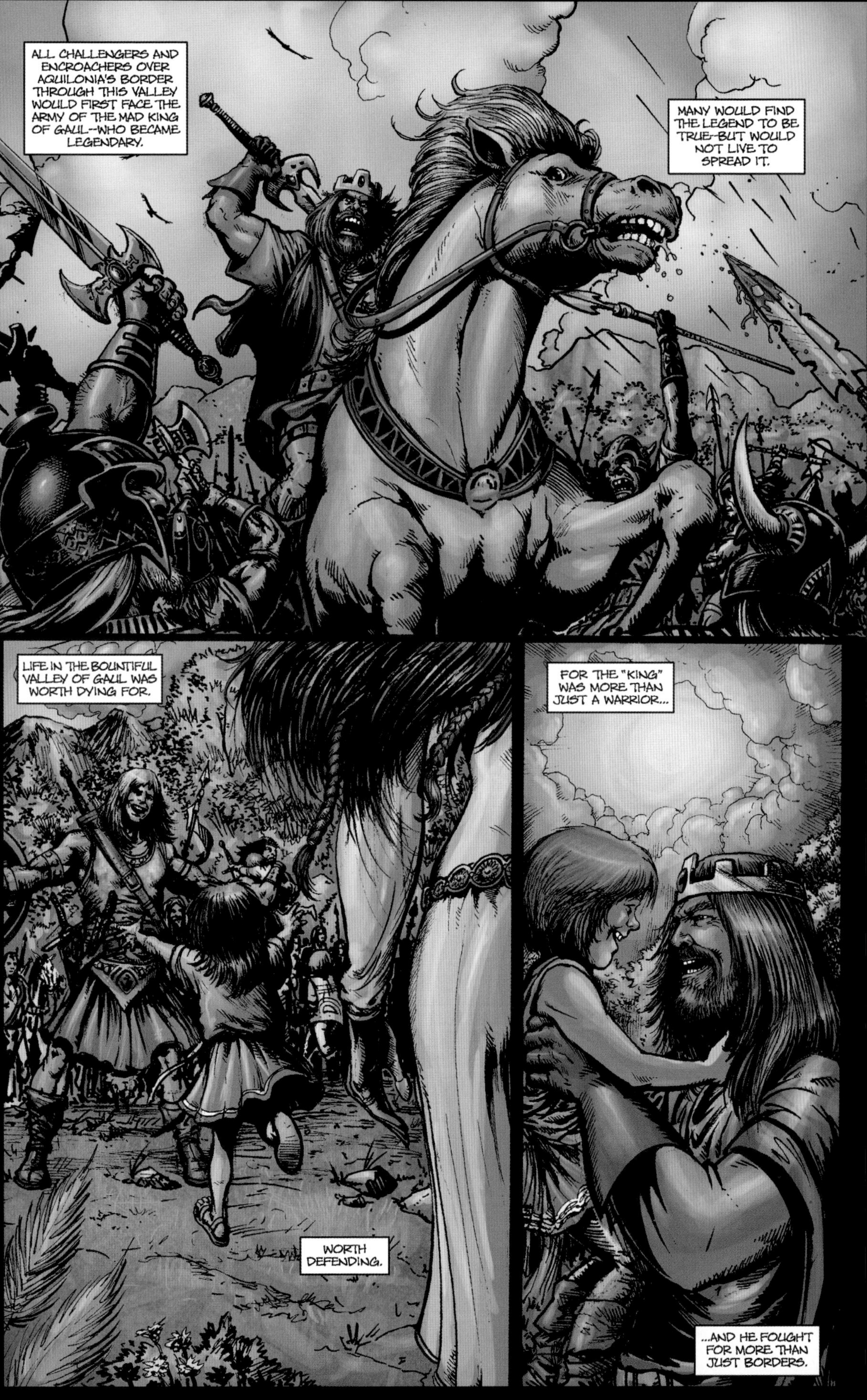
ALL CHALLENGERS AND ENCROACHERS OVER AQUILONIA'S BORDER THROUGH THIS VALLEY WOULD FIRST FACE THE ARMY OF THE MAD KING OF GAUL--WHO BECAME LEGENDARY.
MANY WOULD FIND THE LEGEND TO BE TRUE--BUT WOULD NOT LIVE TO SPREAD IT.
LIFE IN THE BOUNTIFUL VALLEY OF GAUL WAS WORTH DYING FOR.
WORTH DEFENDING.
FOR THE "KING" WAS MORE THAN JUST A WARRIOR...
...AND HE FOUGHT FOR MORE THAN JUST BORDERS.

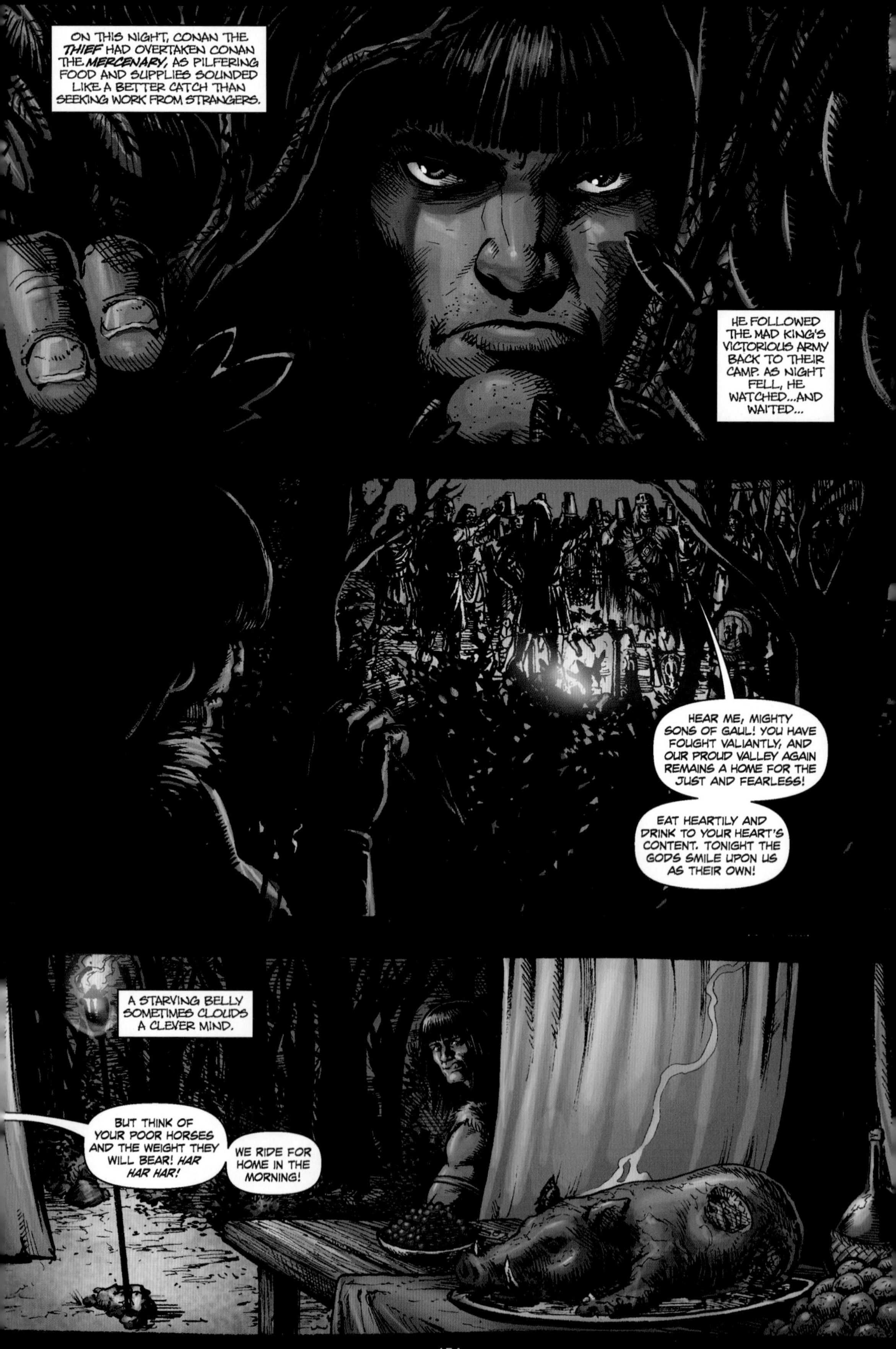
ON THIS NIGHT, CONAN THE *THIEF* HAD OVERTAKEN CONAN THE *MERCENARY,* AS PILFERING FOOD AND SUPPLIES SOUNDED LIKE A BETTER CATCH THAN SEEKING WORK FROM STRANGERS.
HE FOLLOWED THE MAD KING'S VICTORIOUS ARMY BACK TO THEIR CAMP. AS NIGHT FELL, HE WATCHED...AND WAITED...
HEAR ME, MIGHTY SONS OF GAUL! YOU HAVE FOUGHT VALIANTLY, AND OUR PROUD VALLEY AGAIN REMAINS A HOME FOR THE JUST AND FEARLESS!
EAT HEARTILY AND DRINK TO YOUR HEART'S CONTENT. TONIGHT THE GODS SMILE UPON US AS THEIR OWN!
A STARVING BELLY SOMETIMES CLOUDS A CLEVER MIND.
BUT THINK OF YOUR POOR HORSES AND THE WEIGHT THEY WILL BEAR! *HAR HAR HAR!*
WE RIDE FOR HOME IN THE MORNING!

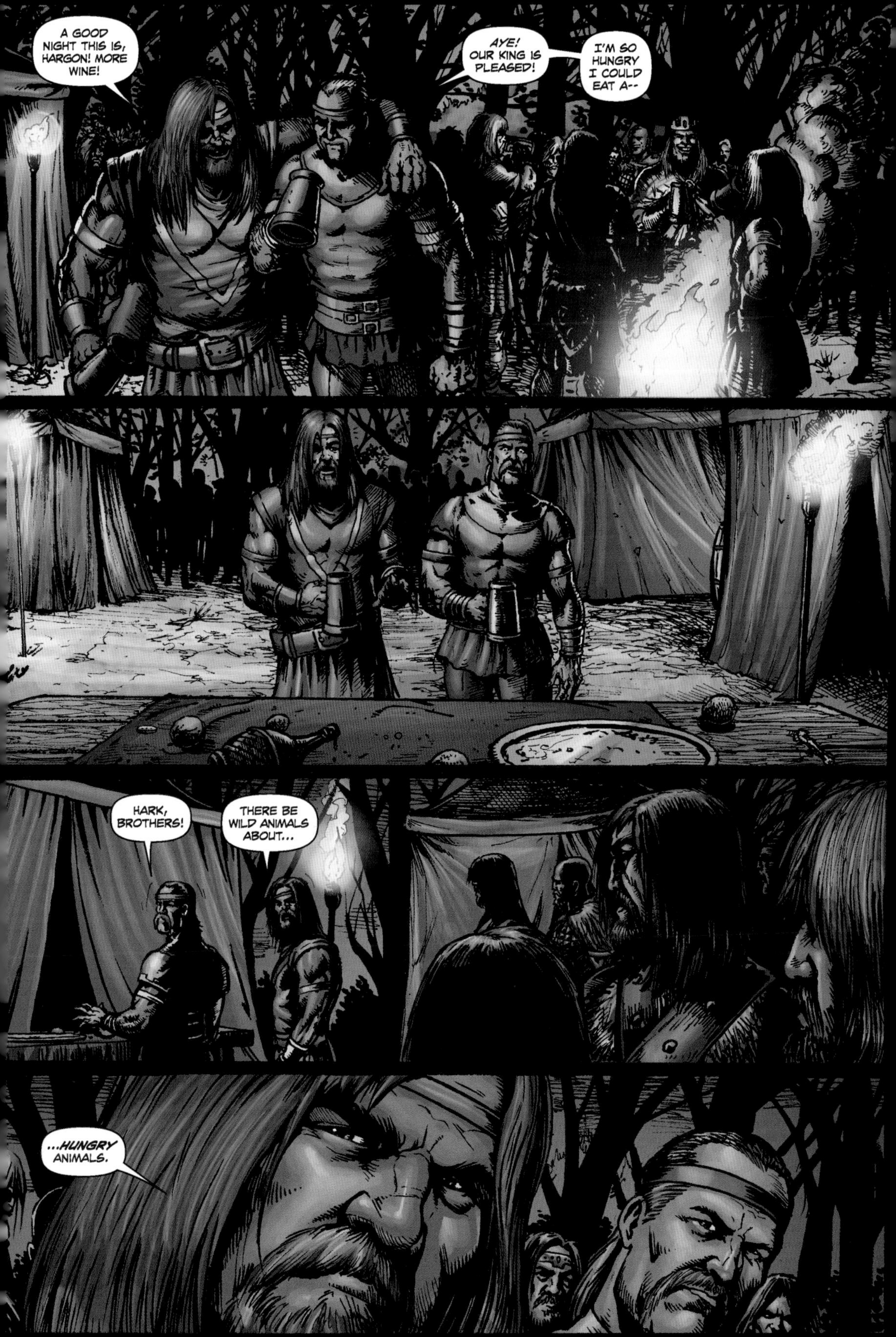
A GOOD NIGHT THIS IS, HARGON! MORE WINE!
AYE! OUR KING IS PLEASED!
I'M SO HUNGRY I COULD EAT A--
HARK, BROTHERS!
THERE BE WILD ANIMALS ABOUT...
...HUNGRY ANIMALS.

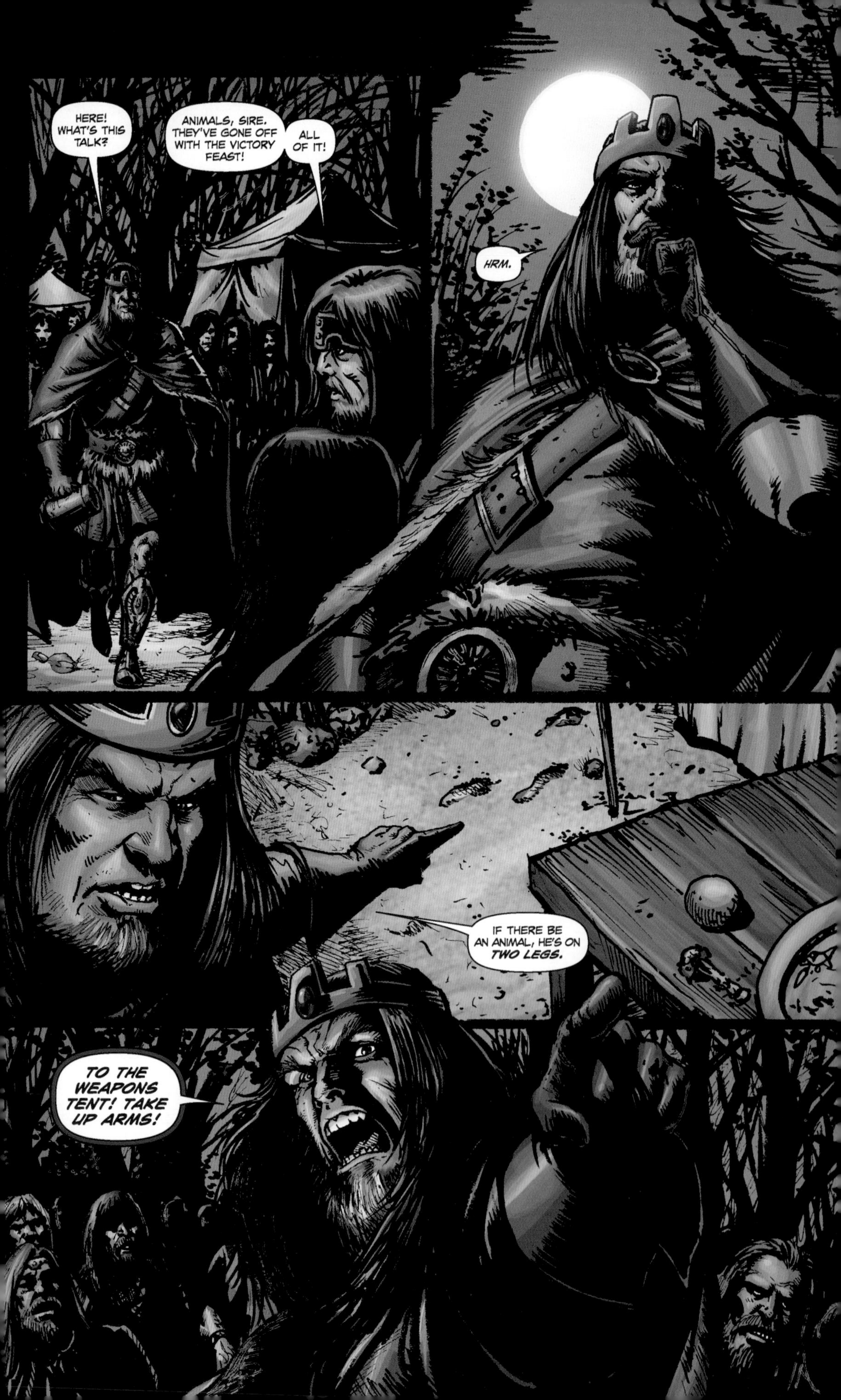
HERE! WHAT'S THIS TALK?
ANIMALS, SIRE. THEY'VE GONE OFF WITH THE VICTORY FEAST!
ALL OF IT!
HRM.
IF THERE BE AN ANIMAL, HE'S ON *TWO LEGS.*
TO THE WEAPONS TENT! TAKE UP ARMS!

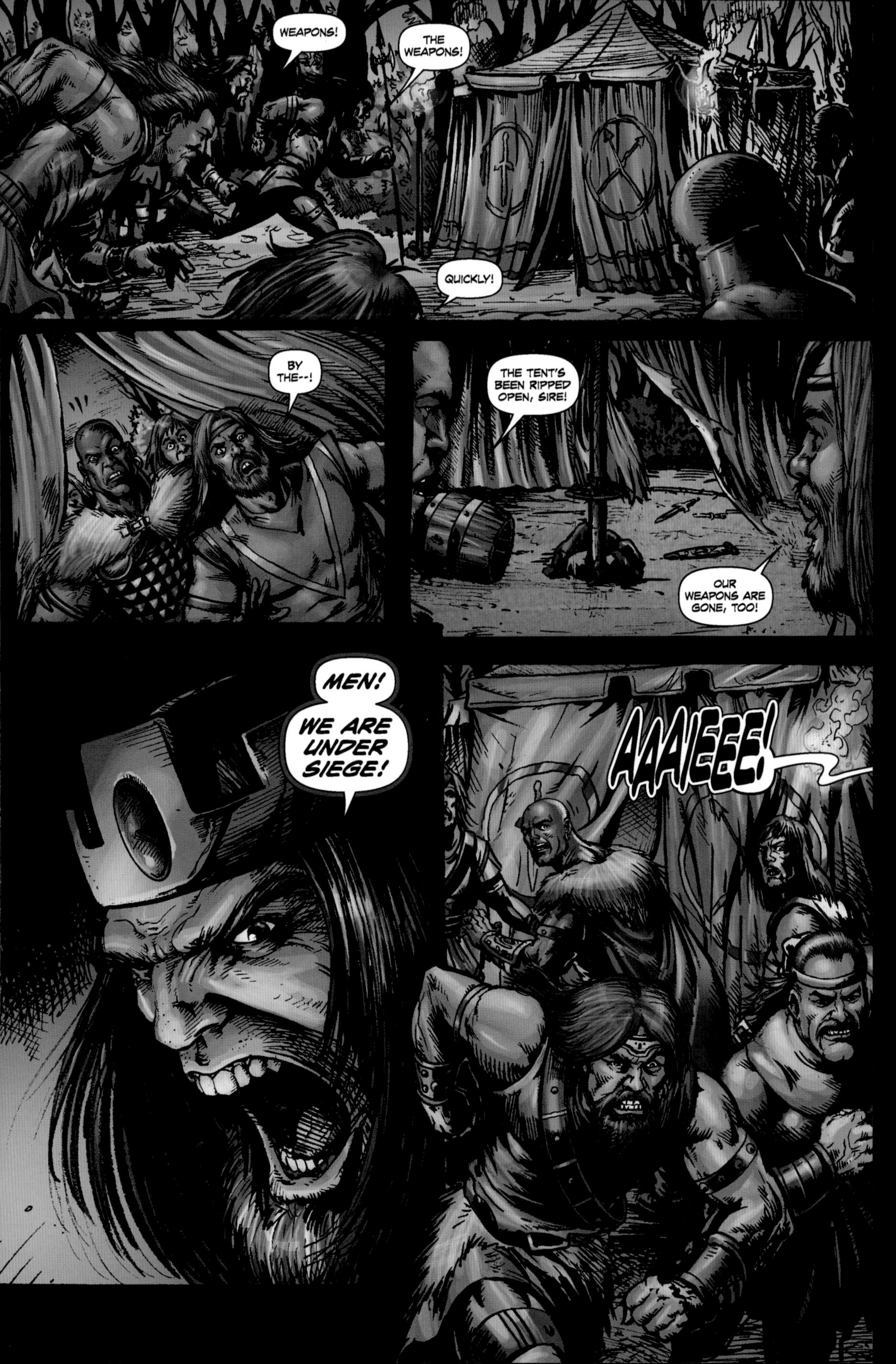
WEAPONS!
THE WEAPONS!
QUICKLY!
BY THE--!
THE TENT'S BEEN RIPPED OPEN, SIRE!
OUR WEAPONS ARE GONE, TOO!
MEN!
WE ARE UNDER SIEGE!
AAAIEEE!

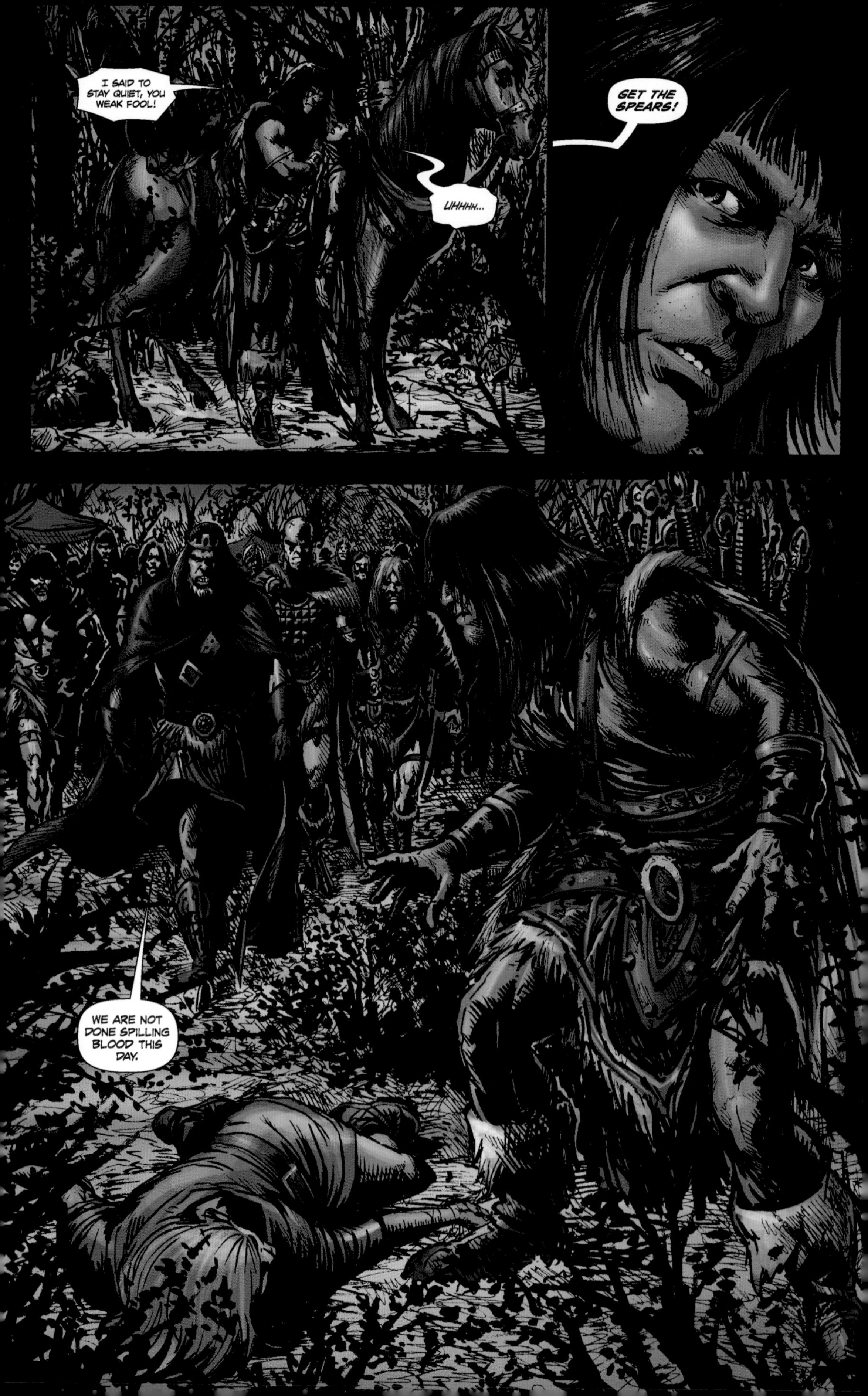
I SAID TO STAY QUIET, YOU WEAK FOOL!
UHHHH...
GET THE SPEARS!
WE ARE NOT DONE SPILLING BLOOD THIS DAY.

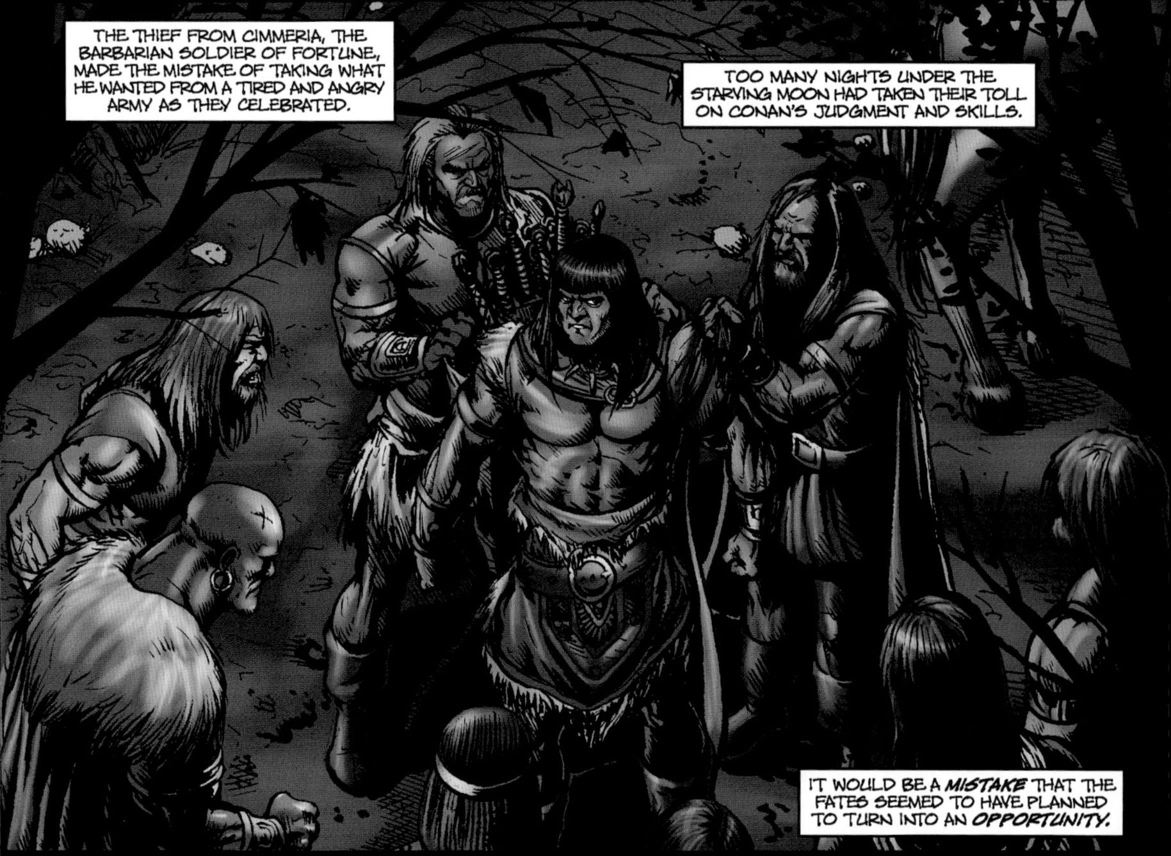
THE THIEF FROM CIMMERIA, THE BARBARIAN SOLDIER OF FORTUNE, MADE THE MISTAKE OF TAKING WHAT HE WANTED FROM A TIRED AND ANGRY ARMY AS THEY CELEBRATED.
TOO MANY NIGHTS UNDER THE STARVING MOON HAD TAKEN THEIR TOLL ON CONAN'S JUDGMENT AND SKILLS.
IT WOULD BE A *MISTAKE* THAT THE FATES SEEMED TO HAVE PLANNED TO TURN INTO AN *OPPORTUNITY.*

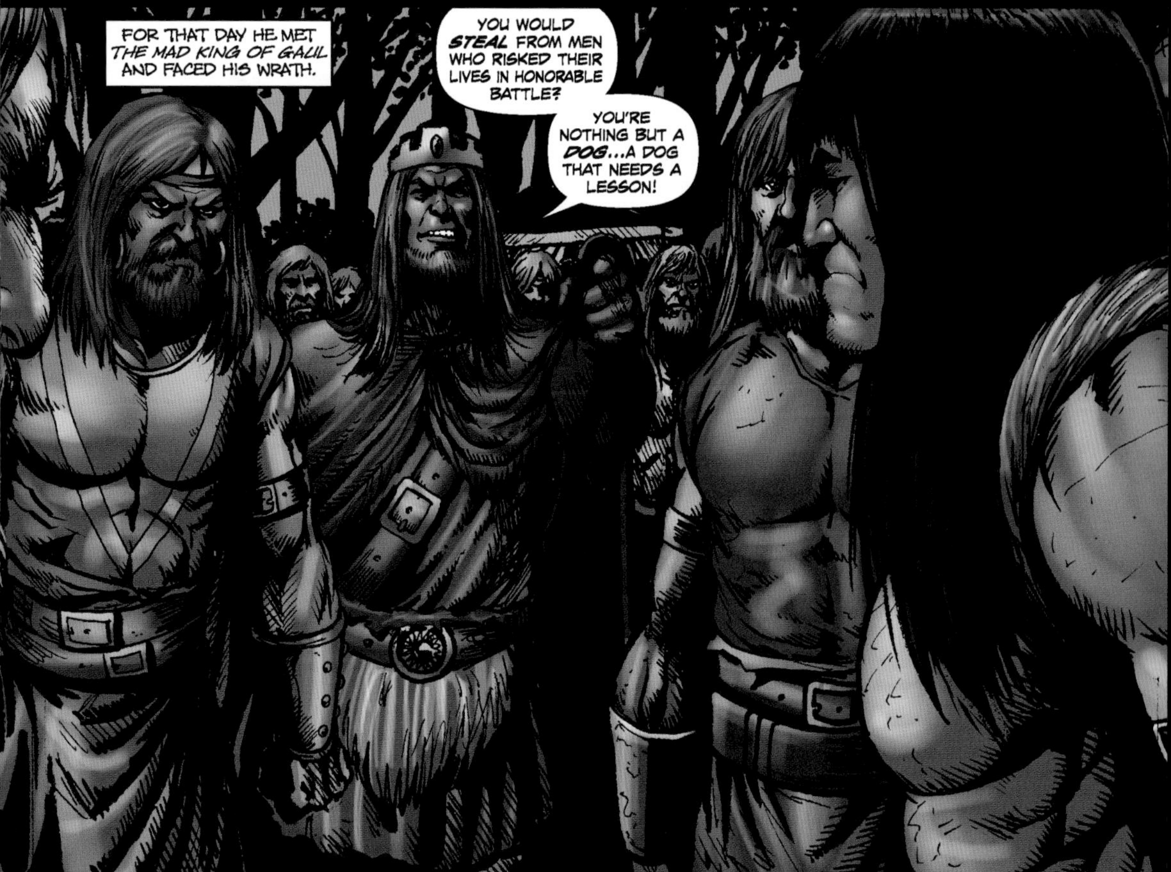
FOR THAT DAY HE MET *THE MAD KING OF GAUL* AND FACED HIS WRATH.
YOU WOULD *STEAL* FROM MEN WHO RISKED THEIR LIVES IN HONORABLE BATTLE?
YOU'RE NOTHING BUT A *DOG*...A DOG THAT NEEDS A LESSON!

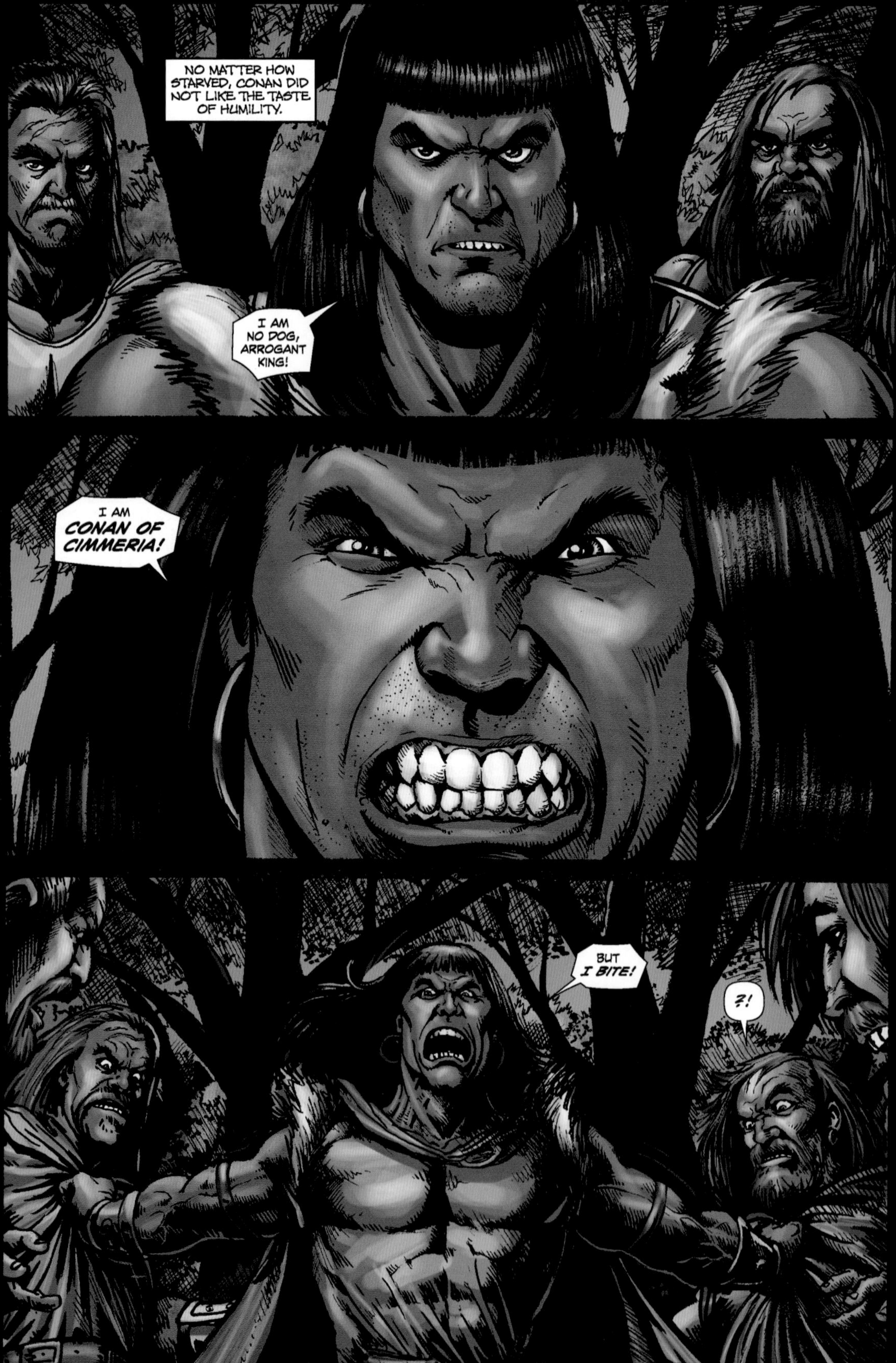
NO MATTER HOW STARVED, CONAN DID NOT LIKE THE TASTE OF HUMILITY.
I AM NO DOG, ARROGANT KING!
I AM *CONAN OF CIMMERIA!*
BUT *I BITE!*
?!

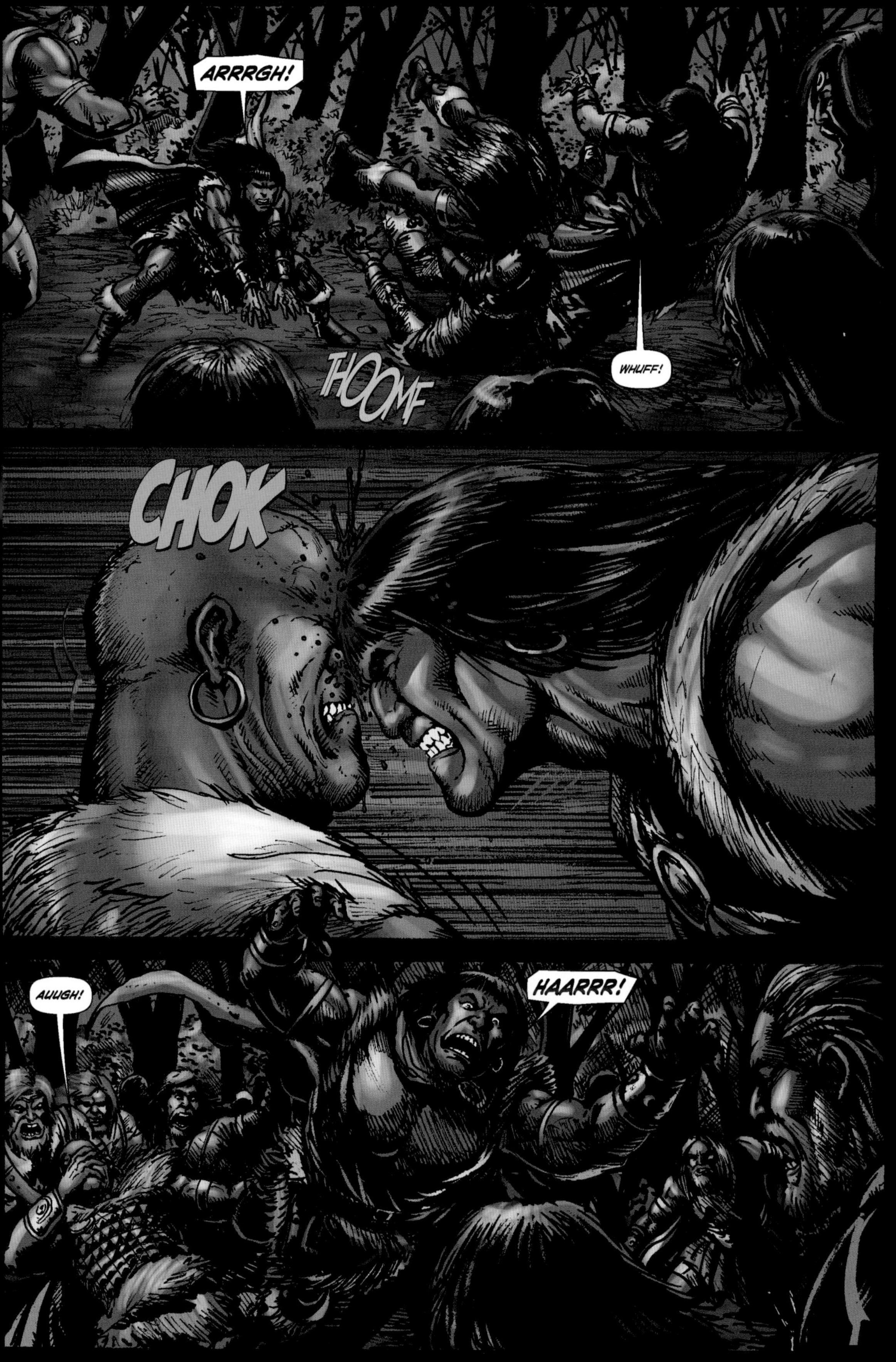
ARRRGH!
THOOMF
WHUFF!
CHOK
AUUGH!
HAARRR!

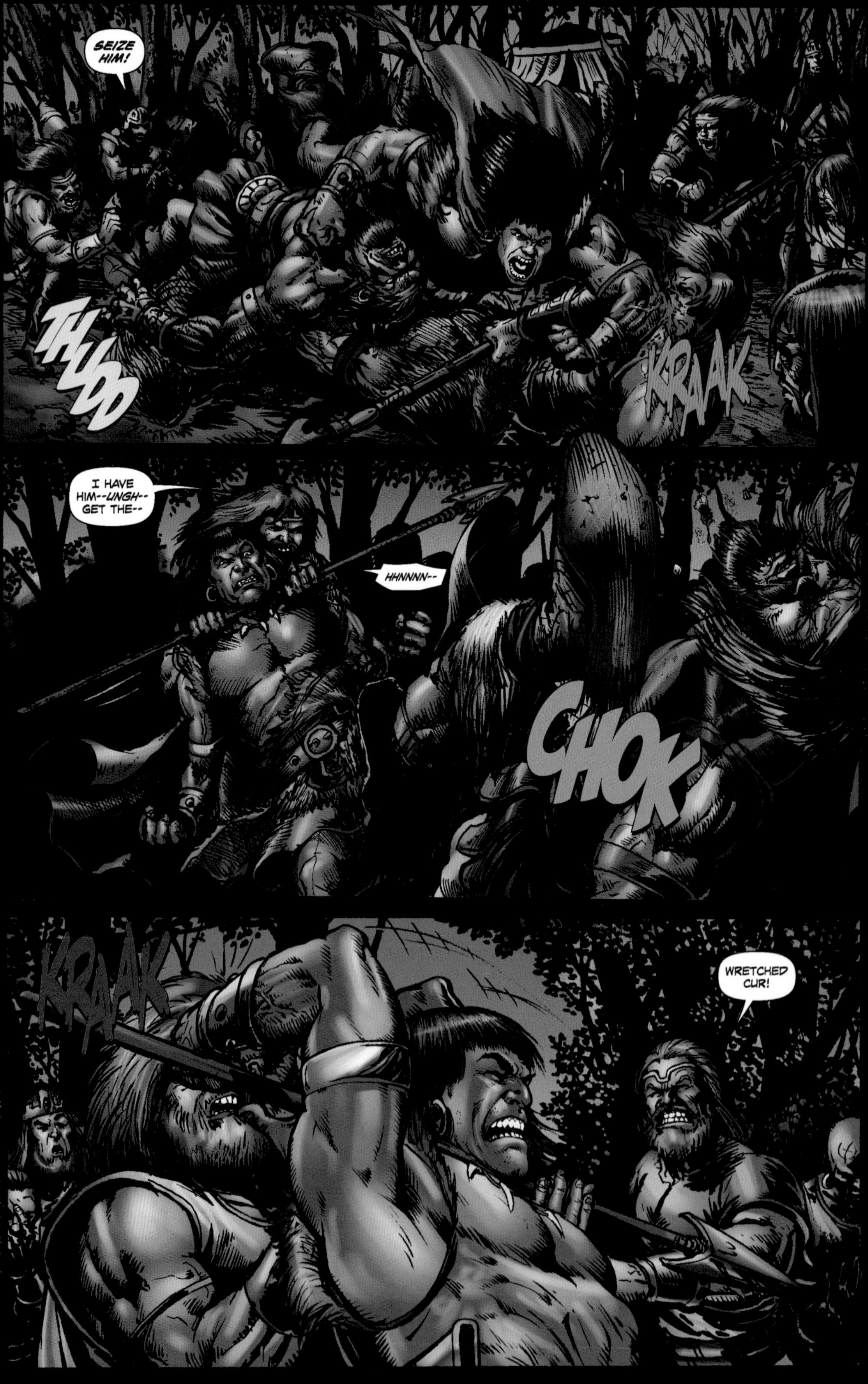
SEIZE HIM!
THUDD
KRAAK
I HAVE HIM--UNGH-- GET THE--
HHNNNN--
CHOK
KRAAK
WRETCHED CUR!

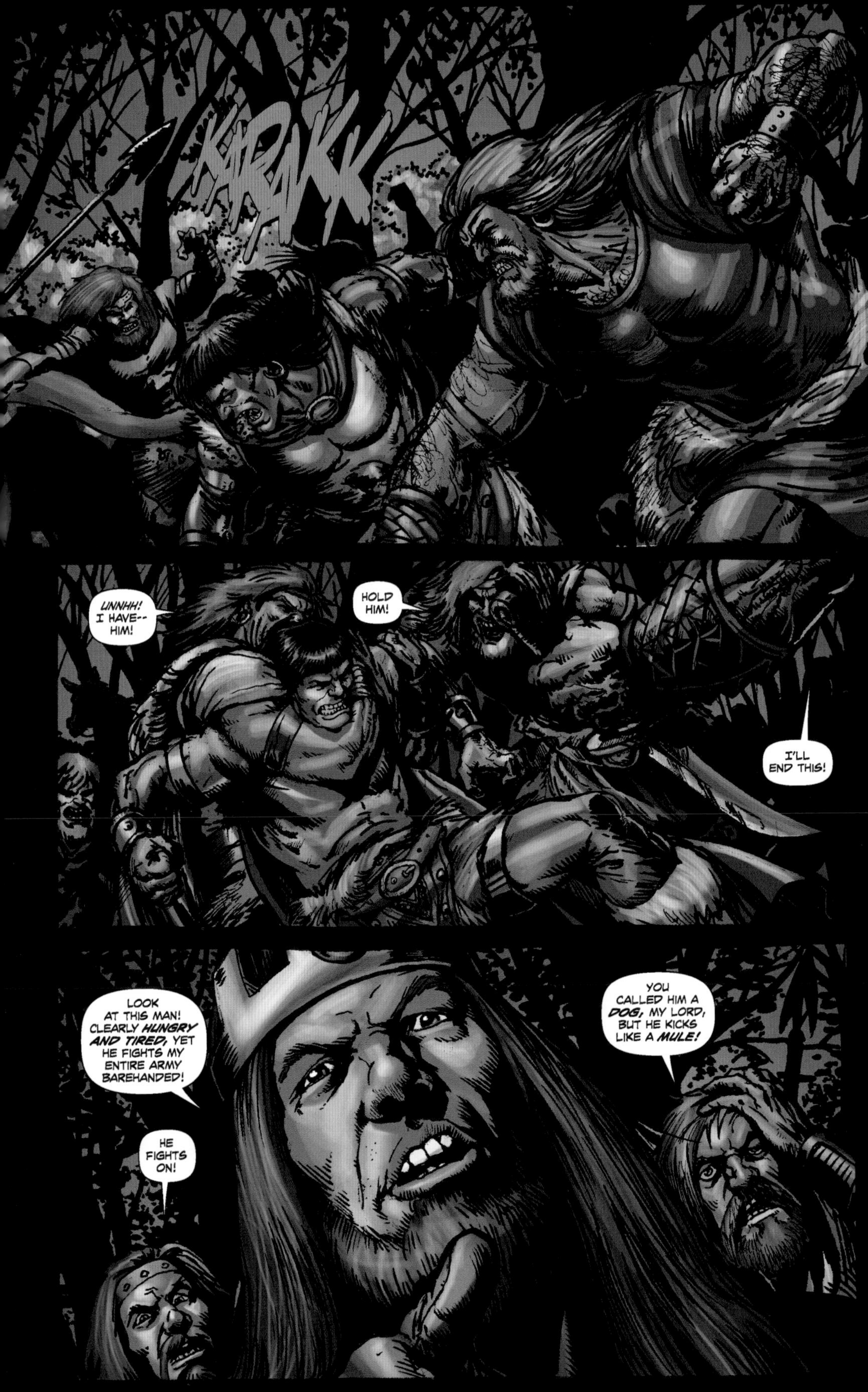
KRAKK
UNNHH! I HAVE--HIM!
HOLD HIM!
I'LL END THIS!
LOOK AT THIS MAN! CLEARLY HUNGRY AND TIRED, YET HE FIGHTS MY ENTIRE ARMY BAREHANDED!
HE FIGHTS ON!
YOU CALLED HIM A DOG, MY LORD, BUT HE KICKS LIKE A MULE!

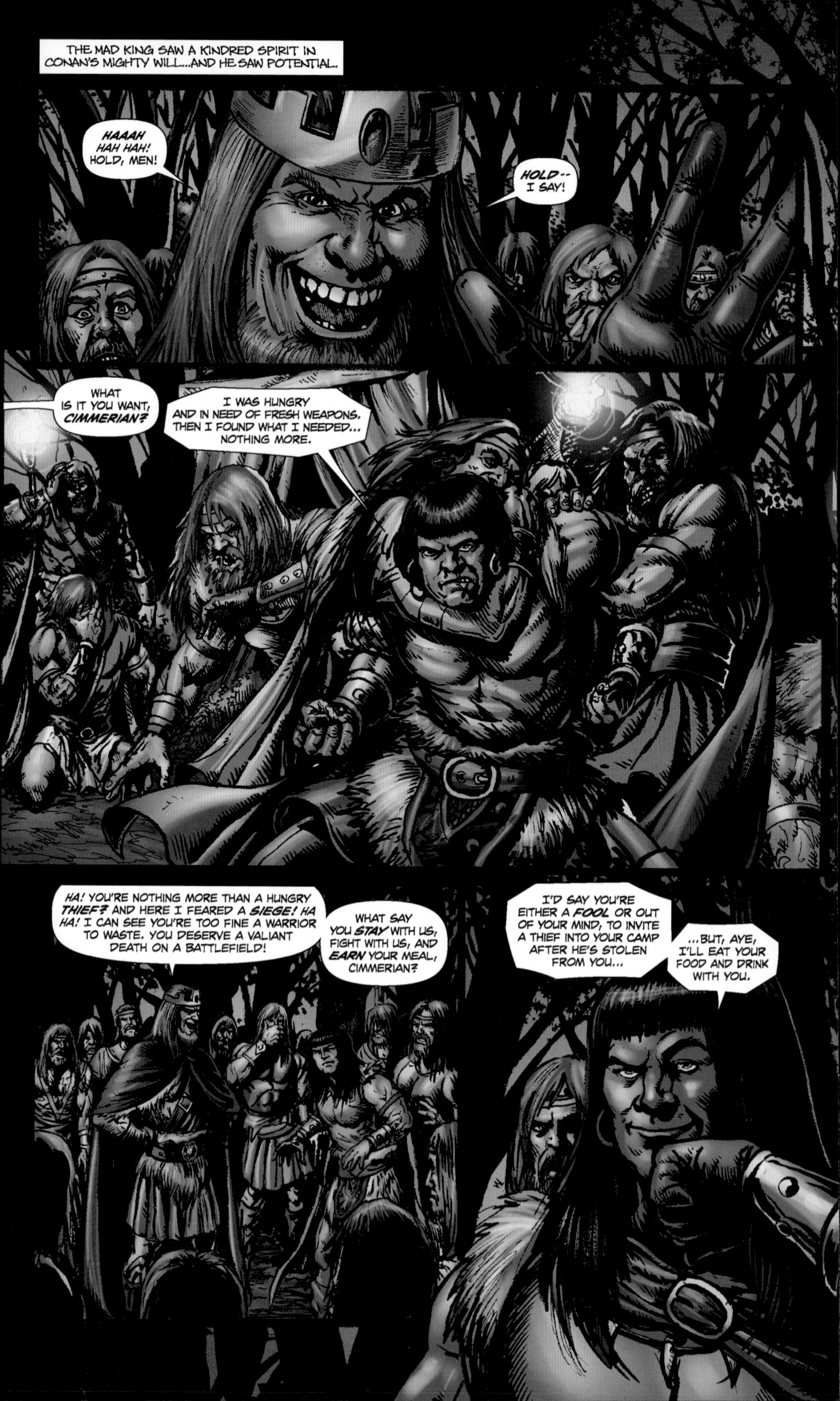
THE MAD KING SAW A KINDRED SPIRIT IN CONAN'S MIGHTY WILL...AND HE SAW POTENTIAL.
HAAAH HAH HAH! HOLD, MEN!
HOLD-- I SAY!
WHAT IS IT YOU WANT, CIMMERIAN?
I WAS HUNGRY AND IN NEED OF FRESH WEAPONS. THEN I FOUND WHAT I NEEDED... NOTHING MORE.
HA! YOU'RE NOTHING MORE THAN A HUNGRY THIEF? AND HERE I FEARED A SIEGE! HA HA! I CAN SEE YOU'RE TOO FINE A WARRIOR TO WASTE. YOU DESERVE A VALIANT DEATH ON A BATTLEFIELD!
WHAT SAY YOU STAY WITH US, FIGHT WITH US, AND EARN YOUR MEAL, CIMMERIAN?
I'D SAY YOU'RE EITHER A FOOL OR OUT OF YOUR MIND, TO INVITE A THIEF INTO YOUR CAMP AFTER HE'S STOLEN FROM YOU...
...BUT, AYE, I'LL EAT YOUR FOOD AND DRINK WITH YOU.

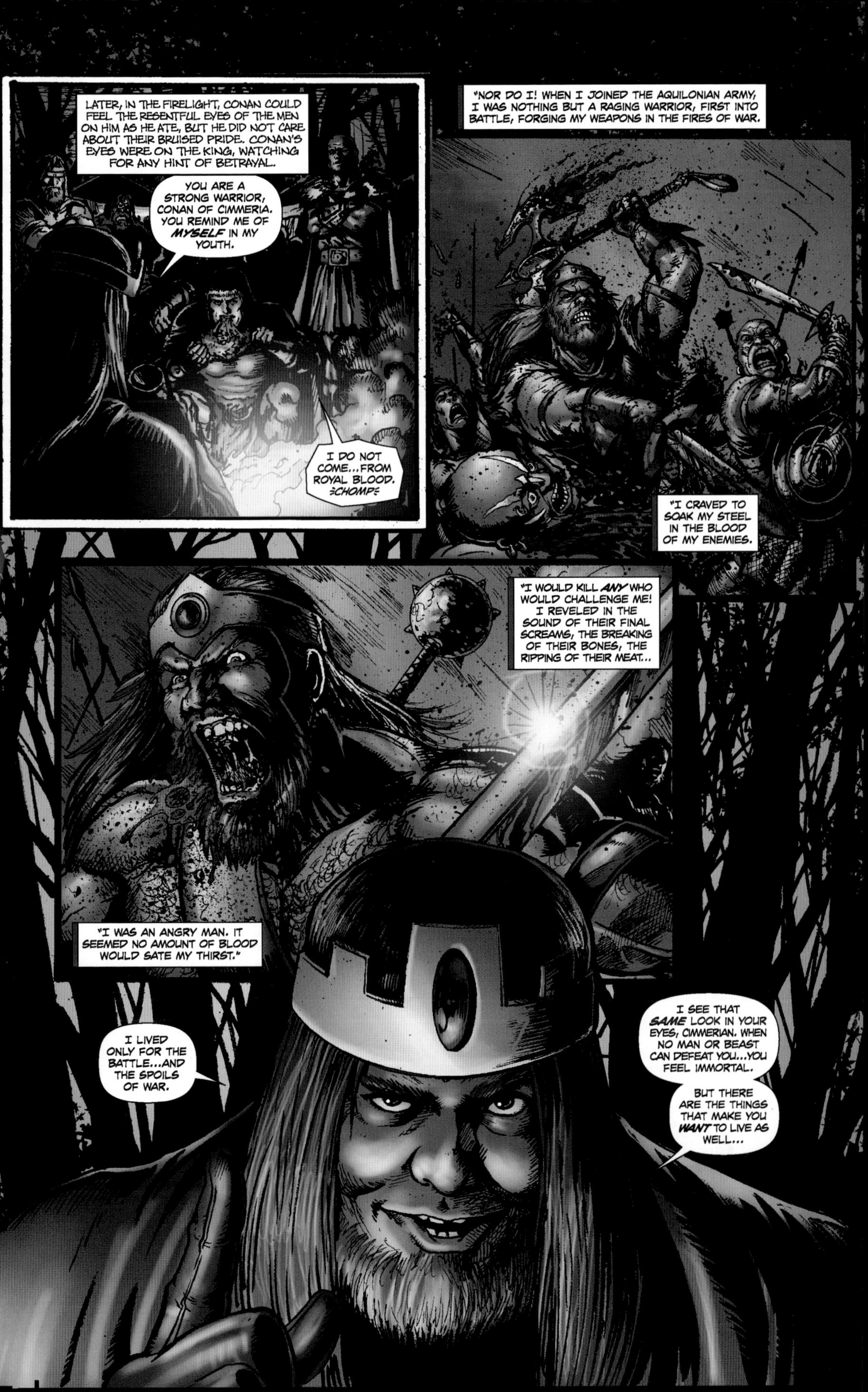
LATER, IN THE FIRELIGHT, CONAN COULD FEEL THE RESENTFUL EYES OF THE MEN ON HIM AS HE ATE, BUT HE DID NOT CARE ABOUT THEIR BRUISED PRIDE. CONAN'S EYES WERE ON THE KING, WATCHING FOR ANY HINT OF BETRAYAL.
YOU ARE A STRONG WARRIOR, CONAN OF CIMMERIA. YOU REMIND ME OF *MYSELF* IN MY YOUTH.
I DO NOT COME...FROM ROYAL BLOOD. *CHOMP*
"NOR DO I! WHEN I JOINED THE AQUILONIAN ARMY, I WAS NOTHING BUT A RAGING WARRIOR, FIRST INTO BATTLE, FORGING MY WEAPONS IN THE FIRES OF WAR.
"I CRAVED TO SOAK MY STEEL IN THE BLOOD OF MY ENEMIES.
"I WOULD KILL *ANY* WHO WOULD CHALLENGE ME! I REVELED IN THE SOUND OF THEIR FINAL SCREAMS, THE BREAKING OF THEIR BONES, THE RIPPING OF THEIR MEAT...
"I WAS AN ANGRY MAN. IT SEEMED NO AMOUNT OF BLOOD WOULD SATE MY THIRST."
I LIVED ONLY FOR THE BATTLE...AND THE SPOILS OF WAR.
I SEE THAT *SAME* LOOK IN YOUR EYES, CIMMERIAN. WHEN NO MAN OR BEAST CAN DEFEAT YOU...YOU FEEL IMMORTAL.
BUT THERE ARE THE THINGS THAT MAKE YOU *WANT* TO LIVE AS WELL...

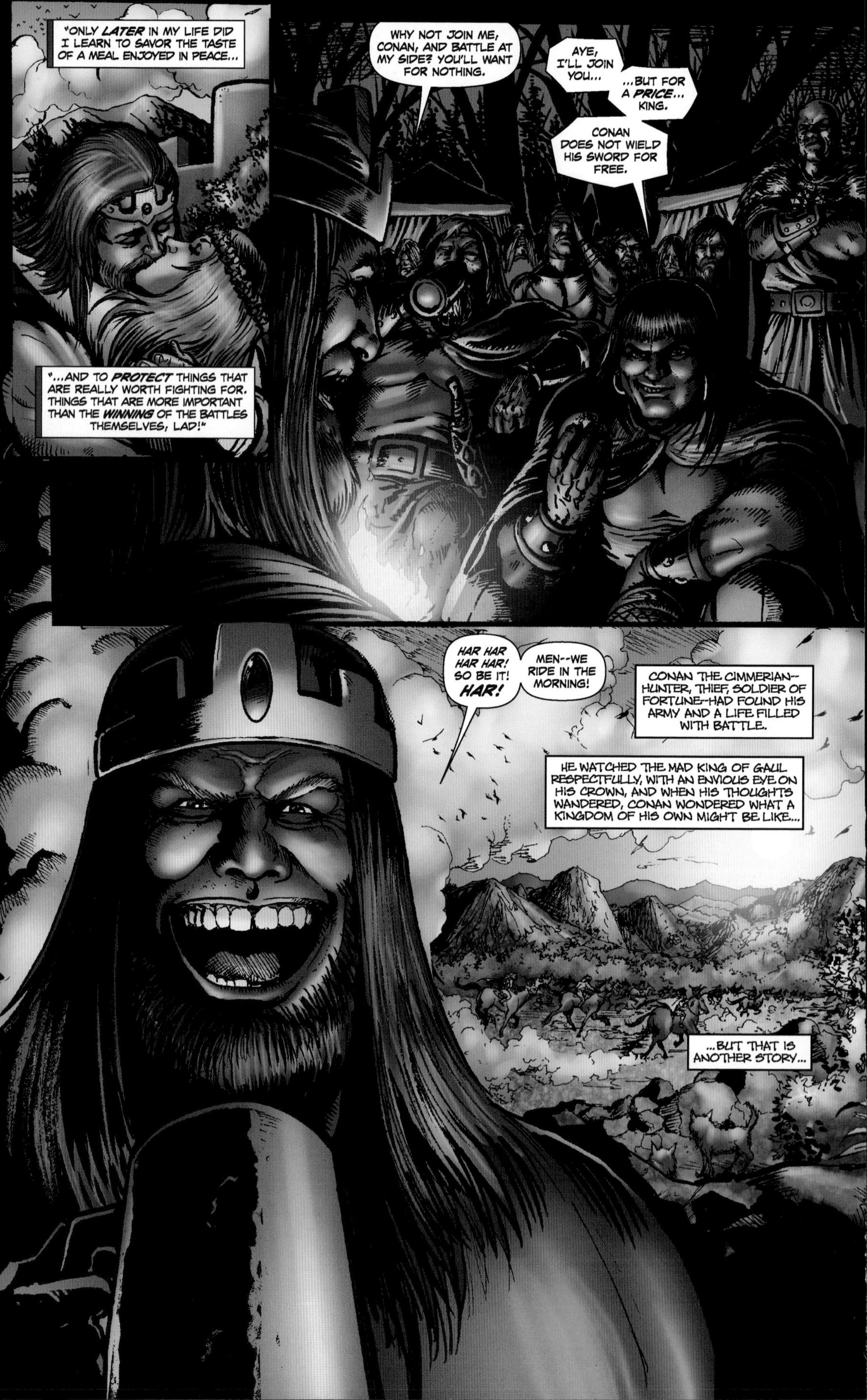
"ONLY LATER IN MY LIFE DID I LEARN TO SAVOR THE TASTE OF A MEAL ENJOYED IN PEACE...
"...AND TO PROTECT THINGS THAT ARE REALLY WORTH FIGHTING FOR. THINGS THAT ARE MORE IMPORTANT THAN THE WINNING OF THE BATTLES THEMSELVES, LAD!"
WHY NOT JOIN ME, CONAN, AND BATTLE AT MY SIDE? YOU'LL WANT FOR NOTHING.
AYE, I'LL JOIN YOU...
...BUT FOR A PRICE... KING.
CONAN DOES NOT WIELD HIS SWORD FOR FREE.
HAR HAR HAR HAR! SO BE IT! HAR!
MEN--WE RIDE IN THE MORNING!
CONAN THE CIMMERIAN--HUNTER, THIEF, SOLDIER OF FORTUNE--HAD FOUND HIS ARMY AND A LIFE FILLED WITH BATTLE.
HE WATCHED THE MAD KING OF GAUL RESPECTFULLY, WITH AN ENVIOUS EYE ON HIS CROWN, AND WHEN HIS THOUGHTS WANDERED, CONAN WONDERED WHAT A KINGDOM OF HIS OWN MIGHT BE LIKE...
...BUT THAT IS ANOTHER STORY...

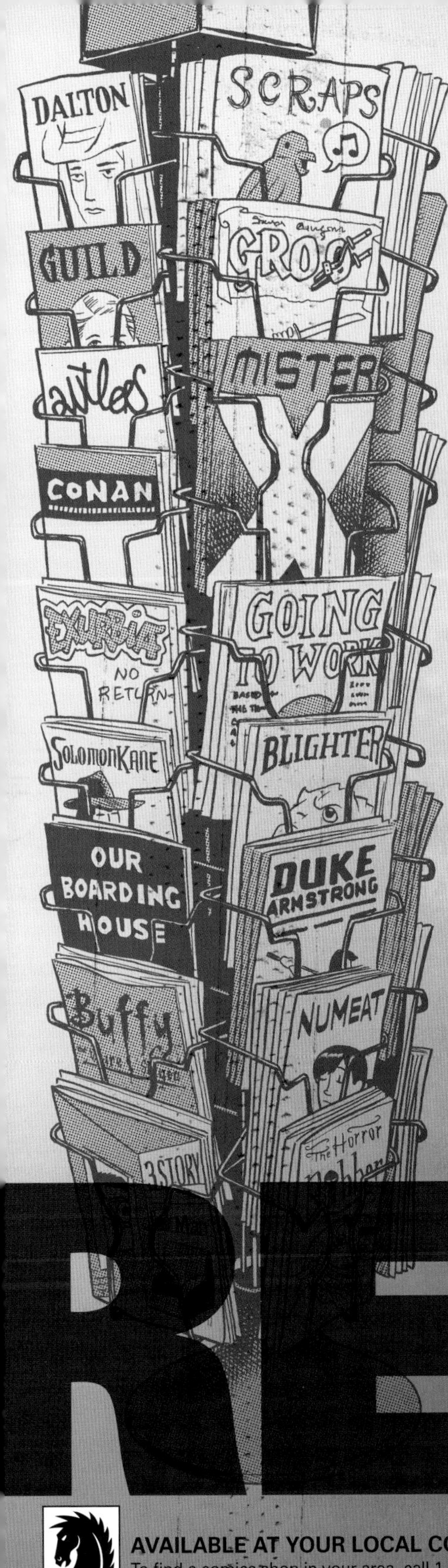
DALTON
SCRAPS
GUILD
GROO
MISTER X
CONAN
EXURBIA
NO RETURN
GOING TO WORK
SolomonKane
BLIGHTER
OUR BOARDING HOUSE
DUKE ARMSTRONG
Buffy
NUMEAT
3STORY

MYSPACE DARK HORSE PRESENTS
Joss Whedon, Mike Mignola, Gerard Way, Steve Niles, Fábio Moon, and others
$19.99 each

Volume 1 978-1-59307-998-7	**Volume 2** 978-1-59582-248-2
Volume 3 978-1-59582-327-4	**Volume 4** 978-1-59582-405-9

BUFFY THE VAMPIRE SLAYER SEASON EIGHT VOLUME 6: RETREAT
Jane Espenson, Georges Jeanty, and Joss Whedon
978-1-59582-415-8 $15.99

FRAY: FUTURE SLAYER
Joss Whedon and Karl Moline
978-1-56971-751-6 $19.99

WONDERMARK VOLUME 1: BEARDS OF OUR FOREFATHERS
David Malki
978-1-59307-984-0 $14.99

BEASTS OF BURDEN
Evan Dorkin and Jill Thompson
978-1-59582-513-1 $19.99

EXURBIA
Scott Allie and Kevin McGovern
978-1-59582-339-7 $9.99

THE NIGHT OF YOUR LIFE
Jesse Reklaw
978-1-59582-183-6 $15.99

READ

AVAILABLE AT YOUR LOCAL COMICS SHOP OR BOOKSTORE
To find a comics shop in your area, call 1-888-266-4226.
For more information or to order direct, visit darkhorse.com or call 1-800-862-0052
Mon. – Fri. 9 AM to 5 PM Pacific Time. *Prices and availability subject to change without notice

FOR MORE COMICS ONLINE, VISIT

Felicia Day: watchtheguild.com (*The Guild* web show)
Ben Dewey: meleecomics.com
Damon Gentry and Aaron Conley: invademyprivacy.com
Matt Kindt: mattkindt.com
David Malki: wondermark.com
Roman Muradov: bluebed.net
Yuko Ota and Ananth Panagariya: johnnywander.com
Jesse Reklaw: slowwave.com
Matt Sundstrom: mattink.com